Transforming British Government

Volume 1: Changing Institutions

Transforming Government

General Editor: **R. A. W. Rhodes**, Professor of Politics, University of Newcastle

This important and authoritative new series arises out of the seminal ESRC Whitehall Programme and seeks to fill the enormous gaps in our knowledge of the key actors and institutions of British government. It examines the many large changes during the postwar period and puts these into comparative context by analysing the experience of the advanced industrial democracies of Europe and the nations of the Commonwealth. The series reports the results of the Whitehall Programme, a four-year project into change in British government in the postwar period, mounted by the Economic and Social Research Council.

Titles include:

Transforming Government
Series Standing Order ISBN 0–333–71580–2
(*outside North America only*)

You can receive future titles in this series as they are published by placing a standing order. Please contact your bookseller or, in case of difficulty, write to us at the address below with your name and address, the title of the series and the ISBN quoted above.

Customer Services Department, Macmillan Distribution Ltd, Houndmills, Basingstoke, Hampshire RG21 6XS, England

Transforming British Government

Volume 1: Changing Institutions

Edited by

R. A. W. Rhodes
Professor of Politics
University of Newcastle

in association with
ECONOMIC AND SOCIAL RESEARCH COUNCIL

Published by PALGRAVE MACMILLAN
Houndmills, Basingstoke, Hampshire RG21 6XS and
175 Fifth Avenue, New York, N. Y. 10010
Companies and representatives throughout the world

PALGRAVE MACMILLAN is the global academic imprint of the Palgrave
Macmillan division of St. Martin's Press, LLC and of Palgrave Macmillan Ltd.
Macmillan® is a registered trademark in the United States, United Kingdom
and other countries. Palgrave is a registered trademark in the European
Union and other countries.

Outside North America
ISBN 0–333–75241–4

In North America
ISBN 0–312–23584–4

This book is printed on paper suitable for recycling and
made from fully managed and sustained forest sources.

A catalogue record for this book is available from the British Library.

Library of Congress Catalog Card Number: 00–039063

Transferred to digital printing 2003

Printed and bound in Great Britain by
Antony Rowe Ltd, Chippenham and Eastbourne

To
Vincent Wright, 1937–1999

Contents

List of Boxes, Figures and Tables

Foreword: the Whitehall Programme

Are the people in Whitehall usually right? How far has the Civil Service been improved by recent changes? Should the whole machinery of central government be added to the checklist of institutions in need of root-and-branch reform? These are some of the questions posed by the Economic and Social Research Council's 'Whitehall Programme', of which these two edited volumes form part.

Like many other products of the Programme, these books are the result of an exercise in team work that reflects a typically quiet and unheralded shift in Britain's political culture. As the reader will discover, a key ingredient has been the support and co-operation of the Civil Service.

The Whitehall Programme was born of a new commitment to what is now called 'transparency'. The idea of outside experts taking an inside look at government processes was not in itself novel: on rare occasions, enterprising investigators were invited in, without too many strings attached. Official histories had occasionally been commissioned, and senior civil servants sometimes spoke about the need for wider scholarly access. But it was not until the 1990s that the notion of a wide-ranging, externally-funded series of studies took concrete form. The catalyst for such a project was a call in 1992 by Sir Robin Butler, then Head of the Civil Service, for a closer association between senior officials and the increasing number of researchers who studied and wrote about what they did.

The ESRC picked up this gauntlet and decided to fund a programme of linked studies of different aspects of the core executive – with the aim of extending knowledge, stimulating debate, and developing a dialogue between academics and practitioners. Later, the Cabinet Office chipped in with additional money for particular topics. The resulting 'Whitehall Programme' has turned into the most ambitious investigation of British central government ever undertaken by independent scholars. A total of 23 projects were awarded grants during 1995.

Much of the research was, of course, conducted in traditional ways: using official and other documentation in the public domain. What made the Whitehall Programme different from previous work was the active welcome it received from every level of the Civil Service, from the top down, and the willingness of officials to make themselves available to researchers. It was an incalculable advantage to the Programme that both Sir Robin and his successor, Sir Richard Wilson, gave it their full encouragement, taking trouble to open doors wherever possible. There was also a collective element: although each project stood and stands on its own, researchers were invited to share their experiences and findings in a variety of workshops, seminars and conferences arranged by

Professor Rod Rhodes, the Programme's inspirational Director. Such 'work-in-progress' events helped to give the shape of a single enterprise, greater than its parts.

Will the Whitehall Programme affect practice? It was not meant as a call to action: or, at least, any single kind of action. Yet there are implicit messages. My prediction is that there will be a cumulative influence. Some of the resulting books and essays will arouse intense interest, others will at first be little noticed. Whatever the initial reaction, I believe that the pioneering Programme, with its remarkable range of authors and topics, will come to be seen as a major landmark in the study and understanding of modern government.

Ben Pimlott
Chairman of the ESRC Whitehall Programme

Editor's Preface and Acknowledgements

There are enormous gaps in our knowledge of the key actors and institutions in British government. We cannot do simple things like describing the work of ministers of state, permanent secretaries and their departments. Also, there have been large changes in British government during the post-war period, such as: the growth of the welfare state; the professionalisation of government; the consequences of recession; the effects of New Right ideology; the impact of the European Union; the effects of new technology; the hollowing out of the state; and the new public management with its separation of policy and administration. We do not know how these changes affected British government. And we cannot understand the effects of these changes by focusing only on Britain. We must also analyse the experience of the advanced industrial democracies of Europe and the Commonwealth.

To repair these gaps in our knowledge and to explain how and why British government changed in the postwar period, the Economic and Social Research Council mounted the Whitehall Programme on 'The Changing Nature of Central Government in Britain'. This Macmillan series, entitled 'Transforming Government', reports the results of that five-year research programme.

The series has five objectives. To:

1. develop theory – to develop new theoretical perspectives that explain why British government changed and why it differs from other countries;
2. understand change – to describe and explain what has changed in British government since 1945;
3. compare – to compare these changes with those in other EU member states and other states with a 'Westminster' system of government;
4. build bridges – to create a common understanding between academics and practitioners;
5. disseminate – to make academic research accessible to a varied audience covering 6th-formers and senior policy makers.

These two volumes, *Transforming British Government*, have one simple objective: to provide a summary of the key findings of all the projects. Volume 1 surveys the main institutional changes while Volume 2 examines the changing roles and relationships of the core executive. Each chapter explains what the researchers did and, where appropriate, identifies the lessons for British government. It is quite impossible to synthesise the 12 projects covered by Volume 1. Nonetheless the 'Introduction' (Chapter 1) tells the history of the Programme while the 'Conclusion' (Chapter 14) provides a personal interpretation of its major lessons.

I am the wrong person to attempt an assessment of the Whitehall Programme, but no matter. Many others will provide a critical analysis and the ESRC itself will ensure that each project as well as the overall Programme is properly evaluated. However, I hope these two volumes will encourage the reader to seek out the books, articles and chapters of individual projects and explore their findings in more detail. Each chapter is only a 'taster' for the 'book of the project', many of which will repay in full your detailed attention.

Acknowledgements

After five years, there are so many people to thank, that it is hard to be both brief and comprehensive. Pride of place must go to my colleagues on the Whitehall Programme. I would like to thank them for their enthusiasm and support in the face of too many requests from me for information about conference papers, seminars and the like. The ESRC funded all of us and its contribution is fully acknowledged in each chapter. Individual members of the ESRC were also great supporters. It is no doubt invidious to single out any individual or section but I must thank Martin Kendor who aided and abetted me in setting up the Programme, Tim Whittaker and his colleagues in 'External Relations' who were unfailingly helpful in staging media events, and Ron Aman who, as Chief Executive of the ESRC, had many others things to occupy his mind but never missed an opportunity to extol the Programme's virtues. In the immortal words of Duke Ellington, 'I love you madly'.

The Programme would not have survived let alone thrived without the help of the civil service. Sir Robin Butler decided there should be better links between the civil service and academia, and it came to pass. His firm, unwavering commitment to the Programme was beyond value. Sir Richard Wilson picked up the baton with what, I suspect, could be described as 'enthusiasm', but I do not seek to give offence. Andrew Whetnall and David Wilkinson provided day-to-day support and advice and tolerated some 50 researchers crawling over Whitehall with great good cheer and no little patience. David Wilkinson developed voracious reading habits which puzzled even him, let alone his civil service colleagues. I am sure he will make a full recovery. I must record my genuine delight at the co-operation of the civil service and senior politicians. Rarely was an interview refused and the conversations were frequently frank and revealing. We are all immensely grateful.

Peter Hennessy was a regular source of advice at the outset and helped this new boy avoid opening his mouth to change feet. Ben Pimlott was always there with a friendly word of advice and ideas about how to best disseminate the findings.

Over the years there were so many conferences and seminars it is impossible to thank everyone who made a helpful contribution by name. I hope all concerned will rest content with this general thank you.

One great opportunity for the Director was to build international research contacts when disseminating the research findings. I was lucky to work with Lotte

Jensen, Torben Beck Jørgensen and Tim Knudsen of the Institute of Political Science, University of Copenhagen; and with Glyn Davis, John Wanna and Pat Weller of the Centre for Australian Public Sector Management, Griffith University, Brisbane. Both Brisbane and Copenhagen are now second homes and the joint work will continue long after the end of the Whitehall Programme. Angela Mulvenna coped with my busy travel schedule and frequent absences with good humour. Janice McMillan provided the usual help. Mark Bevir provided intellectual challenge.

Vincent Wright was the principal investigator for the Whitehall Programme project on core executives and policy co-ordination in six West European countries (see Volume 2, Chapter 2). He died in Oxford on 8 July 1999. He would abhor any fulsome tribute. So, I simply record that these two volumes are dedicated to him as a mark of affection for a friend and respect for a colleague. We all miss him greatly.

ROD RHODES

Notes on the Contributors

Christopher Brady is Director of Studies for the General and Strategic Management MBA at City University Business School. He has previously served as an intelligence officer in the Royal Navy and a Research Fellow with the Institute of Contemporary British History. He has written on issues as diverse as collective responsibility, political management, élite teams and game theory.

Simon Butler is Jean Monnet Professor of European Politics at the University of Manchester. He has published on the governance of the European Union, EU-member state relations and German politics. A full-length study of his work with Martin Burch is forthcoming with Manchester University Press as *Mandarins, Ministers and Europe*.

Martin Burch is Director of the Graduate Centre and Senior Lecturer in Government at the University of Manchester. He has published in the area of British politics and especially on the development and nature of Cabinet government; his most recent book is The *British Cabinet System* (with Ian Holliday).

June Burnham is senior lecturer in European Government at Middlesex University. Her research is on French and British administration. Relevant recent publications include: *Whitehall and the Civil Service* (Politics Association, 2nd edition 1999); and (with J. M. Lee and G. W. Jones), *At the Centre of Whitehall* (Macmillan 1998).

Peter Catterall has been Director of the Institute of Contemporary British History since 1989. He also lectures in history at Queen Mary and Westfield College, University of London and in 1999–2000 will be Fulbright–Robertson visiting professor of British history at Westminster College, Fulton, Missouri. He is the author and editor of numerous books and he co-edits the journals *Contemporary British History* and *National Identities*.

Christopher Clifford was senior Research Officer on the 'History of the Organisation of Central Government Departments', 1995–97. He gave evidence, with Iain McLean, to the Lords Select Committee on the Public Service, HL 68 1996–97. He served as chief editor of the paper output of the project.

Terence Daintith is Dean of the School of Advanced Study of the University of London, and a Professor of Law in the School's Institute of Advanced Legal Studies, of which he was Director between 1988 and 1995. His previous posts were at the Universities of California (Berkeley), Edinburgh and Dundee, and at the European University Institute in Florence. He has published extensively in the fields of UK and comparative public law (especially with reference to economic policy), oil and gas law and European law. His most recent book (with Professor Alan Page) is *The Executive in the Constitution* (1999).

Patricia Day is a senior research fellow in the Department of Social and Policy Sciences at Bath University. She has written numerous journals and monographs on health policy and the NHS as well as regulation and audit in public services. She is co–author (with Rudolf Klein) of *Accountabilities* and *How Organisations Measure Success*.

Neil C. M. Elder is Reader Emeritus, University of Hull. He has written extensively on Swedish politics and government. His books include *The Consensual Democracies?: The Government and Politics of the Scandinavian States* (with Alastair H. Thomas and David Arter), 1988.

Christopher Hood is Professor of Public Administration and Public Policy at the London School of Economics. He was previously Professor of Government and Public Administration at Sydney University. His research interests include the study of government organisation, public management and regulation. Recent publications include *The Art of the State* (1998), *Regulation Inside Government* (co-author, 1999) and *Telecommunications Regulation* (co-author, 1999).

Brian W. Hogwood is Professor of Politics in the Department of Government at the University of Strathclyde, and has published extensively on public policy and public administration. His research interests include agencies and other public bodies, trends in public policy, and regional government in England.

Oliver James is a lecturer in public administration and public policy in the Department of Politics at the University of Exeter. His research interests include public sector reform, regulation of the public and private sectors and political economy models of the public sector. He is co-author of *Regulation Inside Government: Waste Watchers, Quality Police and Sleazebusters* (1999).

G. W. Jones has been Professor of Government at the London School of Economics (LSE) since 1976. He is the author of *Borough Politics; Herbert Morrison; West European Prime Ministers; The Government of London;* and *At the Centre of Whitehall*. He was a member of the Layfield Committee on Local Government Finance (1974–76) and of the National Consumer Council (1991–99). In 1999 he was appointed to the Advisory Panel on Beacon Councils and was awarded an OBE.

David Judge is Professor of Politics in the Department of Government at the University of Strathclyde, and has published extensively on representation and Parliament. His research interests are legislative studies, particularly the British House of Commons and the European Parliament, and UK politics.

Rudolf Klein is Emeritus Professor of Social Policy and Senior Associate of the King's Fund. From 1978–98 he was Professor of Social Policy at the University of Bath and Director of the Centre for the Analysis of Social Policy. He was previously a journalist with the *London Evening Standard* and *The Observer*. His publications include books on public expenditure, accountability, performance indicators and regulation.

Rodney Lowe is Professor of Contemporary History at the University of Bristol. He has published widely on twentieth-century welfare history and his latest books include The *Welfare State in Britain* since 1945 (second edition, 1998), *Welfare Under the Conservatives* 1961–1964 (with Paul Brigden, 1998) and *Welfare Policy in Britain* (with Helen Fawcett, 1999).

Iain McLean is Professor of Politics, Oxford University and Official Fellow of Nuffield College. Interests in UK government including devolution and centre–periphery relations; disaster, corporatism and taking responsibility (based on the Aberfan case study); elections and the properties of electoral systems; history of social choice.

Alistair McMillan was a Research Officer on the 'History of the Organisation of Central Government Departments', 1995–97 and chief editor of electronic output. He is now a doctoral student, Nuffield College, Oxford, working on Indian elections in collaboration with the Centre for the Study of Developing Societies, Delhi.

Murray McVicar, formerly Research Officer in the Department of Government at the University of Strathclyde, is now Senior Research Specialist in the Scottish Parliament Information Centre.

Alan Page has been Professor of Public Law at the University of Dundee since 1985 and has also taught at the Universities of Westminster and Cardiff. He is an Honorary Fellow of the Society for Advanced Legal Studies. His publications include: 'The Citizen's Charter and Administrative Justice' in Harris and Partington (eds) *Administrative Justice in the 21st Century* (1999, Oxford: Hart, pp. 85–98); and 'Controlling Government from Within: a Constitutional Analysis' *Public Policy and Administration* (1998), 13, pp. 85–95. He is the author, with Terence Daintith, of *The Executive in the Constitution: Structure, Autonomy and Internal Control* (1999).

Edward C. Page is Professor of Politics, University of Hull and has written on comparative public administration. His books include *People who run Europe* (1998).

Rod Rhodes is Professor of Politics (Research) at the University of Newcastle upon Tyne; Director of the Economic and Social Research Council's Whitehall Research programme, 1994–1999; and Adjungeret Professor, Institut for Statkundskab, Kobehavns Universitet. He is the author or editor of 20 books including recently: (edited with P. Weller and H. Bakvis), *The Hollow Crown* (Macmillan 1997); *Understanding Governance* (Open University Press 1997); and *Control and Power in Central–Local Government Relations* (Ashgate 1999). He has also published widely in journals such as: *Australian Journal of Public*

Administration, British Journal of Political Science, European Journal of Political Research, Parliamentary Affairs, Political Quarterly, Political Studies, Public Administration, Public Administration Review, and *West European Politics*. He has been editor of *Public Administration* since 1986. He is chair of the Political Studies Association of the United Kingdom.

Astrid Ringe is a research assistant at the University of Bristol. She is currently working on an ESRC-funded project to produce a handbook on the records available at the Public Record Office on economic policy 1951–64. She has published articles on the NEDC.

Neil Rollings is Senior Lecturer in Economic History at the University of Bristol and Associate Professor at the Institute of Economic Research, Hitotsubashi University, Japan. He has published on postwar British economic policy and European integration.

Colin Scott is a Senior Lecturer in Law and member of the Centre for the Analysis of Risk and Regulation at the London School of Economics, specialising in regulation. His publications include the co-authored books *Regulation Inside Government* (1999) and *Telecommunications Regulation: Culture, Chaos and Interdependence Inside the Regulatory Process* (2000).

Martin J. Smith is Professor of Politics at the University of Sheffield. His research interests include the reform of Whitehall and the Labour Party. Recent publications include *The Core Executive in Britain;* and *New Labour in Government* (co-editor).

Tony Travers is Director of Research, Greater London Group, London School of Economics, and co-author of *Failure in British Government: the Politics of the Poll Tax* (1994).

1
Introduction: The ESRC Whitehall Programme: a Guide to Institutional Change

R. A. W. Rhodes

Introduction

This chapter has four parts. First, I provide a brief history of the Economic and Social Research Council's (ESRC) Whitehall Programme.[1] Second, I explain some key concepts and theories. Third, I outline the structure of this volume. Finally, I provide an Appendix of the major publications between 1994 and 2000 of the projects reporting in this volume. It covers books, articles, chapters and discussion papers. It does not cover the many conference papers, newspaper articles and other more ephemeral publications.[2]

A brief history of the Whitehall Programme

The Programme's formal origins lie in a Workshop entitled 'The Changing Nature of the British Executive' funded by the ESRC which I ran at the University of York on 13–14 April 1992. The workshop brought together academics and civil servants and sought to blend theory and practice. In David Marsh's possibly immortal words 'we have here two people who have made substantial contributions to understanding British government, Peter (Hennessy) in spite of his complete lack of theory and Patrick (Dunleavy) despite his excess of it'. The joke captured the good humour and frank exchanges of the workshop. The informal origins of the Programme were conversations in York in November in the snow between Rod Rhodes and Martin Kendor of the ESRC. Having aided and abetted Rod Rhodes in setting up the 'Local Governance' Programme, he was once more finding ways of spending the Society and Politics Development Group's money (Rhodes 1999). But not for long. The penitential cross of finance officer beckoned. The poacher became gamekeeper, or more prosaically, guardian of the budget. So he departed as consultations got underway. The report on the workshop with its proposals for future research were discussed at several conferences and seminars.

Paralleling this academic activity, the (then) Conservative government of John Major was encouraging openness. The Cabinet Office sent an observer to the York Workshop. Sir Robin Butler, Head of the Home Civil Service, gave the Frank Stacey Memorial Lecture at the University of York and signalled his willingness to encourage research on central government (Butler 1992). After exploratory meetings with the Cabinet Office on 7 September and 11 December 1992, the Cabinet Office and the ESRC arranged a further workshop at the Civil Service College. These discussions led to a formal accord between the Cabinet Office and the ESRC with the former taking part in a joint steering and commissioning panel to develop a research programme. The Board of the ESRC agreed to fund the Programme in September 1993 and the Commissioning Panel met on 6 December under its chair, Professor Ben Pimlott (then at Birkbeck College, University of London) to finish the specification and agree the commissioning process. The Programme called for outline proposals in December 1993 and January 1994. At its February meeting, Professor Rod Rhodes was appointed Programme Director for four years. He took up his appointment on 1 April 1994. The Panel met on 7 March 1995 to consider 112 outline proposals. It shortlisted 30. These full proposals were sent to between 4 and 6 referees and at its meeting of 12 September the Panel agreed to fund 16 projects costing £1.5 million. The Office of Public Service and Science (OPSS) in the Cabinet office offered to fund jointly two projects on open government and the history of government departments, each costing £100,000. The Panel did not allocate all its funds in the first round because it was clear there would be gaps in the Programme's coverage, notably studies of prime minister, cabinet, ministers and the core executive. So, there were enough funds for a second round of commissioning. A further 25 applications were received. The Committee funded the two OPSS projects and five commissions to write books on the core executive based on research already completed.

The Programme comprised 23 projects costing £2.1 million. The first project began in March 1995. The last project finished in March 1999. The Director's appointment was extended to June 1999. At its peak, the Programme employed 49 people. It covered the disciplines of politics, law, history and management. The Programme focuses on 'the changing nature of governance in the UK' (*Corporate Plan 1996–2001*: 11; *ESRC Thematic Priorities (Update) 1997*) and, therefore, contributes in its entirety to the ESRC's governance, regulation and accountability priority theme.

The role of the programme director[3]

The Programme Director's role is a classical illustration of the dilemma posed by responsibility without power. The role is best compared to 'herding cats', and I like cats! My formal responsibilities were broad and I quote them more or less verbatim below.

1. To assist the Whitehall Commissioning Panel in the selection of research projects to be recommended for funding.
2. To provide academic leadership for the programme, monitor progress on individual projects within the programme and to provide guidance and assistance where appropriate to researchers on the programme.
3. To organise programme workshops and seminars in order to ensure effective communication between the various projects within the programme. To

ensure opportunities for synergy between multi-disciplinary approaches to the research areas are realised and possibilities for the sharing of data and information explored. The co-ordinator will also be expected to pursue international links on behalf of the programme as appropriate.

4. To report on the progress of the programme to the Programme Steering Committee[4] and the Research Programmes Board, as required, including the provision of written material for meetings of the Committee and the Board. The co-ordinator will be required to submit an annual report on his own work and that of the programme as a whole.

5. The programme will, in addition to the expected generation of academic articles and books, produce results of direct relevance to non-academic audiences. The co-ordinator will be responsible for networking with these groups and with the research community in order to promote the programme and disseminate research outputs that derive from it.

6. To pursue the possibility of external funding and to encourage the close involvement of potential users of the research.

7. To act, as required, in a representative capacity on behalf of the research programme.

8. To provide advice to the Programme Steering Committee on the development of the programme.

I stressed four facets of the job. First, I played a supporting role for the projects. The Programme recruited senior colleagues. Any attempt to 'direct' their research would have been futile as well as counter-productive. I concentrated on helping them and on 'trouble shooting' with the civil service when necessary.

Second, I sought to provide 'academic leadership' through my work on understanding the new governance and on developing an anti-foundational approach to British government (see, for example, Rhodes 1997a).

Third, I cultivated links with the civil service. I visited Whitehall regularly and ensured the civil service took part in all Programme events. Most notably, I organised many élite seminars at which the projects reported on their research to an invited audience of civil servants.

Fourth, as well as devising and implementing a communication strategy, I sought to improve the Programme's visibility among academics and practitioners through a programme of public lectures, national and international. I presented several papers in the USA and undertook lecture tours of Australia (11 presentations) and Scandinavia (7 presentations). I also gave papers in several other countries (France, Italy, the Netherlands, New Zealand, Spain).[5] My objective was to give the Programme a life beyond its individual projects. The 'new governance' was the flagship idea. The public lectures and the élite seminars were the media.

The Programme's objectives

The Programme had seven objectives:

1. To describe, to explain and to create a better understanding of both recent and long-term changes in the nature of British government.

2. To compare these changes with those in other EU member states and other states with a 'Westminster' system of government.
3. To develop new theoretical perspectives and to encourage the use of new research methods in the study of central government.
4. To encourage interdisciplinary work.
5. To foster contacts and create a common understanding between academics and practitioners.
6. To encourage new researchers in this area.
7. To encourage the dissemination of the findings in a form accessible to a wide audience.

The Programme's themes

The Programme had six themes:

1. Developing theory: the new governance.
   Theoretical innovation focused on several key concepts: governance, regulation, core executive.
2. Hollowing out the state.
   Four topics were considered under this heading:
   (a) privatisation and the redefinition of the scope and forms of public intervention;
   (b) the transfer of functions to new service delivery systems, such as agencies and through market testing;
   (c) the transfer of competences by British government to European Union institutions; and
   (d) reduced capacity of the centre to steer.
3. The fragmenting governmental framework.
   The programme provides anthologies of what is going on, especially up-to-date accounts of the impact of change on central departments.
4. Ministers and managers.
   Historical and modern accounts of the relationships between key institutions in the core executive.
5. The evolving constitution.
   Analyses of changing patterns of accountability and of regulation.
6. Delivering services.
   Analyses of contracting out, public consultation and decentralisation.

The Programme, as outlined above, is an example of academic 'curiosity research' which set out to provide an 'anthology of change' in British government. It was explicitly agreed with the ESRC and the Cabinet Office that the Programme's primary objective was not to provide policy-relevant advice. To continue with the language of the civil servants with whom we worked, we were 'holding up a mirror to government' and 'learning each other's language'. Our task was 'to help one another understand the changes'. In practice, the Programme combined basic research on the evolution of British government with policy-relevant research on contemporary practice in Britain and Europe. Those colleagues who were so inclined were free to explore policy-relevant issues; for example, on improving methods of consultation. The Programme's users include not only the higher civil service but also 6th-formers studying A-level politics, university students, and citizens curious about the workings of government.

Some key notions

This section provides an introduction to the concepts and theories used in this volume. I do not seek to provide a critical analysis but to help the reader come to grips with the several chapters and their, at times, distinctive language. Authors were asked to report their research findings and reserve their more theoretical reflections for journal articles. None the less to make sense of their findings, some theory is inevitable. It has been kept to a minimum, however, and I stick to the theories and concepts used by the authors themselves. Where a particular approach is used by one author only, I leave it to that author to explain.[6] Apart from clarity, the objective is also to avoid the same terms having to be defined several times.

As will quickly become clear, the Whitehall Programme travelled in several directions at the same time. There was no one theoretical approach nor, as Programme Director, did I seek to impose one. Without trying to fit my colleagues into arbitrary boxes, the contributors to Volume 1 draw on three organising perspectives or frameworks for analysis which provide a map of how things relate as well as a set of research questions (Gamble 1990: 405; Greenleaf 1983: 3–8). I provide a brief summary, therefore, of: the Westminster model; the new public management (NPM); and governance, with boxed illustrations of each taken from the relevant projects in the Whitehall Programme.

The Westminster model

I begin with the obvious – a dictionary definition of the Westminster model:

> The characteristics of the Westminster model ... include: strong cabinet government based on majority rule; the importance attached to constitutional conventions; a two-party system based on single member constituencies; the assumption that minorities can find expression in one of the major parties; the concept of Her Majesty's loyal opposition; and the doctrine of parliamentary supremacy, which takes precedence over popular sovereignty except during elections. (Verney 1991: 637)

The model has been criticised and adapted and several variants exist (see Bevir and Rhodes 1999; and Volume 2 Chapter 14). But there is a clear baseline to any discussion of the Westminster model and there is strong family likeness between the several varieties. The family lived happily under the roof of the Whitehall Programme (Box 1.1) and of the several variants the 'social science' approach was the more common.

Box 1.1   Variations on the Westminster model*

The findings of several projects, for example on cabinet committees and permanent secretaries, provide critical variations on the central beliefs of the Westminster narrative.

Cabinet committees are effective when there is a clear relationship between the committee and the department carrying out the policy; and a clear sense of political direction about the committee's goals [Brady and Catterall].

The system of cabinet committees does not provide evidence of prime ministerial government but of the frequent failure of prime ministers to exercise leadership. The frequent attempts to strengthen co-ordination reflect the weakness of the Prime Minister in performing his or her key duties [Brady and Catterall].

Permanent secretaries are no longer anonymous 'Mr Fixits' for their minister or the locus of institutional scepticism but the conservators of their department and its public face (Theakston 1999).

Britain does not have prime ministerial or cabinet government but ministerial (or baronial) government [Daintith and Page] (Jones 1998) (Norton Volume 2 Chapter 7).

Britain did enjoy an exceptional degree of continuity and order but it contained two contradictions: between the limited role of the state in practice and the lack of constitutional checks on its unlimited theoretical power; and between the popular conception of state's class neutrality and its partiality when it intervened (Lowe and Rollings Volume 1 Chapter 6).

* In all boxes in Chapters 1 and 14, I paraphrase rather than quote from the projects to save space. The references in square brackets are to either an end of award report or the summary 'Briefing' produced by most projects (see the Appendix at the end of this chapter. The author–date references in parentheses are listed in the Bibliography.

The preferred way of working of the social science approach to studying British government is to frame hypotheses which can, in principle, be refuted or falsified. Gamble (1990: 412) notes that it 'introduced new rigour into British political science and widened the range of research questions but had no alternative organising perspective to propose' so most operate within the Westminster model. However, there was a greater diversity of subjects. Gamble (1990: 414–18) and Tivey (1988) identify five important developments: public policy, political economy, political behaviour especially the several theories of voting behaviour, Thatcherism, and managerialism. This diversity exists in the Whitehall Programme and I describe it below.

The new public management

Hood (1991: 5) argues that new public management (NPM) in Britain has two divergent strands: managerialism and marketisation. Managerialism refers to introducing private sector management in the public sector. It stresses hands-on; professional management; explicit standards and measures of performance; managing by results; value for money; and, more recently, closeness to the customer. It is often referred to as the '3Es': of economy, efficiency and effectiveness. Marketisation refers to introducing incentive structures (such as market competition) into public service provision. It stresses disaggregating bureaucracies; greater competition through contracting-out and quasi-markets; and consumer choice (for a more detailed discussion, see Hood 1991; Pollitt 1993). Before 1988, managerialism was the dominant strand in Britain. After 1988, marketisation became a major source of innovation.

The label NPM now covers many varieties of public sector reform. It is seen as an example of globalisation and marketed by organisations such as the World Bank and the Organisation for Economic Co-operation and Development (OECD). Arguably, it refers to all species of public sector reform (Hood 1995; Rhodes 1999c). At a minimum it covers: privatisation, marketisation, corporate management, regulation and decentralisation. It is the most popular perspective on recent changes (Box 1.2).

Box 1.2 **From Westminster model to New Public Management**

Several projects identify changes in the Westminster model under the impact of NPM.

The story of internal regulation is the story of a plural centre seeking to extend its control [Daintith and Page].

Regulating and auditing quasi-markets is expensive and costs are rarely identified clearly [Whiteside].

The Treasury has a clear set of views on social policy covering not only the levels of spending but also the content. The Treasury's approach is dominated by short-term spending decisions and it has lost the analytical capability to control the link between economic and social policy and to comment on policy content [Parry and Deakin].

The attempt to separate policy from service management has failed. Creating operational agencies increased their policy making role; policy migrated to the agency and policy making became an exercise in managing ambiguous boundaries [Elder and Page] [Day and Klein].

Agencification and managerialism created two cultures – mandarins and managers [Day and Klein].

Governance

The term 'governance' has an unfortunately large number of meanings. It can refer to a *new* process of governing; or a *changed* condition of ordered rule; or the *new* method by which society is governed (see Finer 1970: 3–4). So far, so simple; but the problems of definition become chronic when specifying this new process, condition or method. Elsewhere I have identified at least seven separate uses of governance relevant to the study of Public Administration (Rhodes 1997a: Chapter 3) including, for example, corporate governance, the new public management and international interdependence. Here, governance refers to self-organising, inter-organisational networks with the following characteristics:

1. Interdependence between organisations. Governance is broader than government, covering non-state actors. Changing the boundaries of the state meant the boundaries between public, private and voluntary sectors became shifting and opaque.
2. Continuing interactions between network members, caused by the need to exchange resources and negotiate shared purposes.
3. Game-like interactions, rooted in trust and regulated by rules of the game negotiated and agreed by network participants.
4. A significant degree of autonomy from the state. Networks are not accountable to the state; they are self-organising. Although the state does not occupy a privileged, sovereign position, it can indirectly and imperfectly steer networks. (Rhodes 1997a: Chapter 3)

After 1979, government policy fragmented service delivery systems and compensated for this loss of hands-on controls by centralising financial control. The shift from line bureaucracies to fragmented service delivery systems multiplied the number and type of organisations which need to co-operate in delivering services and increased the centre's dependence on these networks of organisations. There has been a shift from government to governance; from bureaucracy to networks (Box 1.3). So the notion of governance challenges the commonplace notion of Britain as a unitary state with a strong executive and replaces it with the notion of Britain as a maze of institutions and functional authority; the differentiated polity.

Within these broad organising perspectives, projects used several specific theories and concepts. Thus, in Volume 1, the specific social science theories include historic institutionalism and theories of regulation; they are discussed in Chapters 3 and 5 respectively. Other chapters use a shared terminology, namely: the core executive, policy networks, power-dependence and hollowing-out (see Chapters 2, 6, 7, 11 and 14). To avoid undue repetition, I define each briefly here while Chapters 2 and 14 are structured around these ideas and so provide the reader with an extended discussion. I also provide brief résumés for the various theories and concepts used in Volume 2 in the introduction to that volume.

Box 1.3   Characterising governance

Martin Smith (1999) argues the Westminster system has changed from bureaucracy to networks.

Bureaucracy
A high degree of state control, the result of policies such as nationalisation.
A large bureaucratic machine.
Legitimacy to undertake large scale intervention in society.
The incorporation of key economic groups into the policy process.
A high degree of consensus between officials and politicians over their role in governing and decision making.

Networks
A shift from bureaucratic management to decentralised and delayered management.
A tendency to set overall direction of policy rather than detail of policy – a lack of detailed intervention.
Control over a smaller public sector.
The exclusion of economic groups from the policy process.
Loss of consensus between officials and politicians.
Concern with managing networks rather than directing state bureaucracies.

The core executive

Textbooks, commentators and practitioners take it as axiomatic that the British unitary state is characterised by a strong executive (see Birch 1964: 243–4). The Westminster model encourages sterile debates about the relative power of prime minister and Cabinet (Rhodes 1995). In fact, the centre is characterised as much by fragmentation and interdependence as by strength.

> executive authority is neither the sole preserve of prime ministers nor exclusive to political leaders. ... Decision making is fragmented between policy networks with sporadic prime ministerial interventions. Ministers responsible for domestic departments are, to a substantial degree, sovereign in their own turf. Co-ordination is achieved (if at all) and conflicts resolved (or at least suppressed) in and by Cabinet *and* its multifarious committees, supplemented by bureaucratic mechanisms. (Rhodes 1988: 76)

This notion of the segmented executive was subsequently developed to include the 'the core executive':

> We define the core executive functionally to include all those organisations and structures which primarily serve to pull together and integrate central government policies, or act as final arbiters within the executive of conflicts between different elements of the government machine. (Dunleavy and Rhodes 1990: 4; Rhodes 1995)

The point of this notion is that co-ordination and conflict management – joined-up government if you will – are not the exclusive concern of prime minister and cabinet. Just as 'central government' can be seen as a federation of departments, so the 'core' of government, which seeks to tie together the seemingly disparate departments, itself multiplies co-ordinating actors and their attendant procedures and mechanisms. The core executive is not the specific institutions of prime minister and cabinet but the set of networks which police the functional or department-based policy networks.

Policy networks

A policy network is a cluster or complex of organisations connected to one another by resource dependencies (Rhodes 1986: Chapter 2 after Benson 1982: 148). Policy networks matter: they are not another example of otiose social science jargon. All governments confront a vast array of interests. Aggregation of those interests is a functional necessity. Intermediation is a fact of everyday life in government. To describe and explain variations in patterns of intermediation is to explore one of the key governmental and political processes. Policy networks are one way of analysing aggregation and intermediation; they are the oligopoly of the political market-place. They are important for six reasons (see Marsh and Rhodes 1992a; Marsh and Smith 2000).

- They limit participation in the policy process;
- They define the roles of actors;
- They decide which issues will be included and excluded from the policy agenda;
- Through the rules of the game, they shape the behaviour of actors;
- They privilege certain interests not only by according them access but also by favouring their preferred policy outcomes;
- They substitute private government for public accountability.

So, debates about, for example, the dominant interests in networks and the asymmetric power of central departments are not exercises in pedantry. They are about: 'Who rules?', 'How do they rule?', and 'In whose interest do they rule?'. Policy networks are a tool for exploring how power is exercised in modern Britain and who benefits from its exercise (and for a review of the recent literature see Rhodes 1999a: Chapter 8).

Power-dependence

The notion of power-dependence contains five propositions (Rhodes 1981: 98):

(a) Any organisation is *dependent* upon other organisations for *resources*.
(b) In order to achieve their *goals*, the organisations have to exchange resources.
(c) Although decision-making within the organisation is constrained by other organisations, the *dominant coalition* retains some discretion. The *appreciative system* of the dominant coalition influences which relationships are seen as a problem and which resources will be sought.

(d)   The dominant coalition employs strategies within known *rules of the game* to regulate *the process of exchange.*

(e)   Variations in the degree of *discretion* are a product of the goals and the relative power potential of interacting organisations. This relative power potential is a product of the resources of each organisation, of the rules of the game and of the process of exchange between organisations. (Emphasis in original)

So, relations in a network or in the core executive resemble a 'game' in which all actors manoeuvre for advantage. Each deploys its resources – for example, legal, organisational, financial, political or informational – to increase their influence over outcomes while trying to avoid becoming dependent on the other 'players'. It is a complex game in which the various interests, levels and units of government are interdependent and relationships are constantly shifting.

Hollowing-out

This term refers to:

- privatisation and the redefinition of the scope and forms of public intervention;
- the transfer of functions to new service delivery systems, such as agencies and through market testing;
- the transfer of competences by British government to European Community and other international institutions; and
- the reduced capacity of the centre to steer (modified from Rhodes 1994 and 1997c).

So the capacity of the British executive to steer is eroded by power-dependence in the professional–bureaucratic complexes of policy networks and this erosion gained great impetus from, for example, privatisation and Europeanisation.

Organisation

As well as providing a summary of the key findings of all the projects, Volume 1 surveys the main institutional changes and Volume 2 examines the changing roles and relationships of the prime minister, ministers and civil servants. Volume 2 also explores the new ways of delivering services which have evolved over the past 25 years. It is, of course, impossible to explore changing roles and relationships without examining the ways in which such changes are a response to and a cause of institutional change. The differences between the two Volumes is, therefore, one of emphasis and to some degree of discipline with the historians and lawyers predominantly in Volume 1 and the political scientists in Volume 2.

Volume 1 has three parts. Part I examines the changing context of government. Martin Smith (Chapter 2) challenges the Westminster model with its focus on prime minister and Cabinet, arguing for a focus on power-dependence in the core executive. Simon Bulmer and Martin Burch (Chapter 3) explore the impact of Europeanisation on Whitehall trying to explain the UK's distinctive response to pressures common to all member states. Alan Page and Terence Daintith (Chapter 4) explore a neglected features of the British constitution; the growth in the executive's internal controls (of, for example, the civil service). Finally, Christopher Hood and his colleagues (Chapter 5) explore the large and continuing growth of regulatory bodies overseeing government.

Part II explores the historical development of key institutions. Rodney Lowe and Neil Rollings (Chapter 6) look at the modernisation of British government between 1957 and 1964 to argue there was no 'unilinear increase in state intervention after 1900 nor a centralisation'. Astrid Ringe and Neil Rollings (Chapter 7) provide an example of this mix of intervention and governance by examining how fragmentation of the core executive frustrated the reform of the monetary system. Three chapters which focus on specific institutional changes follow. Iain McLean and his colleagues (Chapter 8) describe the changing organisation of central government departments. Peter Catterall and Christopher Brady (Chapter 9) describe the origins, organisation and functioning of cabinet committees. June Burnham and George Jones (Chapter 10) look at patterns of development of the prime minister's office.

Part III focuses on the major institutional innovation of the past 25 years; the introduction of 'Next Steps' agencies. Brian Hogwood and his colleagues (Chapter 11) describe how agencies are called to account, finding both gaps and overload and suggesting too little attention has been paid to the multiple constituencies with an interest in agency accountability; 'No one is accountable for the overall pattern of accountability'. Neil Elder and Edward Page (Chapter 12) compares agencies in Britain, Germany and Sweden, concluding that their characteristics reflect the constitutional–legal conditions of each country. Pat Day and Rudolf Klein look at the internal agency of the Department of Health and ask whether management can be insulated from policy and what is the relationship between steering (department) and rowing (agency)? The short answers are 'no' and 'ambiguous'. The longer answers are in Chapter 13.

Each chapter explains what the researchers did and, where appropriate, identifies the lessons for British government. It is impossible to synthesise here the 23 projects covered by the two volumes. Nonetheless each volume has an 'Introduction' which tells the history of the Programme, introduces the several theories and concepts used in the book, and provides a bibliography (Chapter 1). I also try to provide 'added value' in the guise of a 'Conclusion' (Chapter 14) which gives a personal interpretation of the major findings and lessons of the several projects.

Notes

1. The ESRC is the United Kingdom's leading social science funding agency. It is an independent organisation, financed solely by government. Its activities fall into three groups: research grants, research centres and programmes, and postgraduate training. Research Programmes seek to harness and strengthen the United Kingdom's social science research capacity to address scientific and policy relevant topics of strategic and national importance. Typically, there will be 10 to 15 projects drawn from several social

science disciplines and spread among UK universities. Researchers work independently on individual projects with the support of a Programme Director and his or her advisory Steering Committee.

2. Further information on the Programme and individual projects, along with contact names and addresses, can be found on the Programme's web site http://www.ncl.ac.uk/~npol/whitehall/index/html.

3. After May 1997, the title became 'Programme Director', the terms of reference were revised and the Steering Committees became advisory. The new terms of reference identified seven roles: adding value, providing intellectual leadership, providing a lead on engaging with potential users, providing input to public policy debates, providing inputs to ESRC policy debates, providing a channel of communication between the ESRC and the research community, and providing advice to the ESRC about securing value for money from the programme.

4. The members of the Steering Committee were: Professor Ben Pimlott, Chair, Birkbeck College; Vernon Bogdanor, Brasenose College, Oxford; Professor Peter Hennessy, Queen Mary & Westfield College, University of London; Dr Ian Harden, Faculty of Law, University of Sheffield; Bill Jones, University of Manchester; Nicola Simpson, National Association of Citizens Advice Bureaux; Professor Cyril Tomkins, School of Management University of Bath; David Wilkinson, Office of Public Service, Cabinet Office; and Andrew Whetnall, Office of Public Service, Cabinet Office.

5. The Whitehall Programme has formal links with equivalent research projects in Denmark and Australia. In Denmark the link is with the Institute of Political Science, University of Copenhagen and their Danish Research Council funded project on 'Democracy and Institutional Change'. In Australia the link is with the Centre for Australian Public Sector Management, Griffith University, Brisbane and their Australian Research Council funded project on 'The Governance of Australia'.

6. For example, cultural theory (Thompson *et al.* 1990) underpins the categories used in the chapter by Christopher Hood and his colleagues (Chapter 5) but it is not necessary to understand these theoretical roots to make sense of this summary of their research. The interested reader should consult Hood 1996 and 1998.

Appendix: Programme Publications, 1994–2000

Books

Project publications

Those works marked with an asterisk appear in the 'Transforming Government' series, edited by R. A. W. Rhodes.

Bridgen, P. and Lowe, R. (1998), *Welfare Policy Under the Conservatives 1951–1964*. London: PRO Publications.

Bulmer, S. and Burch, M. (2000), *Mandarins, Ministers and Europe*. Manchester: Manchester University Press.

Burnham, J. (1999), *Whitehall and the Civil Service*. Sheffield: The Politics Association and Sheffield-Hallam University Press.

*Burnham, J. and Jones, G. W. (2000), *Advising Prime Ministers 1868–1998*. London: Macmillan.

*Catterall, P., Brady, C. and Kandiah, M. (2000), *Government by Committee: the Development of the Cabinet Committee System*. London: Macmillan.

*Catterall, P., Brady, C. and Kandiah, M. (2000), *Routine and Crisis: the Operation of the Cabinet Committee System*. London: Macmillan.

Catterall, P., Kaiser, W. and Jordan, U. (eds) (2000), *Political Reform in Twentieth Century Britain: Themes, Ideas, Policies*. London: Cass.

Clifford, C., McMillan A. and McLean, I. (1997), *The Organisation of Central Government Departments 1964–1992: a History*. Oxford: Nuffield College. This book is also available on the web (http://www.nuff.ox.ac.uk/politics/whitehall/index.html) see:

> Volume 1 Project Synopsis
> Volume 2 Departmental Function Transfers
> Volume 3, Pt 1, Departments and ministers: Departmental Functions
> Volume 3 Pt. 2, Departments and Ministers: Internal Structural Change
> Volume 3 Pt. 3, Departments and Ministers: Ministers and Ministerial Office

Daintith, T. (ed.) (1997), *Constitutional Implications of Executive Self-Regulation: the 'New' Administrative Law*. London: Institute of Advanced Legal Studies.

Daintith, T. and Page, A. (1999), *The Executive in the Constitution: Structure, Autonomy and Internal Control*. Oxford: Oxford University Press.

Day, P. and Klein, R. (1997), *Steering but not Rowing? The Transformation of the Department of Health: a Case Study*. Bristol: The Policy Press.

*Elder, N. and Page, E. (2000), *Accountability and Control in Next Steps Agencies*. London: Macmillan.

*Hogwood, B., Judge, D. and McVicar, M. (2000), *Agencies and Accountability*. London: Macmillan.

Hood, C. (1998), *The Art of the State*. Oxford: Clarendon.

Hood, C., Scott, C., James, O., Jones, G. and Travers, T. (1999), *Regulation Inside Government: Waste-Watchers, Quality Police and Sleaze Busters*. Oxford: Oxford University Press.

Lowe, R. (1998), *The Welfare State in Britain*. London: Macmillan.

*Smith, M. (1999), *The Core Executive in Britain*. London: Macmillan.

Director's publications

Rhodes, R. A. W. (1995), *The New Governance: Governing without Government*. London: ESRC/RSA.

Rhodes, R. A. W. (1997), *Understanding Governance: Policy Networks, Governance, Reflexivity and Accountability*. Buckingham: Open University Press.

Rhodes, R. A. W. (ed.) (1995), *British Public Administration: the State of the Discipline* (special issue of *Public Administration*, 73).

Rhodes, R. A. W. (ed.) (1998), *Transforming British Government* (special Issue of *Public Policy and Administration*, 13/4).

Rhodes, R. A. W. (ed.) (1999), *United Kingdom*. Volumes I and II. Aldershot: Ashgate.

*Rhodes, R. A. W. (ed.) (2000), *Transforming British Government*. London: Macmillan.

Volume 1. Changing Institutions
Volume 2. Changing Roles and Relationships

Rhodes, R. A. W. (with Bruno Dente, Marco Cammelli and others) (1995), *Reformare la Pubblica Amministrazione*. Torino: Edizioni della Fondazione Giovanni Agnelli).

Rhodes, R. A. W. and P. Dunleavy (eds) (1995), *Prime Minister, Cabinet and Core Executive*. London: Macmillan.

Rhodes, R. A. W., Peters, B. G. and Wright, V. (eds) (1997), *Adminstrer Le Sommet De L'Exécutif*. (Special issue of *Revue Française d'Administration publique*, July/September, No. 82).

*Rhodes, R. A. W., Peters, G. and Wright, V. (eds) (2000), *Administering the Summit*. London, Macmillan.

Rhodes, R. A. W. and Weller, P. (eds.) (2000), *Mandarin or Valets? The Changing World of Top Officials*. Buckingham: Open University Press.

*Rhodes, R. A. W., Weller. P. and Bakviss H. (eds) (1997), *The Hollow Crown*. London: Macmillan.

Articles

Project publications

Brady, C. and Catterall, P. (1997), 'Managing the Core Executive', *Public Administration*, 75/3: 509–29.

Brady, C. (1999), 'The Management of Cabinet Government during the Suez Crisis', *Contemporary British History*, 1112: 65–93.

Bridgen, P. (2000), 'Making a Mess of Modernisation: the State, Redundancy Pay and Economic Policy Making in the early 1960s', *Twentieth Century British History*, 11: forthcoming.

Bridgen, P. (2000), 'The One Nation Idea and State Welfare: the Conservatives and pensions', *Contemporary British History*, forthcoming.

Bulmer S. and Burch, M. (1997), 'Maastricht II und danach: Großbritannien doch am Herzen Europas?', *Wirtschaftsdienst*, 77. Jg., Nr.7: 381–5.

Bulmer, S. and Burch, M. (1998), 'Organising for Europe: Whitehall, the British State and European Union', *Public Administration*, 76/4: 601–28.

Burnham, J. and Jones, G. W. (1997), 'Policy Advice to the Core Executive', *Public Finance Foundation Review* No. 16: 8–15.

Catterall, P. (1997), 'Handling the Transfer of Power: a note on the origin of the Douglas-Hume Rules', *Contemporary British History*, 11/1: 76–82.

Catterall, P. (1998), 'The Cabinet', *Modern History Review*, 10/1: 15.

Catterall, P. and Brady, C. (1998), 'Cabinet Committees in British Governance', *Public Policy and Administration*, 13/4: 67–84.

Clifford, C. (1997), 'The Rise and Fall of the Department of Economic Affairs', *Contemporary British History*, 11: 94–142.

Daintith, T. (1998), 'The Legal Effects of the Appropriation Act', *Public Law*: 552–7.

Elder, N. C. M. and Page, E. (1998), 'Culture and Agency: Fragmentation and agency structures in Germany and Sweden', *Public Policy and Administration* 13/4: 28–45.

Hogwood, B. W. (1997), 'The Machinery of Government 1979–97', *Political Studies*, 45/4: 704–15.

Hood, C. (1996), 'Control over Bureaucracy: Cultural Theory and Institutional Variety', *Journal of Public Policy*,15: 207–30.

Hood, C. and Scott, C. (1996), 'Bureaucratic Regulation and New Public management in the UK: Mirror Image Developments', *Journal of Law and Society*, 23: 321–45.

Hood, C., James, O., Jones, G., Scott, C. and Travers, T. (1998), 'Regulation Inside Government' Where New Public Management Meets the Audit Explosion', *Public Money and Management*, 18/2: 61–68.

Jones, G. W. (1998), 'Reforming No. 10', *Talking Politics*, 11/1: 21–7. Revised and updated version of an article published in *Public Finance Foundation Review*, No. 16, August 1997: 8–15.

Judge, D., Hogwood, B. W. and McVicar, M. (1997), 'The Pond Life of Executive Agencies', *Public Policy and Administration*, 12/2: 95–115.

Lowe, R. (1996), 'The Influence of Ideas on Social Policy', *Contemporary British History*, 10: 160–77.

Lowe, R. (1997), 'Plumbing New Depths? Contemporary Historians and the Public Record Office', *Twentieth Century British History*, 8: 239–65.

Lowe, R. (1997), 'The Core Executive, Modernisation and the Creation of PESC, 1960–64', *Public Administration*, 75/4: 601–15.

Lowe, R. (1997), 'Milestone or Millstone? The 1959–1961 Plowden Committee and Its Impact on British Welfare State Policy', *The Historical Journal*, 40/2: 463–91.

McLean, I. and Johnes, D. (1999), 'Regulating Gifts of Generosity: the Aberfan Disaster Fund and the Charity Commission', *Legal Studies*, 19: 380–96.

McVicar, M., Judge, D. and Hogwood, B. W. (1998), 'Too Much of a Good Thing?', *The Stakeholder*, 2/1: 10–11.

Page, A. (1998), 'Controlling Government From Within: a Constitutional Analysis', *Public Policy and Administration*, 13/4: 85–95.

Ringe, A. (1998a), 'Background to Neddy: Economic Planning in the 1960s', *Contemporary British History*, 12/1: 82–98.

Ringe, A. (1998b), 'The National Economic Development Council 1962–67', *Contemporary British History*, 12/1: 99–130.

Ringe, A. and Rollings, N. (2000), 'Responding to Relative Decline: the Creation of the NEDC', *Economic History Review*, May.

Rollings, N. (1994), '"Poor Mr Butskell: A Short Life, Wrecked by Schizophrenia"?', *Twentieth Century British History*, 5/2: 183–205.

Smith, M. (1994), 'The Core Executive and the Resignation of Mrs Thatcher', *Public Administration*, 72: 341–64.

Smith, M. J. (1998). 'Theoretical and Empirical Challenges to British Central Government', *Public Administration*, 76/3: 45–72.

Director's publications

Rhodes, R. A. W. (1994), 'Reinventing Excellence: or How Best-Sellers Thwart the Search for Lessons to Transform the Public Sector', *Public Administration*, 72: 279–87.

Rhodes, R. A. W. (1994), 'The Hollowing Out of the State', *The Political Quarterly*, 65: 138–51.

Rhodes, R.A.W. (1995), 'The State of Public Administration: a Professional History of the 1980s', *Public Administration*, 73: 1–16.

Rhodes, R. A. W. (1995), The Changing Face of Public Administration', *Politics*, 15: 117–26.

Rhodes, R. A. W. (1996), 'From Institutions to Dogma: Tradition, Eclecticism and Ideology in the Study of British Public Administration', *Public Administration Review*, 56/6: 507–16.

Rhodes, R. A. W. (1996), 'Looking Beyond Managerialism', *Australian Journal of Public Administration*, 55/2: 1–4.

Rhodes, R. A. W. (1996), 'Agencies in British Government: Revolution or Evolution?', *Diritto Pubblico*, No. 3: 731–54.

Rhodes, R. A. W. (1996), 'The New Governance: Governing without Government', *Political Studies*, 44: 652–67.

Rhodes, R. A. W. (1997), 'Diplomacy in Governance', *Politics Today*, 7/3: 24–7. Edited version reprinted in *Public Finance Foundation Review*, No. 13: 8–10.

Rhodes, R. A. W. (1997), 'It's the Mix that Matters: from Marketisation to Diplomacy' *Australian Journal of Public Administration*, 56: 40–53. Reprinted in *Public Policy and Administration*, 12/3: 31–50.

Rhodes, R. A. W. (1998a), 'Different Roads to Unfamiliar Places: UK Experience in Comparative Perspective', *Australian Journal of Public Administration*, 57: 19–31.

Rhodes, R. A. W. (1998b), 'Diplomacy in Governance', *Politics Today*, 7/3: 24–27.

Rhodes, R. A. W. (1998), 'L'evoluzione del governo centrale in Gran Bretagna: il programma Whitehall dell'ESRC', *Storia Amministrazione Costituzione*, Annale 6: 297–303.

Rhodes, R. A. W. (1998), 'The Changing Nature of Central Government in Britain: The ESRC's Whitehall Programme', *Public Policy and Administration*, 13/4: 1–11.

Rhodes, R. A. W. (1999), 'Traditions and Public Sector Reform', *Scandinavian Political Studies*, 2214: 341–70.

Rhodes, R. A. W. (2000), 'The ESRC Whitehall Programme, 1994–1999', *Public Administration*, forthcoming.

Rhodes R. A. W. and Bevir, M. (1998a), 'Public Administration without Foundations', *Administrative Theory & Praxis*, 20/1: 3–13.

Rhodes, R. A. W. and Bevir, M. (1998b), 'Narratives of "Thatcherism"', *West European Politics*, 21/1: 97–119.

Rhodes, R. A. W. and Bevir, M. (1999a), 'Studying British Government: Recon-structing the Research Agenda', *British Journal of Politics and International Relations*, 1/2: 215–39.

Rhodes, R. A. W. and Bevir, M. (1999b), 'Narratives of Governance', *Revue Française de Science Politique*, 49/6 1999: 355–77.

Rhodes, R. A. W. and Bevir, M. (2000), 'Analysing Networks: from Typologies of Institutions to Narratives of Beliefs', *Revue française d'administration publique*, forthcoming.

Rhodes, R. A. W. and Dargie, C. (1996), 'Traditional Public Administration', *Public Administration*, 74: 325–32.

Rhodes, R. A. W. and Marsh, D. (1995), 'The Concept of Policy Networks in British Political Science: Its Development and Utility', *Talking Politics*, 8: 28–40.

Rhodes, R. A. W., Peters, B. G. and Wright, V. (1997), 'Tendances convergentes et spécificités nationales', *Revue Française d'Administration Publique*, July/September, No. 82: 381–95.

Chapters

Project publications

Brady, C. (1997), 'The Cabinet Office' and 'War Cabinets'. In J. Shafritz (ed.), *International Encyclopaedia of Public Policy and Administration*. New York: Westview.

Buller, J. and Smith, M. J. (1998), 'Civil Service Attitudes to the European Union'. In D. Baker and D. Seawright (eds), *Europe: For and Against*. Oxford: Oxford University Press.

Bulmer, S. (2000), 'The United Kingdom: Between Political Controversy and Administrative Efficiency', in A. Maurer, J. Mihag and W. Wessels (eds), *Fifteen Into One: the European Union and Member States*. Manchester: Manchester University Press.

Bulmer, S., Jeffrey, C. and Paterson, W. (1998), 'Deutschlands europäische Diplomatie: die Entwicklung des regionalen Milieus'. In W. Weidenfeld (ed.), *Deutsche Europapolitik: Optionen wirksamer Interessenvertretung*. Bonn: Europa Union Verlag.

Bulmer, S. and Burch, M. (2000a), 'The Europeanisation of British Central Government'. In R. A. W. Rhodes (ed.), *Transforming British Government. Volume 1. Changing Institutions*. London: Macmillan.

Bulmer, S. and Burch, M. (2000b), 'The "Europeanisation" of British Central Government. In M. Aspinall and G. Schneider (eds), *The Rules of Integration*. Manchester: Manchester University Press.

Burnham, J. and Jones, G. W. (1999), 'Innovators at No. 10 Downing Street'. In K. Theakston (ed.), *Leadership in Whitehall*. London: Macmillan.

Burnham, J. and Jones, G. W. (2000), 'The Evolving Prime Minister's Office: 1868–1997'. In R. A. W. Rhodes (ed.), *Transforming British Government. Volume 1. Changing Institutions*. London: Macmillan.

Catterall, P. (1997), 'Efficiency with Freedom? Debates about the British Constitution in the Twentieth Century'. In P. Catterall, W. Kaiser and U. Jordan (eds), *Political Reform in Twentieth Century Britain: Themes, Ideas, Policies*. London: Cass.

Catterall, P. and Brady, C. (2000), 'The Development and Role of Cabinet Committees in Britain'. In R. A. W. Rhodes (ed.), *Transforming British Government. Volume 1. Changing Institutions*. London: Macmillan.

Daintith, T. (1997), 'Legal Control of Administrative Action'. In T. Daintith (ed.), *Constitutional Implications of Executive Self-Regulation: the 'New' Administrative Law*. London: Institute of Advanced Legal Studies.

Day, P. and Klein, R. (2000), 'The Politics of Managing the NHS'. In R. A. W. Rhodes (ed.), *Transforming British Government. Volume 1. Changing Institutions*. London: Macmillan.

Elder, N. C. and Page, E. (2000), 'Accountability and Control in Next Steps Agencies'. In R. A. W. Rhodes (ed.), *Transforming British Government. Volume 1. Changing Institutions*. London: Macmillan.

Hogwood, B. W. (1998), 'UK Regulatory Institutions: increasing regulation in the "shrinking state"'. In G. B. Doern and S. Wilks (eds), *Regulatory Institutions in Britain and America*. Toronto: University of Toronto Press.

Hogwood, B. W. and Judge, D. (2000), 'Agencification and Ministerial Accountability in the UK'. In E. Schröter and H. Wollman (eds), *Public Sector Modernisation in Britain and Germany*. London: Macmillan.

Hogwood, B. W., Judge, D and McVicar, M. (2000a), 'Agencies and Accountability'. In R. A. W. Rhodes (ed.), *Transforming British Government. Volume 1. Changing Institutions*. London: Macmillan.

Hogwood, B. W., Judge, D and McVicar, M. (2000b), 'Agencies, Ministers and Civil Servants in Britain'. In B. G.Peters and J. Pierre (eds), *Politicians, Bureaucrats and Administrative Reform: the Changing Balance*. London: Routledge.

Hood, C. and James, O. (1997), 'The Central Executive'. In P. Dunleavy *et al.* (eds), *Developments in British Politics 5*. London: Macmillan.

Hood, C., Scott, C. and James, O. (2000), 'Bureaucratic Game Keeping: regulation of UK Public Administration 1976–96'. In R. A. W. Rhodes (ed.), *Transforming British Government. Volume 1. Changing Institutions*. London: Macmillan.

Loughlin, M. and Scott, C. (1997), 'The Regulatory State'. In P. Dunleavy *et al.* (eds), *Developments in British Politics 5*. London: Macmillan.

Lowe, R. (1996), 'The Re-planning of the Welfare State, 1957–64'. In M. Francis *et al.* (eds), *The Conservatives and British Society, 1880–1990*. Cardiff: University of Wales Press.

Lowe, R. and Rollings, N. (2000), 'Modernising Britain 1957–1964: a classic case of Centralisation and Fragmentation?' In R. A. W. Rhodes (ed.), *Transforming British Government. Volume 1. Changing Institutions*. London: Macmillan.

McLean, I., Clifford, C. and McMillan, A. (1999), 'Aberfan at the Public Record Office'. In M. Hughes (ed.), *Aberfan – our Hiraeth – an Anthology of Poetry, Prose and Pictures*. Aberfan, Aberfan & Merthyr Vale Community Co-operative.

McLean, I., Clifford, C. and McMillan, A. (2000), 'The Organisation of Central Government Departments: a History 1964–1992'. In R. A. W. Rhodes (ed.), *Transforming British Government. Volume 1. Changing Institutions*. London: Macmillan.

Page, A. (1997), 'Toolboxes and Blueprints: Controlling the Control of the Executive and the New Administrative law'. In T. Daintith (ed.) *Constitutional Implications of Executive Self-Regulation: the 'New' Administrative Law*. London: Institute of Advanced Legal Studies.

Page, A. (1997), 'The Constitutional Implications of Executive Self-Regulation in the United Kingdom'. In G. Little (ed.) *The Legal Regulation of Economic and Social Order*. Stirling: Scottish Socio-Legal Studies Association.

Page, A. (2000), 'The Citizen's Charter and Administrative Justice'. In Harris and Partington (eds), *Administrative Justice in the 21st Century*. Oxford: Hart.

Page, A. and Daintith, T. (2000), 'Internal Control in the Executive and its Constitutional Significance'. In R. A. W. Rhodes (ed.), *Transforming British Government. Volume 1. Changing Institutions*. London: Macmillan.

Ringe, A. and Rollings, N. (2000), 'Domesticating the 'Market Animal'?: The Treasury and the Bank of England 1955–60.' In R. A. W. Rhodes (ed.), *Transforming British Government. Volume 1. Changing Institutions*. London: Macmillan.

Rollings, N. (1996), 'Butskellism, the Postwar Consensus and the Managed Economy'. In H. Jones and M. Kandiah (eds), *The Myth of Consensus. New Views of British History, 1945–64*. London: Macmillan.

Smith, M. (1995), 'Interpreting the rise and fall of Margaret Thatcher: Power Dependence and the Core Executive'. In R. A. W. Rhodes and P. Dunleavy (eds), *Prime Minister, Cabinet and Core Executive*. London: Macmillan.

Smith, M. (1996), 'Reforming the State'. In S. Ludlam and M. J. Smith (eds), *Contemporary British Conservatism*. London: Macmillan.

Smith, M. J. (1999), 'Centre of Power: the institutions of government'. In I. Holliday *et al.* (eds), *Fundamentals in British Politics*. London: Macmillan.

Smith. M. J. (2000), 'Prime Ministers, Ministers and Civil Servants in the Core Executive'. In R. A. W. Rhodes (ed.), *Transforming British Government. Volume 1. Changing Institutions*. London: Macmillan.

Director's publications

Rhodes, R. A. W. (1995), 'Introducing the Core Executive'. In R. A. W. Rhodes and P. Dunleavy (eds), *Prime Minister, Cabinet and Core Executive*. London: Macmillan.

Rhodes, R. A. W. (1995), 'From Prime Ministerial Power to Core Executive'. In R. A. W. Rhodes and P. Dunleavy (eds), *Prime Minister, Cabinet and Core Executive*. London: Macmillan.

Rhodes, R. A. W. (1995), 'Guide to Further Reading'. In R. A. W. Rhodes and P. Dunleavy (eds), *Prime Minister, Cabinet and Core Executive*. London: Macmillan.

Rhodes, R. A. W. (1995), 'Les reseaux d'action publique en Grande-Bretagne' en *Les Reseaux de Politique Publique. Debat autour des policy networks*. Sous la direction de Patrick LeGales et Mark Thatcher. Paris: Editions L'Harmattan.

Rhodes, R. A. W. (1995) 'The Institutional Approach'. In D. Marsh and G. Stoker (eds), *Theories and Methods in Political Science*. London: Macmillan.

Rhodes, R. A. W. (1995), 'Governance in the Hollow State'. In M. Blunden and M. Dando (eds), *Rethinking Public Policy Making. Questioning Assumptions Challenging Beliefs*. London: Sage.

Rhodes, R. A. W., George, S. and Bache, I. (1996), 'The European Union, Cohesion Policy and Subnational Authorities in the United Kingdom'. In L. Hooghe (ed.), *Cohesion Policy and European Integration*. Oxford: Clarendon Press.

Rhodes, R. A. W. (1996), 'Policy Networks and Policy Making in the European Union: a Critical Appraisal'. In L. Hooghe (ed.), *Cohesion Policy and European Integration*. Oxford: Clarendon Press.

Rhodes, R. A. W., George S. and Bache I. (1997), 'Regionalism in a Unitary State: the Case of the UK'. In J. J. Hesse (ed.), *Regions In Europe II: The Regional Potential*. Baden-Baden: Nomos.

Rhodes, R. A. W. (1997), 'Reinventing Whitehall, 1979–95'. In W. Kickert (ed.), *Public Management and Administrative Reform in Western Europe*. Aldershot: Edward Elgar.

Rhodes, R. A. W. (1997), 'Foreword by Professor R. A. W Rhodes' to W. J. M. Kickert, E. H. Klijn and J. F. M. Koppenjan (eds), *Managing Complex Networks: Strategies for the Public Sector*. London: Sage.

Rhodes, R. A. W. (1997), 'Shackling the Leader? Coherence, Capacity and the Hollow Crown'. In P. Weller, H. Bakvis and R. A. W. Rhodes (eds), *The Hollow Crown*. London: Macmillan.

Rhodes, R. A. W. (1999), 'Foreword: Governance and Networks'. In G. Stoker (ed.) *The New Management of British Local Governance*. London: Macmillan. Edited version reprinted in G. Stoker (ed.), *The New Politics of British Local Governance*. London: Macmillan.

Rhodes, R. A. W. (1999), 'Public Administration and Governance' in J. Pierre (ed.) *Debating Governance*. Oxford: Oxford University Press.

Rhodes, R. A. W. (2000a), 'The ESRC Whitehall Programme: a Guide to Institutional Change'. In R. A. W. Rhodes (ed.), *Transforming British Government. Volume 1. Changing Institutions*. London: Macmillan.

Rhodes, R. A. W. (2000b), 'The Governance Narrative'. In R. A. W. Rhodes (ed.), *Transforming British Government. Volume 1. Changing Institutions*. London: Macmillan.

Rhodes, R. A. W. (2000c), 'The ESRC Whitehall Programme: a Guide to Changing Roles and Relationships'. In R. A. W. Rhodes (ed.), *Transforming British Government. Volume 2. Changing Roles and Relationships*. London: Macmillan.

Rhodes, R. A. W. (2000d), 'Understanding the British Governmental Tradition: an Anti-Foundational Approach'. In R. A. W. Rhodes (ed.), *Transforming British Government. Volume 2. Changing Roles and Relationships*. London: Macmillan.

Rhodes, R. A. W. (2000e), 'Everybody But Us: Departmental Secretaries in Britain 1970–1999'. In R. A. W. Rhodes and P. Weller (eds) (2000), *Mandarin or Valets? The Changing World of Top Officials*. Buckingham: Open University Press.

Rhodes, R. A. W. and Weller, P. (2000), 'Enter Centre Stage – the Departmental Secretaries'. In R. A. W. Rhodes and P. Weller (eds) (2000), *Mandarin or Valets? The Changing World of Top Officials.* Buckingham: Open University Press.

Smith, M. (1996), 'Reforming the State'. In S. Ludlam and M. J. Smith (eds), *Contemporary British Conservatism.* London: Macmillan.

Smith, M. J. (1999), 'Centre of Power: the Institutions of Government'. In I. Holliday *et al.* (eds), *Fundamentals in British Politics.* London: Macmillan.

Discussion papers

Public service seminars

Klaus Goetz, *Challenges to the Public Bureaucracy State – Six Propositions on Administrative Development in Germany.*

Torben Beck Jørgensen, *From Agency to Department and Back Again: Contradictory Developments in Danish Public Administration.*

Patricia W. Ingraham, *Reinventing the American Federal Government: Reform, Redux or Real Change.*

Michael Power, *The Perils of the Audit Society.*

Michael Bichard and Andrew Likierman, *Outsiders and Insiders in Government.*

John Gray, *The Illusion of a Minimum State.*

Vernon Bogdanor, *Constitutional and Administrative Reform: Can Inquiries be Probing, Expeditious and Fair? Scott Compared with Earlier Inquiries.*

Ian Harden, *The Impact of the EU on Constitutional Reform.*

Francis Plowden, *The Appropriate Use of Management Consultants in Government.*

Terence Daintith, *Judicial Review and its Impact on Government.*

Mark Thatcher, *Regulation and Regulators: Is the Current System Working or is There a Need for Rationalisation and Reform?*

Martin Loughlin, *The Constitutional Dimension to Central–Local Relations.*

Christopher Foster, *Constitutional and Administrative Reform: Is the State Under Stress?*

Richard Parry and Nicholas Deakin, *The Treasury and Social Policy.*

Robin Butler, *Retrospective and Looking Forward.*

George Jones, *Reforming No. 10.*

Lord Norton of Louth, *The New Barons? Senior Ministers in British Government.*

Paul Hirst, *How Global is Globalisation? And where does the UK fit in?*

Vernon Bogdanor, *Whither the Union?*

Rod Rhodes, *The Governance Narrative.*

(All papers: Public Policy Group, LSE.)

Other

Bulmer, S. and Burch, M. (1996) 'The British Core Executive and European Integration: a New Institutionalist Research Prospectus' *Manchester Papers in Politics – EPRU Series,* No. 4 (Department of Government, University of Manchester).

Bulmer, S. and Burch, M. (1997), 'Organising for Europe – Whitehall and the EU. An Historical Institutional Approach', *Manchester Papers in Politics – EPRU Series,* No. 1 (Department of Government, University of Manchester).

Bulmer, S. and Burch, M. (1998), 'The "Europeanisation" of Central Government: The UK and Germany in Historical Institutionalist Perspective', *Manchester Papers in Politics – EPRU Series,* No. 6 (Department of Government, University of Manchester).

Hood, C. and James, O. (1996), Regulation Inside British Government: The Inner Face of the Regulatory State?' *Bureaucratic Gamekeeping Discussion Paper No. 1.*

Hood, C. and Scott, C. (1996), 'Bureaucratic Regulation and New Public Management in the UK: Mirror Image Developments?' *Bureaucratic Gamekeeping Discussion Paper No. 2.*

Hood, C. and James, O. (1996), Reconfiguring the UK Executive: From Public Bureaucracy State to Re-Regulated Public Service? *Bureaucratic Gamekeeping Discussion Paper No. 3.*

Hood, C., James, O., Jones, G., Scott, C., Travers, T., and Tunstall, H. (1997), 'Regulation of the UK Public Sector: Mapping the Terrain', *Bureaucratic Gamekeeping Discussion Paper No. 4.*

Hood, C. and James, O. (1997), 'Regulation Inside Government: Problems of Regulatory Failure', *Bureaucratic Gamekeeping Discussion Paper No. 5.*

Hood, C., James, O., Jones, G., Scott, C. and Travers, T. (1997), 'Waste Watchers, Quality Checkers and Sleazebusters', *Bureaucratic Gamekeeping Discussion Paper No. 6.*

(All papers by Christopher Hood and colleagues available from: Department of Government, LSE.)

Briefings

Richard Parry and Nicholas Deakin, *The Treasury and Social Policy.*

Jane Steele and John Seargeant, *Does Consultation Work?*

Noel Whiteside, *Private Agencies and Public Purposes.*

Patricia Day and Rudolf Klein, *Steering But Not Rowing? The Transformation of the Department of Health.*

Neil Elder and Edward Page, *Accountability and Control in Next Steps Agencies: a comparison of Germany, Sweden and the United Kingdom.*

Ken Spencer and John Mawson, *Towards Policy Co-ordination at the Regional Level.*

Kevin Theakston, *Leadership as Conservatorship.*

Martin Smith, *What is the Core Executive?*

Christopher Hood and colleagues, *Wastewatchers, Quality Police and Sleazebusters.*

Chris Brady and Peter Catterall, *Assessing Cabinet Committees 1945–66.*

Brian Hogwood, David Judge and Murray McVicar. *The Audit of Accountability.*

June Burham and George Jones, *The Evolving Prime Minister's Office: 1868–1997.*

Dennis Kavanagh and Anthony Seldon, *Inside Number Ten 1970–98.*

Rodney Lowe and Neil Rollings, *Modernizing Britain.*

Martin Smith, David Richards and David Marsh, *The Changing Role of Central Government Departments.*

Alan Page and Terence Daintith, *Controlling Government from Within*

R. A. W. Rhodes, *The Governance Narrative.*

(All papers edited by Professor R. A. W. Rhodes are available from him at: Department of Politics, University of Newcastle.)

Part I
Context

2
Prime Ministers, Ministers and Civil Servants in the Core Executive[*]

Martin J. Smith

This chapter re-evaluates the operation of central government. Its key argument is that the notion of prime ministerial and Cabinet government is inappropriate for understanding the operation of the core executive. The chapter develops the notion of the core executive in order to provide a more complex account of the relationships within the central state. Discussions and perceptions of British central government have to a large extent been framed by the constitution (Judge 1993). The aim of this chapter is to demonstrate how the constitutional imperative has mis-specified the loci of power within the central state. Much of the debate concerning the centre of government has been about whether the British system is becoming presidential with power increasingly concentrated in the Prime Minister's Office (Pryce 1997). This chapter will argue that such a view misunderstands the nature of power in central government. The chapter will demonstrate that various parts of the core executive have resources and in order to achieve goals different actors and institutions need to exchange resources. Therefore rather than central government being dominated by the prime minister or Cabinet, actors within the centre are dependent on each other. Consequently, power within the core executive is fluid and complex; it does not belong to a single institution. The chapter will conclude by examining how with the reform of government and greater external constraints have affected these dependencies.

The constitutional approach

The study of central government in Britain has revolved around a number of oft repeated questions: has prime ministerial power replaced Cabinet government; who is dominant, ministers or civil servants; and does parliament control the executive? The central theme of this chapter is that these questions are inappropriate and that they derive from a number of distortions and simplifications.

* I would like to acknowledge the ESRC for funding the research (award number: L124261005).

These distortions have developed for a number of reasons. First, they derive from the impact the (uncodified) British constitution had on the study of British central government. According to the constitution, Parliament is sovereign; no parliament is subject to a higher authority and no parliament can be bound by its predecessor. Consequently, power in Britain resides in the Crown-in-Parliament. The crown is represented by Ministers of the Crown whose legislation has to be passed by the Houses of Parliament. Ministers are responsible through ministerial responsibility to Parliament and through collective responsibility all ministers are bound by decisions taken in Cabinet. The constitution presents a mythical account of the operation of British central government but like all myths it partially reflects reality and influences those who believe the myth (Smith 1999).

The principles of parliamentary sovereignty, the public service ethos, ministerial responsibility and collective Cabinet responsibility not only suggest that decision making is confined within the parliamentary system – and in particular the executive – but raise questions concerning the nature of the relationships between ministers and the prime minister and between the executive and Parliament. A set of supplementary questions follow concerning whether officials are usurping the constitutional power of ministers and whether sovereignty is being undermined. Consequently, many analysts of central government have been concerned with answering questions suggested by the constitutional focus rather than the realities of the political process.

Second, analysis of central government has been concerned with discovering the locus of power, seeing power as residing somewhere: with the prime minister, the Cabinet or the civil service. Consequently power is conceived as an object that resides in an institution or an individual rather than something that derives from relationships and is constantly changing. Power – or the achievement of goals – does not reside with the prime minister or the Cabinet. If ministers, the prime minister or officials want to achieve policy goals they do not have to defeat other centres of power, but they do need each other. Each part of the core executive has resources. According to Rhodes (1988: 42), 'The resources of an organisation constitute a potential for the exercise of power'. Resources have to be exchanged in order for actors to achieve goals. Therefore, the policy process is about developing processes of exchange. Goals are achieved as a result of resource exchange that occurs in the relationships between prime minister, Cabinet and other actors within the core executive. Power is dynamic and fluid and based on interdependency, rather than individual volition, within the core executive.

Third, much of the focus on central government has been on the 'heroic' institutions of the prime minister and the Cabinet. Such narrowness has led to an over-concentration on these institutions and a tendency for many analysts to be more concerned with the personality and style of the prime minister than the operation of the processes of central government. Journalistic accounts have dominated perceptions of how government works and the media are by and large more interested in personalities than in the way institutions structure relationships. Consequently it is often suggested that central government changes according to the personal preferences of key ministers.

A number of studies have attempted to get away from highly personalised accounts of central government and to question the traditional constitutional and institutional approaches. In the 1960s and 1970s authors such as John Mackintosh started to question some of the implications of the traditional assumptions concerning prime minister and Cabinet. However, despite much innovative and interesting work by commentators such as Mackintosh (1977a), Anthony King (1985) and George Jones (1975), their terrain was still largely framed by the traditional, constitutionally defined, agenda.

In recent years there has been a move to more analytical accounts of the core executive. One of the earliest was Bruce-Gardyne and Lawson's (1976) detailed case studies in public policy which highlighted the complexity of the policy process below the Cabinet level. More recently Burch and Holliday (1996: 5) have suggested an approach which recognises that:

> Cabinet system actors operate within a series of limits which are both internal and external to that system. Internal limits comprise abiding organisational patterns and established ways of working. They shape behaviour, and provide the immediate context within which opportunities to exercise individual initiative arise. ... External limits comprise the economic, social and political context within which all Cabinet system actors operate. ... In our way of looking at things, the role of the individual is conditioned by and secondary to these limits and constraints.

Burch and Holliday's approach is extremely useful because it emphasises the importance of institutions, rules and values in structuring the behaviour of actors within the central state and consequently highlights the limitation of personality-derived approaches. Perhaps most influential in reassessing such approaches to central government is Dunleavy and Rhodes' call for a more systematic research agenda for core executive studies (Dunleavy and Rhodes 1990; Rhodes and Dunleavy 1995). They suggest that we can improve our understanding of the core by widening the focus of central government studies and applying a range of conceptual and theoretical approaches. The intention of this chapter is to use the notion of the core executive in order to develop an approach to central government that is consciously analytical; concerned with the wider context of central government policy-making; and concerned to highlight how the policy process is based on negotiation not command. Actors and institutions within the core executive are dependent on each other because all parts of the core executive have resources. Some of these resources are structurally determined – the prime minister has certain resources that derive from the position of the prime minister – while others vary according to particular circumstances. For example, authority is an important resource. Authority varies with the success of a minister, the degree of support he or she has in the party and, sometimes, personality. The impact of the prime minister, of a

Cabinet minister, or of an official on policy depends on the structures of dependency that link them to other actors and the resources that each of these actors control. This structure of relationships provides the framework within which the actors of the core executive operate; it does not determine either policy outcomes or the matter of who 'wins'. The effectiveness of actors within the core executive depends on the tactics, choices and strategies they adopt in using their resources. Ministers and prime ministers can build alliances, officials can withhold information or call on other departments to support their arguments. It is not always those with the most resources or the actors who are the least dependent who win. The choices that actors make affect the outcome of policy. Nevertheless, as Burch and Holliday indicate, these choices are made within a set of structured relationships and institutions.

In addition, the freedom of actors to use their resources will depend on the particular context. For example, after an emphatic election victory a prime minister is usually less dependent on his or her Cabinet than when the government is behind in the polls and the prime minister is an unpopular leader. Therefore we can assume that following success the prime minister has more freedom to use resources than at other times. Nevertheless, the prime minister is nearly always constrained by the structures of dependency. It seems that circumstances will have to change greatly for Tony Blair to sack a senior Cabinet colleague, for example, Gordon Brown. Margaret Thatcher, despite her apparently high-handed manner and clear ideological goals, never removed Peter Walker even though they had strong political differences.

Consequently, it is impossible, and indeed fruitless, to try and identify a single site of power within the core executive because, to use a fashionable postmodern notion, it is everywhere. The structures of dependency and the distribution of resources mean that all actors can have some success. No single actor can achieve what he or she wants without exchanging resources and compromise is therefore built into the structure of government. The Scott Report into the sale of arms to Iraq highlighted not only how officials thwarted ministers but also how officials were forced into line by ministers. It demonstrated how officials were often unwilling to act without ministerial cover. Margaret Thatcher, despite being depicted as an authoritarian prime minister, as the epitome of prime ministerial government, and even as Presidential (Pryce 1997), was forced out of office (Smith 1994). Prime Ministers may in particular circumstances ignore or override their ministers but they can only do this if the Cabinet provides them with the necessary authority. They will lose that authority if they continually act alone.

Power within the core executive does not depend on the personality of the prime minister. Thatcher appeared strong in 1987 and John Major appeared weak in 1997 not because Thatcher was a dominant personality and Major was a weak personality but because their circumstances were different. Major was without a majority in parliament, the government was divided and the popular perception was that his government lacked economic competence. In other words, circumstance created Major's indecisiveness; it was not indecisiveness that led to the Conservative defeat.

It is also important to remember that while relationships of dependency and the distribution of resources may be structural they are not permanent and fixed. The resources of actors and their relationship to each other change across time. The relationship of the Treasury to other government departments remained in constant flux throughout the twentieth century and the postwar period has seen the prime minister accrue more resources with the development of the Prime Minister's Office. Therefore, in addition to a contextual approach, it is important to develop an historical account in order to examine how relationships have developed over time and how actions at one particular time can create the strucutural context for later actors.

The core executive in historical perspective

The core executive is, metaphorically, the brain of the state. Therefore its development is inextricably linked to the growth of the state. The period between the late 19th century and the 1950s saw a massive growth in the state both in terms of expenditure and employment which eventually peaked in 1976. With this growth in the state, the core executive developed into a highly institutionalised set of relationships. Before the 1850s, central government operated on an *ad hoc* basis. Cabinet was informal, central co-ordination was weak and government was unbureaucratic. The first significant development was the Northcote–Trevelyan reforms of 1854 which laid the foundations of a modern professional civil service.

The Northcote–Trevelyan reforms established a professional, expert and permanent civil service which had a degree of independence from their political masters. With the increasing size and responsibilities of the state, politicians were unable to make all the decisions and control all the operations of a department. They needed advisers they could trust. First, officials had to sift, organise, and provide ministers with, information on key problems and the available policy options. Second, ministers required high quality staff with the ability to take decisions independently in an increasing number of areas. Third, there was a need for the administrative machinery to implement decisions in an increasing number of areas of civil society. The reforms of government in the nineteenth century 'created a series of mechanisms by which the central machinery of the state could make its decisions locally effective' (Cronin 1991: 19).

Nevertheless, there was much opposition to the Northcote–Trevelyan reforms and it was not until 1870 that open competition for civil service posts was introduced and even then the Home Office and Foreign Office resisted reform for many years (Greenleaf 1987). Moreover, the reforms were evolutionary rather than revolutionary (Hennessy 1990) and did not undermine what was known as the night-watchman state. They did, however, establish the basis of the modern civil service which enabled the creation of a bureaucratic, administrative state. The aim of the reformers was not to expand the state but to make it more economical and efficient (Greenleaf 1987; Hart 1972). Increasing its capabilities was in a sense a side-effect. By abolishing patronage and creating a class of what later became known as policy advisers, the reforms enabled the development of a more effective civil service.

These changes in the civil service were paralleled by changes in other parts of the core executive. During this period the Cabinet became increasingly formalised and power relationships within it changed. From the middle of the nineteenth century 'most government tasks came to be formalised under the effective responsibilities of ministers' (Daalder 1963a: 18). In order to co-ordinate the work of ministers, the Cabinet grew and became increasingly formal in its structure (Daalder 1963b). According to Mackintosh (1977b: 143) the Cabinet was now:

> 'the centre of political power; it was the body which determined policy. It was possible for prime ministers, foreign secretaries and even lesser Ministers to take some decisions on their own, but if there was any dispute or challenge from Parliament or the press, the matter had to be settled in the Cabinet'.

This period also saw the emergence of the Treasury 'as the department crucial to the central control of administrative efficiency and financial accountability' (Thane 1990: 9). It established the basic mechanisms for assessing government expenditure and entrenched, in principle, a system for controlling the level of increase (see Roseveare 1969).

It was the First World War which saw the establishment of the key elements of the modern core executive with the development of new departments and the establishment of formal Cabinet procedures. Between 1914 and 1919 the Cabinet was transformed 'from a political committee into a complex administrative machine' (Turner 1982: 57). Under Asquith's premiership there had been problems of organisation, political conflicts and conflicts of responsibility. Lloyd George, who became prime minister in 1916, sought to define clearly the lines of responsibility by creating a small war Cabinet of five members which was to determine the main lines of policy (Mackintosh 1977b: 371). As the majority of departmental ministers were not included in the War Cabinet, the recording and distribution of decisions became essential. For the first time a Cabinet Secretariat was established which kept and distributed Cabinet minutes. In addition, small *ad hoc* committees were established to deal with particular problems and War Cabinet members chaired standing committees which co-ordinated policy between departments (French 1982). The War saw the establishment of a formal system of Cabinet government with an institutionalised system of committees serviced by a Cabinet Secretariat. These developments, 'undoubtedly lowered the status of departmental ministers. Their work was co-ordinated from above. They had to execute decisions in which they were never consulted' (Daalder 1963a: 46).

Additionally, the War resulted in an increased role for the Treasury. The Treasury established control over the stock exchange, become involved in overseas finance and took over exchange rate policy from the Bank of England (Burk 1982b). But while the absolute power of the Treasury may have increased relative to the departments, Treasury control over staffing and expenditure greatly weakened as departments became increasingly autonomous and declared extra expenditure as necessary for victory (Burk 1982b; Roseveare 1969). In effect the Treasury lost its primacy during the War as the demands of the situation lifted the constraints on state expansion (Cronin 1991).

Such was the impact of the War on government that the government set up the Haldane Committee in 1917 to investigate the machinery of Government. In its report the Committee outlined the three main functions of the Cabinet:

1. the final determination of the policy to be submitted to Parliament;
2. the supreme control of the national executive in accordance with the policy prescribed by Parliament;
3. the continuous co-ordination and delimitation of the activities of several departments of state (Cd 9230 1918: 1).

The committee recommended the Cabinet should at most consist of 12 members, meet frequently and be supplied with the proper provision of information. In the event, the impact of the Haldane Report was limited (Daalder 1963b). Yet, crucially, Haldane did establish the crux of the relationship between ministers and officials, defining them as inextricably linked rather than hierarchical and based on ministerial control (Richards 1997). The next significant change in the nature of the core executive occurred during the Second World War. As Peter Hennessy (1990: 88) emphasises, Adolf Hitler 'obliged the British Government to find new men and new methods overnight'. The Second World War saw a number of significant changes. Authority shifted largely from the Cabinet to the War Cabinet (which had overall authority but particular responsibility for the conduct of the war) and the Lord President's Committee which had responsibility for domestic policy. Consequently the apex of government was dominated by 'a web of ministerial committees' (Cronin 1991; Middlemas 1986). In addition, there was the establishment of a range of new departments, the growth of economic power and a massive increase in the number of outsiders brought into Whitehall.

In the postwar period the core executive had to deal with two contradictory trends: one was an expanding welfare state and increasing demands for government intervention. The second was relative economic and political decline which limited the economic resources and the political autonomy of the central state. Various governments tried to deal with these problems by reasserting Treasury control and modernising the state. Both the Wilson government of 1964–70 and the Heath government of 1970–74 experimented with new departmental arrangements in an attempt to meet the needs of the modern world. Wilson, through the Fulton Committee, instigated a thorough, if largely fruitless review of the civil service and Heath attempted to introduce greater managerialism (Kellner and Crowther Hunt 1980; Hennessy 1990; Radcliffe 1991; Pollitt 1984).

With the continual pressure of relative economic decline and increased demands for government activity, all postwar governments have been concerned with reinforcing Treasury control in the hope of controlling public expenditure. Following a select committee report, the Plowden Committee was established in 1961 to examine the issue of Treasury control. It pointed to the need for 'a more rational and efficient means of planning the use of public money and other wealth' (Greenleaf 1987: 275). The result was the Public Expenditure Survey Committee (PESC) under which departments had to set out their long-term expenditure plans. These had little impact and so were supplemented by Heath with Policy Analysis and Review (PAR) but it was only with the IMF crisis of 1976 that cash limits were introduced and any real impact on departmental expenditure was made.

The development of the state has seen shifting relationships within the core executive. In particular there has been the professionalisaton of the bureaucracy, the establishment of the cabinet system and the variable role of the Treasury. What we have not discussed is the role of the prime minister. Even if we reject the presidentialism thesis it is clear that the resources of the prime minister have changed in the postwar period and the relationship between the prime minister and the Cabinet is crucial in understanding the operation of the core executive.

The prime minister and cabinet

The relationship between the prime minister and the Cabinet has been one of the central issues in the examination of central government in Britain. There is a growing consensus that the period since 1979 has seen the role of the Cabinet decline as it increasingly becomes a dignified part of Britain's written but uncodified constitution (Burch 1988; Hennessy 1986; Lawson 1994) with the cabinet generally being bypassed in the policy-making process and existing merely as a rubber-stamp. The sidelining of the cabinet has seen the parallel development of an increasingly dominant prime minister. For Pryce (1997: 197), 'the presidentialization of electoral politics in Britain has brought in its wake a presidentialization of Britain's governing institutions'. There is little doubt that the resources of the prime minister have increased in the postwar period. In addition to prime ministerial patronage, the size of the Prime Minister's Office has grown, prime ministers have become increasingly involved in the development of policy, there has been a greater tendency for prime ministers to operate bilaterally with ministers and the media has increasingly focused their attention on the premier.

Nevertheless, the central argument of this chapter is that the question of Cabinet or Prime Ministerial government (or presidentialism) is irrelevant because power does not belong to a single institution within the core executive. As has been said, different actors and institutions need each other. Cabinet ministers and prime ministers have resources but in order to achieve goals they need to exchange resources. The process of exchange – the alliances – that are built to some extent depends on the particular context; thus if a prime minister has just won an election he or she is less dependent than one that is very unpopular in the poll but continual overriding of the wishes of the cabinet will in turn undermine that authority. Therefore even dominant prime ministers need to exchange resources.

Clearly, the prime minister has resources that are unavailable to other ministers as well as the traditionally cited formal resources of patronage, control of the cabinet agenda, appointment of cabinet committees and the prime minister's office. The prime minister also has less tangible resources such as the ability to intervene in any policy area. Only the prime minister really has any collective oversight; most ministers lack the interest, time, ability or institutional support to be involved in other areas of policy. This oversight enables prime ministers to involve themselves in any area of policy making that they choose.

Authority is the acceptance of power without needing to exercise formal capabilities (Wrong 1988). A crucial rule of Whitehall is that ministers and civil servants accept the authority of the prime minister. Nevertheless, unlike other resources which are fairly objective, prime ministerial authority is largely relational and will depend on the position of the prime minister him or herself. In particular, the prime minister has greatest authority after an electoral victory and particularly if it is an unexpected one:

> Winning the general election against all expectations enormously boosted Heath's self-confidence. ... Not only was he prime minister but he was prime minister with no debts to anyone and a clear personal mandate to impose his new authority on those who had sniped at him for so long. ... His personal authority was actually greater than it would have been had he entered Downing street a year or two earlier on the back of a sweeping and predicted Tory landslide. (Campbell 1993: 289)

Thatcher's authority was greatest after the Falkland's victory and the subsequent landslide election victory in 1983 which allowed her to remove most of her critics from cabinet and, according to King (1985), it allowed her 'to put her stamp on an extraordinarily wide range of policy decisions'. Major's problem in 1990 was a lack of authority. Although he had authority from his win in the Conservative election leadership, he was not always seen as his own man. His electoral mandate was won by Thatcher and she initially constantly reminded the new prime minister that he was there to implement her agenda. The absence of independent authority limited his cabinet and policy options. For a long period Major was in a position of having to react to problems such as the poll tax and ERM membership rather than setting his own agenda. Conversely, the size of Labour's victory in 1997, which largely was attributed to Tony Blair, meant that the new prime minister had tremendous authority to force through new policies despite some veiled criticism amongst MPs.

Despite formal and informal resources, to understand prime ministerial power it is necessary to examine resource exchange that results from dependency. Even with an array of institutional resources and the authority of the office, a prime minister can achieve nothing on her or his own. In order to translate capabilities into power he or she is dependent on others for advice, information, support and assistance in making policy (Table 2.1). Ministers and civil servants clearly have their own resources, as we will see in the chapter that follows. Perhaps most importantly, ministers have their own sources of authority. Many senior ministers have such high authority that it is almost impossible for a prime minister to dismiss them. For example, in the period around 1987/1988 Nigel Lawson was in an exceptionally strong position. As Chancellor of the Exchequer he controlled significant institutional resources, not least the Treasury, which effectively gave him control of economic policy. Moreover, he was seen as architect of Britain's economic revival and subsequently he had tremendous authority within the Tory Party (Watkins 1991: 96). As he had little ambition to be prime minister he could take political risks. Lawson's stock rose further with his radical 1988 budget which delivered a balanced budget and cuts in taxation. Consequently, despite major disagreements between Thatcher and Lawson, he was, in the prime minister's word, 'unassailable'. Thatcher admitted to Kenneth Baker that she could not have sacked Lawson because 'I might well have had to go as well' (Thatcher quoted in Baker 1993: 315). Likewise, because John Prescott has an independent power base in the Labour Party, it seems highly unlikely that Blair could remove him from cabinet.

Not only is a prime minister confronted with ministerial resources, he or she is also highly dependent on the cabinet for their authority. Authority, depends on legitimacy; it exists only while it is recognised and therefore a prime minister's authority can only extend as far as the cabinet will allow. The limits of authority are illustrated starkly in the case of Thatcher's resignation where the cabinet effectively removed the prime minister's authority. Thatcher would have gone on to a second ballot in the leadership contest had she not realised that cabinet support was slipping away. She admits in her memoirs that once she was convinced that she had lost cabinet support she decided not to stand in the second round:

> a prime minister who knows that his or her cabinet has withheld its support is fatally weakened. I knew – and I am sure that they knew – that I would not willingly remain an hour in 10 Downing street without the real authority to govern. (Thatcher 1993: 851)

This process of exchange is also affected by the particular context. The degree of dependency and the need to exchange resources will depend on the context. If the external context is favourable to the prime minister in terms of economic policy or electorally then the prime minister has less dependence on the cabinet. If the external context is less favourable the prime minister requires more support.

Success in achieving policy goals for both ministers and the prime minister will depend on tactics. How resources are deployed is an important aspect in power and it means that in certain situations ministers with relatively low resources can

Table 2.1   Resources of prime ministers, ministers and officials

Prime minister	Ministers	Officials
Patronage	Political support	Permanence
Authority	Authority	Knowledge
Political support by Party	Department	Time
Political support by	Knowledge	Whitehall network
Electorate	Policy networks	Control over information
Prime Minister's Office	Policy success	Keepers of the constitution
Bilateral policy making		

defeat the prime minister or more highly resourced ministers. The three most recent prime ministers have all had very different strategies and tactics. Thatcher's strategy was generally interventionist; Major was more collectivist and Blair appears directive (Table 2.2)

Thatcher wanted to intervene in the work of departments. As Lord Young confirmed in an interview, Thatcher's impact on the department was: 'Absolutely enormous. I used to be in fear and trembling when I went to see her as she somehow knew more about my department than I did. She worked incredibly hard and had an incredible capacity for detail. It was very difficult to get anything over her, very difficult.'

Patrick Jenkin also accepted that Thatcher had an enormous effect on departments especially when compared to Edward Heath. One former official in the Department of Education said that 'There were occasions in my time in education when policy pronouncements emerged from No. 10 of which we were totally unaware'. But she was often highly tactical in her approach, creating the right cabinet committees, building the necessary alliances or working bilaterally with ministers to bypass cabinet opposition. Even a dominant prime minister like Thatcher is dependent on colleagues if her or she wants to intervene. So, in the first phase of her administration Thatcher had to be, and was, effective at building alliances in order to achieve her goals. She was also effective at using relatively independent figures like Lord Whitelaw and John Wakeham as conduits between herself and cabinet so that compromises could be worked out with neither direct confrontation nor capitulation.

Table 2.2   Strategies and tactics of prime ministers

	Thatcher	Major	Blair
Strategy	Interventionlist	Collectivist	Directive
Tactics	Using small groups of ministers to build support for her goals. Bilateral meetings with ministers.	Working with cabinet to build consensus. Delaying decisions until support.	PM's Office and Cabinet Office to develop strategic direction. Use of 'Cabinet enforcer' to ensure ministers follow direction.

Later, when she found increasing opposition in cabinet, Thatcher's tactic was to operate, to some degree, outside the cabinet system. She depended on her political advisors for support and influenced policy by operating bilaterally with ministers who were not in a position to resist her demands. In Lawson's view, after her defeat over Westland:

> The lesson that Margaret took from it was that her colleagues were trouble-some and her courtiers loyal. From then on she began to distance herself from colleagues who had been closest to her – certainly those who had minds of their own – and to retreat to the Number 10 bunker, where the leading figures were Charles Powell and Bernard Ingham. (Lawson 1992: 680)

With ministers like Whitelaw, Walker and, at certain times, Lawson, Thatcher was more dependent on them than they were on her and so they had consider-able freedom and, in Whitelaw's and Lawson's case, influence. Consequently, even a prime minister with a dominant style who wants to intervene needs to understand the lines of dependence and work out tactics accordingly. For the first half of her period in office, Thatcher's tactics worked relatively well and she was effective at achieving her goals.

Major was clearly in a different structural position to Thatcher, coming into office without his own electoral mandate and with an economy in recession. Consequently, he adopted a different strategy. Thatcher was seen to have been removed from office because she would not listen and ignored her lines of dependency. Therefore the new prime minister was expected to be more colle-giate and Major obliged. He was concerned with reasserting cabinet government. In Anthony Seldon's (1997: 738) assessment:

> Major by temperament and choice was a conciliator. Before he became prime minister, he had found Mrs Thatcher's style of 'macho leadership' personally distasteful. His chairmanship of cabinet and cabinet committees, in contrast, allowed ministers to express their views, and guided them to a conclusion in line with his intentions. Rather than have dissent in the Cabinet he preferred to delay decisions until he could reconcile differences.

These changed tactics were not solely determined by personality but were what the circumstances required. As Seldon (1997: 742) suggests, 'Major's leadership could be argued to have been exactly what was required for the times'. With the removal of Thatcher the party and the cabinet had different visions of Conservatism, and Major had to try to keep the cabinet together. Baker records in his memoirs: 'John's style of chairing the cabinet was quite different from Margaret's. John encouraged discussion and elicited colleagues' views. ... One of John's great talents is his skill in handling difficult meetings and teasing out a consensus.' (Baker 1993: 427).

Although it is too early to be definitive, Blair's strategy appears to be one of setting an overall policy direction with the cabinet under his leadership and then ensuring that the departments follow the broad policy outline. However, it seems he was willing to become closely involved in certain policies such as education, Northern Ireland and even the issue of the 'millennium bug'. The role of first Peter Mandelson and then Jack Cunningham seems to be to ensure that departments are acting in the collective interest of the government. The cabinet enforcer is useful for the prime minister because he can seem not to be interfering directly himself.

However, it also appears that Blair is aware of his dependencies. Two ministers, Gordon Brown and John Prescott are in strong positions. Brown agreed not to challenge Blair for the leadership of the Party and so Blair owes his position, to some extent, to Brown who probably is the one cabinet minister who could challenge Blair. As a result of Brown's support for Blair he has been given control of the government's economic strategy (Draper 1997: 30). According to Draper (1997: 29), Blair knows that his relationship with Brown is a key factor when it comes to the government's success. It is a much closer than usual relationship for a prime minister and chancellor, and the two heavyweights regularly discuss matters that go well beyond the Treasury remit.

Labour's position on membership of European Monetary Union (EMU) is a result of policy worked out between Blair and Brown. Prescott also has a strong position because he was elected by the Party as deputy leader and is seen as protecting the compassionate heart of 'old' Labour. He also provides a useful function for Blair in that he can often convince the party membership that key policy changes such as trade union reform and not renationalising the railways are not at odds with Labour's principles. Prescott has too much party support and is too important in that position for Blair to be able to remove him.

It is also the case that a minister can win battles with the prime minister through clever tactics. Virginia Bottomley saved a threat to the Department of Heritage budget by releasing a letter from the Chancellor saying lottery money would be in addition to not a replacement of existing expenditure. One of the best examples of ministerial tactics is when Lynda Chalker was faced with a large cut in Overseas Development Agency (ODA) expenditure. The department sent out a press release outlining how the proposed cuts in the budget would mean a 5 per cent cut in ODA expenditure and the lowest level of expenditure ever on overseas aid. Indeed, the department pointed out that with the Fundamental Expenditure Review, the real cut in expenditure would be 16 per cent. The department then encouraged the non governmental organisations (NGOs) to lobby the Treasury and the prime minister pointing out how many projects would be affected by these cuts. As a consequence of the lobbying, the cuts were restored.

Prime ministers undoubtedly have more resources than other ministers. However, ministers are in a strong position because they are the head of departments and only departments have the capability both to make and implement detailed policy. Therefore departments are a crucial site of power within the central state.

Ministers, civil servants and departments

Despite the importance of departments to the policy process, most attention has been paid to the issue of who is dominant, ministers or officials. However, again, such an approach misunderstands the nature of the relationship between ministers and officials. They rarely compete for power but are more often dependent on each other.

Ministers and officials operate within a structured world into which each brings different resources and, in order to achieve goals, they need each other (Table 2.3). The relationship is structured by the institutions within which they operate (i.e. the departments; mechanisms of cabinet government and party); different resources which again are institutional and constitutional, and by different perceptions of each other and their respective roles. But while it is a structured relationship it is one in which both parties bring their own unique elements and one, because it is based on perceptions and a constitution that exists through the reproduction of rules rather than on paper, that is open to continual reinterpretation. Ministers and civil servants have various resources; different structural positions and constraints; and varying abilities to act and to achieve their goals. As one former official said of the relationship: 'It seems to me that the essence of it (the relationship) is dynamic interaction, it is not that there is one set of values, propositions, positions or needs that the politicians have and another set that the official system has and they have to sort of compromise, but rather they interact.' Another official saw the relationship working well when it was one of 'give and take'.

Table 2.3 Resources and structures of ministers and civil servants

	Civil servants	*Ministers*
Resources	Time Expertise Experience Knowledge Whitehall network	Access to cabinet Political alliances Political support and legitimacy

Internal structures	Rules of the game
	Constitutional elements –
	  ministerial responsibility
	Neutrality
		Maintenance of
		ministerial hierarchy; ministerial
		  responsibility

External structures	Departmental interests Political demands Economic circumstances	Departmental interests Economic and political constraints

Agency	Interpretation of rules
	Official alliances
	Alliances with ministers
	Ability to take decisions in
	  discrete policy areas
		Ability to make policy
		Authority over officials
		Ability to override organisational
		  and departmental imperatives

Officials and ministers are dependent on each other and so create an evolving and occasionally seamless relationship. Ponting (1986: 14) perceptively states:

> The question of where power lies between ministers and civil servants inside Whitehall can never be answered satisfactorily. The dividing line depends on so many things, the political strength and intellect of the individual minister, the type of decisions being taken, the amount of administrative detail involved, the level of political interest in the outcome of the decision and the personal relationship between the individuals. All these factors mean that boundaries of power are fluctuating continuously.

This point is important and highlights again the need to see power as fluid and relational and not an object. Therefore it is necessary to specify the conditions within which these relations occur and the resources various actors bring to the policy process.

Despite the apparently overwhelming predominance of resources in the hands of officials, they do not dominate the policy process because ministers also have resources. It is often difficult for officials to use their resources without the addition of ministerial resources. The resources of officials are fairly obvious and result from their permanence and control over an organisation with information, experience and time to make, and ultimately to deliver, policy. Without this machinery there is little that a minister could achieve.

While officials have administrative resources, ministers have the political resources essential for policy outcomes. Ministers' political authority and legitimacy enables them to develop support for policies with colleagues, cabinet and the outside world. Without cabinet and Treasury support, departments could achieve little and so officials need ministers to legitimise policy and to gain financial and political support. As one former Permanent Secretary suggested:

> First of all the minister has got to be decisive. He must know what he wants to do. He must be prepared to listen to advice, to question advice and then to make up his mind and go ahead taking things to cabinet and winning his battles in cabinet. So you need someone who is strong. ... He's got to be decisive and strong and if he is not, as I said, the fortunes of the Department fall. There is a misunderstanding, which is quite common, that civil servants like weak ministers because they can rule them, they don't at all. That's no good because when the minister is on his own in cabinet they are not there to rule or do anything else to influence him. So you want someone who is active, intellectual, quite bright of course, can whip things up.

Once ministers have the authority, they work with officials to develop policy and it is the official machinery for making policy that ministers need. In particular the officials have knowledge of who to talk to and how to build the necessary Whitehall consensus. Moreover, most officials are intensely loyal to their minister and they are consequently extremely able at offering political cover both within Whitehall and in the outside world. Officials and ministers are not therefore in conflict but are symbiotic. Ministers need the expertise and officials need ministers with weight who can gain money, time for legislation and interdepartmental support. With a weak minister a department will achieve little.

The centres of co-ordination

The irony is that while the core executive is institutionally strong at departmental level, it is institutionally weak in the centre. Power is much more apparent at departmental level and consequently there is a problem of co-ordination. This problem is exacerbated by the existence of three centres of co-ordination; the Cabinet Office and the Office of Public Service, the Prime Minister's Office and the Treasury. This situation raises the question of whether three co-ordinators can co-ordinate?

The Treasury's co-ordination role derives from its economic and public expenditure responsibilities. The Treasury controls and plans the expenditure of all departments, and before recent reforms it controlled the manpower, pay and gradings of all civil servants, and it has responsibility for macro-economic policy and taxation (Pliatzky 1989). As Nigel Lawson (1992) reveals:

> the Chancellor has his finger in pretty well every pie in government. This follows partly from his responsibility for Government spending and partly from tradition. As a result, he can exert a significant influence on policies which are announced by other ministers and which the public does not associate with the Treasury at all.

Cabinet ministers at the receiving end of Treasury fingers have also confirmed their impact. The former energy minister David Howell told Peter Hennessy (1992) 'the nexus between No. 10 and the Treasury is decisive, it overrules, it is everything. The Treasury also knows that it can win'. Lord Carrington confirmed in an interview: 'The Treasury always wins' and a number of former cabinet ministers said in interviews that the Treasury was the key co-ordinating department. Crucially, the Treasury and the Chancellor have a number of resources that are unavailable to other departments. It is the only department that by right has access to other departments and therefore has some sense of the 'bigger picture' (Thain and Wright 1995: 104). The chancellor also has, in most cases, more authority than any other minister in the government other than the prime minister. Consequently, the prime minister/chancellor axis is a crucial relationship in government. As a result they are extremely dependent on each other but also, if their relationship is strong, they have a great deal of influence over the core executive. It would be rare for any coalition of ministers to defeat an alliance of the chancellor and the prime minister.

Nevertheless, the role of the Treasury in co-ordination has been variable. There was a feeling in the postwar period that it was too weak and that departmental expenditure was out of control. As a result the Thatcher government strengthened the role of the Treasury but the period since the late 1980s has seen a shift in the location of the centre of the core executive. Under Thatcher, resources were shifted to the Prime Minister's Office and the Treasury. The Treasury was given control of the civil service with the abolition of the Civil Service Department (CSD); it controlled economic policy and public expenditure and had detailed control of public expenditure. Thatcher strengthened the role of the No. 10 office and increased the involvement of the prime minister in departments. She also saw herself as being a key player in economic policy. For Thatcher, Treasury weakness in the 1960s and 1970s was one of the key causes of Britain's economic decline and therefore she was intent on reasserting Treasury control. Consequently, with the backing of the prime minister, the Treasury was in a strong position. For much of the 1980s the prime minister–Treasury nexus was the co-ordinating centre of the core executive. As Hennessy (1994: 487) concluded following a participants seminar on cabinet government:

> All (commentators) agreed on the Prime Minister–Chancellor of the Exchequer nexus as the special relationship within modern British government. It was so central and powerful that even such an arch prime ministerialist as Edmund Dell felt that there was no need for a PM's Department as the Treasury and Number 10 'combined form a good basis for the sort of strong centre of government which I would like to see'.

Since the creation of the Office of Public Service and in particular with the role of two individuals, Michael Heseltine and Peter Mandelson, power has shifted away from the Treasury to a new nexus, again focused around No. 10 but this time including the Cabinet Office and the OPS which have been given greater responsibility for the civil service and for co-ordinating the work of government. The Cabinet Office is the formal centre of government; its role is to co-ordinate the work of government departments and to ensure that the cabinet's will is implemented (Seldon 1995). Hennessy (1990: 390) claims 'The Cabinet Office is the crucial junction box of the central government system ... when it comes to formulating policy at the critical stage just before it goes to ministers collectively, all wires lead to No. 70 Whitehall'. Yet as Dynes and Walker point out there is a hole at the centre of British government with the Cabinet Office unable really to impose central co-ordination on the federation of resource-rich and constitutionally independent departments: 'The Cabinet Office is a peculiar department, simultaneously weak and strong ... the Cabinet Office sometimes appears to be less of a nerve centre in Whitehall than a post office' (Dynes and Walker 1995: 21). This hole is being made larger by the apparent hollowing out of the state (see Rhodes 1995; 1997a). With the execution of policy making and implementation being delegated to agencies, regions and the EU it is increasingly difficult for the centre to control the policy process.

The problems for the Cabinet Office are several fold. It lacks resources in terms of either finance, policy making capability or independent authority. If the Cabinet Office is to achieve anything it relies on the backing of the prime minister. On its own, it relies on the co-operation of the departments, but while there is strong dependency between the Treasury and the departments, departments rarely need the Cabinet Office in the same way. Much of what the Cabinet Office does is pure administration: it circulates papers; organises cabinet committees; and distributes agendas. The important work in terms of discussions between departments or work within departments will go on without the Cabinet Office. The Cabinet Office has neither the staff nor the capability to oversee what goes on in departments and while it may believe that it is controlling the work of Whitehall, it sees very little of the day-to-day business even when it is interdepartmental. Therefore, the impact of both the Cabinet Office and the Office of Public Services (OPS) depends on the impact of the Prime Minister's Office. In recent years the prime minister has attempted to tie them more closely to Number 10. However, under Heseltine, the OPS tended to be a competing coordinating centre with the Prime Minister's Office. Heseltine was prepared to use the department as a base on which to speak on any issue in government that attracted his attention. Blair seems to be attempting to avoid this problem by ensuring that the OPS remains largely under his control.

From government to governance?

As we saw above, the constitutional approach locates power firmly within the parliamentary system and in particular within the executive. However, in recent years it has been suggested the state has been 'hollowed out' (Rhodes 1994) and that power is increasingly dispersed amongst a range of state and non-state actors and institutions. This fragmentation is the consequence of two factors: reform and increasing external constraints.

Since the early 1980s, Whitehall has been undergoing a 'dynamic evolution' (Richards 1997) with the introduction of managerialism into central government. Initially, this process involved the introduction of greater efficiency into departments through the Financial Management Initiative and the privatisation of many state-owned industries. In 1988 the Ibbs Report, *The Next Steps*, proposed a division in departments between those who were policy advisers at the core of departments and those concerned with service delivery. This change led to a rapid division between the core and the periphery of the state (Kemp 1993). By 1995/96 there were 109 executive agencies covering 386 000 civil servants (Cm 3579 1996/97). The aim of the new agencies was to break the traditional uniformity of the traditional Whitehall bureaucracy and, consequently, it has resulted in the introduction of open competition for posts and fixed-term contracts. These changes have impacted on the central departments, with the Fundamental Expenditure Reviews and the Senior Management Review cutting the core funding of departments and trying to de-layer the senior levels of the civil service so that the policy process has become more flexible.

A number of commentators have suggested that these changes signify a changing relationship between ministers and officials (Foster and Plowden 1997; Campbell and Wilson 1996). Officials are seen as becoming more managerial and concerned with service delivery rather than as simply policy advisors. Ministers, it is argued, have much more developed ideas concerning the types of policies they want and are therefore much less reliant on officials. Increasingly, policy advice is coming either from think tanks or from political advisors.

Further fragmentation has occurred with increased marketisation and contracting out in areas such as the National Health Service. Increasingly, government is relying on the private sector under contract to deliver public goods. In addition, the government is relying on the voluntary sector to deliver public goods, particularly in the area of welfare services. These changes also have important implications for the distribution of resources and the nature of relationships within the core executive. The growth of the state up to the 1970s saw the development generally of hierarchical line bureaucracies. In departments such as the Department of Social Security, decisions were taken in the centre and implemented uniformly throughout the country according to a set of extremely detailed rules. In other departments, such as Department of Education and Science (DES), the process was more complicated. The department to a large extent relied on local authorities and it was also in close contact with interest groups. Nevertheless the number of actors and institutions involved in the developing and implementing of policy was relatively limited. In the last 15 years the policy process has greatly fragmented. As has been said, ministers are increasingly likely to take advice from think tanks and from other outside bodies; and the decision and implementation process may include the department itself; agencies; a regulatory body; a privatised industry; local authorities; a range of Quangos; and a number of pressure groups. While Thatcher's intention was to limit the role of the state, the impact of the reforms is actually to extend the role of the state and to make it much more difficult to control by the core executive. As Rhodes (1997b) clearly illustrates:

> The fragmentation of British government is plain for all to see. Since 1988 British government has created 109 agencies and the number of special-purpose bodies has multiplied to 5521 involving more than 70 000 government appointments and an estimated £52 billion of public spending. Add in privatization, services contracted to the private and voluntary sector and functions run by the EU and the extent of service fragmentation is still understated.

This process of fragmentation has been taken further by the growth of external constraints on the core executive. Traditionally, the key constraint on the core executive was parliament. Throughout the twentieth century power shifted from the parliamentary arena to a range of bodies including policy networks, sub-government, the judiciary and perhaps most importantly the European Union (EU). Not only does the EU place limits on what national governments can do in certain areas, for example, agricultural policy and trade policy are almost solely European, but it has also changed the nature of the core executive (Buller and Smith 1998). To a certain extent it has increased the role of the Cabinet Office and the Foreign Office who both have a role in co-ordinating Britain's position in Europe but, increasingly, departments are developing their own European expertise. The EU is only one of a range of international organisations that limit the core executive: NATO is crucial in terms of defence policy and the World Trade Organisation has a significant impact on trade policy. Moreover, while its impact is subject to much debate, it is difficult to deny that due to the growth in international trade and the size of currency transaction, national economic policy can only be developed within the context of the world markets – something which often leaves the Treasury with limited room for manoeuvre.

There is some evidence that the state has become increasingly hollow and that the core executive is losing power to other centres. However, before jumping to apocalyptic conclusions about the future of the core executive, it is worth considering a number of points. First, the state has always been constrained and the question of whether the government makes a difference is an old one. Second, Saward (1997: 26) suggests 'the state is being redefined or reshaped, not hollowed out, at least on the internal dimension'. Rhodes' notion of subgovernment raises the question of whether government ever really did control the implementation process and therefore the creation of agencies and regulatory bodies may be a more effective means of executive co-ordination than traditional hierarchy. It is clear that there is a high level of dependency between agencies and departments (see Gains 1998) and government clearly has the ability to increase the powers of regulatory bodies.

However, Saward (1997: 32) does argue that at the international level there is evidence that national governments are more vulnerable to outside pressures and events and 'becoming local governments'. Again, it is important to be cautious. The balance of resources between national and the international arenas has changed and the relationships of dependency may have altered. But as we have seen, dependency is a two-way process and international actors depend on nation states. The EU in particular can achieve little without the support of national governments.

Conclusion

Traditionally, the operation of central government has been understood in terms of cabinet and prime ministerial government. This chapter demonstrates that such an approach is too simplistic. All actors within the core executive have resources and, in order to achieve policy goals, resources have to be exchanged. The chapter highlights that two factors affect the process of exchange: the structures of dependency created by the formal and informal institutionalisation of relationships within the core executive; and the external political and economic context. Both affect the resources that actors control and the structures of dependency that tie them together. Such an account does not deny the importance of agents or even of personality. It is apparent that there is a strong personalist element to the role of a prime minister. However, personality is not the determinant. It is but one variable in determining the operation of central government. More important is a conception of actors as agents who can both determine the rules of the game and, through tactics, affect how resources are deployed.

3
The Europeanisation of British Central Government[*]

Simon Bulmer and Martin Burch

Introduction

On the face of it, the impact of membership of the European Union (EU)[1] on the United Kingdom is both substantial and wide ranging. Areas of policy have been removed from the exclusive domain of the national state to be shared with the EU. European issues are a central feature in party and public debate. Large numbers of national politicians and bureaucrats are now engaged in European policy-making and large parts of the policy agenda of the UK are now set within an EU context. There can be no doubt that the impact of the EU on British politics has been considerable, yet the effect on the system has been less evident. There is a puzzle here as to how the Europeanisation of both politics and policy has been possible without dramatic changes in the structures and processes of national government, a point that has been noted by many observers as equally pertinent to other member states (see Hanf and Soetendorp 1998; Rometsch and Wessels 1996; Wright 1996; Olsen 1995: 25; Page and Wouters 1995). Given that member states have been subject to similar pressures, why has there not been a convergence in governmental systems? Why has national diversity survived to the degree it has?

In our research we set out to consider how this puzzle has worked out in the case of the UK. Our task has been to examine the impact of membership of the EU on the organisation and operation of central government. We have done this through extensive interviewing in all the Whitehall departments (and some of their related agencies), of the central co-ordinating machinery (Cabinet Office European Secretariat [COES] and the Foreign and Commonwealth Office [FCO]) and in the UK Permanent Representation (UKRep) in Brussels. We have also interviewed British nationals and non-British nationals in Brussels, and drawn together comparative material, based on interviews and analyses, covering the situation in

[*] This chapter is based on empirical research funded by the UK ESRC Whitehall Programme, award number L123251001. We are grateful to the ESRC for financial support and to the serving and retired officials and politicians who were willing to be interviewed under 'Chatham House rules'.

Germany and France. In the course of our enquiries we collected primary documentary materials where these were made available to us. We have been particularly concerned with the origins and development of the Whitehall way of handling EU matters and we have examined the relevant Public Record Office files and interviewed many of those who have been involved since the UK's first application for entry in 1961. In conducting our research, we have employed Europeanisation and historical institutionalism as tools of analysis, both of which we have developed in the course of our inquiries. The rest of this chapter deals with some of our key findings. What we have found is that there has been a slow revolution in Whitehall as a result of membership of the EU. This is now a matter of such significance that any comprehensive and sensible analysis of UK central government must explore the European dimension.

Our project is actually the first in-depth study of the development and nature of the Whitehall approach to the EU. If our concerns appear to be with only a small part of British politics, it is worth underlining the fact that the institutions of government occupy a key role in political life. It is ministers and officials from government who are responsible for representing British interests in the EU policy-making process. At a later stage of the policy cycle they usually assume responsibility for the transposition and implementation of EU legislation in the United Kingdom. Government also plays an important intermediating role for other political forces. Hence the impact of EU membership upon government institutions is of crucial importance for the UK.

In this chapter we consider whether central government has been Europeanised. We address the following questions: has central government adopted the organisational logic of the EU? Or has the traditional Whitehall model continued to prevail? We explore these questions by looking at the extent and nature of change in central government, but before proceeding to do so we need to say a little about what we mean by Europeanisation, how we understand the nature of institutional change and how we organise the presentation of our findings.

An important *caveat* must be mentioned at the outset. When examining the impact of EU membership upon the UK it is difficult to detach adaptation of government from the wider political context, not least the contortions of the two main political parties in coming to terms with the European issue (Baker and Seawright 1998). It is important to keep this point in mind and, indeed, we return to it in our conclusion.

Europeanisation

We use the term Europeanisation to characterise the impact of the European integration process upon the national level, and specifically upon the domestic institutions of government (for details see Bulmer and Burch 1998a). Of course the impact of European integration stretches well beyond government institutions. Broadly speaking, Europeanisation affects the political systems of all member states: their politics, policies and polities, including the workings of the institutions of government. We argue that, for each of these three, a two-stage response is necessary: reception and projection. Under the former, the significance of Europeanisation has to be registered and assimilated; under the latter, an effective form of response has to be devised, involving engagement with the EU itself. Reception corresponds most closely to Ladrech's formulation of Europeanisation as a 'process reorienting the direction and shape of politics to the degree that EC political and economic dynamics become part of the *organizational logic of national politics and policy-making*' (Ladrech 1994: 69 – our emphasis). However, Europeanisation involves more than this; it entails the ability to participate in integration so as best to be able to 'project' a national government's concerns into the EU decision-making process.

What broadly conditions these processes of reception and projection is the European Union's own organisational logic which national institutions of government need to adapt to if the opportunities afforded by membership are to be effectively exploited. There are a number of aspects of this that help to shape (but do not determine) responses at the national level. First, the institutions of the EU largely set the content and momentum of European policy business within national governments. If one compares the dynamics of European policy within the national context with those of domestic policy, the most obvious distinction is that the former are driven by a Brussels timetable. While purely domestic business can sometimes be deferred, to attempt postponement of a national response to an EU proposal is simply to risk exclusion from the Brussels debate. Second, the EU style of policy-making and administration, inasmuch as there is one, has only recently become institutionalised. We can perhaps characterise its general features as fluid, open, network-based, rule-guided, multilingual, relatively contained within policy sectors, and subject to significant inter-institutional bargaining (See Bulmer and Burch 1998a; also Wright 1996: 150–3). National government actors not only have to be skilled at operating in this environment but they must also be able to take its requirements into account when engaging in relevant policy discussions at home.

Finally, there is the challenge posed to each member state's ways of operating by the enormous complexity and volume of activity that has to be engaged in at the EU level. In 1997, for example, the Council adopted 243 items of legislation (directives and regulations) as well as taking 146 decisions (Corbett 1998: 47). As shown in Table 3.1, policy-making is undertaken in a hierarchy of committees. In the case of the UK, all levels of the Whitehall hierarchy – from the prime minister to departmental desk officers – are engaged in interaction with the EU. Some, most notably the staff of the UK's Permanent Representation (UKRep) to the EU, are exclusively engaged in such interaction. Matters are often determined at an official level: 70 per cent of decisions are generally held to have been taken at working group level; 15–20 per cent at the level of COREPER (the Committee of Permanent Representatives); and 10–15 per cent by ministers (Hayes-Renshaw and Wallace 1997: 40). In fact, this formal decision-making hierarchy is but part of the picture of Whitehall interaction with the EU. Before Commission proposals are formally adopted considerable consultation takes place in Commission advisory

Table 3.1   Intergovernmental decision-making bodies attended by representatives of the UK government

Institution	UK participant	No. of formations	No. of meetings
European Council	Prime Minister, Foreign Secretary, advisers	1	3 p.a. (1998) (plus 1 informal)
Council of the EU	Minister, advisers	21 (1998)	94 p.a. (1998)
Committee of Permanent Representatives (COREPER)	Permanent Representative/ Deputy Perm. Rep.	2	Weekly (both)
Special Committee on Agriculture (SCA)	Agricultural Counsellor from UKREP	1	Weekly when agriculture ministers not meeting
Working groups	Officials, usually from Whitehall	232 (1998)	3139 meetings p.a. (1998)

Note: for reasons of simplification we have excluded some middle-ranking decisional fora at the same level as the SCA: the important Monetary Committee (dealing with EMU); the Article 113 Committee (on trade); the Political Committee (on foreign policy); and the K4 Committee (on Justice and Home Affairs). To indicate the spread of impact across Whitehall, the UK delegate to the K4 Committee is from the Home Office, and within Whitehall co-ordinates with Customs and Excise and the Lord Chancellor's Department.
Source: data from General-Secretariat, Council of the European Union.

committees: here, national officials although formally involved in a personal capacity, are important participants. Once legislation is agreed there is a completely separate set of committees (409 of them in 1996), known by the overall term comitology, to monitor the Commission's executive powers (Wessels 1997: 276).

Change and institutions

In order to explore the extent and nature of the Europeanisation of Whitehall we develop ideas that are derived from the historical institutionalist literature. These deal both with change and the structure and nature of institutions. On change, we hold that in settled and stable societies, the usual response to new requirements is that existing institutions are adapted rather than new ones created (Thelen and Steinmo 1992: 16–18; Skowronek 1982: 12; Krasner 1988; Ikenberry 1988: 194–5; March and Olsen 1996: 256). Institutional change is, therefore, incremental as well as marginal. It is hardly ever radical, that is, involving a clean break with the past. Nevertheless, institutions can be significantly transformed over time. This happens when the outcomes of small and marginal changes accumulate and crystallise to such an extent that what becomes established is something distinctly and qualitatively different from that which previously existed (see Bulmer and Burch 1998b; Thelen and Steinmo 1992: 13–18). This transformative change is not always over, it is a matter for exploration and judgement, but we hold that while the pattern of institutional change is usually incremental it is essential to try to distinguish moments of transformation within it.

We identify three dimensions of institutional activity along which change can be measured. First, changes in activity as revealed in the growth in the volume of business and the number of personnel in UK government that are drawn into European policy making. Second, changes in policy as revealed in the extent to which EU requirements and policies have affected the determination of UK government policy agendas and goals. Thirdly, changes in administrative practices as shown in the degree to which the EU ways of doing things – its operating procedures and administrative values – have impinged on, and become embedded in, the administrative workings of British central government.

Moreover, in seeking to explore the extent of change along the dimensions mentioned above, we, like some other historical institutionalists, find it useful to concentrate on key moments when departures are made from established patterns (Thelen and Steinmo 1992: 27). It is at these moments that new institutional structures and processes may be set. Collier and Collier (1991: 29) use the term 'critical juncture' which they define 'as a period of significant change ... which is hypothesised to produce distinct legacies'. We go further by distinguishing a critical moment from a critical juncture. A 'critical moment' is when an opportunity arises for significant change. Such opportunities may not be realised and exploited but, if they are, the outcome is a 'critical juncture' at which there is a clear departure from previously established patterns. In theory, at each critical moment the opportunities for institutional innovation are at their widest. Joining the EC in 1973 was one of those critical moments, but was it a critical juncture?

In the rest of the chapter we explore these issues of Europeanisation and institutional change by examining the impact of EU membership along four institutional dimensions, as follows:

- *Systemic* – impact on the constitutional structure or the framework of state and government;
- *Organisational* – impact on the offices and networks and the key positions within them (including any impact on the powers, resources and skills attached to these positions);
- *Processual* – impact on the processes shaping how business is handled, especially the processes for distributing information and determining policy positions;
- *Regulative* – impact on the rules and guidelines about who should do what plus the extent to which there is a strategic capacity both to ensure tasks are fulfilled and to think ahead.

There is a fifth dimension which needs to be taken into account: the *cultural*. This concerns the norms and values that are prevalent within the institution and how these are inculcated. It is slightly different from the other four dimensions because it is present in all of them. Within the systemic dimension culture could refer to overarching issues, such as the understanding of national sovereignty or national identity. Within the organisational it could refer to understandings about who is eligible to fill a position and what they are expected to do. Within the processual it could refer to the traditional Whitehall value of settling business at the lowest possible level. Within the regulative it could refer to values concerning when officials in a ministry should take legal advice on a matter.

In assessing the Europeanisation of Whitehall we make some brief historical observations and then examine each of the institutional dimensions noted above: how far has adaptation occurred in each of these?

British central government and Europeanisation

Historical overview

Before we embark on looking at changes in UK central government in response to the challenge of Europe it is important to consider the pattern of governance that was already present, and in particular the traditional Whitehall values concerning how business should be handled and by whom. These values apply especially within the processual and regulative dimensions and constitute what might be termed Whitehall's way of doing things. So far as processes are concerned the traditional Whitehall approach to handling cross-departmental business centres on the cabinet committee system. Typically, ministerial committees are mirrored by and receive business from lower tiers of official committees. Underlying this formal structure there are three central precepts which ensure the effective handling of business. First, departments with the main policy responsibility will usually have the lead in preparing business and pressing it forward. Secondly, in order to avoid overload, the understanding is that business should be settled at the lowest possible level: preferably within the department itself or between departments without engaging wider, cabinet system, actors. Indeed only those matters which cannot be so settled, or which have widescale cross-departmental implications, or which raise major issues of policy or are significant matters of public concern are expected to go further (Cabinet Office 1997: 3). Third, and this is a feature more distinctive to Whitehall, the operation of the system depends on the expectation that when issues arise in one department which have implications for others, those others will be informed and if necessary consulted. This principle of information-sharing is an essential feature of the traditional Whitehall system and one which distinguishes it from many continental bureaucracies.

These three precepts governing the handling of business are derived from and legitimated in terms of the two key constitutional conventions governing the operation of Whitehall: collective and individual responsibility. Within the regulatory dimension, they are backed up by a series of codes and guidelines. These have developed cumulatively over many decades, and designate, amongst other things, the form in which business should be handled and matters such as to whom it should be sent and when (for details see Burch and Holliday 1996: 56–60). Strategic capacity to ensure that tasks are fulfilled and to think ahead is formally enshrined in the Cabinet and its ministers and those who assist them, though there has traditionally been a great deal of uncertainty about where strategic leadership actually lies and who should exercise it. Traditionally, those officials concerned with the co-ordination of policy across Whitehall have placed great value on the efficient handling of policy business rather than the content of policy itself. However, the system seeks full consultation and, ideally, consensus across Whitehall and, if left to its own devices will tend to seek the common ground between different departmental interests. All of these Whitehall ways of doing things were well established before UK entry into the EC.

Significantly, the UK approach to handling EU business can be traced back at least as far as the first (failed) application for entry in 1961–63 when the rudiments of the structure which is now in operation were first brought into play. That centred on a tiered system of cabinet committees, one ministerial, and two levels of official committees, which brought together and co-ordinated the business for negotiation across Whitehall; a co-ordinating responsibility (located in the Treasury); a staff carrying out the negotiations in Brussels supported by UKDel – the UK delegation to the Communities – but with close liaison back to the inter-departmental committees; and involvement of a high-powered legal team (Tratt 1996; Ludlow 1997). The same structure emerged at the time of the second application to join in 1967 except that responsibility for the co-ordination of the UK approach was moved from the Treasury to a special unit or secretariat in the Cabinet Office. By this time the early manifestations of the pattern of intra-departmental organisation for Europe were beginning to emerge in those departments most affected by EC membership: the Ministry of Agriculture, the Department of Trade, the Treasury and the Foreign Office.

After the negotiations were successfully completed, effectively by the summer of 1971, the government reviewed its approach to the handling of EC matters. The approaches of other member states were investigated, with the French being judged to have the best model of co-ordination. Also examined was the possibility of creating a Ministry for Europe and, briefly, allowing the Foreign and Commonwealth Office (FCO) to take the lead on Community matters across Whitehall (Wallace and Wallace 1973: 254). All these options were rejected and Prime Minister Heath laid down the dictum that 'Departments should think and act European'. He endorsed a system for handling business, in keeping with that used in the negotiations, which entailed co-ordination and light oversight by the Cabinet Office. The main change was in the purpose of the machinery which was now switched to deal with membership as opposed to entry. This led to some enhancement in the number of personnel involved, but the mechanisms and the approach were not substantially altered (Bulmer and Burch 1998b).

Two points are striking from this historical overview. First, the critical juncture in terms of shaping the machinery for developing Britain's European policy was actually at the start of the 1960s and bound up with the decision taken by the Macmillan government in April 1961 to apply for EC membership. The co-ordinating committee structure can be 'read across' to that presently prevailing. Accession to the EC in 1973 was a critical moment, but not a critical juncture, for there was no major change to the machinery. The principal change at that time was the exposure of a larger number of civil servants, diplomats and ministers to the functioning of the EC but within an already established framework. The second observation is that the institutional format had already emerged and it was in keeping with UK traditions. Fundamental reform was examined but turned down. Across all dimensions the arrangements for handling EC business that were adopted, and later built on, were those operative in Whitehall.

We now turn to the details of this machinery as it operates today. For reasons that will become evident we will tackle the *systemic* dimension last, since we argue that the most significant developments in that regard are underway at present and raise key questions for the future handling of EU policy-making.

The organisational dimension

What have been the key developments in the offices, networks and the positions of the key players within Whitehall, and the nature of the connections between them?

One very evident feature of the present set-up is that there is now pretty well universal coverage of central government so far as European business is concerned. Every department has some involvement (as do some executive agencies), and nearly every department has EU co-ordination facilities, but the approach varies as does the effectiveness of the response. Some departments have been particularly slow off the mark in pulling together their approach to EU business and/or have entrusted matters of co-ordination to a relatively weak division. Over and above departmental level there is a well-established official network centred on the COES and its contact list of over one hundred names for official committees. However, there exists an inner core in that the key organisational players remain situated, as they always have been, in the COES, the Foreign and Commonwealth Office (FCO), the Department of Trade and Industry (DTI), the Ministry of Agriculture, Fisheries and Food (MAFF), the Treasury and UKRep. These are the elements that make up the general structure of the European network in Whitehall. The general trend over the period of entry has been one of expansion in terms of the number of offices and positions involved and in the scope of the network.

Since entry, there have been very few formal organisational innovations in the handling of European business above departmental level. Most arrangements have developed from small beginnings as and when the need arises. The possible exception is the COES and its attached team of Cabinet Office Legal Advisers (COLA), based in the Treasury Solicitor's Department. COES is the one long-established pro-active secretariat in the Cabinet Office. The role of the prime minister has also been enhanced over the period. No. 10 has always held an important position in the shaping of European policy, but the establishment of the European Council in 1975, and its subsequent development into the key strategic policy body of the EU, reinforced prime ministerial opportunities for closer involvement. Moreover, the head of COES has become the key official adviser to the prime minister on European policy, though the personalities of both incumbents are important in shaping the nature of this relationship.

Organisationally the system has become more fragmented as subsidiary networks have emerged as business has expanded. These include the lawyers' network which centres on COLA and its web of cross-departmental contacts. Others centre on specific items of business: the EU's Common Foreign and Security Policy (CFSP) centred on the FCO; Justice and Home Affairs (JHA) co-operation centred on the Home Office; monetary union (EMU) centred on the Treasury (and for some time contained within it). These developments have meant that the process of managing business has become more complex, has a number of subsidiary hubs, and, arguably, that oversight has become more problematic. In addition, in recent years the system has become slightly less Whitehall-focused. The 'territorial' departments have geared up to handling Europe and have begun to liaise informally amongst themselves. The phenomenon of minimal decentralisation is also evident in the structural funds field as the English Government Offices in the Regions have, especially since 1994, begun to play a larger role. This development has taken place substantially in response to EU pressure.

So far as the development of skills is concerned, the training of officials has been provided in different ways, including through the Civil Service College. However, budgetary constraints have increasingly led to the parallel emergence of fragmented in-house training programmes. Across Whitehall, language training has become increasingly needed to facilitate the networking skills on which bilateral and multilateral lobbying and negotiating in the EU rely (Maor and Stevens 1997).

In addition to internal organisational arrangements, Whitehall has had to adapt to the fact that EU business requires some input from Westminster. The House of Lords conducts detailed wide ranging enquiries into policy issues, while the House of Commons, by contrast, has set up an elaborate system for monitoring legislation and referring matters deemed significant for debate. These arrangements, together with the power of reserve scrutiny, represent the key responses of the Commons (House of Commons 1996). They are, however, reliant upon information coming from relevant ministries (through Explanatory Memoranda), while the House of Commons has been seeking for a number of years to get its powers extended to cover the burgeoning activity of the EU in the CFSP and in JHA. After the Modernisation Committee grasped this procedural nettle, the relevant extension in the scrutiny power of the Commons committee has recently been granted (House of Commons 1998; Cabinet Office 1998). The consequence of this latest move is to make the handling of European business in Whitehall both more complex and, potentially, more accountable.

How does the evidence on post-accession developments within the organisational dimension correspond to our hypothesis of Whitehall having to adapt to the organisational logic of the EU? Our basic finding is that the system has responded in a largely reactive manner. There has been no widescale official review and no evaluation of its overall effectiveness. At the organisational level, Europeanisation has been partial. It has reflected more the logic of accommodating European business within the practices of Whitehall than of reforming British central government to reflect the different institutional dynamics of the EU.

The processual dimension

On the face of it we would expect there to have been considerable adaptation at the level of the processes shaping EU business. The functional necessity to participate in EU policy-making is present almost regardless of the attitude of the government-in-office to European integration. Has the process of Europeanisation, then, been more pervasive at this level?

As already mentioned, an important conditioning factor for the processes whereby European business is handled is the extent to which the timetable and momentum of business is substantially set at EU level. Within this context of constraint, Whitehall has put in place procedures to ensure that it can respond promptly to material emanating from the EU. The key decision process on European business has always centred upon a three-tier system of ministerial and official cabinet committees, some *ad hoc* meetings and numerous informal contacts. Over time the *ad hoc* meetings and informal elements have tended to become more important. The three-tiered committee system comprises: the Cabinet Sub-Committee on European Affairs (E)DOP; very senior officials EQ(O*) (until 1997 designated EQ[S]); and EQ(O). A connected process is in place to deal with legal issues, convened by the Cabinet Office Legal Adviser either as a formal sub-committee EQ(O)L or on an *ad hoc* basis. The key information flows on European business in Whitehall operate through the contact lists for these committees and, on items of low sensitivity, are expanded out to a wider EU information net with about 250 initial contact points.

An important effect of EU membership has been to extend UK policy processes outside the national state boundaries. This has required the creation of new mechanisms to encompass the element outwith the UK and has seen the emergence of distinct patterns of involvement beyond Whitehall. The main innovation in the European policy process at the top level upon membership was the creation of a 'sweeping-up' Friday meeting in the Cabinet Office to ensure last minute coherence of negotiating positions as well as looking ahead to other up-coming business. Attended by the UK Permanent Representative, this meeting is a key strength in the tactical co-ordination of UK European policy. Beyond that, the policy process spreads out from Whitehall into UKRep in Brussels and more widely into the fora of the EC/EU and especially through the regular participation of UK officials in Council working groups, Commission advisory groups and in comitology meetings (see Table 3.1, above). The result is that significant amounts of policy are shaped in EU arenas rather than in those of the UK.

Informal aspects of process are also vital to the operation of the machinery. Personal contacts between UK officials and their counterparts in member states and EU institutions are essential to effective formulation and projection of the UK position. Success in exercising influence through personal contact is assisted through attention to UK staffing levels in Brussels. Indeed, central government's response to the need to find UK recruits for established posts in the European institutions was rather *ad hoc* in nature until 1990, when a European Staffing Unit was set up in the Office of Public Service. Thereafter the UK has begun to ensure that its quota of permanent posts is taken up. Separately, UKRep seeks to help 'place' UK officials in key positions as Detached National Experts (DNEs) in the Commission. The UK's co-ordinated approach to policy-making has enabled Whitehall officials to make good use of British contacts within the Commission, for example, by exploiting the UK Commissioners' advisers in their own *cabinet*.

The UK/EU policy process raises problems concerning general oversight and accountability. Because the process characteristically centres on detailed and specialised policy questions, officials tend to handle much of this business. Ministers are brought in according to the established Whitehall criteria: on larger policy issues or when a change in policy direction needs to be considered. However, the specialised nature of business, the tendency for decisions to be reached within EU arenas and the importance of informal contacts, raises problems about effective ministerial involvement and the dangers of unforeseen policy development.

In sum, for the processual dimension, too, a Whitehall logic tends to prevail. However, its co-ordinated nature serves central government in good stead in ensuring a coherent articulation of the UK position. At this level of response, therefore, adaptation to the rhythms of the EU policy process has been more extensive but still within a Whitehall logic.

The regulative dimension

What have been the key developments in terms of rules and guidelines concerning who should do what and in respect of strategic capacity?

There has been a cumulative expansion of rules and guidelines at both departmental and inter-departmental level. Most departments now have guidelines and set procedures for dealing with recurrent items of EU business. The COES has accumulated a substantial series of Guidance Notes. These serve to promote conformity across departments on the handling of standard items of business, such as infraction proceedings initiated by the Commission against the UK government. For instance, Humphreys lists 76 notes, combining those issued by the Cabinet Office and by the then Department of the Environment (Humphreys 1996: 237–9).

Less obviously but equally importantly, Treasury rules concerning the EU budget have a pervasive effect on all Whitehall departments which have spending programmes supported from Brussels. These rules have become both more particular and more pervasive – since the late 1970s, as a result of stronger general

Treasury controls, and from the early 1980s, with the creation of EuroPES or the supply of the related public expenditure. The exact functioning of the rules differs according to the policy area. The general principle, however, is the same: the UK's hypothecated contribution to the particular spending programme is deducted from that department's public expenditure survey (PES) settlement. Or, put illustratively, the Office of Science and Technology (OST) suffers a cut in its budget equivalent to the calculated cost to the UK of contributions to the EU spending programmes which OST administers. Since spending departments would rather run programmes whose rules are determined in the UK than those shaped (and compromised) in Brussels, this system lines up all spending departments behind the Treasury in resisting increases to the EU budget. This stance on the budget has an impact on the conduct of UK European policy. The rules are so entrenched that their effect is well known and simply anticipated by officials.

As far as strategic capacity is concerned there has been little Whitehall-wide response. The COES is relatively small, with just nine senior officials, and cannot go much beyond the short- to medium-term tactical considerations of European policy. Occasionally it may convene an *ad hoc* group of officials, for example, to consider the implications of eastwards enlargement but no COES planning staff exists. Capacity at No. 10 has also been rather limited and, of course, dependent upon the European policy of the current prime minister. With relatively few exceptions there has been no government-wide vision concerning the evolution of integration. Two notable exceptions have been the Thatcher government's prosecution of the single market initiative and Blair's 1998 review of UK European policy which is still to come to fruition.

A rounded judgement of the regulative dimension provides a mixed picture. Central government has not responded in a particularly effective way to European integration, where 'kite-flying' and bilateral relationships form an essential part of 'playing the European game'. As regards the EC budget, Treasury rules trump European policy. Except when the EU is conducting a medium-term budget review, the EC budget has simply been part of domestic PES negotiations even though the consequence is to give no ministry an incentive to advocate the development of EC spending policies even if they might have some benefit to the UK. The consequence in both cases is to limit the UK's ability to treat membership of the EU as an opportunity to garner additional resources that it is. In respect of codes and guidelines, the EU has had some impact. These help, *inter alia*, to ensure that the UK government has a good record before the European Court of Justice. But they are detailed in nature and tend to affect the conduct rather than the substance of European policy. Again, EU business has tended to be incorporated into Whitehall's 'logic of appropriateness' rather than prompting a more concerted reform centred on EU logic.

The cultural dimension

As we noted earlier, the cultural dimension is closely linked with each of the others. The essential question here is: how far have the norms, values and culture of the EU come to augment or affect those intrinsic to the established Whitehall way of doing things?

Concerning the organisational dimension, three observations relating to personnel are striking. First, a cadre of European-aware senior officials has emerged over time. They share skills and understandings about how the EU works, and an awareness of what the critical issues are and how business should be handled in both Whitehall and Brussels. Originally located in a small group of ministries, notably the FCO, MAFF, the DTI and to a lesser extent the Treasury, their spread has widened with the extension of EU business. The cadre displays a greater awareness of how to influence the EU policy process at the all-important, early stage: through Commission advisory groups; lobbying of the Commission services; or contacting members of the UK commissioners' cabinets, if necessary by using UKRep as an intermediary. It also reveals a stronger awareness of the need to form alliances with counterparts in other member governments. An awareness, therefore, of the importance of adapting to the EU in a manner suited to having an effective voice in Brussels (projection) is particularly strong in this cadre.

A second observation is that these officials have (through experience) a more informed and realistic view of EU issues than do other colleagues in Whitehall, including some ministers and many contributors to the wider UK debate on EU membership. Without measuring things quantitatively, we detected that officials who had spent periods in Brussels (on secondment as DNEs, in UKRep or in Commission cabinets) were better equipped to appreciate the norms and procedures of the EU, together with the opportunities afforded by it. Since the EU operates in a quite different way from the British political system, this awareness is crucial to an effective representation of British interests in the EU.

Thirdly, the European policy-making network in Whitehall, in which this cadre represents a core, forms a larger grouping of senior civil servants than any other cross-departmental policy group existing on a long-term basis. In other words, EU business brings together more senior Whitehall officials than any other policy domain. This situation is in itself indicative of the slow but transformative change brought about in Whitehall. It also means that the European policy debate within the network is conducted at a distinctly different level from that in the rest of Whitehall and the public domain.

These features reflect the Europeanisation of Whitehall personnel. However, a substantial portion of Whitehall officials still do not have the opportunity to obtain a Brussels perspective. We detected a tendency amongst officials who still lacked experience in Brussels to regard having an early and coherent British policy as a great strength but to neglect the inflexibility in the British negotiating position that may ensue. Since the 1986 Single European Act, as qualified majority voting has become more prevalent in the European Council, so the need for negotiating flexibility has grown. To have a coherent and firm view may suffice in major order negotiations in the EU, where unanimity applies, but such a policy risks marginalisation under conditions of QMV. We also noted that management reform within ministries can serve as a disincentive for officials to take temporary postings in the Commission, and in addition some departments may be unwilling to bear the associated costs.

Within the *processual and regulative* dimensions some of the consequent clashes of culture emerge in the issue of how to handle European policy. Should one follow Whitehall's values both of cross-departmental co-ordination and of all singing from the same hymn-sheet, that is, speaking in accord? Or are there merits in retaining flexibility for end-game negotiations? Co-ordination works because of traditional norms of sharing information across Whitehall. These ensure that there is a strong understanding that intelligence on developments in Brussels is shared amongst departments. It contrasts strongly with the practice in Germany where intelligence is a resource which may be used by one ministry against another. Where an inter-ministerial disagreement over policy develops, there is a strong understanding that the Cabinet Office be brought in to help broker a solution at an early stage to ensure that a single policy is articulated in Brussels. We would argue that this approach is highly successful in the reception stage of European policy-making. However, it is not without disadvantages when it comes to the projection of European policy. As noted, it encourages inflexibility. It also allows other member states to use the British government as a proxy: they are able to hide behind British 'resolution' and avoid any flak.

A further observation relates to transmission of awareness of European matters and approaches to dealing with them through training in individual ministries. Despite the general trends noted above, we found that the decision to raise European awareness in individual departments did not follow any central decision previously taken in Whitehall. A 1991 management review in the Scottish Office (Scottish Office 1991); the arrival of the Europhile John Gummer to become Secretary of State for the Environment (from the Europeanised MAFF); or personnel changes in the Treasury under Kenneth Clarke: such departmental developments occasioned an upgrading of European training. The growth in training is particularly worthy of note. The Treasury is a key player in European policy-making but seems until 1997 to have given little priority to the specific needs of European training.

Perhaps the biggest challenge to the handling of European policy is emerging at the systemic level, something which we have not yet discussed. We have argued elsewhere that the process of devolution may present a serious challenge to the co-ordination of European policy (Bulmer and Burch 1998b). Chains of accountability between the devolved administrations and assemblies will ultimately have to flow into a territorially re-defined Whitehall. The cultural dimension of this development will be closely linked with the emergent institutions (see below). It does not require too much thought to realise that some of the traditional Whitehall values will be placed under serious challenge. The cultural dimension is, however, part of a wider picture of constitutional reform taking place under the Blair government, and it is to this which we now turn.

The systemic dimension

Prior to the election of the Blair government, UK membership of the EC/EU did have a creeping impact on the broad constitutional framework within which central government operates. The key changes were in respect of political and legal aspects of sovereignty. Joining the EC involved a significant loss of sovereignty, although this change is something that has been kept somewhat covert. Arguably, in a gradual way, developments, within the EC have cumulatively begun to erode aspects of the established constitutional framework in the UK. This has been most evident in the consequence of ECJ rulings for the operation of UK legal institutions and in the slow development of a more significant regional voice in national administration in response to the requirements for handling structural funds. Cross-border co-operation in Ireland has had some limited effect on the conditions against which the peace process developed (Teague 1996).

The raft of constitutional reforms that followed on from the election of the Labour government in 1997, in part derived from European developments, seems likely to have significant consequences for Whitehall's approach to handling European policy. This is most evident in the case of devolution, although it is too early to judge the likely ramifications of elections to Scottish and Welsh executives. For example, draft concordats between the Scottish executive and Whitehall will have to find a satisfactory way to handle a key policy area such as fisheries, which is central to Scotland's economy but where MAFF will retain the policy lead. Moreover, the proposed organisation of the Scottish Parliament to deal with EU business rejects the Westminster approach and proposes innovative arrangements, such as a consultative forum of interests working in conjunction with a European Committee (Scottish Office 1998).

The changes to UK constitutional law are not confined to the three elected assemblies. There is the-as-yet unclear nature of regional developments in England. Independence for the Bank of England brought further change at the systemic level, although a decision to join the single currency would have much greater consequences. A shift to proportional representation, even if not (yet) a fact for Westminster elections, is likely to change the cultural context of politics and render the coalition-building in the EU less alien than it seems at present to those trained in the adversarialism of Westminster. Freedom of information legislation, when it comes about, will also have some impact on the Whitehall approach. These constitutional changes have the potential to lead to a fundamental re-shaping of UK politics, the role of Whitehall in it, and, consequently, the foundations of European policy-making.

As a final systemic point we need to consider the whole context of the UK's relations with the EU. At no time during the history of membership has a strong political consensus been built around integration. However, the Labour government came to power on a manifesto commitment of playing a leading role in EU reform. Tony Blair seems to have embarked upon a concerted effort to make a success of this commitment through his call, at a seminar on 28 May 1998, for a fundamental review of European policy. Already this initiative has yielded action both in relation to the development of a more systematic approach to training on European matters for both officials and ministers and through enhanced inter-ministerial co-ordination.

It is too early to tell where these developments will lead but they are likely to alter the framework of policy and with it the institutional arrangements as well. Although the causes of change do not derive from the EU itself, constitutional reform, we suggest, will create such a major change in the practice of European policy-making in the UK that a critical juncture may well ensue.

Conclusion

In this chapter we set out to examine the extent and nature of change in British central government as a result of membership of the EU looking at the effects of Europeanisation on the traditional Whitehall model. We identified two components of Europeanisation: reception and projection. There can be little doubt that British central government has largely performed well in terms of reception. Along the organisational, processual and regulative dimensions an effective machinery has been put in place. However, this pattern of reception has largely been one of adapting the traditional Whitehall approach and absorbing EU business into it. The impact of the EU upon Whitehall–Westminster relations, Treasury rules and the machinery of European policy co-ordination – to take three examples – seems to have been of a type designed to minimise disturbance to traditions in British central government.

The performance of central government in projecting British policy positions into EU arenas in a manner which suits the latter's organisational logic, is a much more modest one. To be sure, UKRep is a highly efficient organisation. The placing of staff in EU institutions, and the exploitation of such contacts, is also efficient. As has been said, there is also a highly informed cadre of EU-aware officials. However, flexibility in negotiations is sometimes lost as a result of the Whitehall imperative of agreeing policy early. The government's strategic planning capacity on European policy is slight. And not least, UK negotiating teams have sometimes been led by ministers who have found integration distasteful and thus have not been disposed to exploit the opportunities afforded by the EU. This political dimension is a crucial part of the mixed performance on the 'projection' side, since it is clear that establishing a planning capacity on European policy, and developing a constructive engagement with the EU policy process, depends on direction from political leaders. At least until 1997, for reasons that are well-known, such governmental leadership has been subject to veto points in both parties.

Overall, our findings are that institutional adaptation has been of two principal forms over the period since 1973: incremental and transformative. By the latter we mean that the cumulative effect of incremental development has been such as to create significant Whitehall-wide organisational change over the longer term. Europeanisation has created something qualitatively different from the situation upon accession. These findings can be demonstrated by reference to our three indicators: activity (i.e. the impact of EU business upon Whitehall); the growth of policy areas where the EU may have the policy 'lead'; and Whitehall's adaptation – albeit partial, as we have seen – to the EU's patterns of administration and governance.

To the extent that there has been a more radical form of change in central government, it was that triggered by the 1961 application for EC membership. This is the only 'critical juncture' we have identified thus far. Moreover, no critical moment has emerged since 1971/72 to stimulate a review of the collective purpose of Whitehall in the EU. A major factor in explaining this path-dependent, incremental approach is the political climate on European policy. The creation of any Whitehall review might at certain stages during the last 25 years have opened up political divisions over the purposes of European integration, never mind of Whitehall in serving them! However, the current constitutional changes in the UK, together with the review of European policy currently in hand, may trigger a further critical juncture in the handling of European business.

Notes

1. For consistency, the designation European Union (EU) is used throughout this chapter unless inappropriate. The European Economic Community (EEC) was established in 1957. After 1965 the phrase 'European Communities' (EC) was used. In 1992 the 'European Community' became a separate entity within the wider European Union (EU).

4
Internal Control in the Executive and its Constitutional Significance*

Alan Page and Terence Daintith

Introduction

Executive self-restraint constitutes one of the essential underpinnings of democracy and the rule of law. Unless there exist structures and powers through which the executive government can control the actions of its component parts, the control powers assigned to other organs under our existing constitution, notably Parliament and the courts, just will not work. The vital importance of internal control in organisations is something that is now taken for granted in discussion of regulation of all kinds, from financial services to health and safety. The point is accepted by lawyers who deal with regulation (Ayres and Braithwaite 1992: Ch. 4), yet it has hardly penetrated constitutional law scholarship. Constitutional lawyers in the United Kingdom have largely neglected the executive, and its internal controls, and instead have concentrated on the more familiar (and more accessible) external controls applied by Parliament and the courts. In our research (Daintith and Page 1999) we set out to repair this gap in our understanding of our constitutional arrangements. The picture that emerges is of a system of internal control which has been shaped by the pluralistic legal structure of the executive branch, but which is in the course of significant change, largely but not solely as a result of the public service reforms pursued by successive governments over the last 20 or so years. In this chapter we draw together the threads of the changes that are affecting internal control, before examining its relationship with the external controls operated by Parliament and the courts. In the final section we offer our conclusions on the constitutional significance of the internal control function in contemporary UK executive government and its recent changes. We begin, however, with the traditional pattern.

The organisation of internal control: the traditional pattern

Arriving at a satisfactory understanding of the internal control function within executive government requires an analysis of the legal structure of the executive

* We would like to acknowledge the ESRC for funding our research (award number L124225003).

branch under the constitution. That analysis (Daintith and Page 1999: Ch. 2) shows legal primacy in general as belonging to departments, not the centre. It is in departments, or more precisely in their ministerial heads, that the powers and duties of modern government are, by law, very largely vested. No less important in practice is the fact that it is rare for ministers to be subject to any higher authority in the exercise of the functions entrusted to them. In the absence of such higher authority it falls to departments as a matter of law and no one else to exercise those functions. It would be wrong to overstate the significance of the formal legal position, but departmental primacy in the organisation of government is reinforced by the underlying principle of ministerial responsibility. We are familiar with the use of the doctrine to ward off control from outside, but it may operate in exactly the same way within the executive branch. The position of departments within the executive is further buttressed by the fact that their ministerial heads are also members of the central executive authority, the Cabinet.

Departmental primacy emerged as the central organising principle of the executive branch in the middle years of the nineteenth century when the ministerial department replaced the board of public officials as the preferred form of executive organisation (Willson 1955). Its corollary was an essentially decentralised system of internal control, the operation of which depended on the ministerial head of each department who in turn was responsible to Parliament. Aside from the minister, the key role in this system was occupied by the permanent head of the department, who was responsible to the minister for its overall organisation, management and staffing (Treasury 1989: para 6.2.1). The role of the 'centre' was one essentially of co-ordination, advice and assistance rather than control. The traditional orthodoxy was that it was better to trust departments than to engage in 'a futile attempt at supervision in detail' (Haldane 1923: 8).

There were exceptions to this pattern. The most important were those in respect of expenditure and establishments, the latter being treated until recently as part of the control of expenditure. Treasury control of money and staff in a plural executive was founded on control of access to resources, reinforced in the case of staff by a mixture of mainly prerogative and to a lesser extent statutory controls. These prerogative controls, derived not from parliamentary authorisation but from the executive's inherent power of self-management under the constitution, were written down and formally delegated to the Treasury for this purpose, most notably by the Civil Service Order in Council 1920.

But although the Treasury has always possessed important powers of control over departments, it has never strayed far from an approach which treats the primary responsibility for financial as well as policy decisions as belonging to spending departments (Woods 1956: 113). No doubt the adoption of that approach reflected a calculation that a system in which the emphasis was on the 'conjoint and co-operative responsibility, under Ministers, of all departmental heads, including the Treasury' (Hamilton 1951: para 86) was likely to be more effective than one in which the emphasis was on the Treasury's powers of control alone. But it also acknowledged the extent to which collective control in a plural executive depended on agreement among departments. Greenleaf reminds us that the reason why Treasury control of public expenditure was never so complete or severe as the conventional wisdom asserts, was because 'departments were important official entities in their own right and headed by ministers with their special authority and responsibility to Parliament. Against this twin array the Treasury could not ultimately stand alone and needed Cabinet support and Parliamentary follow-up' (1987: 253).

One other feature of the traditional system which deserves mention is the part played by monitoring in the operation of central systems of control. The strength of the UK approach to internal control, in contrast to one in which spending decisions must be passed by representatives of the Treasury or Ministry of Finance located in each spending department, as in France or Italy, is that it places the responsibility for compliance firmly on the shoulders of departments. Their sense of responsibility is not diminished as a result of responsibility being seen to belong elsewhere. Its weakness is that it is vulnerable to non-compliance. Where central systems of control have been established, for expenditure and establishments, reliance on the department as the primary agent of control has therefore invariably been accompanied by some form of check on the diligence with which central disciplines are applied. Expenditure control has been backed both by a powerful system of state audit and, in more recent years, by an increasingly sophisticated cash monitoring system (Daintith and Page 1999: Ch. 6). After after the Second World War the decentralisation of responsibility for much of establishment's work was formalised and made permanent, the Treasury 'reaffirmed its right of inspection and of access to departments – the right to go and see for itself – and particularly the right to submit particular branches and posts to closer examination if it should seem to it desirable to do so' (Padmore 1956: 130).

This combination of delegated authority and central monitoring, however, was the exception rather than the rule. Across much of what the executive did the traditional system was one of departmental self-discipline or self-control under the individual and collective supervision of ministers. Seen in this light old problems take on a new air. The reason we have lacked a developed system of administrative law (Ridge v. Baldwin 1964: 72) is not so much due to failures in performance by the courts as to the fact that 'Parliament gave a free hand to half a hundred draftsmen and departmental solicitors to produce whatever appealed to their taste or fancy' (Cooper 1957: 269). Given that latitude, the unsystematic encroachment upon traditional principles about which critics complained was always the likely result.

Growth and change

Forces for change

Departmental self-discipline continues to form the cornerstone of internal control. Over the last 20 years or so, however, the internal control function has undergone significant growth and change. As we have suggested, the main driving force behind this development has been the public service reforms pursued by successive governments over this period. If functions are to be contracted out, if burdens on business are to be reduced, if openness is to be increased, if services are to be made more responsive to their users, if co-ordination across departmental boundaries is to be increased, the centre has to find some means of inducing or compelling departments and agencies to move in the desired directions. In some cases, the increase has resulted not from any growth in the agenda of internal control but from the continued delegation of central functions to departments and agencies. The delegation of responsibility for recruitment, for example, has led to a central Recruitment Code policed by the Civil Service Commissioners (Daintith and Page 1999: Ch. 3). As could be expected, the possibility that departments should simply certify their compliance with the Code was rejected (Cabinet Office 1994: paragraph 5.1). Changes in the constitutional environment have also played a major role. EU membership in particular has produced, in the shape of the European Secretariat, a more vigorous central co-ordination mechanism than exists for the co-ordination of purely domestic issues.

Co-ordination versus centralisation

In all these areas, therefore, new systems of control have emerged. The shape they take reflects who controls the resource with which they are concerned. Only rarely, in our system, has such power been centralised or even concentrated in a single department. The notable exceptions are the Treasury's 'ancient authority' over government's financial resources, and the Cabinet's more recently acquired control over legislative resources, that is, over departmental access to Parliament for legislative purposes. Less well known – except to ambitious barristers, perhaps – is the Attorney-General's power over the appointment of all counsel representing the Crown, and over Crown legal proceedings generally. These 'resource monopolies' within the executive are all conventional in nature, though it is quite possible for such a monopoly to be created by law: the specific powers of control with which the Civil Service Commissioners are still endowed represent the remains of powers which have been in existence since the Civil Service Order in Council 1870 established open competition as the normal method of entry to the service and put the Commissioners in control of it. A body that possesses such a monopoly may use it as an instrument of control. This has always been the endeavour of the Treasury, though both the purpose and the style of the control regime have changed radically over the years. Control over legislative access has likewise been the means by which the Cabinet has pursued, mainly through the Parliamentary Counsel Office, goals of consistency in legislative drafting and a discipline – admittedly limited – over aspects of legislative content. Naturally, where such monopoly power is conventional in origin, it may in the last resort be overridden by *ad hoc* decision-making within the Cabinet system, a possibility that provides an in-built constraint on the over-zealous use of such power. But it remains the case that its holder enjoys a privileged position in shaping the relevant control regime, whether by way of a long-term process of delegation, as with the Treasury, or through turning potential powers of obstruction to constructive use in building norms and expectations, as with the Parliamentary Counsel Office in alliance with the Law Officers.

The new control and co-ordination machinery engendered by public service reform and by changes in the constitutional environment has received little if any support from the creation or extension of resource monopolies. Two examples come to mind. First, the leveraging of the Treasury's running costs control regime to support participation by the Cabinet Office (formerly OPS) in the monitoring of departmental performance (Treasury 1998b). Second, the extension of control powers to control litigation by giving European lawyers in the Treasury solicitors department a monopoly over management of litigation in the ECJ (Daintith and Page 1999: Ch. 9).

Nor has the new machinery been based on prerogative or statutory powers (with the exception of the controls over recruitment which continue to be exercised by the Civil Service Commissioners in their new role as the guardians of the principle of recruitment on merit on the basis of fair and open competition, together with the analogous controls which have been introduced in respect of public appointments). Instead of taking powers of control over departments and agencies to achieve these new ends, government has preferred to build on techniques of co-operation and co-ordination honed in the Cabinet Office over many decades, of which the Cabinet or ministerial committee together with the official committees that sometimes parallel them provide the quintessential institutional expression. The process of co-operation is, however, increasingly driven by a variety of centrally placed units each with a well-defined mission (and, often, a set of norms and standards to go with it). The traditional Cabinet Office maxim, 'There is no policy other than there should be a policy', is being supplemented by a variety of specific policies from its constituent units – efficiency, better regulation, better government – through stimulation, exhortation and co-ordination. These units and their policies depend for their influence directly upon consensus in their favour within the Cabinet system, at the highest political levels of the executive, a consensus which may need to be sustained (or failing that a policy imposed) by the political leadership and power of the prime minister.

This kind of co-ordination technique is no longer confined to questions of how to conduct executive government; it is coming to be used increasingly as a means by which the centre can (seek to) influence substantive policy through the setting up of units or groups within the Cabinet Office to address problems like social exclusion, or industrial innovation and enterprise. It is also being practised in other departments which have an acknowledged co-ordinating role, for example, the institutionalisation of the Government Legal Service under the leadership of the Treasury Solicitor, the creation as part of the service of a Lawyers' Management Unit, and the steady elaboration of a structure of co-ordination led by the Government Legal Service Liaison Group (Daintith and Page 1999: Chs 7 and 9). In the matter of legal resources, the Treasury Solicitor has never achieved the sort of monopoly enjoyed by the Treasury over financial ones, but now, arguably, it exercises stronger leadership over the legal function in the executive than does the Treasury over its accountancy counterpart. Such leadership capacities, however, appear to rest more upon professional cohesion than upon the collective political consensus sustaining the Cabinet Office role in 'directed co-ordination'.

This model of internal control, which has affinities with notions of 'co-operative implementation' (Michael 1996) and 'enforced self-regulation' (Ayres and Braithwaite 1992), continues to be based on departmental self-control, but involves a greater degree of central initiative than in the past. The role of the centre is no longer confined to advice and assistance; it is also increasingly one of encouraging and exhorting departments and agencies to move in desired directions. The foundations of departmental primacy within the executive branch, however – legally vested powers; absence of superiors; ministerial responsibility; Cabinet membership – remain essentially intact. The retention of these guarantees of departmental autonomy means in turn that the exercise of collective control continues to rely heavily on agreement. Where there is agreement, as in the case of recruitment, we may expect it to proceed relatively smoothly. Where there is an absence of agreement, or scope for disagreement, as in the case of deregulation, we may expect it to remain problematic. The Better Regulation Unit may have the support of the prime minister, but it is still powerless to prevent the Minister of Agriculture from introducing new regulations such as banning beef on the bone.

Formalisation

Co-ordination and control which derives from political agreement does not, however, require the continuous maintenance of such agreement. The articulation of such control in the form of explicit rules and procedures eventually furnishes an independent source of legitimacy. Such formalisation may indeed be a useful, perhaps even essential, support for the specific control policies of the new central units in government. A document expressed in terms of standards, or principles, or rules, and hence looking rather like law, may acquire an aura of authority which usefully supplements whatever influence is possessed by the relevant Cabinet Office Unit. The need to legitimate these new control policies may be a significant factor in explaining the clear recent trend to the formalisation of internal control.

Indeed, such formalisation is frequently linked to the reform processes we have described. New internal procedures have been instituted, for example, in respect both of the scrutiny of secondary legislation which amends primary legislation and of legislative proposals which have a potential impact on business. There has been a flood of codes, handbooks, guidance, framework documents, charters, statements of principle and other forms of normative material stemming directly from the public service reforms of recent years. Constitutional change, too, has also played a part. The decision to make rights derived from the European Convention on

Human Rights (ECHR) directly enforceable under United Kingdom law, for example, is leading to provision for the more systematic consideration of the legislative implications of ECHR obligations along lines similar to that undertaken in respect of European Community obligations since accession.

Formalisation, however, has not just been about implementing reform – and buttressing such reform is certainly not its only motive. It has also been about the re-statement and reinforcement of existing expectations in the face of the challenge to those expectations represented by public service reforms. Examples are the growing fragmentation of the public service, increased budgetary pressures, and new modes of delivery of public services. Their re-statement has also been prompted by fears that the existing mechanisms of professional socialisation are breaking down – a breakdown compounded by the growth in recruitment from the private sector. The Civil Service Code, the Recruitment Code, as well as the numerous handbooks and booklets which have been produced both by external and internal watchdogs, all seek to increase the visibility of existing expectations in an effort to reduce the risk of their being ignored. The preparation of the *Agency Chief Executive's Handbook*, for example, was occasioned by the 'need for even greater vigilance about standards throughout the Service'. Its purpose was to ensure that service-wide rules on conduct and financial propriety were always available to chief executives in a 'readily accessible form' (Cabinet Office (Office of Public service) 1996: p. iv). *The Ombudsman in Your Files* (Cabinet Office 1995b) and Regularity and Propriety (Treasury 1997) stem from the same impulse. *The Judge Over Your Shoulder* (Treasury Solicitor's Department 1987, 1995), the model for these booklets, was not only about alerting civil servants to requirements, but it was also a response to the increasing prominence of judicial review rather than the expression of any fear that public service reform might give more opportunity for civil servants to act illegally. To find a comparable upsurge in the codification of the rules relating to government we have to go back to the inter-war period and that too followed a period of dislocation, upheaval and uncertainty.

This codification of expectations has also been about maintaining or restoring public confidence in government; in that regard, it has been as much about reaffirming existing standards and increasing their visibility to allay the scepticism of outsiders as about laying down new and more exacting standards. The need for articulation and codification arose, the Chancellor of the Duchy of Lancaster argued in 1996, not because of any fall-off in respect for the implicit shared rules of public life, but because in 'a far more open society' it was 'right that all citizens should be able to have access to the rules by which their politicians and public servants are expected to behave' (Willetts 1996).

For some observers the increasing formalisation of internal control is to be regretted. The multiplication of codes to ensure probity, Foster and Plowden argue, is leading to a system which will be less effective and more expensive than reliance on 'traditional civil service methods'. The reason for this in their view is that rules simply do not work:

they merely stimulate ways round them, so leading to yet more rules to plug loopholes, leading to a growing climate of regulation of a kind from which the new public management saw the need to escape in the interests of efficiency. There can be no guarantee that reliance on these methods will be more effective or cheaper than relying on traditional civil service methods, based on the traditional Haldane relationship: indeed on both counts, rather the reverse. (Foster and Plowden 1996: 229)

This argument is important, but one which needs to be approached with a degree of caution. It misrepresents the traditional system as 'a system not of rules but of advice' (Foster and Plowden 1996: 77). The nature of the existing British constitution is thus said to be not 'to circumscribe matters with rules but to rely upon the more elastic safeguard of taking advice' (Thomas 1978: 6–7). Perhaps key actors thought of the constitution in this way, or would have liked it to be so seen, but the normative content of the traditional system was considerably greater than this suggests. For example, as we have seen, many of the key principles governing the civil service are traceable in written form to the interwar period or earlier. The form in which they were expressed (see below) may have allowed considerable latitude in their interpretation and application, but there was no question that the civil service had its own code.

Foster and Plowden's argument also neglects the role of rules in the provision of certainty; not absolute certainty, for that is unattainable, but greater certainty than is provided by reliance on unwritten rules. For Kernaghan 'the suggestion that contemporary public servants can rely for ethical guidance simply on unwritten rules in the form of traditions, conventions, understandings and practices is naive, and even dangerous'; a dominant rationale for written rules, he points out, 'is that there is much uncertainty as to what the traditional rules are and what they mean in the day-to-day operation of government' (1993: 27). The traditional objection to codification is that the pretence at clarification is illusory and must be paid for by the loss of flexibility which is the great merit of unwritten law, but as Freund pointed out 'the layman's purpose will often be served by intelligible explicitness falling short of absolute certainty; and this gives the written rule a political and educational value which nations living under codes fully appreciate' (1932: 6).

Finally, it overlooks one of the most significant features of these codes, namely the fact that they are without exception non-statutory. With this in mind we can turn to the relationship between internal control and the external controls operated by Parliament and the courts.

Internal control and external controls

Executive reliance on external control: parliament

The general picture is of the executive relying on its own resources for the purposes of internal control rather than seeking external parliamentary or judicial support. The principal exception is in expenditure control where a relationship of mutual dependence has existed between the Treasury and Parliament from the outset, although there are signs that Treasury dependence on parliamentary disciplines may be beginning to decline (Daintith and Page: Ch. 5). The civil service, on the other hand, with the exception of civil service numbers, has always been regulated as part of the exercise of the executive's prerogative powers.

This pattern has not been radically altered by the public service reforms of recent years. Sometimes the executive has had no choice but to secure legislation in the implementation of those reforms. But wherever possible it has preferred to proceed on the basis of its own powers both in the narrow prerogative sense (the Civil Service Management Code, the Recruitment Code, the Civil Service Code, the Public Appointments Code) and in the sense of the power of 'any Tom, Dick or Harry' (Ferguson 1988) to issue a non-statutory code (the Code of Practice on Access to Government Information). At the same time, the revival of the device of the Secretary of State covering several formerly separate departments (Daintith and Page: Ch. 2) has had the unexpected but welcome effect of reducing executive dependence on legislation in matters of its own organisation by diminishing the need for the formal transfer of functions between departments. It is a mark of the success of the government's policy of avoiding legislation wherever possible that the public service reforms of recent years have generated a total of only three enactments, all directed to the removal of obstacles to the implementation of specific policies: the Government Trading Funds Act 1990, the Civil Service (Management Functions) Act 1992 and the Deregulation and Contracting Out Act 1994.

Several reasons may be suggested why the executive should prefer to rely for internal control purposes on its autonomous powers. Legislative time is in short supply: relying on its own powers wherever possible enables the available time to be devoted to other, presumably more worthwhile, purposes. It also means that at some future point valuable legislative time does not have to be devoted to amending legislation. One reason why parliamentary legislation has recently been so infrequent is that there are few previously erected statutory obstacles to the implementation of public service reform. As well as being time-consuming, recourse to parliamentary legislation may also be risky: a government that relies on its own powers avoids the lottery of legislative amendment. It is also possible that despite the fact that the executive controls access to the legislative process, parliamentary legislation may in fact be beyond it: either there is internal agreement in which case legislation is unnecessary, or there is no agreement in which case parliamentary legislation is not a practical possibility. As in the case of freedom of information, it may be easier to secure internal agreement to a non-statutory code than to an Act of Parliament.

At the same time, non-statutory regulation is commonly regarded as possessing, in this as in other contexts, a number of advantages over its statutory counterpart. It is typically expressed differently: not as the precise and detailed rules of statute, but in the form of a mixture of general principles and subsidiary rules, which those who are bound by them are expected to observe in their spirit as well as their letter. This combination of principles and rules is said to allow the legislative project to be kept within manageable bounds, while at the same time allowing the underlying purpose of obligations to make plain as well as discouraging conduct at or near the margin of unlawfulness; in contrast, we do not expect the underlying principles to 'sing out of' Acts of Parliament (compare Cabinet Office 1994: paragraph 4.17). Such regulation is claimed to be more easily adaptable to changing circumstances or new developments. New cases can be decided by reference to the general principles on which systems are based, and the rules themselves can be changed quickly and with a minimum of formality. It is also said to be quicker and more flexible in its application to individual cases; the rules can be interpreted and applied in a practical common-sense (less legalistic) manner, taking into account their spirit as well as their letter. Statutory regulation, on the other hand is said to invite the inflexible application of rules without regard to their underlying purpose; it 'imports a rigidity into any procedure it touches' (Sisson 1966: 60). Finally, of course, non-statutory regulation in its prerogative form was for a long time not open to challenge in the courts. It thus combined certainty of effect with the avoidance of litigation.

Whether non-statutory regulation has always realised these advantages is open to question. Nor is there any inherent reason why statutory regulation should not be expressed in the form of a mixture of principles and rules. The principal objection to the executive's proceeding on a non-statutory basis, however, is not that the claims made for the non-statutory approach may be exaggerated, but that by doing so it avoids the degree of parliamentary scrutiny and control attendant on the formulation and enactment of legislative proposals. This objection would not have cut much ice with Sir James Stephen who thought it beneath the Queen's dignity to ask Parliament 'to aid her to do that which she can do as effectually without their aid' (1854: 79). Nor is it a theory which has weighed heavily with successive governments, who have preferred to exploit the latitude afforded them by the existing constitutional framework. The last Conservative government acknowledged the view that 'additional authority' would be conferred on the proposed Civil Service Code by a 'statutory approach', but made clear its opposition to such an approach were it to inhibit the 'effective and efficient' management of the service (Cabinet Office 1995a: paragraphs 2.15–2.17). The result, however, is an area of law that is of increasing importance – extending for example to relations between the executive and the individual in matters such as freedom of information – which is governed by the executive's own law rather than parliamentary legislation. We come back to this point in discussing the constitutional significance of the internal control function, below. What it underlines, however, is how narrow in some respects is parliament's formal dominion over the executive.

As part of its programme of constitutional reform, the Labour Government is committed to giving statutory backing to the Civil Service Code. It is also committed to a Freedom of Information Act, although a place on the legislative programme for either has yet to be secured. Regardless of whether or not the statutory element of internal control increases, we would expect the inter-dependence between internal and external agents and mechanisms of control to increase as a result of the expanding public scope of internal control. Through initiatives like the Citizen's Charter or the Better Regulation programme, internal control now addresses the relationship between the executive and the citizen in a way in which traditionally it did not. This has brought with it a need, for example, for independent complaint handling mechanisms, which in some cases has proved capable of being met internally – the Civil Service Commissioners for example have been re-invented as an internal appellate as well as regulatory body – but which in others has had to be addressed through external mecha-nisms. Prominent among these has been the Parliamentary Commissioner for Administration, who as well as being the final rung in the Citizen's Charter complaints ladder is also currently responsible for the investigation of com-plaints arising out of the Code of Practice on Access to Official Information. This extension of the subject-matter of internal control has also brought demands for the independent validation of agency performance against ministerial targets, which again can only be met externally, but which the executive has yet to concede.

Executive reliance on external control: the courts

Despite the executive's preference for proceeding wherever possible on the basis of its own law, there are some examples, mainly in the field of finance, of parliamentary support being sought for internal schemes of control. There are no equivalent examples of executive reliance on the courts. Individual senior judges, it is true, have proved a convenient resource when the executive wants delicate jobs done in an atmosphere of impartiality (Stevens 1993), but this willingness to rely on judicial impartiality and acumen does not extend to courts as institutions. The failure of seventeenth-century experiments with a judicial power within the executive, and the undistinguished record of the ordinary courts as administrative supervisors in the eighteenth and nineteenth centuries doubtless explain, in part at least, the absence of executive recourse to the courts in support of internal control. In more recent years, the attention paid to excluding possibilities of judicial review even where the executive was borrowing from judicial methods in meeting new administrative needs – as in planning and social security – betrays a deep-seated fear that executive effectiveness would be compromised by 'the inept intrusion of the law' (Sisson 1966: 71).

We may assume, therefore, that a key part of the rationale for the executive's reliance on its own law has been to keep the courts as well as parliament out of its 'own affairs'. Following the GCHQ case (*Council of Civil Service Unions v. Minister for the Civil Service* 1985), it can no longer be assumed that internal controls are automatically immune from review. But it does not follow from this that the executive will find itself enmeshed in judicial rulings which somehow fail to take proper account of the needs of the administration. Most disputes are likely to continue to be settled away from the courts. Although judicial review of civil service regulation has been a possibility now for more than a decade, the law of the civil service continues to be made, interpreted and applied, and disputes arising out its application settled, largely within the executive itself. The executive is also better placed in this field than in others to neutralise the precedential effects of judicial decisions simply by changing the rules, and to be able to retain this power where rules are put on a statutory footing. Finally, it cannot be taken for granted that judicial rulings touching on internal control will necessarily be unsympathetic to the needs of the administration: indeed the reverse appears to have been the case (*R. v. Lord Chancellor's Department*, ex parte Nangle 1992; *Ahmed and others v. The United Kingdom* 1998).

The dependence of external controls on internal control

Whether or not the executive can influence their shape and development, the controls operated by Parliament and the courts depend unequivocally on the executive's own machinery for their effectiveness. The evidence of our research bears out Grunow's contention that internal controls are heavily influenced by the external demands – for economy, for legality and, increasingly, for effectiveness as well as responsiveness – to which the executive is subject (Grunow 1986: 647). It is through the system of departmental self-discipline that such controls are mainly transmitted and diffused within the executive. The corollary is that the effectiveness with which they are internalised may vary from department to department, but this possibility is inherent in a decentralised system of voluntary compliance. Defenders of such a system emphasise the relative imprecision of the European Convention as a factor in the United Kingdom's relatively poor record before the European Court on Human Rights, but it is difficult to regard the lack of the central oversight that exists in relation to European Community law as not also a factor. Where by contrast central controls are strong, as in finance, the effectiveness with which external controls are internalised appears to be much greater.

At the same time, as we have seen, the system of internal control is changing. We have suggested that it is public service reforms rather than constitutional developments which are the principal factor behind the strengthening of central control, but constitutional developments have also played an important part. In particular, the expanding network of obligations to which the executive finds itself subject as a result of European Union membership, has resulted in a more proactive central co-ordination mechanism in the guise of the European Secretariat of the Cabinet Office and an increase in the centre's capacity to second-guess departments. Judicial influences have significantly reshaped the internal structure and control of the executive's legal function in recent years. Not so long ago, judges could be relied upon to be understanding (and often politically experienced), judicial intervention was rare and, if unfortunate, could usually be reversed by legislative means. In consequence, government ran its legal services rather like those of a loosely structured conglomerate in which each subsidiary had its own firm of solicitors who might – or might not – consult head office lawyers when things got difficult. European law, and judicial review, have changed all that. The basic structure remains decentralised, but a long-term effort of central co-ordination of legal advice, and of integrating it into policy-making, was initiated in the 1980s and still continues. The incorporation of the European Convention on Human Rights, by making the domestic courts a forum in which the compatibility of executive action with Convention rights can be challenged, further increases its importance. So far, that effort has been directed essentially to managing the consequences of changes in the legal environment of executive action. The executive's capacity to shape that environment remains unproven.

Changes in parliamentary, as opposed to judicial, controls have not had the same impact on the internal control function. Rather, it is the changes the executive has unilaterally made in its own structure and functions that have radically altered the subject-matter of parliamentary control. As a general rule, moreover, parliamentary relations continue to be left to departments, and there is some evidence that they are slipping down the scale of departmental priorities.

The constitutional significance of internal control

For the citizen, the meaning of the constitution lies in how it affects, and reflects, the way of living in the country it governs. For most people in Britain, the question is still the one that was uppermost in the minds of the framers of the constitution of the United States: how can we organise public power to give ourselves – all of us – the best chance of leading a free and prosperous life? The question may seem far removed from an enquiry into how the executive controls itself and the detailed examination of decision-making structures and procedures entailed in such an enquiry. Let us explain why it is not.

What a constitution does for or against basic interests such as freedom, equality or prosperity it does through a combination of the structures it ratifies and the values it represents. 'Democratic' control of the executive through the legislature may be a mixed blessing if the legislature's instincts are more populist or nationalistic than those of the executive, or if the legislature's key institutional values amount to no more than expediency and survival. Judicial independence may be a curse if the courts have less respect for freedom than does the executive. Recent examples from abroad could be adduced to illustrate all these possibilities. We do not argue (which is not to say that we think it unarguable) that such inversions of commonplace expectations about guarantees of democracy and the rule of law exist in the UK. By contrast, we would argue strongly that it is meaningless to say that the constitution enshrines a value like equality or openness unless one knows the answers to several questions: what bodies under the constitution subscribe to that value; what other values each such body may need to set against it in decision-making; and how each such body can secure respect for that balance both by the individuals of which it is made up, and by other bodies within the state that it seeks to control or influence. Our focus on 'control' has been designed in particular to throw light on this last question, of how things get done, and thus to illuminate what has hitherto been both the darkest part of the constitutional structure yet at the same time the part closest to the decisions which will affect the way the citizen lives. In consequence, our exploration has been of the structures, processes, practices and rules encountered within the executive branch (although always with reference to their connections with other branches), rather than with the values for which they are the vehicle. Nonetheless, the recent changes in this area, which we have summarised in this chapter, throw up some points worthy of consideration even by those who do not particularly want to look inside the executive but only to understand evolving relationships between the traditional 'powers' in the state, or whose concern is mainly with the behaviour and impact of the state rather than with its structures.

Three remarks will be enough. First, the reforms of public expenditure which began in the 1960s, and the public service reforms which gathered pace some ten years later, were initiatives conceived within the executive and carried through by the executive with only marginal reference to the other powers in government. They have demonstrated a fact little remarked upon in recent decades: the fact that the executive is a distinct power within the constitution which enjoys the same kind of institutional autonomy as do Parliament and the courts. While the actions of any given government require to be legitimated by parliamentary support for its leaders, and must respect the rule of law, the executive is not thereby rendered a mere mechanical contrivance for the implementation of legislative and judicial decisions. It thinks for itself and has extensive capacities, within the constitution, to translate its thoughts into action. In so doing it may be quite capable of changing the relative importance of constitutional values.

Much recent public service reform, and in particular the Citizen's Charter initiative, now tellingly entitled 'Service First', moves attention away from the special case – the sort of case which once made good material for a parliamentary question – towards normal performance: the sort of standards in administration which all citizens should be able to expect. Whether one sees this as an innately egalitarian rethinking of administration, or as a regrettable slide towards consumerism in provision of public services (as does Jacob 1991), one cannot deny that a process of real constitutional significance is going on. The same can be said of the way in which governments of either political stripe, the one under the technicist rubric of resource accounting, the other through the mystical language of the 'golden rule' (Treasury 1998a), have been modifying the basic financial structures of the constitution so as to accommodate a new approach to fiscal policy, one which gives more weight to medium-term results and to world market opinion and much less to responsiveness to (democratic) political pressure. Of course the executive has always had its own ideas, and those ideas have been powerful and have often decided the fate of our country: Treasury and Foreign Office arrogance in the face of the European Community project, and its unfortunate results, have been well documented (Young 1998). What is new, in recent years, is the explicitness with which those ideas have been formulated, and the executive's readiness to present and operate them as its own, without wrapping itself in the gauzy platitudes of parliamentary sovereignty.

Second, looking at the constitution from the worm's eye view of internal control of the executive, shows the other constitutional organs in an interestingly new light. So far as Parliament is concerned, it helps us to get behind the clichés like 'elective dictatorship' to see what is actually going on. Our constitution is one which actually demands that the leaders of the executive be able to dominate Parliament; if they could not, they would not be eligible as its leaders. It therefore seems perverse to grumble about the use of party discipline to override parliamentary doubt and dissent. Instead, understanding internal control points our attention to the narrow gateways, set by parliamentary powers and procedures, through which it is essential for executive policies to pass if they are to be effective. The positioning of these gateways, and how they are operated, have a profound influence on the internal organisation of government, helping to sustain two of its key points of central control: over the legislative programme and over annual expenditures. In the long run it is more important for Parliament to ensure that these gateways are not enlarged or circumvented than itself to determine what passes through them, because the gateways in themselves structure how the executive exercises control. In fact the current situation could be said to be full of dangers for Parliament. In the legislative field, an increasing volume of important traffic is circumventing the gateway, often because of the choices regarding the mode of implementation of European Community law offered to departments under the European Communities Act 1972. Alternative control mechanisms have been devised within the executive, but do not secure the same opportunities for Parliament. In expenditure, it is the Treasury's gradual withdrawal from its role as keeper of the parliamentary gateway, in favour of other ways of performing its own job, which is making it more difficult for Parliament to exercise overall scrutiny.

As well as suffering this attrition of the bases of its power, Parliament is also witnessing a radical challenge to the relevance of its activity. In the last two decades the executive has carried through, without asking Parliament's consent, a public service reform project which, even if it has not destroyed the bases of traditional ministerial responsibility to Parliament, has profoundly modified the meaning of such responsibility by sweeping away the management and communication structures within the executive on which it relied. As part of this process, the executive has undermined the role of the ordinary MP in redress of grievances by creating a quite new context within which grievances may be framed and redressed, the Citizen's Charter programme. The ordinary MP has no privileged place within this structure; indeed, he or she has no place at all. There seems to be less and less difference between what an MP might do in relation to a complaint about departmental activity on the one hand and local authority services on the other. These internal moves by government mean that if 'calling government to account' is to continue to be an effective parliamentary function, Parliament, and primarily the House of Commons, must find new methods of work and new points of leverage on the reconstituted executive.

By contrast, the position of the courts appears much more positive. The expansion of judicial review over 30 or so years, and other legal developments, have created changed conditions for the exercise of the executive's legal function, such that it has had to respond by changes in its internal control system. Developments such as the incorporation of the European Convention on Human Rights and the continuing ramification of European Union law appear likely to further reinforce the influence of judicial decisions on the substance of state policy, and to restrict executive scope to 'correct' unwelcome judicial decisions through the legislative process. Nonetheless, the judicial function may not be impervious to change resulting from executive-led development of the constitution.

It is possible to imagine the public service reforms we have analysed impinging on the courts in two different ways. The first is under the control of the courts themselves. There seems no reason why the standards of self-regulation that the executive has been so busily developing within the Citizen's Charter programme, the Better Regulation programme, and elsewhere, should not be adopted or assimilated by the courts as elements of our judge-made administrative law. The structures of judicial action, and the principle of judicial independence, suggest, however, that this will happen only if parties regularly argue from these premises in litigation, and it is not yet clear that departments, as the key litigants, see advantages in going down this road. A second effect of executive self-regulation, however, may be to change the pattern of litigation coming before the courts, a process that the judiciary cannot itself control. If expectations of effective redress are displaced from judicial review to internal procedures, as they seem to have been displaced in recent decades – in part at least – from parliamentary question and complaint to judicial review, the landscape of public law litigation may again undergo significant change. If these executive programmes really work, then people who want administrative errors rectified will seek and find the redress they need through such programmes, without invoking any external jurisdiction. It is people who want to make a point about the legality of executive action who will continue to go to the courts. Whatever the rhetoric of administrative law, policy rather than administration may become the primary concern of judicial review.

A third and final point relates to the general structure and theory of the constitution. The executive has been able to play the leading role in modern constitutional development not because we really have no constitution – nor because we have a constitution in which anything goes, as different theorists would have us believe. The executive can so act because basic principles of our constitution recognise it as an autonomous body which can manage its own resources save where Parliament ordains otherwise, and give it co-ordinate power together with Parliament in the all-important area of public expenditure. While other rules subject the executive to the control of Parliament and courts in vital areas of its activity, they leave significant scope for the executive to determine how it is going to operate within those constraints. In seeking to describe and analyse the structures and internal control of the executive, we have in effect been showing how those powers and discretions are transformed by the executive itself into stable rules and procedures for the deployment of resources of government. As modes of concretising and implementing basic principles of our constitution, those rules and procedures are no less a part of our constitutional law than the rules of legislative procedure, or the general rules of administrative jurisdiction.

5
Bureaucratic Gamekeeping: Regulation of UK Public Administration, 1976–96*

Christopher Hood, Oliver James, George Jones, Colin Scott and Tony Travers

Background: why explore regulation in government?

In the introduction to his *Regulation and Deregulation* (1999: 4), Christopher McCrudden recalls that he and Robert Baldwin were doubtful in the mid-1980s if a book with the word 'regulation' in the title would be meaningful to a British audience ('in retrospect, it seems incredible', comments McCrudden (ibid.)). The British literature on the subject at that time was limited and tended to be narrowly focused on judicial review (ibid.). Since then, as McCrudden notes, an academic and practitioner 'industry' has rapidly grown up around the various authorities that regulate business in the UK. Indeed, there is much talk of a 'regulatory state' replacing an earlier emphasis on public enterprise and direct service provision (see Majone 1994; Loughlin and Scott 1997).

However, what applied to regulation of business 15 years ago (in McCrudden's interpretation, at least) still largely applies to regulation of the public sector in the UK. Whereas there is a growing literature on government regulation of business, the literature about regulation inside government – regulation of public bureaucracies by other public bureaucracies – is sparse and fragmented among those who specialise in different discrete organisations, such as ombudsmen or auditors. It certainly overlaps heavily with the literature on accountability, though the focus of the latter, in the UK at least, has traditionally been on accountability to elected officials and the public (see Dowding 1995) rather than the oversight of bureaucrats by other bureaucrats. Before the publication of *Modernising Government* (Cm 2310 1999) UK central government did not recognise a concept of regulation of government at all, and even now 'regulatory denial' remains the normal reaction in Whitehall to the idea that there are analogues within government to the regulation of business. The official view of 'regulation' as exclusively about what government does to business remains entrenched in central government (though not in local government and the outer reaches of the public sector).

* We would like to acknowledge the ESRC for funding our research (award number: L124251015).

Despite this official 'Nelson's eye' approach in Whitehall, regulation is a pheno-menon and an issue found in government as well as in business. Some types of regulation (over health and safety or data protection) apply to public and private organisations alike. But there is also a range of regulators specific to public sector organisations – arms-length bodies outside the direct chain of command but with more than advisory powers (examples include ombudsmen, auditors, professional inspectors and funder–regulator bodies) that set standards, gather information and try to modify the behaviour of the public organisations they oversee. Over 20 years ago Wilson and Rachal (1977) discussed the phenomenon in the USA and speculated that regulation in government was likely to be less effective than regulation of business because prosecutorial sanctions would ordinarily be absent when one public agency oversaw the activities of another. But no systematic research has hitherto been conducted in the UK (and indeed only limited work has been conducted in the USA) analysing the various arms-length overseers of govern-ment from a 'regulatory' perspective and exploring the variety of ways in which they operate.

That gap needed to be filled for at least two reasons. One was that official dis-course on public sector reform in the UK and elsewhere – and much of the acad-emic literature – tended to focus disproportionately on the service-delivery side of government and the various changes being wrought through new structures and techniques for service management (see Flynn 1990). But to gain an overall and balanced perspective on the changes occurring in the public sector during the 'New Public Management' era, corresponding attention needed to be paid to the developments on the regulatory side of government that accompanied the service-delivery changes.

Second, the question raised by Wilson and Rachal two decades earlier, concerning what if anything might distinguish regulation in government from regulation of business, remained to be answered (and their hypothesis remained untested by any systematic study). Themes developed in a whole generation of (largely) socio-legal research on the operation of regulators of business (in particular the idea of 'relational distance' in regulation developed by Grabosky and Braithwaite (1986) from Black's (1976) general theory of law) remained completely unexplored for regulation in the public sector. Nor was there any general framework within which public sector regulation could be placed as part of a wider understanding of different methods of controlling public bureaucracies. Yet casual observation suggested that increased emphasis on, and a changing style of, public sector regulation was a key feature of an emerging style of public management. For such reasons it seemed difficult to justify the lack of systematic attention paid to regulation in the public sector over the decade or so that regulation of business produced the epistemic 'industry' noted by McCrudden.

Research questions

Our research project is distinctive because it did not work within well-known institutional categories but set out to delineate a set of organisations and activities defined in analytical terms, information not readily identifiable in official statistics or publications. And it sought to place those organisations and activities within a wider analytical framework. The study aimed to explore four main questions.

The first question was (superficially at least) a purely empirical issue of investigating the number, size and development of regulatory bodies overseeing government. ('Superficially', because any such investigation necessarily involves the prior development of an analytical framework.) What was the overall size and scope of such regulator organisations? What was the range and variety of institutional forms and practices? How much was invested in public sector regulation, in staff and spending resources? What sorts of control and oversight strategies did the regulators use? How had they changed over 20 years since the mid-1970s? Was there clear evidence of an 'audit explosion' (as suggested by Power (1997) in a much-discussed analysis) and analogous growth in other domains of regulation of government? What were the areas of growth and decline?

The second question concerned how to 'place' regulation of government in a broader analytical and interpretative context. How did such regulation relate to overall developments in public-service management in the recent past (typically characterised by the term 'New Public Management'), which were often presented as changes designed to convey more discretion to public sector managers and liberate them from egregious 'red tape' restrictions? Were Wilson and Rachal (1977) correct to argue that regulation in the public sector was different from regulation of business? And could some of the themes developed in the socio-legal analysis of business regulation over the past 20 years or so be meaningfully applied to regulation of government?

The third question was more specific, firmly rooted in the socio-legal literature on regulation. How could we understand the relationship between the regulators and regulatees in government, and how did social relationships between regulators and regulated bodies affect the regulatory methods used? In particular, did the idea of regulatory styles and approaches as shaped by the 'relational distance' between regulator and regulatee (that is, the distance between the two in social or professional terms) help to explain variety in regulation of government? ('Relational distance' is a theme that crops up in more or less explicit form in most socio-legal studies of regulation and proved to be a powerful predictor of the behaviour of Australian business regulators in Grabosky and Braithwaite's (1986) landmark study.)

The fourth question was rather more diffuse, and concerned the policy and institutional-design implications of our findings. Did the official central-government attitude of 'regulatory denial' towards regulation in government make sense? Could any conclusions be drawn about 'best practice'? Could precepts commonly applied to regulation of business (for instance in regulatory impact assessment analysis) be fruitfully applied to regulation of government? And could any of the disciplines that were commonly imposed by regulators on their charges be usefully imposed on the regulators themselves?

Six major findings

The methods we used to answer the questions set out above are explained in the Appendix to this chapter (see page 94), and broadly involved a mixture of documentary and interview analysis. When we completed our study at the end of 1997, we had six most important findings to report (for a book-length account of those findings, see Hood *et al.* 1999). Three of those findings were broadly quantitative and formed part of our overall 'mapping' of regulators in UK government. Three other major findings concerned behaviour and style, relating to the more qualitative aspects of our inquiry.

The scale of regulation inside UK government

The answer to the first research question set out above appears to be that regulation, however conceived and measured, is a large-scale activity within government. We began by defining 'regulation' of government as a process in which: (a) one public bureaucracy aims to shape the activities of another; (b) the overseeing bureaucracy is at arm's length from the organisation being overseen (that is, not in a direct chain-of-command relationship); (c) the overseer is not simply an adviser, but has some official mandate to scrutinise the behaviour of the 'regulatee' and seek to change it (ibid.: 8–10). On that definition three main features of regulation of UK Government in the mid-1990s can be noted and these are outlined below.

First, an approximate indication of the scale of this activity can be given. Using a conventional and fairly narrow definition of the boundaries of the 'public sector', we identified not less than 135 separate bodies regulating the UK public sector at national-government level. Those organisations directly employed almost 14 000 staff, and cost £766m to run in 1995 – just over 30 pence in every £100 UK government spent at that time (if we take out the biggest transfer payments in the form of debt interest and cyclical social security). Even on the most restrictive definition of the public sector at national-government level, the scale of investment in 'regulation' of UK government in the mid-1990s seemed to be close to the total invested in regulation of business and far greater than that of regulation over the much-discussed privatised utilities.

Second, any account of the scale of regulation in government can be only indicative rather than definitive. Where the 'public sector' begins and ends is itself an issue that has no single answer, and likewise the extent of 'regulation' depends heavily on categorisation and definition. The three-part definition we gave above is a useful analytical starting-point, but (as in all attempts to classify administrative bodies) problem cases exist on the margin. There is a grey zone somewhere between 'advice' or central intelligence and 'regulation', as with the numerous special-purpose units within central agencies. There is also a grey zone between regulation by 'public bureaucracies' (our main focus of interest) and oversight by the law courts and elected members of the legislature. How, for example, should the UK's 70-odd administrative tribunals – special-purpose administrative law courts of first instance – be classified? Such ambiguities are unavoidable, and mean that any single estimate of the scale of regulation inside government can be of only limited value. It makes more sense to think of the phenomena as a set of concentric circles (like an archery target or dartboard), ranging from a minimal 'core' at the centre to a maximum at the periphery. On that basis our estimate of the number of 'regulator' organisations of the national public sector ran from a low of about 130 to a high of over 200; our estimate of regulatory staff ran from a low of about 14 000 to a high of almost 20 000; and our estimate of the direct running costs of the organisations involved from about £700m at the low end to about £1bn at the top end. (The outer edges of the regulatory 'dartboard' included specialised administrative tribunals, regulators of public utilities (since utilities are considered as having a 'public' juridical character under certain circumstances by the European Court of Justice) and supranational regulators at EU level.) But the value of looking at the phenomenon in a 'dartboard' perspective was that it allowed us to conduct a form of sensitivity analysis – that is, to explore how far conclusions about scale or growth of regulation in government turn on the adoption of one particular definition of the boundaries of such regulation. On the basis of such an analysis, our conclusion was that regulation of UK government was a sizeable and growing activity irrespective of whether we chose only to look at the centre of the dartboard or at its outer edges as well.

Third, conventional indicators of bureaucratic size – staff, budgets, organisational units – formed only part of the costs of regulation (whether of business or government) and arguably form only the tip of an iceberg consisting mainly of compliance costs. Compliance costs – the cost to the regulatees of meeting the regulators' demands – added substantially to the costs of regulation in government. Compliance costs of regulation, though much debated in the context of the 'burden' imposed by regulators on business firms, are not systematically logged in the public sector, so they can only be estimated. And even the meaning of 'compliance cost' is debatable, since it raises complex counterfactuals about what a regulatee organisation would do in the absence of any outside regulatory requirements. To minimise – if not avoid – that difficulty, we chose to define compliance costs narrowly as only what it cost regulatees to interact with their regulator (including provision of information requested, consulting the regulator, setting up and acting as guides on visits and inspections), taking no account of substantive policies or practices that might be shaped by regulation. We made an approximate estimate of compliance costs in local government, combining such published information as was available with a study of compliance costs in one inner-London borough and guesstimates obtained from interviewees. It would be misleading to suggest any precise numbers on such a basis. But it seems safe to conclude that compliance costs (even in the narrow sense explained above) made the total cost of regulation of UK government in the mid-1990s at least double the £766m spent directly on regulatory bureaucracies.

The growth of regulation inside UK government

Not only was regulation of government a large-scale activity, but it also appeared to be growing. The two decades up to the mid-1990s are generally supposed to have been an era of bureaucratic 'downsizing' through privatisation and cut-backs. But at a time when public bureaucracies in the UK shrank greatly in staff size, regulation in and of government was even more dramatic in its increase. The number of regulator organisations grew by at least a fifth between 1976 and 1995, and we estimated that, overall, staff numbers of regulators inside government almost doubled over that period, while overall spending grew by a factor of at least two in most cases.

When we examined numbers of regulator organisations in 1976 and 1995 in different parts of the UK public sector, we found a pattern of growth in all those parts. The number of regulator organisations increased more for local government than for central government. The growth in number of regulator organisations was most marked in the mixed public/private sector. (That is, the 'third sector' of public-service provision, which we defined as one in which either the organisations concerned were not wholly owned by central or local government bodies or services were not mainly financed from general tax funds (ibid.: 22)).

Nor was this regulatory growth just a matter of the proliferation of organisational letterheads. Those regulatory organisations seemed, in many cases, to have substantially increased their claims on the public budget. Indeed, where we could reliably ascertain expenditure over time, our study found that spending by regulators (in constant prices) seemed to have grown more than the 'body count' of organisations. Direct spending on public audit bodies at least doubled in real terms over those two decades; it increased by a factor of three for professional inspectorates and grew at least fourfold for other regulators. Only those regulators located within central agencies (notably the Treasury and Cabinet Office) exhibited a relatively stable level of spending in real terms.

Our estimate of overall changes in the staffing of regulatory bodies inside UK government was 90 per cent growth between 1976 and 1995. That pattern contrasted sharply with what happened to staffing in the public sector as a whole, with a fall of more than 30 per cent in the total numbers of civil servants and over 20 per cent in local authority staff over the same period. (Indeed, we were reminded of Parkinson's (1961) observation of an increase in the number of Admiralty clerks during an era when the number of warships in the navy sharply declined.) There were indications from our interviewees of a growth in compliance costs that was commensurate with, or even greater than, the growth in direct costs of regulation.

The variety and incoherence of regulation inside UK government

Regulation inside UK government appeared from the study to be a large and growing set of activities, but it varied substantially across the different domains and organisations of the public sector. When we concluded our study at the end of 1997, there was no common practice on what regulators reported about themselves or in the way their performance was assessed. The industry had grown up topsy-like, with no overall rationalisation, and was itself regulated at best patchily, little exposed to the kinds of disciplines it imposed on its regulatory clients. There was no overall 'policy community' for regulators in government and there was no central point inside government which was able or willing to overview the army of regulators or promote consistency and 'best practice', for example, over compliance costs. While there were government-wide arrangements for assessing the compliance costs of regulating business – these dated back to the mid-1980s and received increased emphasis during the 1990s – there were no such arrangements for assessing the impact of regulation over public sector bodies.

Styles of regulation varied from one organisation to another and from one part of the public sector to another. Regulatory formality ranged from mainly low levels in central government (where elements of the 'mutuality' style of peer group control governing the Whitehall 'village' classically identified by Heclo and Wildavsky (1974) were still observable) to higher levels for local government and the mixed public/private sector. Dynamics of regulatory development were also variable. For example, in the regulation of prisons (a long-established field of regulation of government, dating back to inspection of Irish prisons in the eighteenth century), a historical legacy of prison reviews after riots, escapes or other scandals had added successive new regulators to the existing structure without taking any away. The result is a crowded and largely unco-ordinated regulatory system, but with a pattern of 'redundancy' so that the overall regulatory system did not depend on the independence or effectiveness of any one regulator. The regulation of school education presented a contrasting pattern, with reconstruction rather than accretion and major recent attempts to increase 'relational distance' in the English and Welsh school-inspection system by breaking up what had been seen as a 'cosy' professional world with limited tension between regulator and regulatee. EU regulation of UK government (and the other member-states) presented a different pattern again, with more emphasis on self-regulation and a distinctive mixture of relatively high formality and high politicisation.

The relationship between new public management changes and regulation inside government

As well as the sheer growth in numbers, regulation inside UK government seemed to have grown overall in formality, complexity, intensity and specialisation over the two decades up to the mid-1990s. Linked to this change we found some evidence of greater reliance being placed on legal values and norms in setting frameworks, determining disputes and so on (a process of 'juridification', by which administrative or other values come to be displaced by the legal values).

At first sight this development seemed paradoxical, since conventional wisdom held that UK public management since the late 1970s had witnessed a 'management revolution' intended to (a) cut excessive rules restricting management discretion; (b) give public service managers more freedom to make decisions; and (c) make government management more like business. Our conclusion was that a 'mirror-image' development (largely unintended by some of the topmost political architects of public sector management reform) seemed to have occurred in a number of cases. What we meant by that was that any increased freedom by operational public-service managers from centrally-imposed rules or authorisations from a higher level in the organisation was balanced by more explicit and intrusive interventions by regulators. Greater 'freedom to manage' in terms of more theoretical decentralisation of decisions over pay, hiring, budgets and the like was accompanied by more scrutiny from arms-length bureaucratic structures over probity, efficiency, quality and 'due process'. Seeing those developments as a form of 'mirror-image' built on a rough analogy with processes such as mirror-image dancing where as one partner moves to the left the other moves to the right but it may be easier to think in terms of opposite-sign or reversed-polarity metaphors.

We found some evidence of this pattern of development in most of the regulatory sectors we examined, suggesting that any proper understanding of the changes occurring in UK public services during the 'New Public Management' era needs to take account of regulatory growth as well as more 'managerialism'. Even in central government, one of the most lightly-regulated parts of the public sector in formal oversight, a measure of deregulation in one sphere (the removal of formal central pay and grading rules in the civil service) was accompanied by increasing regulation in others. However, while the 'mirror-image' pattern seemed to be commonly observable across the public sector, there were some exceptions. We found some areas (notably local government in relation to central government) in which, far from a mirror-image process taking place over two decades, increased arms-length regulation was accompanied by increases in direct controls imposed on management by central prescription. We saw this pattern as a 'double whammy' rather than anything approximating to a mirror-image pattern (though 'mirror-image' processes could be observed inside local government, with direct managerial control from the centre being partially replaced by arms-length regulation). If 'mirror-image' processes represent a largely unintended side-effect of public sector managerialism, 'double whammy' processes involve a reverse effect (Sieber 1981). If the double-whammy pattern became widespread, the whole managerial 'project' for public services would come seriously into question.

The relationship between relational distance and regulatory formality

For the most part, regulators in government differed from their business-regulation cousins in not having the power to prosecute regulated bodies (though there are also business regulators that do not have direct powers to prosecute). In that sense Wilson and Rachal's (1977) argument about the distinctiveness of public sector regulation seems justified, though some public sector regulators wielded sanctions that were more draconian than many penalties obtainable through prosecution in business regulation. (Examples included power to recommend closure of institutions or to recommend surcharging or disqualification of local councillors.) We found that regulators varied widely in the formality and 'punitiveness' with which they approached the organisations they oversaw. The degree of formality seemed to be related to how close or distant regulators inside government were to those they regulated in professional-social backgrounds. Where those being regulated shared the same backgrounds as those doing the regulating, we found low regulatory formality. Where the backgrounds were different, formality tended to be higher.

Although this phenomenon of 'relational distance' had been established for business regulation by Grabosky and Braithwaite (1986), our study was the first to find evidence for the relational distance effect in the regulation of government. We assessed the formality of regulators' relationship with regulatees (in the sense of rule-governed rather than discretionary behaviour and the propensity to deploy sanctions) from an in-depth analysis of documents about 42 regulator organisations. We found a link between a composite index of formality drawn from that documentary analysis and relational distance expressed as shared experience between regulators and regulatees and frequency of contact between the two. We followed the link in a general way through our interview programme and more specifically in a study of school inspections. The latter offered a particularly valuable research site for examining the relational distance hypothesis, since it enabled us to study large numbers in a sphere of regulation involving different teams of inspectors and varying regulatory outcomes. When we looked at evidence for over 3000 secondary school inspections in England between 1993 and 1997, we found that schools being inspected by private-sector inspection teams or local authority teams from another local authority area were more likely to be 'failed' in inspection than schools being inspected by a team from their own local authority. We found exceptions to the pattern expected by the relational distance hypothesis, but there was enough evidence for a link between relational distance and regulatory formality to suggest that relational distance was a key element in shaping regulatory behaviour in government.

Regulatory deficits in 'mutuality', 'competition', 'oversight' and 'randomness'

Our main 'policy' finding was that there was a marked disjunction between the regimes and control techniques applied by regulators of government to their charges and those applied to the regulators themselves. Could this disjunction be justified, or was there a case for an 'immanent' critique of the regulatory system on the basis of exposing regulators of government to the kinds of disciplines they impose on those they regulate? Such an 'immanent critique' at least deserved to be investigated. Pursuing this policy–analytic track, we identified four main weaknesses or 'deficits' in the behaviour and organisation of UK public sector regulators in the late 1990s.

The first was a 'mutuality deficit'. To the extent that regulators of government interacted at all, it was only within particular families, such as the British and Irish Ombudsman Association and the forum for public auditors and (more recently) professional inspectorates. There was no career structure cutting across the 130-plus public sector regulator organisations. There was no attempt to develop 'umbrella' regulator structures for government along the lines of the HSE or the Environment Agency (which are designed to combine the advantages of specialised expertise with an upper tier of cross-cutting policy analysis and legal expertise). There were no general fora in which good practice or overall philosophy could be discussed across the various domains of regulation, 'hot spots' examined, behaviour shaped and assumptions challenged. The consequence was a fragmented system that was neither strongly collegial nor strongly competitive.

The second was a competition deficit, in that regulators of government were not themselves systematically exposed to the sort of competition and rivalry they imposed on public-service organisations, particularly in local government, education and health. Indeed, the response of regulators to the overlap among them was often to collaborate rather than compete, particularly over the debatable lands lying between audit, professional inspection and funder-regulation. Hence the picture tended to be one of *ad hoc* turf battles (for example, over oversight of the freedom-of-information regime) or collaborative deals (for example, between the Audit Commisson and professional inspectorates) where responsibilities overlapped, rather than systematic competition. We did not find a case within the UK of a public sector regulator following the EU practice (in DG XIX) of regulators including themselves in the league tables they published for relative performance among their practices. Sunset-testing of regulatory regimes whereby the legislation contains criteria for its own termination was also notable by its absence, and market testing was unusual beyond the work of OFSTED and public auditors. Choosing one's regulator (as in the ability of local authorities to choose their own auditors up to 1982) was almost unknown.

The third was an oversight deficit, in that no central unit in government had overall responsibility for, or capacity to review, this rapidly-growing regulatory 'industry'. It seemed to be a case of 'no-one in charge government' (Bryson and Crosby 1992: 4ff). External reviews were rare and such reviews tended to be on an isolated case-by-case basis. In an age of codes of conduct no general code of conduct was developed for regulators of government. No formal system had developed for logging compliance costs of regulation in government, in sharp contrast to the systems that had developed for assessing business regulation in the UK's Deregulation Unit and the EU's *fiche d'impact* system. Regulators of government tended to see compliance costs as an issue only for business firms, not public sector bodies (though those at the receiving end had a very different perception). No coherent principles had been developed for appraising regulation in government or for determining appropriate levels of investment – practices that most public sector regulators would have been quick to condemn if they found them in the bodies they oversaw.

Finally, and more, tentatively we identified a randomness deficit, a lack of snap inspections or random scrutinies, especially at the top and centre of government. A few regulators only used random investigations or unannounced visits of the kind traditionally associated with the factory inspectorate (cf. Hutter 1997) or tax bureaucracies. Where randomness was used as a tool for selection of regulatee units for scrutiny, it tended to be applied to the regulation of lower-status organisations in public administration – prisons, schools, social-care institutions and routine financial operations. Regulator organisations themselves were never exposed to such regimes, except through the vagaries of politics. In some ways the greatest need for more randomness in oversight seemed to be at the top and the centre, where relational distance between regulator and regulatee tended to be lowest.

The notion that institutional redesign of public sector regulation might fruitfully seek to reduce these four 'deficits' was not advanced as a cure-all. Like Adam Smith's canons of taxation and many other principles of institutional design (Goodin 1996: 40), the four elements pull against one another at the margin, but they may be able to achieve in combination what no one of them could do on its own.

Regulation in government after 1997: from the Blair landslide to modernising government

Our ESRC study was completed at the end of 1997. But the New Labour government elected in that year gave us a chance to explore whether the trends we had identified over the previous two decades would continue into a new political era. Would public sector regulation be transformed under a government committed to reshaping public administration as part of its aspirations to a 'third way' political agenda? During the first two years of the Blair Labour government up to the (long-delayed) publication of its official 'vision' of public management reform in *Modernising Government* (Cm 2310 1999) in the spring of 1999, two features of that government's approach to public sector regulation can be noted.

One is a theme of continued population growth in regulators of government. Up to *Modernising Government* there was only one major death in that population – the demise of the Funding Agency for Schools, the funder-regulator body set up by the Major government to oversee schools that chose to 'opt out' of local authority control into an alternative regime. But in its first two years the Blair administration announced plans for a dozen or so major new organisations for regulating government. Those organisations included two major new regulators of the National Health Service (the National Institute of Clinical Excellence and the Commission for Health Improvement for England and Wales) and a new 'Best Value' inspectorate that in effect made the Audit Commission a general regulator of local government (involving new cost and quality standards for service delivery and the extension of inspection to services including housing, libraries, planning and transport (DETR 1998, Ch. 7 sec. 7.39)). While it revamped the previous government's Compulsory Competitive Tendering regime into a new 'Better Value' regime, New Labour enthusiastically embraced and extended several Conservative-created regulatory regimes, including the OFSTED school inspection regime in England, the Citizen's Charter regime and the Conservative-created Deregulation Unit (later rebadged and refocused through the addition of a high-powered task force). At the least it seems safe to conclude that the pace of regulatory growth in government was not slackening during New Labour's first two years as measured in resources, and it seems to have been markedly quickening in numbers of organisations being created.

The other theme is some indication of a change in style, at least in official doctrine. *Modernising Government* and other Blair government initiatives marked a departure from previous practice over public sector regulation in at least three ways. One was a tentative acknowledgement for the first time in *Modernising Government* (Cm 4310 1999: 31 and 38) that regulatory compliance costs could be a problem for regulatees in government as well as in business. (But the term 'compliance costs' did not appear, and no specific machinery was proposed for assessing compliance costs, in contrast to the regulatory-impact system for business regulation. In fact *Modernising Government* announced several extensions of regulation in government with no discussion of the compliance costs involved.) A second theme, related to the Blair administration's much-discussed search for co-ordination or 'joined-up government', was concern over consistency of practice and linkages between different regulators (ibid.: 23). But here too there were few tangible measures proposed to 'join up' the different organisations beyond a forum for the various inspectorates involved in the 'Best Value' regime that replaced Compulsory Competitive Tendering for local government. A third theme was official enunciation of a doctrine of what Ayres and Braithwaite (1992: 116) call 'enforced self-regulation' for the public sector. The idea of more formal and external regulation for public sector organisations perceived as poor performers while good performers were to be rewarded with lighter oversight regimes, had appeared in plans and designs announced by the Blair government in several domains of public sector regulation. *Modernising Government* generalised the idea into an overall doctrine of intervening 'in inverse proportion to success' and striking 'an appropriate balance between intervening where services are failing and giving successful organisations the freedom to manage' (Cm 4310 1999: 30–1).

Whether the 'enforced self-regulation' doctrine will prove effective remains to be seen. In principle it offers a way of checking the growth of regulation in government by abandoning one-size-fits-all approaches. It extends the rhetorical stance adopted by both the Blair government and its predecessor over schools, of combining tough-sounding 'zero tolerance' language about low public-service standards with limited deployment of available sanctions in practice. But whether effectiveness can be more than rhetorical is a more open question. EU practice suggests that where regulation is heavily politicised, threats of heavy crackdowns on poor performers – a central requirement for an effective enforced self-regulation regime – may ring hollow (see Hood *et al.* 1999: 182–3). Capacity to deploy heavy sanctions is inevitably limited in both political and organisational terms. Where non-compliance is central to the culture of the regulatee (as applied to at least one regulatory regime we examined), sanctions applied by the regulator may become badges of glory. They can be welcomed as a way of establishing 'street credibility' in a community which sees its values as pitted against those of the regulator, rather than as incentives to change behaviour.

Apart from the development of the 'enforced self-regulation' doctrine, *Modernising Government* and the other Blair government initiatives that emerged in its first two years did little to remedy the four 'deficits' in the organisation and behaviour of public sector regulators that were noted above. *Modernising Government* made only a limited and half-hearted attack on the 'mutuality' and 'oversight' deficits and did not even consider the 'competition' or 'randomness' deficits. Many of the trends and characteristics of public sector regulation that we observed over the previous 20 years – such as overall growth, tendencies towards greater formality, the concentration of the heaviest regulatory tackle on those parts of the public sector outside Whitehall – seemed just as strongly entrenched under the Blair New Labour administration as in its predecessors. Those characteristics are evidently not exclusive to a Conservative style of public management.

Conclusion

Regulation inside UK government seems set for continued growth in some dimensions, though its style may change if aspirations for more general adoption of 'enforced self-regulation' in the public sector succeed. Indeed, more developed regulation seems a stronger theme of contemporary public-service developments in the UK than 'freedom to manage', and may well prove to be a more lasting epitaph of the 'New Public Management' era. The analytical issues that were highlighted in this study – of how public sector regulators are to be organised, and how they are to relate to one another and to those they regulate – are questions central to the institutional design of modern UK government.

Any relatively short research project can focus on only a limited set of questions about the object of study, and our study is no exception. This project is the first ever to paint a picture of the overall scale of regulation in contemporary UK government. Even though that picture is inevitably blurred at the edges, we can plead the pioneer's defence of its limitations. Our project has also sought to integrate the analysis of 'New Public Management' changes with regulatory developments in government. We do not claim to be the first or only scholars to have worked on that theme (see, for instance, Hoggett 1996; Power 1997; Laughlin and Broadbent 1993, 1996 and 1997). But our 'mirror-image/double whammy' analysis and our location of public sector regulation within a broader analytical framework for understanding control over public bureaucracy represents the most developed (and only book-length) examination of that theme to date. We have sought to explore regulation in government in the light of themes developed for the analysis of regulation in other contexts (and particularly the 'relational distance' approach stemming from criminology and socio-legal studies). The study goes some way towards answering the questions about the distinctiveness or otherwise of regulation in government that were posed (though at best only impressionistically answered) by Wilson and Rachal over 20 years ago.

However, there inevitably remains much that we still do not know about regulation in government. Our focus was mainly on developments over two decades commonly associated with a new phase of public sector reform. We did look at longer-term developments in five regulatory domains (local government, central government, EU regulation of national government, education and prisons). But a general history of public sector regulation in the UK, critically exploring earlier periods of 'audit explosion' and regulatory expansion as well as the contemporary one, remains to be written, and our study has indicated some of the questions that deserve to be explored in historical perspective.

Our focus was on public sector regulation in the UK alone, because the ESRC Whitehall Programme wanted us to map out patterns and trends in the UK (and even then the greater part of our in-depth work was conducted in England, for time, cost and logistical reasons). Such a focus necessarily means we can say little about what is distinctive or typical about the UK's experience of regulation in government in a cross-national context. Was the 'mirror-image' pattern of service-delivery changes linked to regulatory growth that we observed in a number of domains in the UK paralleled in other similar countries in the 'New Public Management' era, or did it represent a response rooted in the UK's particular administrative history, as historical institutionalists might expect? (Possible candidates for UK distinctiveness in a historical-institutionalist frame include its traditionally centralised government structure, fragmented public service and limited 'juridification' of public administration.) Did changes in the size and style of public sector regulation mean the UK was in some ways catching up with a Continental European pattern, or striking out in a different direction? As yet no-one has come up with more than highly impressionistic answers to that question. A cross-national study of public sector regulation across a range of different countries with varying exposure to contemporary public sector reform doctrines remains to be conducted. Our study has indicated some of the issues that need to be investigated in a comparative perspective.

Even for the contemporary era and for the UK, the study has left gaps that need deeper investigation. In particular, we have not attempted a systematic assessment of the effects of changing public sector regulation, to answer questions as to whether increasing regulation 'worked' in cutting costs or raising quality (such evidence as we found suggested a very mixed picture), what side- or reverse-effects it produced and what was the overall return on the increased investment in regulation. In avoiding these gaps, our defence is not only the conventional plea of limited time and resources but also the standard argument that the fruitfulness of research is measured as much in the new questions and puzzles it uncovers as in other types of results. Research is not only about answering questions. It is also about establishing new questions and moving towards parametric and away from systemic uncertainty (cf. Green, Tunstall and Fordham 1991: 228) – that is, to a position of knowing what we don't know from not knowing what we don't know. We would be content for that to be our epitaph for this project as much as for the questions we answered.

Appendix: methods of the study

To answer the first question we mapped all the national-level 'regulators' inside UK government – all those arms-length bodies (such as complaint-handlers, auditors, inspectors and other overseers) that set standards, gather information and try to modify the behaviour of public servants in central government, local government and quangos. That was essentially a 'bureaumetric' exercise (updating and modifying the data-collection methods used in Hood and Dunsire 1981) and consisted largely of analysing regulators' numbers, resources and reporting patterns from official documents, supplemented by direct contacts with the organisations concerned. (Those contacts were needed for the many cases where the mass of official documents produced by goverment on its activities did not include the simple numbers about size and cost that we needed.) Using 1995 as a base year, we collected and assessed data for 135 regulator bodies, analysed according to institutional type and sector (distinguishing regulators of central government, local government and the mixed public/private sector and identifying seven different 'families' of regulators). We calculated some aggregate figures for the scale of EU regulation over UK public bodies and drew some comparisons between the overall investment in public sector and private-sector regulators, including regulators of privatised utilities. We also analysed changes in staffing and budgets of public sector regulators over 1976–95, exploring differences among institutional types and sectors and relating the changes to overall trends in public spending.

However, to answer the other questions set out above, we needed to go beyond the standard bureaumetric method in two ways. One was a qualitative analysis of official documents and the other was an interview programme carried out with practitioners. The qualitative analysis of documentary material was needed to help us identify and explore variations in regulatory methods. So we pored over a mass of annual reports, business or corporate plans, external reviews and internal documents (including such written frameworks or guidelines for regulatory operations as we could obtain), to explore variations in reporting patterns, variations in the use of declared performance indicators and variations in efforts to measure compliance costs. From our larger set of regulator organisations, we selected 42 to explore in depth what the documents recorded about how they went about standard-setting, information-gathering and behaviour-modification, and made a comparison with a selected set of business regulators. We also used this in-depth document-based study of 42 regulators to evaluate the relational distance hypothesis about the link between regulatory style and the social relations between regulators and regulatees. We devised qualitative indicators of regulatory formality from the documentary analysis, ranked the organisations on those indicators, put them in three ordered groups and tested four relational distance hypotheses, using the simple *tau*-b proportional reduction in error test for ordinal data calculated from bivariate tables. In addition, we examined data from 3599 school inspections from the OFSTED system of contracted-out inspection of schools over a four-year period to mid-1997. We used this data to supplement our analysis and examine our two relational distance hypotheses (relating to experience and contact frequency).

This qualitative documentary analysis was complemented (and 'triangulated') by an extensive interview programme with a group of public sector practitioners comprising both those who did the regulating and those who were on the receiving end. On the basis of the same sampling frame used for the in-depth documentary analysis, we selected 28 case studies for in-depth interviewing and conducted 81 semi-structured élite interviews with key participants (including ten interviews with EU-level regulators of UK public bodies) to gain a practitioner perspective. (We used two symmetrical interview frameworks, one for regulators and one for regulatees, with some 'customisation' of the framework to fit each organisation.) These interviews were conducted on a 'Chatham House rules' basis, meaning we could not attribute quotations to named sources. We supplemented those interviews with a group forum (in which a number of key regulators of UK government met one another for the first time) and we used other opportunities (such as meetings or seminars to which we were invited) as they arose to elicit responses from senior public servants.

Analysis of qualitative case-study material, both from interviews and documents, raises major and familiar issues of observer bias, inter-coder reliability and general interpretation. Observer bias was a far from trivial problem for us, since (much to our surprise) what began as a recondite academic study attracted a great deal of media interest in the course of our work, including not only heavyweight coverage in the *Financial Times*, but also one leader and an article in the mass-market *Daily Mail* (23.9.97) – not normally noted for its coverage of ESRC research projects. Regulation in government proved to be central to many critical institutional developments during the period of our study, including the new 'sleazebusters' that were created in the aftermath of the 1994 Nolan Report on Standards in Public Life, and new developments in the health service and education that highlighted 'regulation' and separated it from other activities in government. (And, as we suggested above, the New Labour government took these trends further with an explicit commitment to more inspection and public sector regulation.) We had to be careful to allow for the observer-bias effect, and we tried to standardise our interpretation of the qualitative case-study material by intensively discussing the emerging patterns and analytical issues on a team basis, challenging and modifying interpretations in an iterative way.

Part II
The World We Knew

6
Modernising Britain, 1957-64[*]: a Classic Case of Centralisation and Fragmentation?[1]

Rodney Lowe and Neil Rollings

The growth of government has been a principal feature of all western societies in the twentieth century. Britain is no exception. General histories, however, have tended to evade the institutional consequences. This is true even of the latest authoritative survey, Peter Clarke's *Hope and Glory: Britain 1900–1990* (1996), despite the fact that the author is himself an expert on the institutional impediments to the acceptance of Keynesianism. The index provides only two references to the civil service H. A. L. Fisher is cited but not Sir Warren Fisher, Rupert Brooke but not Sir Norman Brook. 'Statesmen in disguise', in short, are permitted to retain their disguise except when, as in the case of Sir Horace Wilson or Sir William Armstrong, they have publicly exposed their activities.

Such evasion, it is true, could be a conscious or subconscious endorsement of the current conviction within political science about the relative powerlessness, and thus relative unimportance, of the 'hollowed out' state in a 'centreless society'. It is not. Rather it reflects the continuing dominance amongst historians of the 'Westminster narrative' with its implicit assumption about the unprob-lematic nature of the policy process: a neutral bureaucracy dutifully implements policy within a unitary state characterised by parliamentary sovereignty and strong Cabinet government. As a result the 'domesticated' history of contempo-rary Britain with its emphasis on continuity and order can be reaffirmed. There is no place for the chaos and discontinuity of a 'differentiated polity' which many political scientists (not to mention practitioners – and not least those trained in history) more easily recognise.[2]

To bridge the gap between these rival interpretations of the past and the present, more active collaboration between historians and political scientists is required. Such collaboration need not be one-sided because, although they may set the explicit agenda, political scientists have long recognised the importance of historical knowledge and an historical perspective (Rhodes 1988: 5). Moreover, historians have valuable skills of their own. With, for example, their

* We would like to acknowledge the ESRC for funding our research (award number: L124251019).

greater concern for the past in its own right, rather than as a primitive stage in the evolution of the present, they are able to reconstruct it more fully. With their greater access to declassified material (however intrinsically incomplete) they are also better equipped than those working on the present-day to map the 'multi-form maze of government' which characterises the 'differentiated polity'. This is important for the analysis of both policy networks and the equally numerous 'organisations and procedures' which make up the core executive – through which some degree of central co-ordination and control is effected. In short, historians have much to offer since they are less subject to the tyranny of immediate relevance and can have a keener sense of the essentially transient nature of the present.

One recognised avenue of interdisciplinary collaboration is the analysis of key historical disjunctures. The attempted modernisation of Britain between 1957 and 1964, during which the first sustained attempt was made to adjust to the changed economic, social and political realities of the postwar world, was just such a disjuncture. It will be briefly placed here in the context of the longstanding tension in Britain between centralisation and fragmentation, or between the rival concepts and realities of 'government' and 'governance'. The pressures for and the attainment of greater centralisation will then be examined, followed by the problems this process both encountered and engendered. Analysis will focus on welfare policy, broadly defined. This is in part because it was the engine which drove government growth in terms of both function and size; in part because, by jointly analysing economic and social policy (where, reputedly, prime-ministerial power is respectively strong and weak), it provides a ready test for the concept of the 'segmented' nature of government. Evidence will also largely be drawn from the records of the core executive. This is because the mile of records accessioned by the Public Record Office every year provides the richest single source of evidence for both the core executive itself *and* the policy networks of which individual ministries are often, although not exclusively, the heart. However, they are, as they must be, balanced by contemporary published sources, the records of other institutions and oral testimony (Lowe 1997a). What emerges is a modifica-tion of claims for the exceptional nature of the present and a greater appreciation of the attempt to 'fill out' the postwar state, to which the 'hollowing out' of the 1980s was a direct reaction.

Historic tensions

In relation to other advanced industrialised societies, Britain until the 1940s did enjoy an exceptional degree of continuity and order. The fundamental reasons for this, however, lay not so much in the nature of government – as the Whitehall model might suggest – as in the nature of broader society, or gover-nance in its fullest definition as a 'socio-cybernetic system' (Rhodes 1997, 50–1). In the nineteenth-century ideal (which cast its shadow long into the twentieth century) the role of the 'state' was very restricted. In contrast to continental thought, as Harris has argued, it was 'civil society' that was seen as the highest sphere of human existence in which men enjoyed some form of absolute rights. 'The State', by contrast, was an institution of secondary importance ... which existed mainly to serve the convenience and protect the rights of individuals in private life. ... The corporate life of society was seen as expressed through voluntary association and the local community rather than through the persona of the state. ... More extensive government was widely viewed as not merely undesirable but unnecessary, in the sense that most of the functions performed by government in other societies were performed in Britain by coteries of citizens governing themselves. (Harris 1990: 67–8)

This view was held independently at all levels of society and supported by an agreed set of values which included a belief in 'common citizenship, the fairness of the rules of the game and the class-neutrality of the major institutions of the state' (McKibbin 1990: 24–5). The perceived superiority of the British 'race', for instance, which found powerful expression in the 1942 Beveridge Report, was based not on any sense of genetic superiority but on a pride in these values, and their attendant civil institutions, which were seen as crucial to the maintenance and expansion of democracy throughout the world (Harris 1997: 488–90).

The balance between government and governance which underpinned continuity and order in the nineteenth century was, however, characterised by two contradictions; and each became increasingly apparent after 1900, as doubts about the continuing ability of 'coteries of citizens' governing themselves escalated. The first contradiction was that between the limited role of central government in practice and its unlimited power in theory. In contrast to the situation in the continent of Europe, there was neither an alternative tier of government nor a range of corporatist bodies which could effectively constrain the centre. The lack of a constitutional check was due *inter alia* to the unique convention of *ultra vires* (which denied local government any powers other than those expressly sanctioned by parliament); local government's chronic lack of independent income; and the denial of tax-varying powers to the two regions which enjoyed some administrative autonomy (Scotland and Northern Ireland). The lack of corporatist agencies was a consequence of the strict rules of public finance introduced by Gladstone.[3] Whereas the decentralised delivery of policy was facilitated on the Continent by a wide range of subsidies, grants and tax-breaks, in Britain such incentives were so limited and so closely monitored that it was neither palatable nor profitable – as the history of social insurance after 1911 demonstrated – for agencies such as friendly societies, trade unions or even whole industries to become involved (Whiteside 1983). The second contradiction was that between the popular conception of the 'class-neutrality' of the state and the partiality it had inevitably to show were it to intervene on a controversial economic or social issue. However great its theoretical power, therefore, government's actual ability to act was severely constrained by the absence of any effective intermediary agencies and the fact that any action to maintain order endangered the very foundation of the popular culture that was in reality sustaining order.

These contradictions became apparent in the Edwardian period when an increased awareness of extensive poverty and of declining economic competitiveness first raised doubts about the efficacy of the broader governance. State intervention along European lines started to appear more rational. Hence the enactment of the Liberal welfare reforms, with the consequent appointment of a nucleus of 'secret dictators' in Whitehall, and the partial creation of a 'developmental state' under Lloyd George (Halevy 1961: 265; Turner 1992). These experiments in bureaucracy and corporatism, however, were notable neither for their efficiency nor for the popular support they attracted. On the contrary, they became a focus for political and social unrest – and thus a temporary hiatus between 1919 and 1921 in the tradition of continuity and order. They did not survive Lloyd George's premiership.

One change, however, did permanently survive Lloyd George's premiership: the creation of a greatly strengthened core executive. Before 1914, the civil service could hardly be called a single service. The older departments enjoyed and jealousy guarded a considerable degree of autonomy, for example, and the interdepartmental transfer of senior officials was virtually unknown. Central co-ordination of policy was also rudimentary, as Beveridge's description of the chaos of wartime manpower policy reveals. 'There being', he wrote

> no secretary to the Cabinet then, and no minutes kept, the only way was to ask the Prime Minister and another member of the Cabinet. To make sure, we asked three separate ministers what had been decided and we received three different answers. ... We chose the answer that seemed to us to be the most desirable in the national interest. (Beveridge 1953: 133–4)

The postwar reforms masterminded by Sir Warren Fisher revolutionised the situation. The Cabinet Secretariat, established temporarily in 1916, was made permanent; and the Treasury's role as the central co-ordinating department was strengthened, not least by the creation of a network of establishment and finance officers to standardise practice throughout Whitehall. With the standardisation of administrative classes, the departmental interchange of staff at all levels became routine and a common ethos based on the principle of public service was actively fostered. The irony was that this ethos fully endorsed the Victorian ideal of government. As has been written, for example, of the interwar civil service:

> theirs has been a liberal view. It has trusted democracy and distrusted the expert. It has placed confidence in reserved powers and not in concentrated power. It has believed in improvisation and self-reliance. ... Their ideal [has been] to encourage common citizens to govern themselves by learning as

much as their leaders, and applying it in their daily pursuits. (Dimmock in Thomas 1978: xii–xv)

The effectiveness of this new, highly centralised machine to initiate and administer interventionist policy went, therefore, largely untested. The heroic attempts between 1906 and 1922 to resolve problems of government and governance, which were to return to haunt government after 1945, may have failed; but the political and economic pressures generated, amongst other things, by universal suffrage and the depression, ensured that there would have to be some pragmatic adjustment. In social policy, an effective new accommodation was reached at least on one level. The voluntary provision of welfare, for example, was able to flourish because central government relieved it of a responsibility (the eradication of primary poverty) which it had patently been unable to discharge. In return, its proponents embraced an 'idealist' philosophy which enabled them to accept that state intervention could underpin, rather than undermine, self-sufficiency. They came to believe, in the words of Jose Harris (1992: 177) that:

it was not the material fact of a social-welfare benefit that was important, but its inner meaning and context. A benefit was allowable (even a state benefit) if it took place in an ethical context (that is, a reciprocal personal relationship between giver and receiver) and if its end was rational (that is, the promotion of independent citizenship in the recipient).

The National Council of Social Services was the foremost symbol of this 'new philanthropy': founded in 1919 as a self-regulating umbrella body to encourage the greater co-ordination and professionalisation of private charity, it was actively supported by government at first administratively and then financially (Braithwaite 1938; Brasnett 1969).

At another level of social policy, however, the brittleness of the accommodation between government and governance was fully exposed. This was particularly true of the evolving relationship between central and local government. Whatever the formal constitutional position, local government had traditionally enjoyed considerable scope for initiative; but this was rapidly eroded. Local self-sufficiency, for example, required larger units of government; and after the 1880s the more dynamic urban areas, the county boroughs, had accordingly been allowed to expand at the expense of the more conservative county councils. This trend was abruptly halted in 1926. In 1929 a major reform of local government finance was enacted but, rather than establishing a new source of buoyant independent income, it introduced a 'block' grant which placed an effective ceiling on local government expenditure. Finally, in 1934, the poor law, the leading symbol of defiance of centralisation since the 1830s, was largely removed from local control with the transfer of direct responsibility for the relief of the able-bodied unemployed to central government. Some attempt was made to sustain an appearance of decentralisation. The formulation of policy within broad principle laid down by Parliament was entrusted to an executive agency, the Unemployment Assistance Board (UAB), and its implementation was monitored by local advisory committees and tribunals. With the first street protest against centralised uniformity, however, Cabinet intervened (unconstitutionally) to suspend the Board's proposed relief scales. The Board's chairman, boldly and independently, replied that 'the Board were in effect officials of the Government and cannot act in the last resort contrary to the policy of government' (quoted in Lowe 1986: 176). Likewise the extreme care with which members of the advisory committees and tribunals were selected made plain that there was to be no attempt to share real power or authority.

Why was there this erosion of local autonomy by politicians and civil servants supposedly committed to preserving self-sufficiency? One obvious answer is that they perceived a threat to continuity and order. The level of unemployment pay was then as now seen to be critical to the effective working of the market: if it exceeded the level of unskilled wages the will to work could be undermined. It was therefore regarded as being as crucial to the maintenance of the economic and social order as was the police force – over which, significantly, local control was simultaneously being eroded (Morgan 1987: 277). Could local authorities be trusted with such a responsibility now that an increasing number were coming under Labour Party control? Their conclusion clearly was negative. Greater centralisation, however, threatened to jeopardise the popular perception of the 'class-neutrality' of the state upon which continuity and order more fundamentally depended. Here, together with the revelation of the essential client status of executive agencies, lay serious portents for postwar government.

In economic policy there was a parallel, but significantly different, adjustment to political and economic pressures. To maintain control over electoral demands for increased public expenditure, and over the newly centralised civil service, the Treasury remained committed to balancing the budget at the lowest acceptable level (the minimal budget balance rule). The fiscal crises immediately after the war and again in the early 1930s, however, alerted it to the need to sustain revenue as well as to restrict expenditure. This gave it a departmental interest in supporting a limited degree of intervention, albeit specifically not for Keynesian reasons (Middleton 1996: 322; Booth 1987: 502–3). At the same time the patent inability of industry to modernise itself within an open economy created a powerful political case for intervention. Intervention when it came, however, did not relieve industry of any specific responsibility. Nor did it restrict the role of industry (as with local government). Rather, it was designed actively to promote – rather than, as in the past, passively facilitate – industrial self-sufficiency and a 'private enterprise' recovery. This meant, in practice, increased pressure both within and upon independent agencies to act (an example being the Bank of England through the Bankers' Industrial Development Company); or, failing that, through an increasingly active if covert 'industrial diplomacy' to foster greater co-operation within industries or regions (as with the creation of the Lancashire Industrial Development Corporation) (Lowe and Roberts 1987; Dupree 1987). Overt intervention, such as the introduction of tariffs in 1932 and financial inducements to industry to locate in depressed areas in 1936 (after unwelcome lobbying from the chief executive of the Special Areas Commission), was limited and undertaken with reluctance.

The advantages and disadvantages of this approach were recognised and well expressed in 1930 when the then Labour government briefly considered establishing a ministry of industry with greater planning powers. As was argued:

> If on the one hand industry was to be left to put its own house in order ... progress was bound to be slow. If on the other hand the element of compulsion was to be introduced, violent controversy would be provoked and the work already done would sustain an immediate check. (PRO 1930)

Government action, in other words, was constrained by a clear appreciation of the traditional means by which continuity and order were maintained. If the profit motive were compromised – however temporarily – by state planning, how would the market function in the future? Moreover, if government itself became directly involved in any of the tough measures which industrial restructuring required – such as redundancy – how could it maintain its reputation for class-neutrality? Covert diplomacy, with the object of strengthening existing institutions within the broader governance, was therefore far preferable; and should government have to become more directly involved, the damage could be limited by a severe restriction of grants (as with regional aid) or the devolution of responsibility to an overtly independent agency (such as the Import Duties Advisory Committee) whose actual independence – as with the UAB – was compromised by the government's firm control over its membership and finance (Mercer 1995). The clear disadvantage of this policy was the slowness, or even absence, of industry's constructive response to these diplomatic sallies (Trentmann 1996, 1044; Garside and Greaves, 1996).

The legacy bequeathed to postwar government, therefore, was complex and contradictory. Britain had traditionally enjoyed an exceptional degree of continuity and order but this was the achievement of governance, broadly defined, rather than government. Central government was in theory all powerful; and in emergencies it could act accordingly. As has been written of the Second World War, for example:

> centralised control over people and resources far exceeded that of any other combatant power with the possible exception of Russia. By a strange irony of history, the United Kingdom with her tradition of scepticism and hostility towards state power generated a far more powerful wartime state than any of her more metaphysically minded, state-exalted enemies. (Harris 1990, 91)

A highly centralised civil service and an acceptable form of taxation existed to administer and finance interventionist policy. In practice, however, the British state in peacetime was – and remained despite the war – severely constrained.

There was an absence of agencies either in sub-central government or in 'civil' society with which power in relation to both social and economic issues could be openly shared and vigorously promoted. Popular compliance, including the payment of taxes, also depended on a perception of its 'class neutrality' which was threatened by any intervention on a controversial matter (Daunton 1996). A tentative reappraisal and temporary solution of this dilemma had been required in the interwar period by political and economic pressure; but the perceived radicalisation of popular politics in 1940 and the resultant demand for government actively to eradicate poverty and maintain a 'high and stable' level of employment demanded a more 'heroic' answer on the lines of that attempted in the first two decades of the century. This was the historic challenge facing postwar government.

Centralisation as modernisation

The Second World War is conventionally regarded as 'the high point of achievement in the history of the British civil service' and thus of the Whitehall model of government (Hennessy 1989: 88); and there were plentiful contemporary suggestions as to how perceived success in the co-ordination and delivery of policy could be maintained in peacetime. Many of these suggestions were first addressed to the 1942 Anderson Committee on the Machinery of Government and they continued to be aired until 1968 when, in very different circumstances, the Fulton Committee delivered its pointed attack on the service's inability to adapt from a 'passive and regulatory' to an 'active and positive' role (Lee 1977; Fry 1993; Theakston 1995: Ch. 3). Such an attack, as is well recognised, was not fully justified. In the late 1950s and early 1960s there had been a belated adjustment to both the nature and organisation of government which one informed outsider at the time entitled the 'great reappraisal' (Brittan 1964: Ch. 7). It is on this reappraisal that the rest of this chapter will largely focus.

Between the mid 1940s and mid 1950s the formal responsibility of central government and the complexity of policy co-ordination undoubtedly increased; but, especially at the top, there was only a limited political, administrative and cultural response. This can best be illustrated by the reaction to one of the most challenging reconstruction ideals: the all-party commitment in 1944 to the maintenance of a 'high and stable level' of employment. The original white paper, whatever its retrospective reputation as an expression of consensus (e.g. Marquand 1988: Ch. 1), in fact epitomised the fragmentation of wartime government. The Treasury and Keynesian economists in the Economic Section of the Cabinet held very different views on the causes, and thus the remedies, of unemployment; and the White Paper represented a fudged compromise between the two, hurriedly agreed to beat the publication of Beveridge's *Full Employment in a Free Society* (Peden 1983; Lowe 1998: Ch. 5.1). It contained few practical proposals and even they were swept aside by the incoming Labour government with its election pledge to 'plan from the ground up'.

However, as the Labour Party soon discovered, wartime precedent was of limited value. The TUC opposed the peacetime use of manpower controls (Brooke 1991). Employers also placed strict limits on the scope of state intervention as the price for their co-operation; and in this they were abetted by officials not only at the policy-implementation but also at the policy-making level (Mercer, Rollings and Tomlinson 1992: 8, 19). Owing to resistance from the most senior officials, indeed, nothing was so ill-planned as the planning machinery itself (Hennessy 1989: Ch. 4; Theakston 1999). Before 1947 the annual plan, the *Economic Survey*, was drafted by working parties in five separate departments and co-ordinated first by a steering committee of senior officials from each interested department (who had little time and even less expertise to compensate for the absence of a dedicated secretariat) and finally by the Lord President's Committee (which similarly had little time or expertise, let alone authority over all relevant policy areas – such as overseas economic policy). A Central Economic Planning Staff (CEPS), to draft the *Survey* and oversee its implementation, was finally established in 1947; but even then it owed less to foresight than the accidents of the fuel and convertibility crises, successive challenges to Attlee's leadership and Dalton's resignation as chancellor. Its staff, moreover, never exceeded 17 and were not always of the highest calibre. It could therefore do little to check departmentalism, the most notorious example of which was the Treasury's continuing insistence to plan the budget over the fiscal year while the *Survey* worked to a calendar year. Whatever co-ordination was achieved was the result not so much of the formal machine but of transient factors such as the authority of the Chancellor of the Exchequer, the personality of the Chief Planning Officer and the placing of CEPS staff on as many committees as possible (Alford, Lowe and Rollings 1992: Ch. 1).

Such popular and administrative reservations about intervention accorded with a considerable degree of political thinking within the Labour government. This was well expressed in the foreword to the 1947 *Economic Survey*, written by the Chancellor of the Exchequer, Sir Stafford Cripps. It made an explicit distinction between totalitarian and democratic planning which had to 'preserve the maximum possible freedom of choice ... and the essential flexibility of our economic life' (Cmd 7046, paragraphs 8–10). The government opted for the latter; and so, for example, its failure both to adopt wage planning and to use the extensive range of economic controls at its disposal in no way represented a defeat. Rather they reflected its views about the positive virtues of free collective bargaining and the desirability of industrialists taking key allocative decisions for themselves – be it via trade associations or, in relation to nationalised industries, in public corporations insulated from persistent political interference (Tomlinson 1997: 298–300). Even the increasing acceptance of Keynesian demand management after 1947 may be interpreted not so much as an extension of governmental power but a 'retreat' into a more modest form of intervention whereby central government remained responsible for the conditions under which the market worked but did not dictate what it should produce (but see Mercer, Rollings and Tomlinson 1992: Ch. 2). In other words, despite its interventionist rhetoric, its new formal responsibilities and the nature of the war economy which it had inherited, the Labour government did – and intentionally did – remarkably little to centralise power in Whitehall.[4]

A similar conclusion can be drawn from social policy. The final acceptance of the Beveridge Report, for example, can be interpreted as a *limitation* of government intervention because, in contrast to the Continent, state responsibility was restricted to the mere provision of a subsistence income (Tomlinson 1998). If individuals wished to maintain their accustomed living standards they had to insure themselves privately. In education and health policy, the story was the same. The Ministry of Education might have been granted the power to 'direct and control' local education authorities but it rarely used it positively (Geen 1981; Simon 1991). Similarly, the nationalisation of hospitals may have reduced the power of the voluntary sector and local authorities, but with a very restricted administrative staff, the Ministry of Health could hardly impose cost-effective regimes on doctors whose clinical freedom, not to mention their entrenched position on Hospital Boards, gave them effective control over the budget (which amounted to almost 10 per cent of public expenditure).

Resistance to greater centralisation continued under the Conservatives until the highly symbolic resignation of Thorneycroft as Chancellor of the Exchequer in January 1958. At the political level, there was an even balance between 'reluctant' and 'anti – collectivists' within the Churchill and Eden cabinets (Jones 1992). In the constituencies, right-wing activism led to the creation of splinter groups such as the Middle Class Alliance. Within the Conservative Research Department (CRD) a sustained attempt was also made to establish a clear ideological justification for 'rolling back' the state. In an increasingly affluent society, it was argued, personal responsibility should be encouraged and the consumers of welfare empowered against its producers. Consequently, direct taxes should be cut and individuals required to pay the full cost of services, be they provided by the market or (when occasionally it was the more efficient) by the state. This policy would, in the NHS, for example, entail the privatisation of non-core services (such as dentistry), the raising of insurance premiums to their proper actuarial level and full charges for services such as hospital stays. In education, vouchers and student loans would be introduced and, in housing, economic rents charged.

At the administrative level, Treasury officials (although highly suspicious of the 'ideologues' in the CRD) championed similar proposals; and in 1956 they secured the appointment of a Cabinet committee on the social services through which, it was hoped, they could win the collective support of welfare ministers for what they euphemistically termed a policy of 'constructive modification'. Their hopes, however, were dashed *inter alia* by the refusal of the Minister of Housing (Sandys) to attend and the rejection by the other ministers of the group's underlying logic. The Committee had hastily to be abandoned before the drafting of a report which would have required an explicit justification of the Treasury's views on the relative contribution of tax cuts and public expenditure to 'national efficiency' (Lowe 1989). The unintended consequence of the

Committee, therefore, was the creation of a ministerial coalition which – in direct conflict with the CRD and the Treasury – supported a more robust defence of state welfare. This coalition served to defeat Thorneycroft when, in the following year, he sought another 'constructive modification' of policy. This defeat also forestalled any further disengagement from the active management of the economy in line with the attempt to float sterling in 1952 (the Robot scheme, see Cairncross 1985: Ch. 9) and the acceptance of contra-cyclical measures to control inflation although not necessarily to relieve unemployment (Rollings 1988).

Thorneycroft's resignation may thus be seen as the historic occasion after which the need for more positive action by central government to resolve the problems of national efficiency, first identified in the Edwardian period, started finally and fully to be accepted at both a political and administrative level within government.[5] The person to seize the initiative was the prime minister, Harold Macmillan. Alert to the need to restructure both his Party's electoral base (following the Suez fiasco) and the economy (given the increasing evidence of relative decline) he had the vision to see the advantages as well as the disadvantages of state intervention. He also had the courage to confront the vested interests blocking change both in and outside government. Consequently, over the following five years, he presided over a radical reappraisal of the role and machinery of central government, culminating in October 1962 with an explicit programme to 'modernise' Britain. It was launched in Cabinet with the following challenge:

> Do we, or do we not, set out to control the pattern of events, to direct development, to plan growth, to use the instruments of government to influence or determine private decisions? Believe that this is inevitable. Forces at work now too complicated, risks of set back too great to leave to market forces and laissez faire. Dirigisme. But it must be creative dirigisme. (PRO 1962)

Macmillan's principal means of securing change was the creation of a coherent body of informed support through the fusion of ministers, party officials and civil servants and private advisers into a 'single policy-making community' (Turner 1994: 226). He personally sought, for example, a wide range of official and unofficial advice. He gave younger ministers their head with, for example, the appointment of Iain Macleod as head of the Policy Study Group between February 1957 and June 1959 to rethink 'progressive Toryism' and as Party chairman in 1961. He closely involved CRD officials with ministers in the extended Steering Committees which drafted the election manifestos between 1957–59 and 1963–64. Brainstorming meetings were held at Chequers. All this activity provided him with a wealth of information and ideas with which to bombard vested interests (such as the Treasury) and the opportunity to absorb their replies into his extended policy-making network. Macmillan was also critically supported by his deputy, R. A. Butler, who chaired the CRD and key cabinet and party committees, and was thus able to co-ordinate the legislative and research programmes as well as to give members at all levels within the party the impression at least that they were participating in policy-making (Lowe 1997b).

The impact which Macmillan's programme of centralisation and modernisation had on the formulation of welfare policy can be gauged from the advice offered by the Cabinet Secretary to his successor in 1964. In sharp contrast to the views of the Treasury and the CRD in the mid 1950s, he argued:

(a) an increase in public expenditure – and therefore in tax – is not necessarily a bad thing, in so far as it provides better social benefits for the less fortunate members of the community and eliminates the grosser disparities of wealth;

(b) by any reliable criterion of value for money, it is not always public expenditure that needs to be reduced. The private sector, particularly private consumption, may be the villain of the piece; and in so far as an increase of tax on 'luxuries' is unavoidable, it may now be preferable to an arbitrary cut in programmes of e.g. housing and new schools. (PRO 1964)

In recognition of its potential to correct market failure and to contribute to – rather than handicap – economic growth, every area of state welfare was significantly expanded (for fuller details, see Lowe 1996; Bridgen and Lowe 1998). To create a healthy, trained and mobile workforce, for example, an ambitious ten-year plan was launched to restructure the provision of hospitals. Seven new universities were built even before the acceptance of the Robbins commitment to double student numbers. Ambitious targets for house-building were also restored and a National Building Authority established to capitalise on the government's 'monopoly' position to force through the construction industry's modernisation. To improve the 'status and security' of the workforce, the Contracts of Employment and the Industrial Training Acts were passed and plans made for the provision of redundancy pay. In economic policy, more coercive powers were taken in the Local Employment Acts of 1960 and 1963 to prevent both the 'human tragedy and waste' of unemployment and the under-utilisation of productive potential (Roseveare 1997, but see also Rollings 1996). Counter-cyclical action was also taken in the downturns of 1958 and 1962 and new devices, such as special deposits and the regulator, were introduced to make the management of the economy more effective.

Equally radical were the changes to the machinery of government designed to minimise the tensions within and outside government which such an expansion of state intervention inevitably created. Three examples must suffice. First, there was the creation of the Public Expenditure Survey Committee in 1961, an innovation which was subsequently hailed as the 'most important innovation in its field in any western nation' (Heclo and Wildavsky 1974: xvii; see also Lowe 1997c). PESC was a committee of principal finance officers from each spending department within Whitehall, chaired by the Treasury, with the remit to review departmental plans for expenditure annually in the light of estimated economic growth. Its objective was to ensure that they could be adequately funded and, if they could not, to determine priorities. Ideally, its work was to be overseen by a ministerial committee on public expenditure (as between 1961 and 1962) whose members could then combine in Cabinet to resist short-term pressures or special pleading for 'uneconomic' expenditure. PESC was specifically designed, therefore, to strengthen the core executive: administratively, it was explicitly to foster 'joint working in a common enterprise' while, politically, the ministerial committee was to 'make the theory of collective responsibility a reality' (Cmnd 1432, paragraph 79; PRO 1960). Should governments feel able to publish their expenditure plans, an added bonus would be the creation of a better informed public.

The main innovation designed to inform public opinion and to strengthen the relationship between the core executive and interests *outside* government, however, was the National Economic Development Council (NEDC). The NEDC, which was established in 1962, was a triumph for Macmillan's extended policy network because, at the critical moment, it was suggested not by a powerful government department or political grouping but by the deputy secretary to the Cabinet, F. W. Bishop (Ringe and Rollings: forthcoming). It was a body of some 22 people, including six representatives each of the government, industry and the trade unions, two representatives of nationalised industries and two independent members. It was also attended by the director of NEDO, a research agency with some 60 staff which it had finally been agreed should be answerable independently to the Council. It quickly became, as its early participants later testified, a crucial public forum in which 'heavyweights' from government and industry were able to have full and frank discussions on the complete range of issues affecting Britain's economic performance, based on expert opinion prepared both within and independently of Whitehall. In the formal and informal sessions alike, mutual suspicions were allayed and mutual education enhanced. The serious reporting of the research it sponsored and the conclusions it reached also greatly informed public opinion (Ringe 1998). In short, the NEDC had the potential to provide the vital institutional framework – which Britain had traditionally lacked – for an equal and open relationship between government and non-government agencies. It thus offered an opportunity for the successful implementation of a British variant of the active labour market policies, which were widely perceived to lie at the root of the economic 'miracles' abroad.

The third organisational revolution transformed the Treasury. On the advice of the 1959–61 Plowden Committee on the control of public expenditure, which had also recommended the establishment of PESC, it was totally restructured with the transfer of some 1300 staff. Its responsibilities for the management of the economy and of the civil service were separated (in anticipation of the later Fulton Report) and officials responsible for economic policy divided into three functional groups: Finance, the Public Sector and the National Economy Group. The latter was the most innovative, bringing together – economists and administrators in accordance with persistent calls since the war for the better mix of experts and generalists to frame 'advice and plans concerning the balance of the economy as a whole, whether short or long term' (Bridgen and Lowe 1998: 28–9). In November 1962 a new modernising permanent secretary was also appointed (William Armstrong) virtually at the same time as the two other most senior positions in the civil service (the head of the civil service and the cabinet secretary) changed hands.

The appointment which best typified Macmillan's style and vision, however, was the one which had to be ended in 1962 because of ill health: the promotion to the Treasury as permanent secretary of its leading critic before the Plowden Committee, Sir Frank Lee. The significance of this appointment became apparent two years later at the NEDC. On taking office, Lee set up a committee of senior permanent secretaries to oversee a working party on economic growth; and its report in July 1961 demonstrated a readiness by the Treasury to take the initiative in surveying the full range of obstacles to growth and in confronting the 'difficult' battles against vested interests (PRO 1961: especially paragraph 39). This report, somewhat modified, was submitted to the NEDC and, although instinctively dismissed as 'Treasury trash', it later formed the basis for NEDO's 'orange book', *Conditions Favourable to Economic Growth*, which many still regard as the best analysis of Britain's continuing economic problems (Ringe and Rollings forthcoming; Ringe 1998). From being a perceived impediment to growth in the 1950s the Treasury thus became a more positive force in the attempts by the core executive to co-ordinate an effective solution to relative decline.

Between 1958 and 1964, therefore, there was anything but a 'hollowing out' of the state. Such a possibility had been considered in the mid 1950s but it had been emphatically rejected. Instead there was an ambitious attempt to build the necessary institutions and networks to develop and deliver from the centre a 'positive' welfare policy, the need for which had been first recognised around the First World War and nominally accepted during the Second. Through his extended policy-making network, the reorganisation of the Treasury and the creation of PESC, Macmillan sought to strengthen the effectiveness of the core executive. Through the NEDC and NEDO an avenue was at last established for an open and equal sharing of views between government and industry, in an attempt to minimise chaos within a 'differentiated polity'. The trouble was, however, that these organisational changes were not met by immediate political and administrative success. The extended network through which Macmillan had assiduously built support for 'creative dirigsme' was unable to prevent the outbreak of another battle within the Conservative Party over the proper role of the state. Departmentalism grew in tandem with government responsibilities. Outside interess also retained their traditional suspicion of the state. In consequence, centralisation did not contain but coincided, so it could be argued, with greater fragmentation and differentiation. This apparent contradiction can best be illustrated not just by organisational change but by specific attempts to deliver new 'positive' policies: in social policy, the reform of pensions between 1957 and 1959 (Bridgen forthcoming) and of redundancy pay between 1962 and

1964 (Bridgen 1999), and in economic policy the continuing battles with the Bank of England and industry to agree an effective monetary and wages policy (Ringe and Rollings 2000; Ringe forthcoming).

Fragmentation and differentiation

During the drive for modernisation and centralisation, four features of government became particularly apparent: the simultaneous strength and weakness of both the prime minister and the Treasury; the debilitating effect of interdepartmental battles on government's ability to act positively; and the continuing ambivalence of outside interest groups towards state intervention.

Macmillan's power as prime minister was well demonstrated by the defeat of his right-wing in 1958, his steady erosion of traditional Treasury dogma and his installation in power by 1962 (particularly following the 'night of the long knives') of a new generation of officials and ministers sympathetic to 'positive' government action. However, as the brainstorming at Chequers in April 1963 demonstrated, the Party once again became split between its liberal and dirigiste wings (CRD papers). The particular areas of dispute were the relative advantages of 'active planning' and universalism on the one hand and of a 'vigorous private enterprise economy' and selectivity on the other. Such fundamental disagreement seriously constrained Macmillan's ability to act.

Any prime minister's authority in welfare policy depends not just on party unity but on a personal capacity and grasp of detail. These served Macmillan well up to 1961 – although in the early battle for pensions reform he was admittedly defeated. Characteristically, he initially backed Macleod's attempt to establish a distinctive Conservative policy (which equally characteristically has since been adopted by New Labour): the requirement that everyone should take out a second, private pension regulated by government to ensure the continuation of their accustomed living standards in retirement. In the face of opposition from the Treasury (which feared lost income from insurance contributions and tax concessions) and the private pensions industry (which feared regulation) he then changed horses – only to be defeated by a combination of junior ministers and party activists on the principle of contracting-out (Bridgen forthcoming).

After 1961, however, his health began to fail. So too did his political authority. Butler's transfer to overseas policy loosened his control over the parliamentary party and constituencies, the more so because the new party chairman (Macleod) was not so emollient towards either right-wing activists (whom he despised) or fellow ministers (with whom he was locked in battle over Macmillan's succession). Macmillan himself was also distracted by foreign crises such as the erection of the Berlin Wall and the Cuban missile crisis which, with uncanny precision, coincided respectively with the launching of NEDC and his address to cabinet on modernisation. This enervation inevitably made it the harder for him to win support from the Cabinet, let alone from both sides of industry, for the core of his modernisation programme – an active labour market policy proposing wage restraint (monitored by a National Incomes Commission) in return for improved working conditions (including redundancy pay). Redundancy pay should have been a practical political proposition because it was coincidentally being championed by the NEDC as a means of encouraging labour mobility. It accordingly acquired symbolic importance as the first test of the Council's ability to translate agreements in principle into practice. Detailed technical problems, however, then struck. The Cabinet agreed a national redundancy fund to make one-off lump sum payments. Both sides of industry, however, rejected the fund in favour of a bolder scheme of earnings-related unemployment pay; but this the Cabinet could not accept because such an extension of universal social security would have conflicted with Party's increasing interest in selectivity. Stalemate ensued. Fragmenting party unity and political leadership, in other words, kept policy fragmented (Bridgen 1999).

A similar mixture of strength and weakness was displayed by the other key player within the core executive, the Treasury. Every welfare policy continued to bear signs of its influence; but, in contrast to the interwar period when it had greater powers of patronage over a more compact service and there was political support for retrenchment, its direct power became more limited. It had instead to resort to a series of committees through which to argue its case, be this inside government (as with the 1956 Cabinet committee on social services, the Plowden committee, PESC and the Ministerial Committee on Public Expenditure) or outside government (as with the 1957–62 Committee on Prices, Productivity and Incomes in wages policy or NEDC). Each of these committees was meant to follow a common pattern. They were to be chaired by a Treasury representative (as in PESC, the MCPE and NEDC) or a known Treasury sympathiser (as in Plowden or COPPI). They were to receive information only from the Treasury, as was the practice on PESC and the MCPE and the intention behind NEDC. They were also to have a Treasury official as their secretary, who would ideally write the reports (as with Plowden and the second COPPI report). Thus there was to be no genuine debate. The Treasury had no intention of compromising its views on such issues as the restriction of public expenditure to a fixed percentage of GNP (as in 1956 and again with Plowden and PESC), the setting of a wage norm (as with COPPI) or the imposition of wage restraint as a precondition for growth (as with NEDC). So, the committees just represented the imposition of the Treasury view by other means. Its officials remained firm believers in the top-down model of policy-making, as validated by the Whitehall model: interdependence, in situations where they had to act, could not be countenanced.

Such intransigence accounted in part for the Treasury's weakness because if there was anything these committees actually did have in common it was the fact that they invariably rebounded against the Treasury. In 1956, as has been seen, a ministerial coalition was formed within the Social Services Committee against retrenchment. COPPI consolidated the opposition of both sides of industry to an incomes policy. The MCPE, the body on which Macleod successfully fought his battle for an increase in welfare policy, was a *precondition* for growth, and officials followed his lead on PESC (Lowe 1997b: 610–13). The NEDC, as has been seen, also dismissed the Treasury's initial brief as 'trash'.

Treasury weakness also stemmed from another source: its continuing reluctance, despite strongly held views, to assume any 'positive' responsibilities itself.
In the 1940s this had been apparent with economic planning; and despite
nationalisation it was discovered in the 1950s, when a tighter wages and
monetary policy was sought, that insufficient powers had been taken to direct
both industries, such as coal, to limit wage increases and the Bank of England to
vary bank rate by specific amounts. The latter issue was referred to the 1957–59
Radcliffe Committee and for once, to the Bank's 'blank amazement', a committee
ruled in the Treasury's favour. 'Bank rate', the Governor continued to insist, 'is
an integral part of the Central Bank's own business' (Ringe and Rollings 2000).
Even then, however, the Treasury did not press home its advantage. Indeed,
Bank officials were now admitted to key policy-making committees in order to
educate them in broader economic considerations and this actually strengthened
their influence. This reluctance, even after 1961, to assume positive power
reflected a continuation of the Treasury's interwar scepticism about the efficacy
of state intervention; and its readiness to act (preferably through another agency)
was often only triggered by a desperation to prevent something worse. Such a
mixture of intransigence and reticence did not serve the co-ordinating functions
of the core executive well or make for good policy.

The Treasury's relative weakness permitted individual departments to revert in
some measure to the factionalism which had existed before the reforms instigated
by Sir Warren Fisher. Macmillan noted in 1957 that the Treasury and the Ministry
of Pensions and National Insurance were fighting over pensions 'like the followers
of the Montagues and Capulets'. The Treasury's wages policy was sabotaged by the
Ministries of Labour and Transport, determined to maintain the independence of
both the conciliation service and the nationalised industries. Even reference to
the Chancellor was unable to resolve the dispute between the Treasury and the
Inland Revenue over who should have responsibility for research into the
economic and social consequences of taxation (Bridgen and Lowe 1998: 31). The
battle over redundancy pay between the Ministries of Labour and National
Insurance even led the British Employers Confederation openly to demand that
the government should speak with one voice. To an extent this factionalism
reflected the power of some formidable officials who were antipathetic to any
major policy reappraisal, such as Sir Eric Bowyer at MPNI and Sir Alexander
Johnston at the Inland Revenue. However, it also exposed a more fundamental
problem associated with the management of an expanded government which, in
the short term, PESC could not relieve. As Sir Keith Joseph was still complaining
in 1964 to anyone prepared to listen, 'we really must have a system of priorities
for expenditure. ... The lack of any clear set of explicable priorities seems to me to
be fatal to economic management and to coherent national policy' (quoted in
Lowe 1997b: 604).

Such political and administrative fragmentation may have sapped the ability of
the core executive to co-ordinate a strong central policy, but the fundamental
impediment to modernisation remained the power of vested interests within the
broader governance. By the late 1950s they had been popularly identified,

together with the government, as the principal obstacles to economic growth; but they demonstrated far less willingness to reform. This reluctance was particularly true of two areas where 'coteries of citizens' had a strong tradition of governing themselves: banking and industrial relations. Specific government attempts to control credit were continually frustrated by the clearing banks, under the protection of the Bank of England, even after the introduction of special deposits; and wages policy was similarly frustrated by a fierce defence of free collective bargaining. The Radcliffe Committee and NEDC did improve things to an extent, although the different ambitions harboured for the NEDC underlined fundamental differences between employers and the TUC (Ringe and Rollings forthcoming). So too did the eventual failure to reach agreement on its first concrete initiative, redundancy pay. The government, as has been seen, was depicted as the villain but, in addition, there was a basic disagreement between the TUC (which wanted an earnings-related scheme to raise the benefits of all) and the British Employers Confederation (who wanted the scheme to extend the right of management to reward 'deserving' workers). The negotiating freedom of both peak organisations was also severely constrained by the need to carry their more conservative members. The battle over redundancy pay was significant for one further reason: the evidence it provides for the impact of greater centralisation on the relationship between government departments and the policy networks of which they were often at the centre. Before 1962, the Ministry of Labour had been happy, on behalf of industry, to champion free collective bargaining against the Treasury. Thereafter it became frustrated by industry's conservatism. It explicitly adopted a 'more direct approach to ... good personnel practices. In future the Ministry may be expected not only to publicise such practices but also to tell industry that it *should* adopt them. The new approach ... would be more like that of overseas ministries' (quoted in Bridgen and Lowe 1998: 34).

Conclusion

By the mid 1950s, continuity and order were breaking down in Britain for a variety of reasons. These included Suez, growing affluence together with an awareness of relative decline. The breakdown has conventionally been perceived as an example of government failure, particularly in relation to economic decline where Continental states appeared to be acting with greater efficiency. This perception is highly questionable. Given the absence of constitutional checks and its potential administrative and tax-raising capacity, it is true that British government was theoretically even more powerful than its Continental rivals. It used this power during both world wars and to create an exceptionally centralised social security system. In practice, however, the 'positive' powers of government were extremely limited because – except in an emergency – public compliance depended on their non-use. Thus, after the experiments in bureaucracy and corporatism around the First World War, state intervention (with differing degrees of transparency in social and economic policy) was restricted to the support of existing agencies within the broader governance. Consequently, the breakdown of the mid 1950s was one of governance. The question then arose about how central government should, and could, react. Positive action, which the reconstruction rhetoric and legislation in the 1940s appeared to promise, risked non-compliance. Collaborative action, as on the Continent, was impossible because of the absence of appropriate sub-central and industrial agencies. Eventually, despite considerable pressure from within the Conservative Party and the civil service, it was decided that the organisation and collaborative capacity of central government should be greatly strengthened. Modernisation, it was agreed, required centralisation. However, the efficacy of greater centralisation was soon compromised, perhaps inevitably, by the political and administrative fragmentation of the core executive; and while with some justification obloquy was – and has since been – poured on government, vested interests within the broader governance were able to evade both fundamental reform and much retrospective criticism.

For historians, the fuller examination of the 'modernisation' programme is important in order to dispel crude notions of government failure. It highlights the full complexity of the problems facing Britain and the real constraints of compliance and organisation on government. This in turn underlines the key methodological issue that while research, especially on government papers, should properly examine competing policy networks within government, it should remain ever alert to the 'real evidence' they contain for the world outside (McDonald, quoted in Lowe 1997a: 240). For political scientists also, the concentration on government requires to be modified. Traditionally, in Britain, governance (in its broadest sense as a socio-cybernetic system) has always been of the greatest importance. A 'centreless' society was the preferred option. It should, in addition, dispel assumptions about a unilinear increase in state intervention after 1900 or in the 'hollowing out' of the state after 1945. After a premature experiment in centralisation at the start of the century, there was a rolling back of the state in the interwar period; and between 1957 and 1964 far from there being a hollowing-out of the state there was a heroic attempt at centralisation. Lexicographers should perhaps have the last word. Governance was a core concept at the start of the century. In the 1920s it was classed as 'incipiently' obsolete. In the 1960s it was then declared wholly obsolete (Fowler 1926, 1965). Its current reinvention needs to be placed in a proper historical context.

Notes

1. The chapter is designed as a response, and therefore owes a considerable debt, to the work of Rod Rhodes and in particular to the papers within the Whitehall programme targeted at historians, most notably R. A. W. Rhodes and M. Bevir (1999) on 'Narratives of British Government'.
2. 'You could not give an accurate account of twenty four hours there, especially in times of crisis (i.e. most days). It was a painful re-education of an Oxford educated history student'. Private information from a former principal private secretary at No. 10, equating postmodernism with Henry Ford's conclusion that 'history is bunk'.

3. Traditional hostility to the ceding of control over the expenditure of any public money to an outside body was well summarised during the First World War by the official who was later to oversee the creation of the UAB: 'the problem is not really one of deciding whether an industry should be allowed to fend for itself ... but of deciding whether an industry should be allowed to set up a sort of *imperium in imperio* with compulsory powers conferred by the state, and a state contribution, but without presumably the measure of state control which would ordinarily be a concomitant of these privileges' (PRO 1917).

4. Even then policy was subject to a classic Whitehall stalling mechanism. Demand management was simply placed in the hands of two officials, Sir Bernard Gilbert who 'does not believe in Employment Policy and Hale, who ... does so even less' (Booth 1983: 118). Similarly, Sir Thomas Sheepshanks was overheard to denounce the Beveridge Report as a fraud and so was immediately commissioned to translate it into a White Paper (Harris 1997: 426).

5. There is a certain disagreement amongst historians, and within the project, over the significance of Thorneycroft's resignation. Certainly it permanently changed the balance of opinion in Cabinet and Whitehall in relation to reductions in social expenditure and, at least to the extent that this influenced public expenditure, it also affected economic policy.

7
Domesticating the 'Market Animal'? The Treasury and the Bank of England, 1955–60[*]

Astrid Ringe and Neil Rollings

Introduction

Gordon Brown's surprise decision to set the Bank of England free to operate monetary policy independently of the Treasury has been popular with many commentators. It represented the culmination of a gradually growing demand for change (Elgie and Thompson 1998: 17). An independent central bank is now widely regarded as the guarantor of a depoliticised monetary policy which avoids intervention by government in the interest of short-term political objectives. According to this argument, a depoliticised monetary policy conducted by an apolitical central bank, will result in a 'better' economic policy (*Economist* 1997; Wood, Mills and Capie 1993). The tendency to shield economic policy-making from politicisation has a long-established tradition in this country and is most clearly expressed in the secrecy that surrounds the Budget and the exclusion of most government departments and ministers from participation in the budgetary process (Dowding 1995: 119; Brittan 1969: 60).

This desire for depoliticisation of economic policy-making originates foremost in the Treasury itself but is also strongly present in a Bank of England that traditionally shields its own affairs and those of the City against the intrusion of outside interests (Bank of England 1997a: 107–12 and 1997b: 316). Both institutions have been able to maintain a high degree of autonomy from the rest of the policy-making machinery despite many challenges to their position. The budgetary process remained essentially unchanged even when the adoption of Keynesian demand management policies greatly expanded the Treasury's responsibilities in the steering of the economy. Economic policy, which then relied on fiscal and monetary policy as chief instruments, was therefore very much a product of the chancellor of the exchequer, his officials and the Bank of England, with some participation from the prime minister. In the name of budget secrecy, the Cabinet was only introduced to the full Budget proposals on the day before their announcement in the House of Commons (Brittan 1969: 42

[*] We would like to acknowledge the ESRC for funding our research (award number: L124251019).

and 69). This process virtually excluded other ministers from the policy process of shaping the budget.

In the same way, monetary policy was decided without consultation with the rest of the Cabinet as its key element, changes in bank rate, were agreed between the chancellor of the exchequer and the Bank of England. This might represent an erosion of the Bank's independence and autonomy compared with the nineteenth century, but still represented a significant degree of autonomy compared with policy formulation in other policy areas (Moran 1986: 22 – 3). This is particularly so given the significance frequently attached to monetary policy in the achievement of various governments' economic policy objectives.

In contrast to current attitudes to bank independence, this exclusive form of economic policy-making has been used to explain the maintenance of policies perceived as detrimental to the growth of the economy. Pollard and others have argued that the needs of industry have been consistently ignored and that the Treasury and the Bank have been furthering the financial interests of the City (Pollard 1982; Ingham 1984: 207–9; Hall 1986: 61; Hutton 1995: 135). This criticism of an anti-industry bias in which the Bank and the Treasury are presented as 'collaborators' has been rejected from a variety of angles (Capie and Collins 1992; Thain 1984). However, both sides of this debate have tended to view the issue of autonomy, or, put more generally, the institutional arrangements of the policy process, as a means to an end: ultimately the focus has been the perceived policy objectives of the Bank and Treasury and their intellectual basis.

Here, a rather different approach is adopted. Our project, of which this case study is a part (see Chapter 6), was devised to assess the nature of policy-making in the field of welfare policy, broadly defined, from the 1940s to the mid-1960s. In particular, we have focused on attempts to modernise the machinery of government in the late 1950s and early 1960s when there was a concerted effort to reform various policy areas.[1] This has involved a series of case studies (Bridgen 1999; Bridgen forthcoming; Lowe 1996; Lowe 1997a; Lowe 1997b; Ringe 1998; Ringe forthcoming; Ringe and Rollings forthcoming). Chapter 6 puts these case studies in a wider context (Lowe and Rollings 2000). There, it is argued that while government responsibilities in welfare policy, broadly defined, grew, centralisation was slow to occur because of a desire to maintain the existing system of governance. When the tensions in this continuity came to a head in the 1950s, attempts were made to centralise and modernise government. However, these efforts were compromised by the fragmented nature of the core executive. With regard to the formulation of monetary policy, this meant that, despite the 1946 nationalisation of the Bank of England, there was little fundamental change in the process by which monetary policy was formulated. During the 1950s there was a growing awareness of the tension between this unreformed policy process and the need for the formulation and implementation of effective demand management policies. However, when the Radcliffe Committee on the Working of the Monetary System reported in favour of reform of the policy process by giving precedence in the formulation of monetary policy to the

Treasury rather than to the Bank of England, the Treasury shied away from this outcome and no fundamental reform occurred. This, it is argued, was because of these tensions between government and governance. First, despite growing government intervention in the field of monetary policy, historically it remained an area where the policy process operated through a system of governance. Treasury officials, perhaps with the notable exception of the economists in the Economic Section, continued to favour such an approach. Secondly, there was fragmentation within the core executive. The Treasury was unwilling to see interference in what it regarded as its core activities. It preferred to maintain its independent position in Whitehall although effective demand management policies required reform of the policy.

The wartime economy

During the Second World War the British economy was centrally managed in order to sustain the war effort. This transformation was never completely reversed after the war. For a transitional period, at least, many direct controls were continued (Rollings 1992). The commitment of the postwar Labour government to the welfare state, full employment and a programme of nationalisation, introduced changes into the domestic economy that resulted in more involvement of the state in the management of the economy. The government was increasingly perceived to have responsibilities in steering the economy towards the achievement of certain goals, that is, full employment, price stability, a balance of payments equilibrium and, later, economic growth. Simultaneously, the share of the government's consumption of GDP increased and therewith its influence and potential ability to manage the economy by, for example, varying investment levels in the nationalised industries, increasing or decreasing taxes, and government spending on public programmes (Cairncross 1994: 49–52).

The impact of government finance on the money markets and the City of London was also greatly increased. This had two causes in particular: the nationalisation programme brought a host of capital-intensive industries into public ownership and their investment programmes as well as those of local authorities were financed by government borrowing, and secondly there were large government debts, arising from the war effort and the expansion of the public sector after the war. While the overall size of the government debt was a matter of concern to bankers, the management of that debt had a significant impact on the liquidity of the financial sector and offered a means of influencing it (Hawtrey 1961: 147; Howson 1994: 229; Dow 1965: 230).

Thus the context for monetary policy formulation was significantly different from that of the interwar period. The nationalisation of the Bank of England in 1946 was significant, therefore, in formalising the relationship between the Treasury and the Bank of England (Elgie and Thompson 1998: 50). The Nationalisation Act concerned the setting of the bank rate after consultation with the chancellor of the exchequer, the appointment of the governor, deputy governor and the directors of the Bank and the right of the Treasury to give directions to the Bank (Fforde 1992: Ch. 1; Howson 1993: Ch. 2). Nevertheless, it is doubtful if the act marked a new era in the relationship. Both the Treasury and the Bank regarded the nationalisation as having little impact on their relationship as it had developed since the late 1930s. The Bank remained institutionally and operationally independent of the Treasury but accepted overall Treasury responsibility for monetary policy. As before nationalisation, the bank rate was only changed after consultation between the chancellor and the governor and the Bank still retained considerable influence over the shaping of the decision. The initiative for a change in bank rate still came from the Bank and the final decision was taken by the Bank's Court after the chancellor of the exchequer's approval had been ascertained. The Treasury's right to give directions to the Bank was never exercised and the relationship continued on the basis of consultation. Nationalisation also gave the Bank statutory powers to direct the high street banks but it chose to continue to rely on 'custom and tradition' in its conduct of business with the banking community (Fforde 1992: 15 and 18).[2] Indeed, Peter Thorneycroft, from his experience as chancellor of the exchequer in the 1950s, agreed with the Radcliffe Committee on the Working of the Monetary System, that the act may have increased Bank independence in some respects (Thorneycroft 1960: 13; Radcliffe Report 1959: paragraph 766).

During a transitory period after the end of war the Bank grudgingly consented to an abstention from the use of traditional instruments of monetary policy such as variations in bank rate, in order to keep the cost of government debts at bay and prevent an anticipated postwar slump. After the 1949 devaluation, the Bank became increasingly restive about the restoration of domestic monetary flexibility and the change of government in 1951 was a welcome opportunity to accomplish this. On the recommendation of the Bank, there were two changes in bank rate in 1951 and 1952. In both cases the chancellor of the exchequer followed the advice of the Bank although the Economic Section and other officials had expressed doubts about the size of the increases. Thereafter Treasury officials and their Chancellors were not entirely in agreement with the Bank's development of monetary policy which raised fundamental issues on the question of the respective powers of the Bank and the Treasury in directing monetary policy (Rollings 1994: 200; Forde 1992: 362, 364–8, 386). These issues, in particular were,

1. What were the Bank's and what were the Treasury's functions in the formulation and conduct of monetary policy?
2. What powers did the Treasury have to direct the Court of the Bank to make changes in bank rate and to issue directions to the banks, i.e. use its statutory power over the banks?
3. How far did the government have rights to interfere with the internal arrangements of the Bank, i.e. to influence the way in which bank rate decisions were taken inside the Bank?
4. What information on the banking sector the Treasury should be provided with by the Bank to assist the formation of monetary policy?[3]

In this context, the Bank of England Act of 1946 was increasingly regarded by Treasury officials and ministers as an inadequate piece of legislation that failed to provide the Treasury with the necessary instruments to use monetary policy to steer the economy.

The postwar economy

There was no active use of bank rate to influence demand under the 1945–51 Labour government but instead budget surpluses were used to limit the money supply and clearing banks were 'requested' to limit lending (Howson 1993). From 1951, the Conservative government broadly upheld the commitment to managing the economy but was at the same time prepared to give market forces more room by dismantling price and other controls. Monetary policy was increasingly regarded as a – if not the – key instrument to control the economy. Although comparatively small changes in bank rate were made at first, and were supplemented by hire purchase controls as well as requests to banks to restrict credit, bank rate changes were increasingly given centre stage in efforts to control inflation (Cairncross 1987: 16).

On the one hand, the reliance on monetary policy was welcomed by the Bank of England as it wished to return to its traditional role and use bank rate flexibly to influence the money markets as its main instrument of policy. On the other hand, with monetary policy becoming an essential instrument of economic policy, the Bank's right to manoeuvre independently of Treasury policies was increasingly challenged. A return to an idealised time, when the Bank was the depoliticised 'market animal' and was unconstrained by government policy objectives, was blocked by the political tool that monetary policy had become.[4] In the interest of its independence, the Bank rejected the notion that monetary policy could play such a key role in the steering of the economy. They insisted on being merely the government's banker and general adviser in the monetary field, not a subordinated policy instrument. Hence the governor's adamant defence of the proposition that the fixing of the bank rate was Bank and not Treasury business (Radcliffe Committee 1960: question 12847; Cairncross 1987: 17).

However, these problems only began to emerge in 1955 and 1956: the methods used between 1951 and 1955 appeared to be relatively successful in the eyes of ministers and Treasury officials – a view that was not, however, shared by the Economic Section of the Treasury (Cairncross and Watts 1989: 217–19). The Bank hoped that a flexible bank rate policy would soon become less timid and allow requests to banks to limit advances to be abandoned. Nevertheless, in spite of the greater use that was made of the bank rate and its generally higher level, the volume of money that was injected into the economy continued to rise in 1954 and 1955 and the Treasury's Economic Section were concerned that inflation would increase further rather than be brought under control. Two rises in bank rate at the beginning of 1955 were judged as ineffective in controlling the rise in bank advances and the new monetary policy was increasingly discredited

(Cairncross and Watts 1989: 221). The conflict between the Bank and the Treasury finally erupted when the Chancellor of the Exchequer, Butler, introduced an expansionary budget and expected the banks to restrict credit decisively in order to check inflationary pressure. The Court of the Bank demanded that the government pursue general economic policies that would soon make a relaxation of credit policy possible, but Butler ignored the Bank. Shortly afterwards the government again requested the banks to restrict advances (Fforde 1992: 632; Dimsdale 1991: 101).

By August 1955 Treasury officials had become disillusioned by the monetary policies pursued thus far, as bank advances continued to rise and still more bank money was injected into the economy. The Committee of London Clearing Bankers was equally disillusioned but for different reasons. It informed the governor of the Bank of England that the policy of restriction of bank credit could not by itself be expected to cure the present excessive consumption at home and that such a policy must be accompanied by decisive and effective measures of retrenchment in the public sector of the economy, that is positive and specific action to reduce the level of expenditure of the government, local authorities and the nationalised industries.[5]

The Treasury and the Bank of England

The apparent ineffectiveness of the monetary techniques used so far generated a consciousness in the Treasury and the Economic Section that monetary techniques and their application were not very well understood within the Treasury and that it was necessary to take a more professional approach. Contact between the Treasury and the Bank, as far as domestic monetary policy was concerned, was characterised by a 'relative paucity of relationships below the Governor level' which 'discouraged debate with Whitehall about policy or about the whole subject of monetary policy – how it worked and how it should be operated' (Fforde 1992: 611). Officials were concerned about shortcomings in three different areas. Firstly, they thought that the Treasury did not receive sufficient information and statistical material from the Bank to allow them to assess how specific monetary measures worked, for example, at the level of the individual bank. Here the secretive behaviour of the Bank was seen to be hindering the development of effective monetary policy measures.[6] Secondly, there was concern that the monetary policy instruments that were being used were ineffective and that new tools were necessary, for example, the prescription of liquidity ratios. Moreover, it was believed that it was impossible to judge the likely effectiveness of these new tools without more information.[7] Thirdly, Treasury officials, and particularly the Chancellors, Macmillan and Thorneycroft, were increasingly dissatisfied with the Bank's mediation between the government and the London Clearing Bankers. A direct approach to, and direct 'negotiations' with, the banking community were therefore regarded as necessary (Cairncross 1987: 16).

Under Thorneycroft's chancellorship the conflict between the Treasury and the Bank became more intense. Acting on a proposal of his Economic Secretary, Nigel Birch, Thorneycroft attempted to commit the Bank to formulate jointly, with the Treasury, monetary policy measures which were to include an agreement on the future course of short-term and long-term interest rates. This proposal entailed active participation of the Bank in policy formulation and was a clear attempt to politicise the Bank's role. It also meant that there would have to be formal meetings of Bank staff and Treasury officials in which both sides would be expected to discuss the monetary development and draw conclusions for the coming Budget.[8] Although the Economic Section was concerned about having to rely on the advice of the Bank and was suspicious of the Bank's policy objectives that were underlying their conduct of monetary policy, the proposal finally went ahead in the autumn of 1957. The chancellor charged this new set-up also with the search for new methods to control the lending policy of the banks, because the Bank of England had made it clear to the government that it disagreed with the policy of requests to restrict credit.[9]

Thorneycroft nevertheless did not have much confidence in a change of attitude within the Bank which would result in greater co-operation between the Bank and the Treasury. Therefore, Treasury officials secretly made enquiries as to what powers were available to the Treasury to force the Bank and the clearing banks to comply with government policy. The Treasury Solicitor was asked whether:

1. the Treasury had powers to direct the Bank of England to give directions to bankers;
2. the Treasury had power under subsection (1) of Section 4 of the 1946 Act to give such directions to the Bank of England that it would be forced itself to give directions to the bankers in pursuance of subsection (3) (dealing with the Bank of England's powers to give directions to bankers);
3. the Treasury had powers to dismiss the Court of Directors of the Bank; and
4. what action could be taken against the Bank, should the Bank fail to comply with directions given to them by the Treasury in pursuance of subsection (1) of section (4) of the 1946 act.

None of these questions were either answered in the affirmative by the Treasury Solicitor or offered the Treasury any practicable lever to bring pressure to bear on the Bank and the bankers.[10]

The 'Independent' Bank

Even under such intense pressure the Bank only made the motions of co-operation and did not concede anything of substance. From the Bank's point of view, there was no need to change their information policy as they believed the Treasury had more facilities than the banks to get hold of the desired information. Secretly, the Bank had even withheld information on bank advances it received from the British Bankers' Association. Bank officials insisted that there should be no direct line of communication between the Treasury, or indeed the government, and City institutions (Fforde 1992: 641–2). The Bank co-operated in the search for a new method of controlling Bank advances but reserved its position with respect to the various proposals that were generated in discussions between Treasury officials and Bank staff. It was particularly adamant in rejecting any proposals that involved the use of their statutory power over the banks as in the case of the enforcement of minimum liquidity ratios, a measure discussed in early 1956. To create a precedent in the use of power to issue directions to the banks was regarded as highly dangerous territory by the Bank: it opened up the pathway to a situation where the Treasury could direct the Bank to issue directions to the banks on policies to be pursued.[11] The Bank was also reluctant to put forward any new methods of credit control because they were concerned that these would provide less incentive for the Treasury to control government debt.[12] It wanted the Treasury to impose stricter spending limits on government departments and to reduce the floating debt not simply to allow the bank rate to become more effective but also to avoid the introduction of new methods to control bank liquidity. Bringing increased government involvement, such steps would threaten the maintenance of the system of informal control of the banking community that the Bank relied upon in their dealings with City institutions.

In 1956 and 1957 the Bank participated in two different internal reviews investigating new instruments of monetary control. The first review, conducted by a Treasury/Bank working group without ministerial participation, did not satisfy the Chancellor of the Exchequer's expectations, although the Governor of the Bank agreed with the conclusion of the report. It stated, that 'the government must manage its finances so that it does not have to rely on the floating debt, and that if this is done it should be possible to get full co-operation of the banks in carrying out government policy, by mutual agreement (including agreed requests) rather than by direction'.[13] This outcome ultimately did not satisfy Treasury officials either because it forced them to continue the unsatisfactory and not very successful policies pursued so far. They could only recommend to the chancellor a further attempt at 'requests to limit advances' as a measure of monetary restraint.[14]

The internal inquiry set in motion by Thorneycroft, in 1957, was of a different quality, because of ministerial participation and the potentially more confrontational terms of reference: 'to consider ... what steps are required to get effective control of the credit level'.[15] The resulting report was supported only by Treasury officials and Thorneycroft's favourite economist, Lionel Robbins. The report favoured the introduction of the prescription of liquidity ratios in conjunction with a requirement for the banks to take up certain amounts of a new non-liquid government security. The Economic Secretary, Birch, recommended to the Chancellor that fresh legislation should be introduced to give the Treasury the appropriate powers to compel the banking system to take up the government's debt together with a self-denying ordinance to impose a limit on government borrowing.[16] Under pressure, and after a period of resistance, the Bank agreed to work out a 'plan of action' with the Treasury, proposing more effective measures to limit bank advances. The Bank insisted on making the so-called 'special deposits scheme', a scheme that it had discussed in the process of giving evidence to the Radcliffe Committee, the basis of this discussion between the Bank and the Treasury. This scheme was later developed and put into practice but was largely ineffective and did not endow Treasury officials with the monetary policy instrument for which they craved.[17]

In an attempt to regain the initiative and to pre-empt developments that threatened the independence and autonomy of the Bank, the Governor of the Bank, Cameron Cobbold, proposed the setting up of a committee which would consider monetary policy. An all-party parliamentary and industrial group led by Robert Boothby and Nicholas Davenport had demanded such a committee in March 1956 but then both the Bank and the Treasury had blocked the initiative. The demands of Boothby's group were very similar to Birch's recommendations to the Chancellor: they demanded the re-introduction of Treasury Deposit Receipts and powers for the Treasury to vary the banks' cash and liquidity ratios.[18]

Cobbold's proposal envisaged a small committee, set up by Treasury Minute, which thus would not be a Royal Commission to keep its profile low. He had already drawn up a list of membership of the committee, with Lord Radcliffe as chairman. After some quarrelling over whether Lionel Robbins should be included, the membership was agreed.[19] As to the terms of reference of the committee, there was agreement between Cobbold and the Permanent Secretary of the Treasury, Makins, that the terms should be drawn up in such a way as to exclude the consideration of exchange rate policy. Makins made the following proposal: 'to enquire into the working of the monetary system, with particular attention to the influence thereon of public finance: and to make recommendations directed to maintaining the value of the currency both internally and externally'. He wished the enquiry to be free to raise questions of 'improvement of structure'.[20] Robert Hall, of the Economic Section, warned that the Governor's and Makins' stress on the influence of public finance might pre-judge the issue. Hall's own proposal for the terms of reference for the committee acknowledged the importance of public finance for the enquiry but stressed the aspect of co-ordination of monetary policy as presumably pursued by the Bank, and economic policies as initiated by the government. He proposed: 'to enquire into the working of the monetary and credit system, the influence thereon of public finance, and the relation of monetary policy to general economic policy: and to make recommendations'.[21] Hall's tentative attempt to include something of the original grievance of the Boothby group, which had stressed that monetary policy should serve the development of the industrial sector of the economy, was not entirely accepted by either the Bank or officials in the Treasury and led to a watering down of the committee's terms of reference.

The differences over the terms of reference for the proposed committee were finally resolved in a meeting between the Deputy Governor, Treasury officials and Robert Hall, concluding on a depoliticised and open wording: 'to enquire into the working of the monetary and credit system, and to make recommendations'. It was also agreed that deliberations over exchange rate policy should be excluded from the enquiry.[22] This was in line with the opinion of Treasury officials who were concerned the inquiry should not cover the external and internal objectives of monetary policy, in other words trying to maintain a fixed and stable exchange rate and to contain inflation.[23]

The Radcliffe Committee and Reform

The Radcliffe Committee reported in August 1959 and its recommendations did not support the Bank's view of how monetary policy should function. As Robert Hall, the government's chief economic adviser, put it in his diary:

> The recommendations about the relations between the Treasury and the Bank of England suit me very well as they want the primacy of the Chancellor to be clearly recognised. ... Generally speaking, the Report suits me very well and endorses all the things I have stood for in recent years: ... The recommendations about the Bank of England would be the ones to get the headlines as these clearly reduced the Bank's importance and especially that of part-time directors. The Governor did not like this at all and took it (as he should have done) as an expression of some lack of confidence. (Cairncross 1991: 209)

The Radcliffe Committee's recommendation caused 'blank amazement' in the Bank, given the proposed transfer of certain powers to the Treasury that had hitherto been exercised by the Bank.[24] To give effect to the notion that government was determining policy, the committee proposed that the Chancellor, not the Court of the Bank, should decide changes in bank rate (Radcliffe Committee 1959, paragraph 771). The committee further sought to remedy the underlying problems regarding differences in the assessment of the economic and monetary situation between the Treasury and the Bank by proposing the establishment of a standing committee which would advise the authorities on all matters relating to the co-ordination of monetary policy as a whole. A committee of 12, chaired by the Chancellor, or his representative, was envisaged to include two representatives of the Board of Trade alongside six Treasury members, including the Chancellor and the Economic Secretary, and four Bank representatives, led by the Governor and the Deputy Governor, an arrangement that put the Bank in the minority (Radcliffe Committee 1959: paragraphs 773–5). The tendency of the Radcliffe Committee's advice was to subordinate the Bank to the influence of the Treasury, to widen the policy horizon of the Bank by exposing it to stronger influence from government departments, and facilitating a more transparent form of policy discussion between the Bank and their counterparts in government. The Bank's former insistence on the point that monetary policy required them to make flexible decisions in answer to market developments, was rejected by the committee in so far as its recommendations aimed at integrating the Bank's monetary policy activities with the government's supposed longer term economic policy objectives.

The Governor and the Deputy Governor of the Bank were of the opinion that the recommendations of the Radcliffe Committee were 'awkward' and meant 'a good deal of trouble', particularly the recommendation on the bank rate decision. Cobbold perceived, however, that the government would not make any decisive move on Radcliffe's recommendations. The Permanent Secretary to the Treasury, Makins, had indicated to Cobbold that the standing committee would not get anywhere, as no Chancellor of the Exchequer would accept the Board of Trade as a partner in economic policy making (see also Cairncross 1991: 209). Makins had also indicated that the bank rate recommendation might be treated rather as a matter of form than of substance and that the government would say and do nothing before an election. Cobbold concluded that the best approach that the Bank could take would be to 'lie low and saying nothing'.[25] This approach was positively reaffirmed by the Chancellor of the Exchequer who also hoped that the Bank would not feel it necessary to take any public position and let the election pass first.[26] In subsequent discussion with Treasury officials, the Governor suggested that the Bank should try to get out of the Radcliffe Committee's recommendation on bank rate decisions and to water down the recommendation on the standing committee.[27] Denying the significance of bank rate decisions for general economic policy, Cobbold insisted that 'bank rate is an integral part of the Central Bank's own business. To place on the Chancellor direct responsibility for what is essentially a market and operational decision would blur the real responsibilities'. To defuse the power of the standing committee as an advisory body on current policies, he interpreted the Radcliffe recommendation as meaning that such a body should deal with long-term questions and not with immediate practical decisions. The body could therefore be created by an extension of membership and functions of the Economic Planning Board.[28] Cobbold was convinced that the government themselves would only pay lip-service to the standing committee recommendation and that therefore the Bank did not need to be unduly bothered that the committee would interfere with the arrangements for immediate practical decisions on matters such as bank rate and government debt operations. He even planned to use the committee as a means of keeping up pressure on government on such matters as the general credit position and the borrowing requirement of the public sector. The standing committee could become a means of defence against too much being expected from the banking system.[29]

The Bank was correct in their assessment of the Treasury reaction to the Radcliffe recommendations. In a Treasury paper sent to the Bank, the proposal for a new committee to integrate monetary and economic policy advice was watered down even further. The paper agreed with the objective of the proposal but attempted to guard the Treasury's sphere of influence against any encroachment from the Board of Trade: 'Monetary policy is not the concern of the Board of Trade any more than of other economic departments outside the Treasury, and it would be anomalous that anyone owing allegiance to another Minister should have formal responsibility for advising the Chancellor on it'.[30] Makins proposed to make the Bank a formal member of the various official committees dealing with economic policy, particularly the Economic Steering Committee and the Budget Committee. To set up a new committee was only to be considered if public/political pressure was such that it would become necessary.[31] The chancellor of the exchequer followed Makins' advice and opted for an internal review of machinery that would appear to comply with Radcliffe's recommendations without setting up the standing committee. He also decided that the direction-giving power of the Treasury should only be a weapon of last resort in case of irreconcilable disagreement.[32]

The new procedure for the announcement of bank rate changes that was subsequently agreed between the Treasury and the Bank was regarded as close to the existing practice and hailed by the Bank's Court of Directors as a personal triumph for both the governor and his deputy. The new procedure strengthened the role of the Governor of the Bank at the expense of the Court, which had to accept a change that had been settled between the Chancellor and the Governor. However, the procedure preserved previous practice in so far as the Court was consulted before the Chancellor's and the Governor's decision was taken and the announcement of the change remained with the Bank of England. The Chancellor of the Exchequer also agreed to the proposition that the initiative for changes in bank rate would normally come from the Bank.[33]

Treasury–Bank relations in a new context

The Treasury never utilised the Radcliffe Committee recommendations to extend their power over the Bank. On the contrary, officials were almost embarrassed about the kind of support that the Treasury received from the committee. They contented themselves with some concessions the Bank made regarding the improvement of statistics and the setting up of the special deposit scheme mentioned above.[34] The Bank was also added to the membership of a number of committees, which was certainly contrary to the interwar policy of the then Governor of the Bank, Montagu Norman, because it represented an element of incorporation into Whitehall (Moran 1986: 24–5). Nevertheless, the Treasury/ Bank conflict and the two years of monetary enquiry of the Radcliffe Committee resulted in little substantive change in the way in which monetary policy was formulated.

Why was the Treasury's response so reserved? There are three points which we wish to emphasise. First, the existence of the report's conclusions provided a new context for Treasury–Bank relations. Robert Hall noted in the December after its publication that 'the Bank is being far more open with the Treasury than it has ever been before' (Cairncross 1991: 221). However, this co-operation was relatively short-lived. Only two months later he had become 'a bit disappointed lately that the good effects [he] had hoped for from Radcliffe have been getting less' (Cairncross 1991: 231). Indeed, the tension between the Bank and the

Treasury continued very much on the same lines as before Radcliffe. It quickly emerged that the newly created instrument, the special deposit scheme, was not at the disposal of the Treasury in the way it had been anticipated. The Bank was only prepared to use the scheme as a threat and denied – as ever – that the Treasury had any powers to direct the Bank to give directions to the commercial banks.[35]

Soon after the report the necessity to amend the Bank of England Act in order to extend the Treasury's powers towards the Bank was discussed again. Within the Treasury the difference between officials and the Economic Section with regard to the handling of the Bank became more pronounced, with the Section pressing for a more radical approach.[36] However, neither Heathcoat Amory nor Lloyd, the Conservative Chancellors succeeding Thorneycroft, pressed the issue of new legislation.[37]

This in turn relates to the second point. Historically, the relationship between the Treasury and the Bank had been informal (Thorneycroft 1960: 12–13; Moran 1986: 18). Monetary policy had traditionally been formulated within a system of governance rather than one of government. Thus, despite all the criticisms and complaints about the Bank, Treasury officials had little wish to see the relationship formalised or for the Bank to be incorporated into Whitehall. In this respect there was a tension between the pressures for control and centralisation flowing from the government's increased responsibilities in the economy, and the traditional form of policy process. There was a reluctance to reform the existing institutional arrangements if some suitable accommodation could be found.

Finally, the proposals in the Radcliffe Report, in particular that for a standing committee, also threatened elements of the Treasury's own highly-prized autonomy. The participation of the Board of Trade implied the sharing of power and information with other departments and the need to justify policy decisions in a more politicised context. In particular, budgetary policy decisions would have to be laid open or discussed within the standing committee and this would have implied an intrusion of other interests into the Treasury's core activity. The 'settlement' after Radcliffe enabled both the Bank and the Treasury to defend their core activities from interference by other agencies. Although the Bank had to make changes in the procedure for bank rate changes, it did not concede other methods of control, becoming formally established as effective monetary instruments, and it was successful in fencing off the City from direct Treasury interference. The Treasury maintained its independence in economic policy-making within Whitehall. However, its accommodation with the Bank to defuse the more radical proposals of the Radcliffe Committee maintained a kind of isolation that, on the one hand, preserved Treasury integrity and power but, on the other, limited their power by upholding the Bank's separate sphere of influence. The Treasury itself forwent the control over monetary policy that it regarded as necessary to achieve government policy objectives.

This tension was not restricted to relations with the Bank. Another striking example of this dilemma was the attempt to develop an incomes policy in co-operation with the Ministry of Labour and the departments involved with the public sector. The Ministry of Labour was particularly intransigent because it perceived the Treasury's policy as an attempt to take control of its industrial relations territory. Equally, the attempt at co-ordinating economic policy in the National Economic Development Council failed because the Treasury was not prepared to enter such a relationship on a co-operative basis (Ringe forthcoming; Ringe and Rollings forthcoming).

In this sense, the institutional arrangements within which the policy process occurred had still not adapted to the requirements of managing the economy. Demand management politicised the process of economic policy making because, on the one hand, it gave the state a larger role in steering the economy and, on the other, it drew new actors, whose interests central government was expected to accommodate, into the policy process. Yet, on the level of practical policy making, there appeared to be a tendency in the opposite direction. Disaggregation and fragmentation of the core executive of government hampered the policy process; and the maintenance of a supposedly depoliticised process of policy formulation generated what were perceived as ineffective policies and a lack of control over policy instruments.

Three more general conclusions spring from this analysis. First, this case study has illustrated that in the field of economic policy, there was a continued mixture of government and governance in Britain after the Second World War (Lowe and Rollings 2000). The war had revealed the abilities of the state and from then on new responsibilities were taken on. However, there was remarkably little reform of government to establish new institutions to cope with its extended responsibilities: the preference remained limited government, focusing on certain core activities, and the maintenance of a wider system of governance. In the late 1950s early 1960s, when it became clear that modernisation of government was necessary, it proved difficult to achieve and its success was limited.

Secondly, the study highlights the importance of understanding the policy process, and the institutional arrangements which underpin it. It is common to blame government for poor economic performance. However, simplistic notions of governmental failure ignore the complex nature of the policy process and the interdependencies which exist both within Whitehall and with other economic actors. The policy process itself is an important factor in the formulation of policy and has a bearing on the effectiveness of policy.

Thirdly, 'depoliticisation' has a long history in economic policy-making. For much of this century the Treasury has been reluctant to take overt and positive responsibility for policy and where it has had responsibility it has tried to present policy formulation as technical rather than political (Lowe and Rollings 2000). However, once it became widely perceived after the Second World War that government was responsible for the state of the economy, this position became increasingly fragile. The Treasury remained reluctant to take overt responsibility but was increasingly being criticised and blamed from the late 1950s for the state of the economy (Balogh 1959). From this sprang demands for the reform of government, first in the form of the National Economic Development Council (Ringe and Rollings forthcoming), and secondly with the establishment of the

Department of Economic Affairs by the new Labour government in 1964. Neither of these achieved as much as had been originally intended but both challenged the Treasury's position. Returning to our starting point of Gordon Brown's decision to 'depoliticise' the setting of monetary policy: ironically, the result of this move was that political criticism was deflected away from the government and the political spotlight turned on to the Bank. Political pressure has been put on the Bank to act, as in the recent case of job losses in industry that were attributed to the strong pound (*The Guardian* 1998: 24). The actions of the Bank of England have, in this sense, become more politicised.

Notes

1. The research for this chapter was carried out with the support of the ESRC Whitehall Programme 'From Anderson to Fulton: Policy-making in Whitehall 1942–66'.
2. PRO, T 233/1205, 'The relationship between the Treasury and the Bank of England', 1955; T 230/711, 'Talks on the Treasury, 2. The Finance Group, by Sir Dennis Rickett, Relations with the Bank', 1962; T 233/1202, 'Note for the record, bank rate change, 19 September, 1957', 18 Nov. 1957.
3. PRO T 233/1206, Extract from the Proceedings of the Parker Tribunal in relation to the Governor of the Bank of England. Annex, Statement by the Governor of the Bank of England, 16 Dec. 1957; T 233/1203, Harold Kent to Sir Edmund Compton, 31 Jan. 1958.
4. BOE G 15/9, C. F. Cobbold to Lord Radcliffe, 20 Jan. 1958.
5. BOE C40/689, David Robarts, Committee of London Clearing Bankers to Cobbold, 28 July 1955.
6. BOE C40/689, L. K. O'Brien to Sir Kenneth Peppiatt and the Deputy Governor, 23 Nov. 1955; PRO T 230/471, Robert Hall, 'Draft: Inquiry into monetary mechanism', 9 Apr. 1956.
7. PRO T 233/1665, 'Draft note on methods of reducing the quantity of bank credit and bank advances', 2 Aug. 1955; T 230/471, Hall, 'Draft: Inquiry into monetary mechanism', 9 Apr. 1956.
8. PRO T 230/472, Nigel Birch to Thorneycroft, 30 Jan. 1957; T230/472, Hall to Sir Roger Makins, 'Monetary Policy', 31 Jan. 1957; T 230/472, Makins, 'Record of Conversation: Credit Control', 8 Mar. 1957; T 233/1669, E. W. M to Thorneycroft, 12 Mar. 1957.
9. BOE C 40/694, Thorneycroft to Cobbold, 19 Mar. 1957; C 40/695, Cobbold to Thorneycroft, 4 Apr. 1957.
10. PRO T 233/1664, R. J. B. Anderson to William Armstrong, 5 Sept. 1957.
11. PRO T 233/1665, 'Draft note on methods of reducing the quantity of bank credit and bank advances', 2 Aug. 1955; BOE C 40/690, Draft letter to Sir Herbert Brittain, 18 Jan. 1956.
12. BOE C 40/691, O'Brien to Peppiatt, 'Monetary prospects 1956/57', 5 June 1956.
13. PRO T 233/1668, Edward Bridges to Petch, 'Monetary policy', 29 June 1956.
14. Ibid.
15. PRO T 233/2122, Birch to Thorneycroft, 7 Oct. 1957.
16. Ibid.
17. BOE G 15/8, Thorneycroft to Cobbold, 14 Oct. 1957; C 40/704, 'Plan of action', 25 Nov. 1957; PRO T 233/1670, E. G. Compton to Sir Thomas Padmore, 'Interest rates, funding and Exchequer lending policy', 31 Dec. 1957.
18. BOE G 15/8, 'Informal committee of Treasury records', 6 Feb. 1957; PRO T 233/1686, 'Note of meeting with deputation led by Sir R. Boothby, Annexes A and B, 20 Mar. 1956.

19. PRO T 233/1686, Makins to Thorneycroft, 2 Feb. 1957, Makins to Thorneycroft, 7 Feb. 1957, and Makins, 'Monetary enquiry', 22 Feb. 1957.
20. Ibid., Makins, 'Draft', 5 Feb. 1957.
21. Ibid., Hall to Makins, 'Monetary enquiry, terms of reference', 19 Jan 1957.
22. PRO T 233/1686, 'Monetary enquiry', 1 Mar. 1957.
23. BOE C40/897, Compton, 'Operations in 1956/57', 6 Mar. 1957.
24. BOE G15/9, Mynors to Cobbold, 31 July 1959.
25. BOE G 15/9, Cobbold to Mynors, 5 Aug.
26. Ibid., Governor's Note, 'Radcliffe', 7 Aug. 1959.
27. Ibid., O. E. N. to Cobbold, 4 Aug. 1959.
28. Ibid., Cobbold to Makins, 'Informal note of initial reaction to Radcliffe report', 17 Aug. 1959.
29. Ibid., Mynors, 'Governor's note', 21 Aug. 1959.
30. Ibid., Treasury, 'Radcliffe Committee, The relations between the Treasury and the Bank of England', 18 Sept. 1959.
31. Ibid.
32. Ibid., Mynors, 'Radcliffe Committee', 21 Oct. 1959; PRO PREM 11/2668, Heathcoat Amory to Macmillan, 27 Oct. 1959 and Annex.
33. BOE G15/9: 29 October, 1959, 'Informal record of a discussion by the Court of Directors' 29 Oct. 1959, and 'Informal record of the Governor's statement to the Court of Directors held on 19th November, 1959', 19 Nov. 1959.
34. PRO PREM 11/2668, Heathcoat Amory to Macmillan, 27 Oct. 1959 and Annex.
35. PRO T 230/474, A. S. Mackintosh, 'Special deposits', 14 Jan. 1960; BOE C 40/705, Mynors to Sir Cyril Hawker, 'Special Deposits', 8 Jan. 1960.
36. PRO T 230/512, Treasury, 'Credit control', 27 May 1960; T230/561, A. S. Mackintosh, 'Special deposits', 8 Sept. 1960, William Armstrong to Padmore, 'Special deposits: the Prime Minister's Minutes of 1st and 13th August', 14 Sept. 1960, and Hall to Sir Frank Lee, 'Special deposits', 20 Sept. 1960.
37. PRO T 230/512, Treasury, 'Credit control', 27 May 1960.

8
The Organisation of Central Government Departments: a History, 1964-92*

Iain McLean, Chris Clifford and Alistair McMillan

Introduction

Our project was essentially descriptive, not evaluative. The original invitation to tender made it clear that, in the words of Mr Gradgrind, 'What we want is FACTS'. Having received strong signals that we should eschew theory, we did so. We saw our role as providing the data to enable others to formulate and test theories about the growth or shrinkage of government, its size, shape and direction.

In this chapter we describe how our data were collected and how to access them. We discuss strengths and limitations of the data – where they may help to test theories of government growth and shrinkage, and where they may be misleading. Although it was no part of our purpose to discuss even whether central government has grown or shrunk, let alone why, we proceed to some very tentative remarks about trends in growth and shrinkage.

How our data were collected

The Machinery of Government and Standards Group of the Cabinet Office, who had found that their own records of machinery of government changes since 1964 were incomplete, provided principal funding for the project. Intermediate users, including the Public Record Office (PRO) (and its Scottish and Northern Irish equivalents, SRO and PRONI), and end users, such as readers at the three record offices, need an easily accessible record of ministerial responsibilities and internal structure of ministries and agencies. When we started, no such record had been maintained since Chester and Willson (1968). Andrew McDonald from the Public Records Office, whose help was invaluable, put it pithily in a lecture to beginning graduate students in politics in 1996: 'You may not be interested in the structure of government departments in its own right – indeed, I hope that

* We would like to acknowledge the ESRC for funding our research as part of its Whitehall Programme (award number: L124251054).

most of you are not – but knowing about the structure of a department is a prerequisite for work on the department's records'.

The aim of the project, as we originally stated it, was 'to produce a reliable and readable description of changes in function by department'. We began by setting up two pilot studies, one on trade and industry and the other on Scotland. The pilot studies were designed to evaluate the usefulness of possible data sources. We visited the Departmental Record Officers (DROs) of various departments at this stage. The Scottish Record Office would have liked us to take forward their incomplete guide to their holdings, and so would we. But there were only three of us and we were only funded for two years, so we had to cut our ambitions to fit our resources.

The pilots resulted in the decision to restrict information sources to printed material. This was for two reasons. Material held by DROs was not of an even quality or coverage; and we had no direct access to records not yet in the public domain. Although the Cabinet Office had kindly arranged for access to its machinery of government files through an intermediary who had the requisite security clearance, it was impractical for us to give him clear instruction for what to search for, nor for him to know in advance what we would like to find if we knew it was there. In any case, the pilots also showed that the sheer volume of data precluded an approach based on unpublished documents.

We limited our researches therefore to the primary and secondary printed sources listed in Appendix 8.1 (see page 154). These documents were assembled with the kind assistance of various librarians and archivists. We talked to The Australian Archives (AA – the equivalent Australian Federal Department to the PRO), because we admired the idea of their Thesaurus of Government Functions. We envisaged trying to draw up such a thesaurus for British government functions. However, AA staff told us that it had proved too laborious for them to keep up. We therefore decided to concentrate our efforts on making our database searchable on strings of characters defined by the user, while putting warnings about difficult and confusing departmental titles ('Chancellor of the Duchy of Lancaster', 'Paymaster-General', the generic title of 'Secretary of State') in our introductory literature.

Defining the outer boundary and unit of analysis

We were persuaded by Hood *et al.*'s (1978) classic paper, 'So you think you know what a government department is' that any attempt to draw our outer boundary by constitutional or statutory criteria would be doomed to failure. The first step for us was therefore to define the outer boundaries of the project and the most detailed unit of analysis. We started with a number of the classifications of 'central government' in the literature, such as this one from Dunleavy (1989: 289):

(i)   ministerial and non-ministerial Whitehall departments;
(ii) agencies directly controlled by ministers, staffed by civil servants, yet not counted as ministries;
(iii) agencies staffed by civil servants but not directly controlled by ministers;

(iv) agencies directly controlled by ministers but not staffed by civil servants;
(v) agencies neither directly controlled by ministers nor staffed by civil servants.

We speedily found that no extant scheme, including this one, that put 'central government' into such mutually exclusive and jointly exhaustive boxes, actually worked: the real pattern was too messy to fit any such scheme. Why this is so, we explain below.

As our database is intended for use by the public record offices and their readers, we had to consider seriously drawing our outer ring around the set of bodies that are required to deposit their records under the terms of the Public Records Act 1958. With regret, we had to discard this idea for practical reasons. There are central government bodies that fall outside the defined set and non-central-government bodies that fall inside. Examples of the first are the Scottish and Northern Ireland departments, which are not covered by the 1958 Act. Examples of the second are bodies that have been privatised, where the act imposes an unrepealed but unenforceable obligation for their records to remain as public records. (An interesting example is the National Coal Board. For the 1960s, their record classes, including the highly confidential papers of the chairman's private office, are now in the public domain – see in particular class COAL 73 at the PRO. We have used them in the research on the 1966 Aberfan disaster that spun off from this project – see McLean 1997 and our web site (http://www.nuff.ox.ac.uk/politics/aberfan/home.htm). It is hard to imagine that researchers in the 2010s will have equally unfettered access to the archives of the publically owned British Coal, let alone to those of its successor, the privately owned RJB Mining plc.)

We therefore fell back on the tautological principle that CENTRAL GOVERNMENT IS WHAT THE CENTRAL GOVERNMENT SAYS IT IS. Even this does not close the matter, for the source documents tabulated in Appendix 8.1 do not always agree on what ministerial departments exist in a given year. Not all the discrepancies can be removed by discarding non-executive sources (such as the Ombudsman and Hansard) from the list. For non-departmental public bodies (NDPBs), as might be expected, the situation is even less clear: it seems to be up to departments, paradoxically, to decide which non-departmental bodies to put on official lists. As nothing seems to give one of the official lists more authority than the others, we took one set for which there is an unbroken annual series – The *British Imperial Calendar* and Civil Service List and its successor *The Civil Service Year Book* – as the master set, and collated it with our other sources as we went along. The fact that the *Civil Service Year Book* is produced for a purely practical purpose – that of enabling civil servants to locate and contact one another – increases its evidentiary value.

We also had to decide to what level of detail we were able to go. This was likewise a purely practical decision. We knew how much staff time we had available and were able to project from our pilot studies how long it would take for organisations to be entered at each possible level of detail. Organisation charts sometimes show hierarchies within departments and agencies (this was especially the case in our more modern sources), but the only source available throughout our period is that provided by the layout and typography of the *Civil Service Year Book*. Although we realise that this is arbitrary, it enabled us to classify units as 'top', 'second', 'third' and 'fourth' level. We started by entering data on levels down to the fourth. After doing so for around a month, we established that we would not have time to cover the entire civil service at this level of detail, and therefore restricted ourselves to the top three hierarchical levels of each organisation covered thereafter. However, we retained the fourth-level data for those agencies for which we had collected it.

The data are accessible in two forms: through the database interface and through a web interface. Both can be reached at the following URL (http://www.nuff.ox.ac.uk/politics/whitehall/index.html). A paper version is also available (Clifford, McMillan and McLean 1998). These are merely different methods of accessing the information that is contained in the underlying tables that make up the database.

The database has been structured to conform to basic principles of database design. At its heart is a searchable version of the *British Imperial Calendar/Civil Service Year Book*, giving details of ministers, government departments and departmental structure. Other information (details of statutory instruments, lists of ministerial responsibilities, historical descriptions from the public record offices, details of functional changes, etc.) has been tied in with this to produce what we hope is an informative, complete, and consistent account of government changes between 1964 and 1992. However, we could not transcend the limitations of our sources. The historical descriptions of government functions and departments provided by the public record offices were incomplete and tended to be out of date. This was partly due to different approaches from the different bodies involved. When we started, the PRO in Northern Ireland had no information on departmental histories (for the current position see http://proni.nics.gov.uk/records/records.htm and http://proni.nics.gov.uk/records/records.htm). The Scottish Record Office (which in January 1999 changed its name to National Archives of Scotland) had only some MS drafts drawn up in the mid-1970s.

All three record offices are geared towards the organisation of records dealing with events 30 years ago. The PRO at Kew, who have the most complete and useful records, are currently restructuring their organisation of records, and changing the format of the PRO Guide which includes histories of government departments. As the PRO develop their on-line version of the Guide, it may become possible to either link the two data sets, or have some method of co-ordination so that our records of PRO histories can be updated as necessary.

The variety of government organisations

Everybody who writes on this subject has felt the need to classify government organisations. Most have looked at structures; some at functions. Some however (for example, Wilding 1982; Hogwood 1995) have doubted the very possibility of developing a classification system for British governmental organisations. We think they are right. This section tries to explain why.

The words 'classification scheme', 'taxonomy', and 'typology' are often (incorrectly) used interchangeably (Carper and Stalker 1980). Doty and Glick (1994: 232) offer a distinction. Classification schemes or taxonomies 'categorize phenomena into mutually exclusive and exhaustive sets with a series of discrete decision rules', whereas typologies 'identify multiple ideal types, each of which represents a unique combination of the organizational attributes that are believed to determine the relevant outcome(s)'. Taxonomies are therefore more useful than typologies. Can we get a taxonomy of UK government organisations?

A useful starting point is Chester's (1953) distinction between 'ministerial departments', 'local authorities' and the 'rest'. He defines a ministerial department as 'a Minister of the Crown to whom powers have been given either explicitly by name of his office or in the name of a body which by convention or declaration is clearly understood to mean that Minister' (so that, for this purpose, a Minister is his/her department). A local authority is defined as 'a council with its powers and duties confined to a local area and elected by the electors of that area'. Chester's residual formula is: 'any governmental administrative body which has its own statutory powers and responsibilities and is neither a Minister nor a local authority is part of the "rest". It does not matter if this includes a number of bodies which are in practice completely or very nearly subordinate branches of a ministerial department'.

Local authorities, in terms of structure, are relatively uncontroversial. But even they give rise to a taxonomic problem. From their very name, they are not part of central government. Therefore, a function transferred to local authorities is transferred from the central state. It is not transferred from 'the state' – at least in Marxist, and some non-Marxist, definitions of that term. During our study period, especially the last ten years of it, there was a trend towards reducing the financial and legal independence of local government, sometimes even while transferring functions to it. A researcher into (for instance) the 'hollowing out of the state' will come to fundamentally different conclusions if he or she treats local authorities as part of the state than if he or she does not.

Chester's first and third categories, then, are inherently controversial.

Ministerial departments

The search for a definition of a government department in the British system of government is an elusive and difficult one (Hood, Dunsire and Thompson 1978). Yet at the same time departments remain a focus for research (Smith, Marsh and Richards 1993). Hood and Dunsire (1981) looked unsuccessfully – on their own admission – for determinants which governed the pattern of departments. They drew attention to the lack of any single definition of a 'central government agency' in Britain for use as a basic unit of analysis.

The total number of departments at any one time differed according to which listings were consulted. Various listings gave different results. Different institutional definitions of government departments, as listed in *The Civil Service Year Book*, are given in Appendix 8.2 (see page 154).

Hood and his colleagues drew up a typology (not a taxonomy). They distinguished between five-, four- and three-star departments on the basis that five-star departments appeared on all listings, while three-star departments appeared on only a few or one. Jordan has come up with a different scheme based on ministerial control and ministerial rank (Jordan 1995: 15–26):

- Five-star departments: departments headed by a Secretary of State, or called, 'Cabinet-Minister-led departments'. The two might not necessarily be coterminous however. The Minister of Agriculture, although of Cabinet-rank, is not a Secretary of State.
- Second division or non-Cabinet-headed departments: departments not headed by Cabinet-rank but junior ministers, e.g. Law Officer's Department, Overseas Development Administration, Paymaster General's Office.
- Bureaucratic-led departments: certain bodies listed as departments are headed by bureaucrats and some have a specified relationship to the Secretary of State. The Board of Inland Revenue in this respect 'advised the Chancellor of the Exchequer on policy questions'.

Jordan stresses that 'the list of components (in the scheme) changes from year to year as the margins are drawn to suit a sort of common-sense demand that the Cabinet be not larger than 22 rather than the fact that there are real differences between smaller, lower profile, departments and those of Cabinet status' (Jordan 1995: 24). He draws attention to the blurred boundary between those organisations defined as departments and those listed in the *Civil Service Year Book* as 'other organisations'. The Advisory Conciliation and Arbitration Service, for instance, is counted as an 'other organisation', yet it is staffed by civil servants. This particular example draws attention to the difficulties in defining what the outer boundaries are of 'central government' itself. For instance, Dunleavy's scheme (see above) excludes all quasi-non-governmental organisations as he defines them, all agencies being 'fully public sector bodies, constituted by legislation or orders in council, funded by the Exchequer, and subject to some measure of direct parliamentary and ministerial control'.

The concept of 'families' has recently been introduced into the vocabulary of Public Administration as a more useful unit of analysis (Hogwood 1995: 513). 'Families' have their focus on main departments headed by ministers and include the following:

- Non-ministerial departments reporting to ministers, but for which ministers normally did not and do not have responsibility for detailed operational matters.
- Associated executive non-departmental public bodies.
- Other statutory bodies carrying out policy delivery.
- Other bodies carrying out statutory or other functions not recognised by government as public bodies, but functionally acting as though they were.

Hogwood identifies a range of 'family types', differentiated by the extent to which the core of the ministerial department is surrounded by executive agencies that were previously non-ministerial departments or not, or non-departmental public bodies. The range of permutations include:

- simple core-agency families;
- families with cores but also other organisations;
- families with few staff in agencies in the main department;
- families with residues larger than core functions and with complex structures;
- families with large organisations outside the civil service; and
- federal families;
- non-departmental public bodies.

Bodies in this last category have been variously named: 'non-departmental organisation, non-departmental agency, public body, interstitial organisation, *ad hoc* agency, statutory authority, paragovernmental agency, parastatal agency, fringe body and intermediate body' to name but a selection of the possibilities (Hogwood 1995: 208). Numerous typologies exist in this area. Friedmann distinguished between three groupings (Friedmann 1951):

(i)   commercial operations 'designed to run an industry or public utility according to economic and commercial principles ...';
(ii) social service corporations 'designed to carry out a particular social service on behalf of the Government';
(iii) supervisory public corporations having 'essentially administrative and supervisory functions'. They do not engage in commercial transactions either to fulfil their main objective or incidentally to the performance of a social service.

The above types were later given the titles of 'managerial-economic', 'managerial-social', and 'regulatory-social' bodies (Street and Griffith 1952: 271–275). Greaves proposed four types of bodies: 'regional', e.g. the many Port Authorities; 'quasi-judicial', e.g. the Civil Service Commission, the Import Duties Advisory Committee, and the Electricity Commission; 'trusteeship' bodies (for the management of property on behalf of others), e.g. the Charity Commissioners; and 'administrative or managerial' (of a national service), e.g. the National Coal Board (Greaves 1947: 104ff). A later attempt by Hague, Mackenzie and Barker was made to distinguish between 'governmental', 'quasi-governmental', 'quasi-non-governmental', and 'non-governmental' organisations (Hague, Mackenzie and Barker 1975). The result and practical usefulness of this typology was limited. Significant problems existed in delimiting their categories. Anthony Barker, one of those who claim to have originated the term 'quango', later called it 'overused and uselessly vague'. (A glance at the OED will show that the earliest uses found are American; and that it is quite unclear whether the acronym stands for quasi non-government(al) organisation or for quasi-autonomous national government organisation.) Many 'fringe' bodies are far from being 'non-governmental'.

Official attempts to classify bodies in this category began with Gordon Bowen's survey commissioned by the Civil Service Department in 1978. The survey was based upon a questionnaire circulated to departments. Departments were left to decide what constituted a fringe body. This self-reporting was criticised for being a haphazard approach to the subject (Chester 1979). Bowen excluded bodies such as nationalised industries, tribunals, judicial and quasi-judicial bodies, and also those bodies responsible for health services which shared many of the characteristics of other fringe bodies studied. Bowen listed seven characteristics that were found in the bodies he surveyed:

1. set up by Act of Parliament;
2. non-Crown;
3. financed by grants-in-aid;
4. chairman appointed by a minister;
5. staff are non-civil servants, recruited and employed by the board or council of a fringe body;
6. annual accounts submitted to the sponsoring minister and laid before parliament;
7. annual report published.

Out of 252 bodies surveyed, only 33 displayed all seven characteristics listed above.

Sir Leo Pliatzky (1980) suggested the term 'non-departmental public body'. He distinguished between 'executive bodies', 'advisory bodies', 'tribunals' and 'other bodies'. Pliatzky excluded from his study nationalised industries, some other public corporations, and NHS bodies. He recognised the difficulties associated with producing a robust typology of fringe bodies due to there being 'no legal definitions to determine what should go in these lists or into some other category'. He identified 489 executive bodies, 1561 advisory bodies and 67 tribunal systems – reflecting the arbitrary nature of systems of classification.

Official classifications of 'fringe' bodies differ. *Public Bodies 1995* follows Pliatzky's distinction between executive bodies, advisory bodies, tribunals and other bodies while including details of nationalised industries and other commercial organisations, certain public corporations and NHS bodies. This annual publication provides a working definition of a non-departmental public body (the preferred term, which we use): 'an NDPB is a body which has a role in the processes of national government, but is not a government department or part of one, and which accordingly operates to a greater or lesser extent at arm's length from Ministers'. Yet at the same time, the government's own advice to departments on NDPBs separates out Royal Commissions under a separate heading (Cabinet Office undated). This document reflects the difficulty in establishing any agreed criteria upon which to classify individual bodies. In describing the creation of NDPBs, the guide hesitates in making anything other than generalisations:

- Advisory bodies are normally set up by administrative action;
- Royal Commissions are set up under a Royal Warrant under the auspices of the relevant Secretary of State;
- Tribunals are set up by statute, usually in the context of a wider legal framework establishing citizens' rights and obligations;
- Executive, etc. bodies are usually legally incorporated by one of the following:
  (a) legislation;
  (b) Royal Charter;
  (c) registration under the Companies Act.

In our study period, the last of these has been the commonest. It is now severely unclear what a Royal Charter is for, nor what it protects the body from. Not dissolution, as the fate of the Royal Institution of Public Administration shows.

Executive agencies

Executive agencies have, with some exceptions, been formed from activities carried out by ministerial and non-ministerial Whitehall departments. Most agencies remain legally part of the parent ministerial department. (The Royal Mint, which was an institutionally-defined department in its own right prior to receiving agency status, is an exception). However, many now exist as entities with trading funds in their own right; many have delegated powers in the areas of personnel management; thus they have developed organisational identities of their own. The setting up of executive agencies – colloquially known as 'Next Steps' agencies after the title of the report that proposed the model – has created another set of analytical and classification problems. Hogwood (1993: 5–9) differentiates them in terms of the following eight criteria, noting that in terms of organisational origins, some were previously departments in their own right, some were separate units within departments, some were made up of units from two separate departments, some already had trading fund status, and some had previously been non-departmental bodies.

1. staff numbers;
2. status of chief executive and nature of appointment;
3. organisational origins;
4. funding; gross-cost, net-cost or trading fund regimes;
5. staffing: whether they employ non-industrial or industrial civil servants, or both, or neither;
6. existence of boards;
7. monopoly status;
8. single or multiple function and task.

He does not, however, attempt to produce a system of classification.

The Fraser Report attempted to classify executive agencies primarily according to the role and functions they carried out (Efficiency Unit 1991). It distinguished among:

1. mainstream agencies: which are fundamental to the main policy orientation of the parent department, e.g. the Employment Service;
2. regulatory and statutory agencies: execute statutory functions derived from the main aims of the parent department, e.g. Vehicle Inspectorate;
3. specialist service agencies: providing services to departments and other executive agencies, e.g. Information Technology Services Agency;
4. peripheral agencies: not linked to the main aims of a department but report to a minister, e.g. HMSO (as it then was).

Greer (1992) tried to differentiate between agencies on the basis of:

1. financial regime: whether the agencies were self-financing or not; and
2. market share: whether the agencies were monopoly providers.

In his research on bureau-shaping models of bureaucratic behaviour, Dunleavy (1985, 1989) identified five main types of bureaux and three additional categories, related to particular configuration of bureaux budgets. In this sense, there is a relationship between structure (the bureau's budget) and function. Dunleavy's scheme, like the others reviewed so far, is a typology, not a taxonomy. The main types of agency identified are: delivery; regulatory; transfer; contracts; control; taxing; trading; and servicing.

Classifying by function

Government organisations carry out a range of activities, some derived from statutory powers, some not. The notion of a government function is imprecise. Less imprecise are legally defined powers defined by legislation or prerogative powers. Statutes confer powers on ministers individually and executive power is consequently fragmented. The machinery of government change often involves a reallocation of functions between government bodies. One element of this might be the reallocation of statutory powers. Functions and activities carried out by government are often derived from statute, although all governments engage in activities which are not directly related to any statutory provision. For instance, the promotion of Citizen's Charters by the Citizen's Charter Unit was not the product of legislative action. Nevertheless, it is a function or activity of government, which has the potential for transfer. Tracking statutory powers might, in theory at least, be practicable but for the lack of any documentary source which keeps a record of these movements. No publication indicates which statutory powers are allocated to each individual minister, either at a given point in time or over a particular period.

Perhaps the first systematic examination of machinery of government arrangements was made by Bentham in his Constitutional Code (1983 [1830]). Bentham distinguished between 13 ministers and sub-departments: (1) election; (2) legislation; (3) army; (4) navy; (5) preventive service; (6) interior communication; (7) indigence relief; (8) education; (9) domain; (10) health; (11) foreign relations; (12) trade; and (13) finance (Rosen 1983). The 1918 Haldane Inquiry was set up to 'enquire into the responsibilities of the various Departments of the central executive Government, and to advise in what manner the exercise and distribution by the Government of its functions should be improved' (Haldane 1918: 4). The committee went on to ask, 'Upon what principles are the functions of Departments to be determined and allocated?' (Haldane 1918: 7). The report considered both the principle of allocating functions according to the persons or classes to be dealt with and that of allocation according to the services to be performed. The report argued against the first of these on the basis that it would be difficult to limit the number of individual departments that would be needed to cover all possibilities. Haldane favoured the second principle and put forward a scheme along these lines. The report did acknowledge, however, that the drawing of clearly delineated lines around a department's activities was in practice an impossible task such was the need for 'co-operation between Departments in dealing with business of common interest' (Haldane 1918: 16). The report nevertheless proposed ten main divisions:

I	Finance;
II and III	National Defence and External Affairs;
IV	Research and Information;
V	Production (including Agriculture, Forestry, and Fisheries), Transport and Commerce;
VI	Employment;
VII	Supplies;
VIII	Education;
IX	Health;
X	Justice.

Haldane's ten divisions, however, were merely the arbitrary divisions of government as it appeared, in 1918, to an acute civil servant. They were retained by Chester and Willson (1968), but they have no particular authority now in conditions vastly different to those of 1918.

A later, American, attempt (Gulick 1937), suggested the four basic criteria: purposes; processes employed; clientele served; and area served. Gulick's examples are:

- Purpose: such as furnishing water, controlling crime, or conducting education;
- Process: such as engineering, medicine, carpentry, stenography, statistics, accounting;

- Persons dealt with or served: such as immigrants, veterans, Indians, forests, mines, parks, orphans, farmers, automobiles, or the poor;
- Place where service is rendered: such as Hawaii, Boston, Washington, the Dust Bowl, Alabama, or Central High School.

This apparently neat typology provoked Simon (1947: 28) to say:

> this principle is internally inconsistent; for purpose, process, clientele, and place are competing bases of organization, and at any given point of division the advantages of three must be sacrificed to secure the advantages of the fourth.

Hogwood (1992: 65–167) uses Gulick's classification.

There is currently no UK government ministry or department organised according to the principle of process. Client group organisation was used, for example, in the creation of the Ministry of Pensions and some others proposed (e.g. a Ministry for Women).[1] The territorial principle is used for the Scottish, Welsh and Northern Ireland Offices. However, within these, functions are allocated according to other principles in the departmental subdivisions. The allocation of activities according to broad purpose or function served is more common. Nevertheless, as Hogwood points out (1992: 166):

> activities of government are very numerous and varied. They do not all fall into convenient groupings. Even when there are a number of groups of functions which seem to be related, it is not always clear whether these should be the responsibility of a number of small departments or a single large one. Further, the concept of function has inadequacies as a description of how policy responsibilities are in fact allocated and also in the way in which the term is sometimes used in discussions about proposed changes in responsibility.

The Australian Archives (AA) already mentioned developed a Thesaurus of Functions and attempted to classify the federal records for which they are responsible by function. But they found it very hard to pin down functions, either in practice or in theory. Agencies' statements tended to be less than useful, as in this example:

> The Department of ... has the objective of developing as a responsive, responsible, effective and efficient organisation implementing Government policy for maximising long-term economic development for Victoria through ... in ways that are consistent with sustainable and efficient use of resources and equitably meeting the priority needs of Victorians in ... . (Victorian Government Directory 1989)

Replacing the word 'agriculture' with the three ellipses makes the statement totally meaningless. By April 1996, the AA had decided to stop trying to maintain a thesaurus of functions.

Biology

Organisation charts look like trees: not merely (a little bit) like real trees on their sides or upside-down, but (much more) like the family trees drawn by biologists which give a taxonomy for every organism from those of the primeval soup to *Homo sapiens*, or of any subset of the set of living and fossil organisms. There are important similarities between a taxonomy of organisms and one of organisations. But there are even more important differences. Unless we fully understand the differences, we may be distracted into a search for 'One right answer'. One right answer exists in biology, but not in human organisations.

From Aristotle through Linnaeus until the mid-twentieth-century, biological taxonomy was indeed closer to the operation we are trying to do than it is now. Animals or plants could be classified by either their structure (i.e. their morphology); their function; or their descent. A new species would be recognised when it was established that its members could no longer interbreed with those of an existing species.

Taxonomical schools fell into two main groups – those interested in a sense of lineage and evolution between organisms, and those that conducted their taxonomy without reference to evolutionary processes. Dawkins (1986: Ch. 11) labels these the 'phyleticists' and 'pure-resemblance measurers'. Until recently, there was always room for doubt. Should the Tasmanian marsupial wolf be classified (by structure and function) along with other wolves, or (by descent) separately? Gradually, the idea of classification by descent came to dominate other ideas. However, only since the marriage of Mendelian genetics to Darwinism – arranged by R. A. Fisher and a few other mathematical biologists in the 1930s – has the outline of the One Right Answer become completely clear, and only since the revolution in genetics since 1953 could the detail be filled in. Only in 1998 has a complete reclassification of plants, which in effect overthrows the Linnaean categories and substitutes genetically-derived ones, been made.

Since 1953, the decoding of DNA has enabled geneticists to read the protein sequence coded by the DNA of any organism. The four-character language of DNA codes for amino acids, which are the building blocks of the proteins which determine the function of each cell. Mutations in the coding regions produce variations. Most of these variations are fatal; many are neutral; a few are beneficial. Natural selection ensures that only the latter two variation types survive to be propagated. If they find an evolutionary niche, they may persist to generate a new species.

The genome of any organism also contains long strings of DNA sequence that do not seem to 'mean' anything – i. e. which do not code for amino acids. Mutations in these non-coding regions usually have no effect on the appearance or functioning of the organism. However, they do constitute a biological clock. Once the clock has been calibrated by estimating the frequency of these presumptively neutral mutations, the similarity or difference of any pair of organisms can be calculated by comparing their DNA. Therefore, in principle, an evolutionary tree for any set of organisms can be composed on the simple principle that the more similar their DNA, the more recent was their last common ancestor. *Homo sapiens* and chimpanzees share 99.5 per cent of their genetic code; the time elapsed since their most recent common ancestor is much shorter than the time from that point back to the earlier divergence of the chimpanzees from other monkeys.

Although it involves stupendously laborious calculations which only the most recent generation of computing power makes feasible, it is relatively easy in principle to construct the most probable family tree for any set of organisms in this manner. For 3 organisms, there are 3 such trees. The number of trees increases very rapidly. For 20 organisms, there are 8 × 1021 possible evolutionary trees, all but one of them wrong, one correct (Dawkins 1986: 273).

Human organisations

A consequence of the new genetic taxonomy is that there is what Dawkins (1986: 259) calls 'perfect nesting'. Dawkins captures the essential difference between biological and social taxonomy:

> We write the names of any set of animals on a large sheet of paper and draw rings round related sets. For example, rat and mouse would be united in a small ring indicating that they are close cousins, with a recent common ancestor. ... The rat/mouse ring and the guinea-pig/capybara ring would, in turn, be united with each other ... in a larger ring labelled with its own name, rodents. Inner rings are said to be 'nested' inside larger, outer, rings. ... Cats, dogs, weasels, bears, etc., would all be united, in a series of rings within rings, in a single large ring labelled carnivores. ... The important thing about this system of rings within rings is that it is perfectly nested. Never, not on a single solitary occasion, will the rings we draw intersect each other. ... This property of perfect taxonomic nesting is not exhibited by books, languages, soil types, or schools of thought in philosophy. If a librarian draws a ring round the biology books and another ring round the theology books, he will find that the two rings overlap. In the zone of overlap are books with titles like 'Biology and Christian Belief'. (Dawkins 1986: 259)

Hood and Dunsire's *Bureaumetrics* (1981) attempted something similar to the phenetocists' complex methods for producing indices of resemblance, measuring government departments along a number of dimensions, coming up with a range of different 'faces' as a pictorial representation. But there does not seem to be any sense of clusters of organisations with similar overall characteristics. None of the attempts to classify government departments, either by structure or by function, that we have listed above, has any more intellectual authority than any other. Thus our arbitrary decisions, described above, are no more arbitrary than anyone else's.

Trends since 1964

Departments, like their ministers, come and go according to fad and fashion. Machinery of government (MG) 'innovation' has often had a strong sense of déja vu about it. The Department of International Development (1997) has machinery of government antecedents in similar departments created by two previous Labour administrations (the first created in November 1964, the second in August 1974 when Labour resumed power). The Department of the Environment, Transport and the Regions (DETR) is a recreation in part of the 1970 Department of the Environment (DOE) with combined transport responsibilities. The DOE in turn was created in October 1970 with the combined functions of the Ministry of Housing, Ministry of Transport, Ministry of Public Building and Works, and the functions of the Secretary of State for Local Government and Regional Planning. It lost its transport functions to the newly created Department of Transport in November 1976. Labour's current concern to strengthen the Cabinet Office mirrors the debates within the Conservative Party in the late 1960s on how to create a 'central capability'. Titular changes, mergers and demergers may not necessarily imply changes, however, in the scale and scope of their programmes. Programme change can occur in the absence of organisational change (Davies and Rose 1988). Hood, Huby and Dunsire (1985) found that reorganisational changes have little obvious effect on bureaucratic structure and working and that these organisational changes produce neither economies or diseconomies.

While at a departmental level the pattern of ministerial departments remained largely unchanged, a number of significant trends are observable at a sub-departmental level.

Hiving-off

In the late 1960s, the Conservative Party's Public Sector Research Unit and the Fulton Report both examined the feasibility and desirability of creating 'agencies' from existing departmental structures. The Conservatives on the whole saw hiving-off as indicating large-scale divestment of state activities. In the parliamentary debate on the Fulton Report, David Howell, then a member of the Conservatives' Public Sector Research Unit (PSRU) made a far-sighted speech claiming that: 'technical necessity will force Governments in the coming decade and in the 1980s into divesting themselves of a vast range of activities and decentralising responsibility' (*Hansard* 21 November 1968, col. 1635). 'Hiving-off' for Howell was to be a logical consequence of the introduction of a form of programme budgeting into British public administration.

The Fulton investigation into the civil service drew analogies with the Swedish form of government agencies that had existed for several hundred years. Fulton's Management Consultants' report, however, drew heavily on ideas of accountable management and management by objectives which were in vogue amongst American management thinkers. An early list of 'agency' candidates was included in the PSRU's 'Black Book' (a grey dossier in fact) (CRD 3/13/8). Early examples of hiving-off included the Property Services Agency, the Defence

Procurement Executive and the Employment Service Agency. A full list is given in Jordan (1976). By January 1976 departmental agencies accounted for over 23 per cent of total civil servants, numbering some 739,000. Jordan correctly notes, however, that this was in fact a process of 'hiving-in', in that it did not entail the same clear-cut distinction between responsibilities for policy and operational matters: 'it was thought impossible to reconcile real freedom and real political control and responsibility' (Jordan 1992: 20).

Nicholas Ridley argued in 1973 that:

> The first essential for tackling this problem is to separate the functions of policy making from administration. Granted that it is not always easy to draw the line between these two, there are in fact a whole mass of functions which can easily be classified as administrative; and hived off to be run by a public agency. Employment exchanges, the administration of the social services, regional and industrial grants, road building, Companies House, insurance control, prison management, are but a few of the many examples that could be given. Each of these functions should be separated from direct control by Whitehall, and set up as a separate agency with its own Chief Executive. The Chief Executive should operate with precise terms of reference, and be personally responsible for this agency's standard of efficiency, including any mistakes made by his subordinates. He should make periodic reports to Parliament. (Ridley 1973: 11–12)

Regionalisation

The discussion of physical dispersal processes dates from the 1930s, but actual action did not begin in any large way until the Second World War (Hammond 1967: 266; Cross 1970). Some of this wartime relocation was reversed so that by the 1960s, the Civil Service was still highly concentrated in London. The first significant waves of relocation occurred in the 1960s and 1970s (following the unpublished Fleming Report and published Hardman Report in 1973), with a slowing down in the early 1980s and speeding up again in the late 1980s. Between 1963 and 1973, 32 000 civil servants were planned for dispersal. The Hardman dispersal wave ground to a halt in the late 1970s with only 5000 jobs dispersed between 1979 and 1988. For Labour, the point was to revive regional economies by moving white-collar jobs there. For the Conservatives, the point was to reduce office costs. On the whole, however, the Conservative governments cut staff numbers rather than relocating existing employees. From 1987, significant dispersals included the Patent Office's move to Newport, Companies House head office's move to Cardiff, and significant head office functions of the Department of Health and Social Security moving to Leeds (see Jefferson and Trainor 1996; Marshall 1996; Marshall 1990; Marshall and Alderman 1991; Pardoe and Williamson 1979; Winkler 1990). An oddity of the Companies House move is that companies are officially described as 'registered in England', when they are actually registered in Wales.

Europeanisation

Since the UK joined the European Economic Community in 1973, government departments have developed sub-structures to deal with European policy, particularly those departments in mainstream European policy areas such as Ministry of Agriculture Fisheries and Food (MAFF), the Foreign and Commonwealth Office (FCO), and, increasingly since the passage of the Single European Act, the Department of Trade and Industry. Early entry negotiations were handled by the FCO and the Cabinet Office (Wallace 1973). Upon entry, the Cabinet Office created a European Secretariat to handle policy co-ordination across government departments (Dowding 1995: 129–52). Hennessy (1990: 405) speculates that Mrs Thatcher considered creating a European Affairs department, believing the FCO to be too Europhile.

Next steps agencies

Next Steps agencies have largely been created from sub-structures of government departments (Hogwood 1995; Hogwood 1993). (For exceptions such as the Royal Mint and HMSO, see above.) A number of these agencies have also taken on the legal status of Government Trading Funds.[2] The central idea was the separation of policy from operational management, well expressed by Nicholas Ridley in the passage quoted above. But the distinction cannot be easily drawn, particularly for agencies carrying out functions in sensitive areas such as social welfare and penal policy. For early scepticism, see Caulcott and Mountfield (1974: 53). Caulcott and Mountfield, civil servants interested in Fulton's hiving-off ideas, came back from a trip to Sweden 'satisfied that it could not simply be transplanted to British soil ... because all its elements lock so closely: the lack of direct ministerial responsibility, the limitation of parliamentary control, the personal legal responsibility of the civil servant, the separation of powers, the use of guidelines and control devices, plural sources of advice and the "openness"'.

Connoisseurs will relish the inverted commas round 'openness'. Mayne (1990) predicted that in a crisis, 'political control' would be ceded to the minister. In reality there have been temptations for ministers to abdicate responsibility rather than take control (Barker 1998; Cooper 1995; Talbot 1996; Dudley 1994; Lewis 1997). Chief executives were to be held accountable for the performance of their executive agency and were meant to have full responsibility for its operational control. Operational control meant a variety of financial and personnel management freedoms, as well as freedom to determine service delivery. Financial freedoms were enhanced in a number of cases by the granting of Trading Fund status to a small number of agencies.

Privatisation and regulation

Privatisation of central government departments is relatively recent. At the time of Next Steps, some commentators speculated that executive agencies were created simply as a first step towards the privatisation of portions of Civil Service activities. Early pre-agency privatisations included the sale of the state management districts at Carlisle, Invergordon and Cromarty under the Licensing

(Abolition of State Management) Act 1971 c.65, and those of the Royal Ordnance Factories in 1985 and Devonport and Rosyth Dockyards in 1987, the latter two both previously part of the Ministry of Defence. In December 1991 the short-term credit insurance business of the Export Credits Guarantees Department was sold to Nederlandsche Credietverkering Maatschappij (NCM) and a new company, NCM Credit Insurance (UK), was constituted.[3]

Aside from the market-testing and contracting out of many Civil Service activities since the 1991 White Paper, *Competing for Quality*, privatisation has advanced through the sale of a number of executive agencies. Table 8.1 shows the position as at October 1997.

That privatising an industry may increase, not decrease, the need for a public agency to regulate it was a truth painfully (re-)learnt at the end of our study period. Because our closing date is 1992, the utility (and other) regulators that are such a prominent part of the UK state in 1998 barely feature in our database – a mark of how some changes in British government actually do come swiftly and silently.

Well, has the state been hollowed out? We don't know; nor was our project designed for us to find out. But it was designed for others to use our data in order to answer that question, and many others. But we can sound a warning note after being immersed in our data for two years. It all depends what you mean by 'the state'. In particular, as noted above, your answer will be vastly different according to whether you count local authorities, and/or services administered locally by guidelines set by central government, as part of 'the state'. Of course, for more than half of our study period (1970–74 and 1979–92), the governing party has been ideologically committed to reducing the size of the state. But then those years include the period after the Heath administrations' change of heart (or at least of policy), marked by the interventionist Industry Act 1972. Also, as frequently remarked, the Thatcher administrations' privatisations did not start in earnest until the second term. From 1964–70 and 1974–79, the governing party had no ideology relating to reducing the size of the state, and some ministers were committed to increasing it, either actively or as an incidental consequence of their policies. And it is much easier to create a governing function than to destroy one. Once a function has been defined by statute, somebody has to be responsible for it.

Another well-known maxim of measurement is that the measuring rod distorts that which it purports to measure. If you measure the efficiency of the NHS by the length of waiting lists, waiting lists will shorten. If you measure the efficiency of government by the number of civil servants, the number of civil servants will decline. That tells us nothing about the efficiency of the NHS or of government. Our cataloguing project is the result of 46 person-months work by the full-time staff, plus substantial amounts of the project director's time and additional bought-in student labour. What you see is what you get from that. *Caveat emptor.*

Table 8.1 Sources for details of machinery of government changes since 1964

Executive agency	Date of privatisation announcement	Outcome	Source
DVOIT	17.12.93	Sale to EDS	NSBN: 1st September 1995
National Engineering Laboratory	End 1995	Sale to Assessment Services Ltd (subsidiary of Siemens UK)	NSBN: 1st September 1995
Transport Research Laboratory	February 1996	Sale to Transport Research Foundation	NSBN: 1st September 1995
Laboratory of the Government Chemist	31.3.96	Established as non-profit distributing company	NSBN: 1st September 1995
Chessington Computer Centre	01.08.96	Sale to consortium of a Management Buyout Team, Integris UK and Close Brothers	NSBN: October 1996
Occupational Health and Safety Agency	18.09.96	Sale to BMI Health Services	NSBN: October 1996
Her Majesty's Stationery Office	30.09.98	Sale to the National Publishing Group	NSBN: October 1996
Natural Resources Institute	01.05.96	Sale to Greenwich University	NSBN: October 1996
Recruitment and Assessment Services	30.09.96	Sale to Capita Group plc	NSBN: October 1996
Building Research Establishment	19.03.97	Sale to the Management Buyout Team	NSBN: October 1997
Paymaster	01.04.97	Sale to EDS and Hogg Robinson	NSBN: October 1997
ADAS (main functions: Farming and Rural Conservation Agency formed to house residual functions)	02.04.97	Sale to the Management Buyout Team	NSBN: October 1997
Defence Evaluation and Research Agency (Support Services Division)	25.04.97	Sale to Cinven	NSBN: October 1997

Source: Next Steps Briefing Notes.

Appendix 8.1

Primary sources

The *British Imperial Calendar* and Civil Service List
The *Civil Service Year Book*
Statutory Instruments (SIs) containing Transfer of Functions Orders (TFOs)
Primary and secondary legislation: statutes defining departmental responsibilities
PRO Current Guide summaries
Official Documents: White Papers, Hansard, *ad hoc* committee reports, Select Committee Reports
List of Ministerial Responsibilities (since 1974)
Newspapers: e.g. *The Times*
Periodical literature: e.g. *Economist*
Departmental annual reports
Civil Service Statistics
Executive agency annual reports and documents

Secondary sources

Ministerial diaries, memoirs, biographies, autobiographies
Histories of government administrations
Reference works
Works on policy areas
Accounts of administrative and management reforms
New Whitehall Series (as baselines)
Internal departmental histories
Official histories
Academic departmental histories
Accounts by officials
Thesis material

Appendix 8.2

Civil Service Statistics
Annual list of Parliamentary Commissioners for Administration under 1947 Crown Proceedings Act
List produced by Property Services Agency of 'Allied Services Departments' and 'Repayment Departments'
Index of Hansard
Treasury Memorandum on the Supply Estimates
Audited accounts by Comptroller and Auditor General (about 50 per cent counted as departments)
HM Ministers and Senior Staff in Public Departments
Departments under direct ministerial control listed in the List of Ministerial Responsibilities published since 1974

Notes

1. Note the Labour Party's pre-election suggestions of using client group organisation. Gordon Brown suggested grouping departmental functions into superministries designed to deal with different age groups. A Ministry for the First Age would cover

education up to 16, a Ministry for the Second Age would have responsibility for further and higher education, training, employment and social security, and a Ministry for the Third Age would tackle community care and pensions (Elliott and Thomas 1996). Apart from the unhappy history of the minister with special responsibility for women's issues, nothing has been heard of this since 1.5.1997.

2. Trading Fund status originated with the passage of the 1973 Government Trading Funds Act 1973 c. 63 and originally included the Royal Ordnance Factories, Royal Dockyards, Royal Mint, Her Majesty's Stationery Office and the Crown Suppliers. This was amended by the Government Trading Act 1990 c.30 to allow for a greater range of executive agencies to operate as Funds – see HMSO, The Financing and Accountability of Next Steps Agencies Cm 914 (London: HMSO, 1989). Trading Fund status confers the right to carry-over unspent monies at a year-end, rather than see their return to the Consolidated Fund.

3. This was carried out under the Export and Investment Guarantees Act 1991.

9
The Development and Role of Cabinet Committees in Britain*

Peter Catterall and Christopher Brady

Introduction

This chapter reviews the origins, organisation and functioning of the British Cabinet committee system. It argues that the prime factor in its development was not the creation of the postwar Welfare State but the elaboration of the Edwardian warfare state. The principal requirements for the effectiveness of this system, if it can be dignified by such a term, are shown to be the quality of the relationship with departments and a clear sense of political direction. The cardinal source of this political direction is the prime minister. Thus, while the committee system enhances the potential power of the prime minister it also depends upon that power and authority for its effective functioning.

The development and role of Cabinet Committees in Britain

In 1960 Max Beloff remarked on 'the evolution of British government from a Cabinet system to what is virtually a Presidential system' (Beloff 1960). At the same time R. K. Hinton concluded that the prime minister had become an 'elected monarch' (Hinton 1960). With subsequent publications by Richard Crossman and J. P. Mackintosh (Crossman 1963; Mackintosh 1962), whether Cabinet had been replaced by prime ministerial government became, in the early 1960s, a full-scale debate. The Cabinet Secretary, Sir Norman Brook, himself noted in 1961 'that we are doing rather less of our collective business at formal meetings of the Cabinet', though he was reluctant 'to draw any firm deductions'. The explanation offered by the then prime minister, Harold Macmillan, is, however, instructive. 'I think we are using "meetings of Ministers" more than before. There are dangers, of course, in this. But on the whole I think Ministers feel reasonably in the picture'.[1] Indeed, it was already established as 'the exception, rather than the rule, for [committees] to have to render a "report" to the Cabinet'.[2]

* This chapter derives from research undertaken on a project entitled 'Inside the Engine Room: Assessing Cabinet Committees 1945–66'. We would like gratefully to acknowledge the support of the ESRC, Award number L124251002.

The perceived dangers, as Macmillan's final sentence makes clear, were to the doctrine of collective responsibility. This was not just a matter of constitutional proprieties, that government should be seen to be answerable collectively to Parliament, through the Cabinet. It was also one of administration, that those responsible for carrying out policy should share in the decision-making process. If, however, decision-making takes place in small groupings of ministers this cannot be guaranteed, hence the dissatisfaction of Lord Hailsham, who complained in the aftermath of Suez, 'I am finding it increasingly difficult to commit myself in advance to decisions on which I have a strong departmental and personal interest on which I have never been consulted'.[3] Even the prime minister could be caught out. Regarding press reports that £10 million for sport had been turned down, Macmillan's private secretary queried in 1961, 'The prime minister wonders whether this has been considered by any committee or the Cabinet, as he is not conscious that he has turned anything down. Perhaps the Treasury can throw some light on the matter'.[4] Macmillan's difficulty might reflect this apparently increasing tendency to decide policy in fora other than full Cabinet. Whether it also supports the conclusion drawn by critics such as Crossman, that the net effect of this tendency was to enhance the power of the prime minister at the expense of the Cabinet, is however another issue.

Nevertheless, this kind of perspective has hitherto dominated scholarly consideration of Cabinet committees. Committees have been examined in order to explore either the locus or the deployment of power. The bureaumetric approach pioneered by Dunleavy remains popular as a means of trying to assess the pecking order of the contemporary Cabinet. Then there have been a number of studies of particular committees or groups of committees, especially on the defence side (Ehrman 1958; Johnson 1960; Howson and Winch 1977). The apparent proliferation of committees after 1945 has been much remarked upon; indeed, the Attlee style of Cabinet government has been portrayed as an abrupt change (James 1992: viii). Attempts have been made to count an inexorable rise in the number of committees from the Attlee years onwards (Hennessy 1985), an expansion which has been attributed to the 'overload' generated, at least in part, by the creation of the Welfare State (Hennessy 1986). Above all, scholarly interest has focused on whether or not committees have, as Colin Seymour-Ure maintains, contributed to the rise of prime ministerial power (Seymour-Ure 1971). Cabinet committees have thus tended to be studied in terms of how they relate to other debates – the power of the prime minister or the process of military policy making – rather than in their own right.

What is a Cabinet committee?

The first problem encountered in any attempt to rectify this situation is the need to clarify what in fact a Cabinet committee is. After all, no formal records, as opposed to scattered papers or references in private collections or the Public

Record Office's CAB 37 series, exist for committees before 1915. It was not until the establishment of what was to become the Cabinet Office the following year that a body responsible for oversight of Cabinet committees came into being. Even then there was no attempt formally to log committees until the establishment of a committee book in 1927,[5] and even then that only covered the defence side of the core executive which came within the purview of the Committee of Imperial Defence [CID] established in 1903–4. It was not until after the outbreak of the Second World War, in October 1939, that attempts at a more comprehensive guide to Cabinet committees were made.[6] Despite this innovation, even in the Cabinet Office, it still was not always easy to tell what ought to be included. Compiling the July 1945 committee list was, W. S. Murrie found, complicated by the hotch potch of files it was necessary to consult, involving the risk, not least, of losing the reasons why a particular committee was constituted.[7] A year later the situation was no clearer. William Armstrong wrote that, 'so far as I know there is no definition of what constitutes a Cabinet Committee and ... I am far from certain that the distinction [between Cabinet and non-Cabinet committees] is worth making'.[8] He nevertheless made the attempt, distinguishing between Cabinet committees and the throng of inter-departmental 'official' committees, which at points during the Second World War numbered close to 800, on the basis that Cabinet committees were those where the Cabinet Office provided the secretariat. This became generally, though not invariably,[9] true from the 1940s, but was by no means so clear cut beforehand. In the inter-war years, for instance, some committees with departmental secretariat were nevertheless generally accepted as Cabinet committees. Perhaps a better distinction was provided by Peter Baldwin when he argued that the Balance of Payments Committee should no longer be treated as a Cabinet committee because it was 'entirely technical and contains no policy'.[10]

Even the rule of thumb provided by what the Cabinet Office formally recorded as being Cabinet committees in the committee book series is of limited help. Not only were these books clearly far from comprehensive, being subject to constant revision. They are also somewhat unreliable, some of the committees listed being defunct long before they were removed from the record. Furthermore, they only tell part of the story, that of the standing committees.

Standing committees began to emerge with the establishment of secretarial machinery to service them, first for the CID in the Edwardian years and then for the Cabinet as a whole during the First World War. Nevertheless, there also remained a large penumbra of often ephemeral *ad hoc* committees; indeed it was only after 1924 that a formal distinction between *ad hoc* and standing committees began to be applied.[11] Even then, into the postwar years the distinction was often blurred, for instance, under Harold Wilson committees frequently began as *ad hocs* before being converted into standing committees.

Standing and *ad hoc* committees, however, are not the only categories. There were also officially designated working parties or working groups. These were usually composed of lower-level officials preparing briefs on matters of detail for superior committees.[12] Brook did suggest that the distinction was also between working parties could and could not include outside representatives but,[13] as mentioned below, this distinction does not seem to have been a generally observed rule.

Then there are even more informal bodies. Lloyd George made extensive use of what were called ministerial conferences after the restoration of a peacetime Cabinet in November 1919. In a sense a perpetuation of his War Cabinet by other means, these were in large measure a necessary expedient during the prolonged absences of the prime minister in Versailles, a sort of informal steering committee which acted as a clearing house and crisis management machine, for instance, during the 1922 Chanak crisis. To a considerable extent this echoes the similar tendency of the Cabinets of the mid-eighteenth century to meet in smaller groups to tackle particular issues (Turner 1930: 26–35). In 1939, Sir Edward Bridges was still referring to 'the somewhat indeterminate Conferences of Ministers which are sometimes held'.[14] Thereafter the practice seems to have become more variegated. During the Second World War Churchill was to make extensive use of informal ministerial meetings at Chequers without secretariat (Churchill 1948: 365).[15] In the postwar years as well, Macmillan and Wilson, in particular, readily resorted to these, either to prepare business,[16] or to act, Lloyd George-style, as a substitute Cabinet.[17] Senior ministers, such as Butler, might also convene such meetings.[18] Contrary to popular wisdom, such procedures were by no means the innovation of Mrs Thatcher but were certainly revived by her.

Finally, there is the question of whether the Cabinet itself should be considered a committee. That, after all, is how it originated from the Privy Council in the seventeenth century. Over time, however, an increasingly unwieldy Cabinet came to replicate the Privy Council's earlier need to delegate some of its functions to subordinate bodies. As a committee for discussing general policy the Cabinet, however, left much to be desired. As Harold Macmillan (when Foreign Secretary) acerbically noted in July 1955, 'The last item on the agenda was a Foreign Office item – the vast and complicated problem of Arab/Israel relations. ... However, the item in front was the suggested road changes at Hyde Park Corner. So we never got as far as Egypt and Palestine'.[19] Attention instead readily focused on matters of political or departmental significance. Even at the turn of the century such political differences could paralyse business in full Cabinet (Otte 1996), especially as the tariff reform storm gathered. Beatrice Webb noted in her diary in April 1902 a chaotic Cabinet 'breaking up into little groups, talking to each other without anyone to formulate or register the collective opinion' (Chester 1950: 113).

With the growth of government responsibilities, departmental tensions could be equally apt to divide Cabinets. This was, however, already apparent before 1945. As a result, according to Amery, the Cabinet was no longer able to discuss general policy but instead acted as a 'standing conference of departmental chiefs' (Amery 1938). Nor was this a new problem in 1938. The search for a more effective device than full Cabinet to co-ordinate these departments had long since been a major factor in the development of Cabinet committees. This was particularly true on the defence side.

The origins of Cabinet committees

Not only was there an inner Cabinet which acted as a steering committee during, for instance, the Wars of Spanish and Austrian Succession in the eighteenth century, but there is evidence of *ad hoc* meetings, mainly on defence related matters, at that time as well (Jubb 1982; Plumb 1957; Sedgwick 1919). It was not, however, until the late nineteenth century that the need for better co-ordination between the Admiralty and the War Office highlighted by the 1890 Hartington Commission prompted the development of standing defence committees, culminating in the founding of CID. In addition to tackling defence-related matters, this was seen as relieving the Cabinet of onerous responsibilities. As Lord Esher put it in 1905, CID could investigate and plan, while

> The Cabinet, composed of men absorbed in administrative and parliamentary duties growing heavier year by year, cannot undertake to enquire into, nor to construct elaborate schemes involving much technical consideration. (Brett 1934: 114–15).

Thus it was not so much the rise of the Welfare State after the Second World War but the demands of defence before the First that led to an elaboration of the Cabinet committee system. By 1914 CID already had a network of some 30 standing and *ad hoc* sub-committees which, suitably elaborated in the interwar years, continued to be reflected in the defence side of the Cabinet committee system at least until the 1960s.

Committee development on the domestic side was slower. There was no standing domestic committee until the innovation of the Home Affairs Committee to tackle the home front in June 1918. *Ad hocs* were, however, increasingly resorted to as means of clearing grounds for legislation or siphoning out controversy. This was first apparent in the preparation of the Great Reform Bill in 1830, but was to be developed much more into a regular practice of government under Asquith before the First World War. As Herbert Samuel subsequently recalled,

> What frequently happened was that, if a disagreement could not be resolved in Cabinet, the prime minister would ask the two or three ministers who were in disagreement to meet informally by themselves and try to thrash things out before the next meeting of the Cabinet.[20]

By the interwar years, such arrangements had become more formalised.

However, there was still, as Sir Edward Bridges pointed out in his submission to the wartime Anderson Committee on the machinery of government, 'no regular system ... designed to provide a forum to which subjects of common interest to several Departments in the main fields of Government policy could be taken for discussion before submission to the Cabinet'.[21]

Anderson's report in 1945 instead suggested six standing committees to deal with discrete areas of policy; defence, national development, economic relations, external affairs, social services and legislation, all of which had been covered by standing committees in the past, but never all at the same time. This, it was felt, would streamline policy making and relieve pressure on the Cabinet:

> Many Ministers and ex-Ministers have testified that under the pre-war system, with urgent departmental problems always crowding the Cabinet agenda, the Cabinet never had an opportunity to discuss general policy on broad lines; a Standing Committee system should certainly make this more possible.[22]

It was by innovation in this direction that a system that was already established by 1945 was to evolve under Attlee. Attlee's first list of standing committees reflected Anderson's suggestions. However, the importance of particular of these committees continued to rise and fall for pragmatic reasons: for instance, the Lord President's Committee, effectively a domestic Cabinet since its introduction in 1940, withered after 1947. By the end of the Attlee government the committee structure diverged substantially from Anderson's ideal.

Nor did Attlee introduce the absolute increase in the number of main standing committees he is often credited with. In 1950 his government had 14 of these, a number that was equalled or exceeded in the 1930s until a cull under Chamberlain at the end of that decade. Attlee's ministers may have had the perception that the burden of committees was growing. However, as the Cabinet Secretary, Sir Norman Brook, repeatedly pointed out in analysing the period 1947–51, the figures 'do not support the view that Committee work is increasing'.[23] As a point of reference it might be noted that the Blair government had 33 ministerial committees. In addition to the 12 standing committees there were 11 sub-committees, 9 MISC committees (designated 'Ministerial Groups') and the Joint Consultative Committee with the Liberal Democrats (at February 2000).

The purpose of Cabinet committees

It was not Attlee but the crises of war which most contributed to the growth of the workload referred to above. The need for rapid decisions across a complex, intersecting range of issues which, initially at least, did not fall neatly within existing departmental boundaries,[24] led in both World Wars to the creation of small War Cabinets which delegated much of their detailed work to dedicated committees. Committees thus served both to relieve the pressure on the Cabinet and to tackle the new co-ordination problems posed by war, and were to continue to do so into peacetime. As such, Cabinet committees serve two main purposes – political and administrative. Their *political* functions are twofold: firstly, to relieve the Cabinet, either of routine matters which can and should be decided in lesser fora, or by siphoning controversy out of the Cabinet, not least to square, side-track or side-step important colleagues; and secondly, for public relations purposes, either to reassure by announcing the formation of a committee that a matter of public concern is being addressed,[25] or to prepare the presentation of a particular policy. Committees can thus play a significant role both in the internal and external political management of governments.

As *administrative* bodies, Cabinet committees serve either to co-ordinate policy or to clear the ground for legislation. In the pursuit of these objectives they have four main roles:

- *advisory*, to provide technical guidance, assess options and prepare scenarios;
- *policy formulation*, the preparation of policy or legislation;
- *executive*, the taking of decisions, with or without reference to Cabinet for approval;
- *implementation*, the oversight of the drawing up of plans and their being put into operation in Departments.

Committees did not always fall neatly into one or other of the above categories. For instance, although the CID and its network of sub-committees were all supposedly advisory, and therefore not a threat to the responsibility of Cabinet or departmental ministers, in practice all four functions were carried out within the CID system.

Nor does the familiar formal division of Cabinet committees into standing or *ad hoc* correspond closely to these various roles. Both standing and *ad hoc* committees have been created for each of these roles, and sometimes for a mixture of them. In fact, the distinction between whether a committee is standing or *ad hoc* more usually reflects the length of time it is likely to be required and the breadth or otherwise of its terms of reference. For instance, crises usually generate a plethora of *ad hoc* committees which may or may not be transformed into standing committees, one outstanding example being the handling of Rhodesia's unilateral declaration of independence under the Wilson government.

The composition of committees

Nor is there a necessary correlation between these roles and whether a committee is ministerial or official. However, only ministerial committees will serve the political purposes outlined above. Ministerial committees, whether standing or *ad hoc*, will also generally be concerned either with policy formulation or execution, very often with an official shadow, sometimes supported by a penumbra of official sub-committees, to prepare briefs for its consideration. Official committees therefore are generally far more numerous than ministerial ones. On occasion they pre-date the establishment of the ministerial committee. For example, the ministerial group on the Future Policy inquiry into foreign affairs in 1959–60 was only established after the officials under Brook had completed their report. Ministerial direction could thus be fairly loose, in this instance established only by a general and wide-ranging brief set by the prime minister.[26] Official committees might indeed continue to hold watching briefs on particular policy areas, such as relations with the Common Market in the 1950s, even when the ministerial committees are dormant. Or high-powered official committees might be established to implement decisions already taken by ministers, for instance on coal policy in 1946.[27]

However, on other occasions it was the official committee which could prove surplus to requirements. In 1961, for instance, it was decided to abolish the official committee on colonial policy, experience having shown 'that in dealing with many colonial problems the ordinary process of interdepartmental consultation is sufficient for the production of a paper which can go directly to the Ministerial committee'.[28] Which of these variants obtained depended to a large extent on the complexity of the issues involved and the degree of political salience, a variable which could lead officials to want to retain official committees for when ministerial interest revived.[29]

In some cases it was even deemed expedient to have mixed committees composed both of ministers and officials. Harold Wilson was particularly prone to these, seeing them as policy formulation devices clearing the ground either for the Cabinet or for major standing committees.[30] But although his use of them was more extensive, mixed committees had long been a feature of Cabinet practice. In the interwar years, for instance, a number of the most important CID sub-committees, such as Man-Power, because of their political sensitivity, had ministerial chairmen. This was also the case with the most important CID sub-committee of them all, the Chiefs of Staff (COS). This was chaired (at least when the agenda was significant enough to compel him to attend) by the prime minister. The establishment of COS in 1924 was thus felt to have ensured that the service chiefs would be able to render their expert advice without the political interference that was deemed to have gagged them during the Great War.

Although most committees were not mixed in terms of their formal membership, the *formal* membership is often only part of the story. All committees except the most lowly could attract a penumbra of attenders. This was usually because their expertise or departmental interests were related to particular items on the agenda. Even if they were not, plausible claims could usually be made and often were, particularly with respect to the most important committees. The result was the observable tendency of these committees to expand, at least in terms of attendance and sometimes in terms of formal membership as well, for instance, Eden's Egypt Committee during the Suez Crisis (Brady 1997: 66–7). In response to the demands both of ministers and Dominions for representation on the supposedly small policymaking elite of the War Cabinet, Churchill protested in exasperation, 'We shall have to take the Albert Hall for our war cabinet meetings'.[31] It was to avoid this tendency that Macmillan decided not to make his Steering Group on the 'Modernisation of Britain' a formal Cabinet committee.[32] Nor were ministers alone in becoming 'constant attenders'. Ten officials and eight military personnel attended the Egypt Committee, some of whom, such as Brook, were present throughout all its meetings, both for their advice and because of their role in policy implementation. *De facto* then, it was a mixed committee.

The work of some seemingly important committees could become completely clogged by the natural desire of ministers and officials to be represented on them. This in turn could lead to their being bypassed by other committees which, regardless of their formal status, are highpowered bodies set up on specific issues with agendas driven through because of the political imperatives of their members, whether ministers or officials. For instance, far more important in stimulating rearmament in the 1930s was the small official Defence Requirements Committee set up in 1933, rather than an unwieldy CID. Wilson's use of *ad hocs* could similarly be seen as an attempt to guard against this tendency towards institutionalised log-jams.

What makes a committee important, then, is not its formal terms of reference. Nor is it the formal membership. Some committees clearly attracted far more attenders than their formal membership would suggest, others rather less. Even an apparently significant committee, such as the interwar Home Affairs Committee, was often far from quorate. Individual committees may appear important. However, it is the attendance which gives a better indication of whether they were considered to be so by ministers or officials. The indicator of importance, and thus a key determinant of outcomes, is not how the system is organised but how it is used by those within it. As such, bureaumetric attempts (Dunleavy 1994) to measure influence by positions within the system are futile. Some committees, for instance, reflect the personal interests of particular ministers, and may not, as in the case of Population and Employment in 1963, survive their departure.[33] In other words, committees acquire significance because of their personnel and how they use them, not *vice versa*.

In the same way, Cabinet reshuffles invariably lead to a reconfiguration of the committee system. But, it should be noted, it is the changes in personnel which drive the reallocation of committees and their memberships, and not the other way around. For instance, in the autumn of 1961, officials produced a list of amendments to committees 'which would be necessary as a result of the recent Ministerial changes'.[34]

The only committee which actually confers status upon its members is the Cabinet itself. Otherwise the significance of particular committees is not inherent, but is determined either by their composition, or by the use to be made of them. Ministers, for instance, will want to be on committees which relate to their departmental interests. Whether they get on particular committees is a matter of selection. Some committees effectively select their own membership. Numerous official committees will require representation from various departments and this can also be true of very high level committees. However, the relationship with other departments was by no means the only criterion. Party considerations can be another factor, as can Parliament itself: the Minister of Works was put on the Committee on Atomic Energy in 1953 'in view of his responsibility for answering questions in the House of Commons'.[35] Above all, the selection has to reflect the purpose of the committee, the objectives, whether political or administrative, for which it has been established. This can be illustrated by reference to the high-powered ministerial committees at the time of the 1961–63 European negotiations, particularly in comparison with the low-level composition of the committees which dealt with the Messina negotiations of 1955, prior to the 1957 signing – but not by Britain – of the Treaty of Rome.

The task of personnel selection is essentially that of the prime minister. However, the composition will often be on the advice of, or even delegated to, the Cabinet Secretary.[36] The Cabinet Secretary may, in turn, be subject to advice from departments, which often will have legitimate interests involved. Some committees even require outside expertise, a sensitive matter given the political concerns frequently dealt with in committees. There were therefore doubts in the 1950s, eventually overcome, as to whether bodies like the British Council could be represented on a Cabinet committee.[37] However, there were precedents, though those on the defence side of the Cabinet Office were more likely to be aware of them.[38] CID had featured outside experts such as Lord Esher from the earliest days and respected figures such as Balfour or Haldane continued to be involved, even when in Opposition. And some technical committees, such as that on oil from coal in the late 1930s, were composed entirely of outside experts. The 1951–53 Persia Committee was attended both by Anglo-Iranian Oil Corporation and American officials.[39] For its supporters, the flexibility of a system which was able to accommodate so many inputs and variations was one of its principal virtues.

CID allowed not only for outside experts but for Dominion representation, though the amount of imperial involvement was in practice strictly limited (Catterall 1998). Notwithstanding devolution, this was even more true for Northern Ireland. One official noted in 1961:

> There is no absolute ban on Northern Ireland officials attending Cabinet (Official) committees, but the case would have to be exceptional – *vide* Precedent Book, Part II, para 32. As a general rule the Home Office do not send documents or minutes of Cabinet committees to Northern Ireland (although their gist might be reflected to Northern Ireland without revealing the origins of the information).[40]

While understandable in the case of committees dealing with reserved powers, this was also true for committees tackling matters which did impinge upon Northern Ireland, such as those handling the Common Market negotiations. This may, however, be because of the general policy of disengagement from Northern Ireland (Catterall and McDougall 1996), rather than necessarily indicative of how committees will operate in relation to the devolved administrations in Scotland, Wales and Northern Ireland that are currently being introduced.

The organisation of committees

The elaboration of the network of committees was made possible by the establishment of a secretariat to manage it. The need for such a body had been explicitly recognised by the Esher Report which led to the setting up of CID. This pointed out that:

> a Committee which contains no permanent nucleus and which is composed of political and professional members, each preoccupied with administrative

duties widely differing, cannot deal adequately with the complex questions of Imperial Defence. Valuable as is the work which this Committee has accomplished, the fact remains that there is no one charged with the duty of making a continuous study of these questions, of exercising due foresight in regard to the changing conditions produced by external developments, and of drawing from the several Departments of State, and arranging in convenient form for the use of the Cabinet such information as may at any moment be required. (Esher 1904)

But a permanent nucleus was needed to manage standing committees such as CID and its principal sub-committees to ensure that departmental plans were incorporated in the War Book, otherwise all that was possible was the informal *ad hocery* which continued to characterise domestic committees until towards the end of the Great War. The CID secretariat was therefore established in 1904 and in 1916 became the Cabinet Secretariat with the formation of Lloyd George's War Cabinet.

This effectively created a guardian of the committee system in the form of the Cabinet Secretary. The holder of this post, especially in the case of Sir Maurice Hankey, its first occupant, was also a significant influence upon its design. This role was indeed formally recognised by the Anderson Committee.[41] However, the development of permanent committees from the establishment of CID onwards also enhanced the authority of the prime minister. Since they existed to transcend the often fraught relationships between the service ministries, authority for these committees had ultimately to rest with the higher authority of the prime minister, who was also clearly the final court of appeal. The prime minister was thus established as the ultimate architect of the committee structure. The extent of the prime minister's control (as opposed to authority) over the system is, however, unclear.

Formally, it may be that 'the prime minister can shuffle the pack any way he chooses'.[42] Prime ministerial authority is required for setting up or dissolving all but the lowliest of committees. However, this was frequently exercised more as the confirmation of the recommendations of the Cabinet Secretary. These in turn were usually compiled on the basis of recommendations from Cabinet Office and departmental officials. In terms of reconfiguring the system to suit their own ideas even prime ministers with strong views on the subject, such as Attlee or Churchill, made only limited headway. This was not just because of, for instance, Brook's dislike for Churchill's 'Overlords' experiment of 1951–53. Cabinet Office resistance reflected the concerns of departments.[43] These were not passive recipients of *fiats* from on high. Instead, departments both played an active role in proposing the establishment of committees and in agreeing or resisting their demise. Wilson's taste for *ad hocs* indeed seems to have been driven in part by the view that the Ministry of Defence were so in control of the defence side of the committee system that they needed to be circumvented somehow (Wilson 1964: 19). Churchill, in his drive for a committee cull on coming to office in 1951 made less progress – as he complained ironically to Brook.[44] Prime ministers thus had more limited powers of initiative over both the creation and the culling of committees than at first might seem the case. They were better equipped to resist the creation of committees they regarded as undesirable, but even then, powerful premiers – as with Chamberlain over supply in the late 1930s or Churchill over commercial television in the early 1950s – could still be defeated by strong coalitions of interest within the Cabinet.

This is not to deny the prime minister's influence. The person of the prime minister was the greatest variable factor in the calibration of the committee system from one government to the next. It was certainly a more significant factor than party. Party affiliation obviously has had some impact upon the subjects committees were set up to look at. There have also been some instances where it shaped the way they operated. For instance, the Committee of Civil Research (CCR) set up by the Conservatives in 1925 operated on a case by case basis, very often with the object of resolving intra-party disputes. The Economic Advisory Council, which their Labour successors replaced it with in 1930, was instead an uneasy compromise between the objective of an economic information and advice think-tank and that of some sort of Council of Industry.

However, such examples were rare. This was not just because of the continuity the Cabinet Office provided and had a vested interest, not least for administrative reasons, in preserving. It was also because such changes as successive prime ministers contemplated or implemented reflected their personal predilections and their views as to what made administrative sense, rather than more ideological convictions. A case in point is Wilson. If anything his enthusiasm for mixed committees reflected an unideological respect for the Civil Service, of which he was a former member. Undoubtedly, there were ideologically informed critics of the Cabinet on the Left of the Edwardian Labour Party (Barrow and Bullock 1996: 196–9; Hanson 1956). However, such views do not seem to have survived the First World War and gone on to shape the subsequent practice of Cabinet government by the party.

Clearly there is no single controlling agency over the Cabinet committee structure. It is not the prime minister – even committees established at prime ministerial behest could be abolished 'although the prime minister has not been formally consulted'.[45] But nor is it the Cabinet Secretary. The latter's oversight of the running of the machinery could give considerable powers of initiative. Brook, for instance, in view of the failings of the ministerial Overseas Reconstruction Committee in 1946, was instrumental in splitting it into two panels.[46] The Cabinet Secretary also had a key role in identifying which committees to prune. But this should not be taken to indicate control. The organograms periodically produced within the Cabinet Office were, as often as not, attempts to capture a sense of the current situation, rather than descriptions of ideal structures they sought to implement. Committees, particularly at official level, could appear in response to a host of other stimuli.[47] These include issue-specific pressures from either ministers or officials, departmental interests, significant reports or concern in parliament or the press. Any of these, or a combination thereof, could lead to the creation of committees, often with very narrow briefs. In 1959 the Conservative government, largely at the behest of Hailsham, even established a committee to look at Labour's policy on nuclear weapons.[48]

Some of these committees were highly ephemeral. It is therefore not surprising that the Cabinet Office did not always find it easy to keep track either of all the committees or of their levels of activity. And the formal disappearance of a committee may only be logged long after it has effectively ceased to exist. Accordingly, Cabinet Office attempts to measure the workload tended to record the number of meetings and, more occasionally, the number of papers circulated, rather than the number of committees apparently extant at a given moment. This last is both difficult to count and an unreliable guide to activity.

Committees folded for a variety of reasons. Sometimes it was because they were reconstituted or superseded. Culling, as noted above, does not seem to have been an important factor. Departmental interests could ensure that even dormant committees resisted attempted culls. Accordingly, the demise of a committee often required something more than this, such as a loss of interest on the part of departments, the departure of key personnel or the re-routeing of business through other channels. There was, in other words, no set system as such. Of course, some parts remained reasonably stable for many years, an example being defence. But even major components of the committee network – for instance, the Lord President's Committee in 1947 – could be substantially overhauled if they were seen to be failing. What drove the life cycle of committees then, was not so much their place within some kind of idealised structure as their perceived purpose and effectiveness. In a system which is necessarily closely related both to departmental considerations and to the pressure of events, this is hardly surprising.

The effectiveness of committees

The effectiveness of Cabinet committees rests upon two key requirements:

- a *clear relationship* between the committee and the departments which actually implement policy; and
- a *clear sense* of political direction concerning the policy goals towards which the committee is working.

Without these conditions, there is a risk that the committee, however important it might appear to be, will operate in a vacuum and achieve little. Committees are not autonomous entities: their agenda largely reflect the concerns of the departments represented on them. Without effective links to those departments, then, there is not only a risk of flaws in the advisory and formulation processes but it may not be clear how and where the decisions that emerge are to be implemented. As one official commented in 1936, it was the duty of departments to ensure CID recommendations were entered in the War Book, but 'in many cases the responsibility is divided between two or more departments, which probably results in its not being done'.[49] No wonder the wartime Cabinet Secretary, Sir Edward Bridges, emphasised that committee secretaries were responsible not only for clarifying where responsibility for implementation lay but 'to their Chairmen for ensuring that matters remitted for further consideration or for report are not lost sight of and that no undue delays occur'.[50] Even so, the Cabinet Office did not generally chase up matters once remitted to departments.[51]

On the other hand, too close a relationship with departments has long been seen as a problem. Ministers from Gaitskell in the 1940s to Whitelaw in the 1980s have been apt to criticise the use of committees, not for the meeting of minds and making of decisions, but for the dreary repetition of departmental briefs (Williams 1983: 36; Whitelaw 1989: 251). To avoid this and resolve interdepartmental disputes committees need either a political steer to begin with or, eventually, the application of political authority. Otherwise, as with the Committee on Education and Research Policy in the Douglas-Home government in 1964, unresolved disputes and frustrations are simply taken outside of the confines of the committee and referred to the prime minister.[52] This problem is particularly illustrated by the history of the wartime Food Policy Committee. Not only was it continually bedevilled by bickering between the Ministries of Food and Agriculture, simply by being there it seemed to encourage this, by providing a forum for their squabbles. Indeed, their quarrel was only resolved when the prime minister agreed to lay down general lines of policy.[53]

Sometimes the committees themselves overlap. This is not generally conducive to efficiency – Hankey complained of the 'considerable delay and duplication of work' resulting from the overlapping of committees dealing with unemployment in the first Labour government.[54] It is, however, a problem which can easily emerge given the *ad hoc* accretion of committees with different sponsors but similar functions, and the natural tendency of departments to pick and choose which committees they wished to fight their battles in.[55] Meanwhile, significant gaps sometimes remained. One official commented of the official committees on overseas policy in 1957 that 'the combination of geographical and subject-matter committees works rather uncertainly. The Foreign Office are particularly conscious of the absence of an official body at a sufficiently high level to be able to submit to ministers an agreed recommendation'.[56]

Both of these problems reflect a tendency towards bureaucratic or political infighting in the absence of clear political direction. Advice cannot operate in a vacuum. As the Chief of the Imperial General Staff, Sir William Robertson commented in 1915, 'The Government must … know its own mind and what it is trying to accomplish, before its military and naval advisers can give the necessary advice'.[57] This was another reason why some official committees were given ministerial chairmen. However, even then there could still be problems. It was felt, for instance, that the junior minister chairing the Materials Committee, which dealt with the important task of allocating scarce resources in the difficult economic circumstances following the Second World War, 'was too much inclined to act in a judicial capacity, and was too much aloof from Cabinet views on policy'.[58] Political direction was still absent.

It is political direction that provides the motor to drive the whole committee system from the Cabinet downwards. Without it even the most elaborate networks of committees can be rendered nugatory. For instance, although there was a variety of official committees dealing with European policy in the 1950s, their levels of activity were essentially reactive, rising and falling according to the political priorities of the government. The influence of the Economic Steering (Europe) Committee under Sir Frank Lee in the late 1950s was thus not intrinsic, but was due to the shift in governmental priorities following the failure of the Free Trade Area negotiations in 1958. More poignantly, the same point can be made with reference to Suez. Concern about the vulnerability of Britain's interest in the Canal was voiced in the Middle East (Official) Committee [ME(O)] early in 1956.[59] However, there was no ministerial concern at the time. When Nasser demonstrated that vulnerability by nationalising the Canal it was already too late, and all ministers could do was seek to manage the consequences. In this case, the absence of political direction rendered good advice non-effective. The concerns in ME(O) went no further up the system and had no influence on policy.

Political direction comes from ministers. But the ultimate source of that direction is the prime minister. Ministers may supply direction for particular policy areas, but only the prime minister can supply it for the government as a whole. If then, as has been alleged, the committee system enhances the authority of the prime minister, that is because the committee system needs the exercise of that authority in order to function. In inter-departmental disputes, for instance, the prime minister is the only ultimate arbiter. This was indeed already recognised in the foundation of CID, as a committee which consisted of the prime minister and whosoever else he chose to appoint to it.

However, as Hankey knew only too well, this authority was not always exercised. He complained in 1923,

> The real weakness of the existing system is that it does not provide for any central initiative. The CID ... and all the sub-committees are purely consultative. The only person who can take any central initiative is the prime minister himself, and my experience of several prime ministers is that they are always too busy to be bothering with it.[60]

This remained a problem in the postwar years. It meant that in some cases ministers or the cabinet secretary were driven to taking difficulties to the prime minister for resolution. It could also create opportunities for policy entrepreneurs, whether ministerial or official. In the Attlee government, for instance, Herbert Morrison, as Lord President chaired a number of key committees, and was not averse both to nominating himself to even further committees and to transferring issues from one to another in order to try and get the right result. There could even be attempts to circumvent committees. Burke Trend, in 1957, identified a tendency amongst ministers to try to short-circuit the policy process by direct deals with the prime minister before consultations with colleagues,[61] a tendency which was apparently to become much more common under Thatcher (Lawson and Armstrong 1994: 443–4).

The perceived flaws in political direction were also a major reason for the repeated tinkerings with the system. These schemes for reform almost invariably involved smaller Cabinets or inner Cabinets, thus reducing the number of departments represented in the Cabinet, either by merging departments or by creating co-ordinating ministers whose responsibilities spanned several departments. Small Cabinets were seen as being better able to plan broad strategy, though both Macmillan and Wilson experimented with the alternative of holding strategic Cabinet meetings instead. The object in all cases was to create a tighter decision-making group to deliver policy co-ordination and direction. In other words, they reflect an attempt to provide a fail-safe mechanism for policymaking in the event of Prime Ministerial inadequacy. Non-departmental ministers, Gaitskell's favoured solution to the problems he encountered, are effectively surrogates for the Prime Minister. Indeed, Beveridge described the essentially non-departmental Lloyd George War Cabinet, the classic model of a small Cabinet, as 'putting the office of Prime Minister ... into commission' (Beveridge 1942).

However, such attempts to improve political direction often conflict with the other cardinal requirement of good linkage with the departments. Otherwise such ministers and any committees they might chair can become free-floating think-tanks divorced from both the expertise and implementation procedures in departments. However, the need to tackle this problem with departmental 'constant attenders' could, as attempts from Lloyd George onwards demonstrate, render the smallness of these bodies entirely theoretical. Co-ordinating ministers could also prove to be ineffective in tackling departmental disputes. Even when the co-ordination took place through the committee structure rather than through the formal and in some cases rather disparate range of ministries grouped under Churchill's Overlords there was a constant need for reaffirmation of prime ministerial support. The Lord President's Committee might have worked as a sort of domestic Cabinet during the Second World War, but any minister attempting such a co-ordinating role in peacetime was rarely tolerated.

Committees, in the circumstances, were a generally acceptable compromise. Brook argued that they broadly met the requirements mentioned above by securing 'first that plans should be evolved by those who will have to carry them out; and secondly that the power of decision should be confined to the smallest possible body of people' (Brook 1961: 14). This is not to say that the system as a whole, or groups of committees within it, have not been periodically challenged. This has happened in two ways. Firstly, committees have not always proved the most appropriate policy-making vehicles. The fact, for instance, that all the functions given to the new Ministries created during the First World War had originally been tackled by committees demonstrates that on occasion ministries were deemed more virtuous, both because they were accountable to parliament and because of relative ease of executive action.[62]

Secondly, there have been repeated calls for reform in order to facilitate long-term planning. For instance, a Conservative inquiry, when in opposition in the 1960s, argued that committees too often proved simply to be fora for inter-departmental disputes, and called instead for them to be used for 'exploratory forays into the fields of future policy'.[63] This, in turn, was not a new idea. It bore some resemblance both to the prewar CCR and to the scheme of the wartime Anderson Committee for a system of standing committees, which was seen by its supporters as a means of reducing the size of the Cabinet and providing 'an opportunity to discuss general policy on broad lines'.[64] However, as one official complained,

> Neither the Foreign Secretary nor the Commonwealth Secretary (nor the First Secretary of State for that matter) relish discussions of general policy even in so restricted a group. They prefer to talk directly to the prime minister and confine discussion in the Overseas Policy Committee, and still more in Cabinet, to concrete issues.[65]

As a result, these committees did not achieve the virtuous objectives expected. Politics, as ever, intruded upon what may have seemed to be administratively ideal.

Conclusions

There are an almost infinite variety of ideal solutions to the problems of governance in huge organisations, and organisations do not come much bigger than government itself. However, eventually these solutions are best seen as precisely that – ideal. In 1964 one official put it into perspective when he commented that:

> it is an illusion to suppose that, whatever arrangements are made, it will ever be possible to arrange the business of the Cabinet and its committees on the ideally tidy and orderly basis which the critics seem to have in mind – if only because a large part of the subject matter with which these bodies have to deal is only partially under their control.[66]

Our research confirms this analysis. Irrespective of any formal structures for effective governance, it is the informal factors which determine usage of the system. Structure, in the form described by detailed organisational charts, serves one purpose only, and that is the allocation of blame (Beer 1981: 80). What matters is not structure but an ability to respond flexibly to policy-related, contingent issues. This is certainly what mattered to the architects of the system: as one future Cabinet Secretary put it, 'The Committee structure should be regarded as a means of facilitating the despatch of Government business and not as an end in itself. It should therefore be used flexibly'.[67] After Sir John Hunt became Cabinet Secretary in 1973 he was to find that the resultant tendency of the prime minister (and others) to create new committees for policy or political purposes thwarted his attempts even to institute periodic reviews of the structure.[68]

In these circumstances, coherence is provided not by structure but by political direction. That, ultimately, has to come from the prime minister. The consequence of this is a mutualistic symbiosis between the prime minister and the committee system. The proliferation of the committee system and the development of the means of managing it, the Cabinet Office, can be said to have enhanced the power of the prime minister, as the parliamentary critics who sought the dismantling of the Cabinet Office in 1922 were keenly aware.[69] On the other hand, that system needs to be legitimated, and if possible directed, by the prime minister in order to function effectively. How far this is achieved will depend on the political and bureaucratic constraints upon and personal limitations of the individual prime minister.

The concern of some of the participants in the debate initiated by Beloff was that these restraints were not enough. Constitutionally, the restraints should be parliamentary. Tory MP Bob Boothby therefore argued for functional parliamentary committees (Boothby 1960). In doing so he unconsciously echoed the scheme of the early Labour MP, Fred Jowett, to replace the Cabinet with a parliamentary General Purposes Committee and a series of functional committees. Jowett saw the problem as being the power of the Cabinet rather than specifically that of the prime minister, but the nature of that problem was the same; the oligarchic control of a party government with a majority in the Commons (Hanson 1956). It might indeed be argued that a cardinal factor in the evolution of the Cabinet and its committees is the existence of that majoritarian system. However, it remains to be seen, if that system were to be replaced, whether a committee structure more to Jowett's liking might in turn evolve. Even so, it would in all probability still need the political direction supplied by some sort of prime minister figure.

Notes

1. Public Record Office, Kew [henceforward PRO]: CAB 21/4340, Brook to Macmillan, 4 January 1961, Macmillan to Brook, 5 January 1961.
2. PRO: CAB 21/4341, Trend to Brook, 13 June 1958. It should be noted that this was effectively true of most committees as early as the 1920s, see PRO: CAB 21/294, Rawlins to Howorth, 15 December 1924.
3. PRO: CAB 21/4324, Hailsham to Butler, 3 December 1956.
4. PRO: CAB 21/4471, Bligh to Hubback, 6 February 1961.
5. See PRO: CAB 59/1–6.
6. See PRO: CAB 21/2717.
7. PRO: CAB 21/822, W. S. Murrie memorandum, 2 July 1945.
8. PRO: CAB 21/1703.
9. For instance, many of the official economic committees were managed by the Treasury in the 1950s, see PRO: CAB 21/4555, J. B. Hunt, 'Economic Aspects of the Work of the Cabinet Office', 16 October 1957, pp. 3–7.
10. PRO: CAB 21/4777, Baldwin to Cary, 26 July 1962.
11. PRO: CAB 21/276, Hankey, 'Instructions to the Secretary', p. 6.
12. PRO: CAB 21/4774, King to Cleary, 4 July 1961.
13. PRO: CAB 21/4593, Brook to Hoyer Millar, 31 May 1960.
14. PRO: CAB 21/479, Bridges to Webb, 14 January 1939.

15. National Library of Wales, Aberystwyth [Henceforward NLW]: Dr Thomas Jones CH Papers, Class A, vol. 1, doc. 45, Bridges to Jones, 7 January 1948.
16. See PRO: CAB 21/4340, Macmillan to Thorneycroft, 25 January 1957.
17. PRO: PREM 13/237, note on conclusions of a meeting at Chequers, 21 November 1964.
18. PRO: CAB 21/4774.
19. Harold Macmillan's Diaries, Bodleian Library, Oxford: 26 July 1955.
20. PRO: CAB 21/4332, Lord Samuel, 19 May 1950, p. 2.
21. PRO: CAB 21/1084, 'Functions of the Cabinet Secretariat', 14 September 1944, p. 11.
22. PRO: CAB 87/75, MG(45)5, 'The Post-War Cabinet', 2 February 1945, pp. 6–7.
23. PRO: PREM 8/434, Brook to Attlee, 27 January 1947. See also PRO: CAB 21/1702, table, 25 January 1951.
24. PRO: CAB 21/101, Hankey to Oliver, 10 January 1918.
25. Despite the notion that committees were shrouded in secrecy until the Major government decided to publish the ministerial committees in 1992, this was a device which has long been used to relieve political pressure on the government.
26. See PRO: CAB 21/3840.
27. PRO: PREM 8/152.
28. PRO: CAB 21/4373, A. M. to Robertson, 30 November 1961.
29. For instance, the committee on atomic energy, see PRO: CAB 21/2954, Baker to Bishop, 22 October 1959
30. See PRO: CAB 130/213 (MISC17), 13 June 1965.
31. PRO: PREM 4/43A/14, note on India Office to Churchill, 6 June 1942.
32. PRO: CAB 21/4951, James to Cary, 12 December 1962.
33. PRO: PREM 11/4654, Bligh to Macmillan, 9 May 1963.
34. PRO: CAB 21/4575.
35. PRO: CAB 21/2954, letter to Brook, 29 November 1953.
36. Sending the list of committee changes consequent on the July 1962 'Night of the Long Knives' reshuffle to the prime minister's secretary, Brook wrote, 'I leave it to you to decide whether it is necessary to consult the prime minister'. The reply was negative; PRO: CAB 21/4777, Brook to Bligh, Bligh to Brook, 18 July 1962.
37. PRO: CAB 21/4375, King to Stephen, 21 August 1959.
38. See PRO: CAB 21/3931, Orme to Brook, 7 January 1959.
39. PRO: CAB 21/4490, Grant to Glaves-Smith, 12 September 1960.
40. PRO: CAB 21/4642, Hutchison to Glaves-Smith, 11 October 1961.
41. PRO: CAB 87/71, MG (42), 5th meeting.
42. PRO: PREM 11/4836, Rippon to Redmayne, 15 September 1964.
43. An anxiety which had also been apparent at the time of earlier wartime experiments, see PRO: CAB 21/4050.
44. PRO: PREM 11/174, Churchill to Brook, 23 November 1951.
45. PRO: CAB 21/4589, McKenzie to Cary, 21 September 1962.
46. See PRO: PREM 8/154.
47. And the Cabinet Secretary did not always need to be consulted before they were established, see PRO: CAB 21/4777, Cary to committee secretaries, 31 October 1962.
48. See PRO: CAB 21/3909.
49. PRO: CAB 21/479, Warburton to Deputy Secretary, 8 July 1936.
50. PRO: CAB 21/2276, Bridges memorandum, 27 May 1941.
51. PRO: CAB 21/4728, Stephen to Bishop, 5 February 1959.
52. PRO: PREM 11/4655.
53. PRO: PREM 4/6/9, Bridges to Seal, 10 March 1941.
54. PRO: CAB 21/276, CP 480 (24).
55. PRO: CAB 21/4815, Lucas to Owen, 12 January 1962.
56. PRO: CAB 21/4717, Trend to Brook, 4 November 1957.
57. Quoted in PRO: CAB 104/121, Hankey, 'The Coordination and Control of Defence Operations', 13 May 1937, p. 8.

58. PRO: CAB 21/1713, Brook to Plowden, 3 September 1947.
59. PRO: CAB 134/1297, ME(O), 25 May 1956.
60. PRO: CAB 21/268, Hankey to Creedy, 12 April 1923.
61. PRO: CAB 21/4333, Trend to Macmillan, 2 December 1957.
62. See PRO: CAB 40/1, Byrne to Smuts, 5 March 1918.
63. Conservative Party Archive, Bodleian Library, Oxford: CRD 3/14/2, 'The Cabinet System', 3rd draft, 19 December 1966, p. 22.
64. PRO: PREM 4/6/9, Anderson, 'The Post-War Cabinet', 2 February 1945, p. 6.
65. PRO: CAB 21/4781, Cary to Robertson, 26 November 1962.
66. PRO: PREM 11/4838, McIndoe, 'Organisation of the Cabinet and Its Committees'.
67. PRO: CAB 21/4555, J. B. Hunt, 'Economic Aspects of the Work of the Cabinet Office', 16 October 1957, p. 9.
68. British Library of Political and Economic Science, London: ICBH 174, interview with Sir John Hunt, 30 June 1980.
69. See *House of Commons Debates*, 5th ser., vol. 155, col. 213–78, 13 June 1922.

10
The Evolving Prime Minister's Office: 1868–1997[*]

June Burnham and G. W. Jones

The aim of our Whitehall Programme project was to understand how the Prime Minister's Office at No. 10 had developed from the informal assistance given by a few aides in the 1860s to the more specialised and structured arrangements of the 1990s. We saw the 'Downing Streets' of Gladstone, Disraeli and their successors not as a set of interesting case studies from the past but as a means of discovering the factors promoting or constraining the reform of the most central of British central institutions. The analogy is less with the static displays of dinosaurs in a museum than with the anthropologist's effort to discover how we have arrived at *Homo sapiens* the better to comprehend the moulding forces and perhaps to predict our future direction. As Figure 10.1 shows, though the nature of the evidence forces us into a 'prime minister by prime minister' framework, putting under the microscope a sequence of individual specimens, our approach sets each Prime Minister's Office into the longitudinal context provided by its forebears.

The Prime Minister's staff has made surprising growth in 130 years, given the physical restrictions imposed by its environment. On the other hand, its expansion from two in 1868 to 100 in 1997 has been relatively small, both in comparison with the offices of some other chief executives, and in relation to the growth and complexity of modern government business. How has No. 10 adapted to the changing political climate over the decades? Have there been smooth evolutionary processes in which prime ministers and aides adopt and gently modify patterns set by their predecessors, or does change proceed in a jerkier fashion, more subject to the impulses of individual prime ministers or the pressures of particular events? Can the present arrangements for the performance of particular tasks or for the Prime Minister's Office as a whole be seen as effective? Or are there tasks which still fall short of an adequate response to meeting the needs of the prime minister?

---

[*] We would like to acknowledge the ESRC for funding our research (award number: L124261001/6). We should also like to thank Elly Shodell for collection of primary material, and the many interviewees who provided the empirical basis for this chapter.

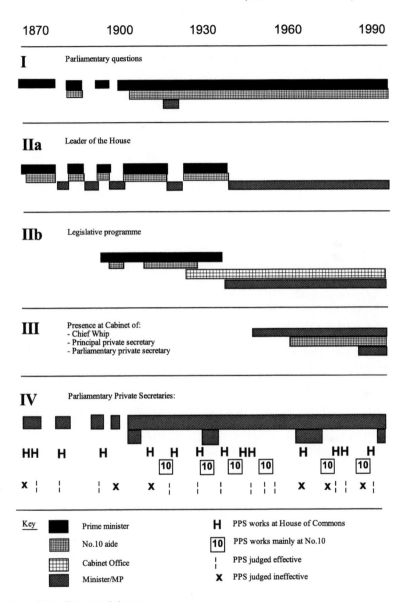

Figure 10.1   Patterns of change

Context, method and theses

These questions were addressed through a survey of the changing arrangements made since 1868 for providing particular categories of personal advice and assistance to prime ministers. By looking systematically for evidence on the ease or otherwise with which innovative changes were made to established procedures, the research sought conclusions on the extent to which an incoming prime minister has the capacity to organise No. 10 to meet his or her needs. It completed and synthesised work on the role of aides in No. 10 that had started in the 1970s, and this chapter deals primarily with aspects of No. 10 that were revealed by the new research. So we pay less attention here to sections of work which can be found in our previous publications, such as the recruitment and careers of aides in No. 10 (Jones 1976; Burnham and Jones 1993); and the work of No. 10 under Callaghan and Thatcher (Jones 1985). Nor do we discuss the gradual delineation of the offices within No. 10: the private office, the political office, the press office and the policy unit, with their specialised but co-ordinated activities (see Lee *et al.* 1998), or the way in which aides attached to sinecure ministers in the central offices have worked with No. 10 aides to promote Cabinet government (Lee *et al.* 1998).

Our primary empirical source for the 1916–97 period was a series of interviews with aides who had served in No. 10 and some other 'core' offices. In brief, data were selected from the interviews about the aides' dealings with a particular institution (parliament, Cabinet, Whitehall, party, Crown or media) to examine the changes, if any, down the years. The equivalent information for earlier prime ministers, and supplementary information for all prime ministers, was sought from collections of correspondence, diaries and memoirs by prime ministers, their aides and advisers, and by the people with whom they came into contact. Special attention was paid to changes in the arrangements and to the context of change, to evaluate the potential impact of individual prime ministers or advisers on institutionalised procedures or structures; that is, whether and under what conditions arrangements that 'had stood the test of time' can be overturned by new incumbents of No. 10 who wanted something different.

The propositions about prime ministers' aides and advisers tested by this study comprised allegations and assumptions made by ourselves and others. Petrie (1958) summed up his own views in the title of his book, *The Powers behind the Prime Ministers* which described the work of Montagu Corry (private secretary to Disraeli), Algernon West (private secretary to Gladstone), Jack Sandars (private secretary to Balfour), Maurice Bonham Carter (private secretary to Asquith), Tom Jones (Cabinet Office deputy secretary and adviser to Baldwin), J. C. C. Davidson (private secretary to Bonar Law; 'private secretary, parliamentary private secretary and everything else' to Baldwin), Rose Rosenberg (personal and political secretary to MacDonald), and Horace Wilson (policy adviser and later head of the civil service to Baldwin and Chamberlain). Petrie asserts that his subjects '... may not unjustly be termed "The Powers behind the Prime Ministers". It is not suggested for a moment that this influence has been improperly exercised, for those concerned have always acted on behalf of the Premier of the day.' (1958: 7). Our starting hypothesis was that Petrie's second statement was nearer the case than his first; that is, the prime minister's staff always acted on behalf of the premier. They were not powers behind the prime minister because they exercised no separate power. Our examination of the evidence found only three cases among 370 aides where that conclusion may possibly not hold: Balfour's private secretary, Sandars, and Campbell-Bannerman's private secretaries, Ponsonby and Nash.

A second line of enquiry responded to propositions made about the Prime Minister's Office as a whole, and the structure and functions it should have within the central institutions. The suggestion that a more substantial Prime Minister's Department was needed if a modern prime minister were to have adequate support was put best by Weller (1983), and in a modified form by Mandelson and Liddle (1996: 240–2). A former Cabinet Secretary (Hunt 1987) thought one already existed in all but name. Early conclusions from the interviews were that No. 10 was inherently more flexible and less bureaucratic than a larger department would be. It had all the requisite connections to other parts of the governmental system, which could be called into play at any moment. Since the prime minister had the power to change the provisions, within limits set by political and constitutional constraints which it would be counter-productive to disturb, a radical upheaval would serve little purpose (Jones 1983).

The research endeavoured to test the hypotheses put forward in these debates which would set important conditions on the future reform of the central institutions. They can be set out as four sets of assertions, together with the questions they stimulate, and are set out thus below.

First, prime ministers control the recruitment of staff to No. 10 and the tasks they perform, and therefore can obtain the type of assistance they require. But how free is their choice? Where are the limits? Who sets them or changes them and in what circumstances?

Second, No. 10 has increased in efficiency and effectiveness over the years, without the need for great expansion, through 'hiving-off' and specialisation. But what are the factors which encourage or hinder devolution of tasks and specialisation? Is each specialised task handled equally effectively? What disadvantages are there to specialisation?

Third, in principle there can be no powers behind the prime minister stronger than the prime minister or ministers, since aides work at the bidding of the prime minister, and because alternative advice from a No. 10 adviser on departmental matters challenges the authority of Cabinet ministers as the prime minister's collaborators and departmental ministers. But how good is the evidence on the power of prime-ministerial aides? Have they and their advice challenged Cabinet and ministerial government since 1868?

Fourth, and overall, there is no need for a larger, more formal, less flexible Prime Minister's Department, since prime ministers can determine the pattern of aid provided from No. 10, which has good collaborative networks with the relevant institutions. Prime ministers and No. 10 aides can rely on a wide variety of sources of advice, from which they can choose the most appropriate to the topic in question. But we need to ask whether prime ministers have used these networks to the best effect, to provide themselves with the advice, support and collaboration they require.

Findings of the project

Recruitment

Statistics on the size of No. 10 in themselves tell us little about the optimum size of No. 10 or whether the growth in staffing from Disraeli's two in 1868 to John Major's 100 in 1997 is large or small. They do not inform us whether prime ministers are able to extend No. 10 to meet their needs, though the 50 per cent increase from 100 to 150 achieved by Tony Blair between 1997 and 1998 suggests there are nowadays few obstacles to recruitment. Even when we try to compare like for like and note that Major's 100 comprised 22 support staff, including office messengers, whereas Mrs Thatcher's 67 in the 1980s did not (such massengers existed but were paid by the Cabinet Office), and that Disraeli and Gladstone had the use of Treasury and Foreign Office messengers, is the size of the support staff important, or are we justified in comparing only the numbers of senior staff, whose growth is less noteworthy?

The limitations on the prime minister's capacity to recruit staff seem always to have been as much personal and political as legal and constitutional. In the nineteenth century the rules on 'official' appointments could be sidestepped by 'unofficial' appointments of family or party colleagues (providing they shared the payments or were not paid from public funds), and by some deliberate blurring of the figures. Thus, when Gladstone took over from Disraeli in 1868, his large family and close ties to young members of the Whig aristocracy provided him with cheap and enthusiastic labour not available to Disraeli. In similar fashion, Macmillan, in 1957, easily inserted into the No. 10 office of private secretaries his wealthy and congenial supporter, Wyndham, as a 'shilling-a-day man', and most recent prime ministers seem to have found desks in No. 10 for party staff not paid from public funds, not officially listed and who therefore go uncounted. Equally significant, when Gladstone and Disraeli found plausible arguments to increase the number of public, paid appointments Treasury minutes could easily be written to that effect. Gladstone alleged that his supplementary post of Lord Privy Seal, with no responsibilities, required another paid private secretary in case the Seal should in future be brought back into use. Nevertheless these prime ministers had to provide justification, and there were political limits to what could be tried. Gladstone would have liked to appoint his son, already acting as private secretary, to a paid junior Treasury post but retreated when his colleague, Granville, advised that parliament would find fault. The principle has changed little. Blair's decision to appoint non-civil servants, such as Jonathan Powell and Alistair Campbell, to No. 10, with authority to give instructions to civil servants, required the discreet publication of an official but virtually valueless document, an Order in [Privy] Council, and a political judgment of what parliament could accept. Churchill, with or without paperwork, had sufficient charisma to obtain a doubling up of staffing so there was someone on call at any hour, not only during the war but more surprisingly when he returned to No. 10 in 1951 and there was no public need for this level of establishment. Yet, to ensure his parliamentary liaison was effective, he had been obliged even in wartime to accept a chief whip and a parliamentary private secretary (PPS) he did not personally like. In short, the political limits to what parliament, and perhaps the public, will bear have more impact on the prime minister than the statutory limits.

Perhaps even more important in evaluating the real size of the Office is understanding the type and volume of tasks its staff undertook for the prime minister, and the implications for the success of the prime minister and the government as a whole. Disraeli reduced the value of his two or three staff by his unwillingness to instruct and then trust the junior officials – he preferred to decipher his telegrams himself. In comparison, Gladstone made the most of his four or five secretaries – except for the appointment of bishops – by his use of 'devolution' and efficient techniques. However, the constitutional conventions of the time always restrict the tasks an official can be expected to perform (or can be seen to perform), and therefore the value of extending the office. Until the 1930s it was considered constitutionally unacceptable for officials to observe Cabinet meetings, let alone take minutes (though a Cabinet official was already taking minutes). Between the late nineteenth century and the 1950s a prime minister's aide might at most be called in momentarily to clarify for the prime minister a point of fact. Yet, on the other hand, a clear if discreet political allegiance of civil servants in No. 10 was acceptable in Victorian times. They could more easily than now take on 'sounding-out' roles with government and opposition leaders, facilitating Cabinet formation or ministerial agreement, or the search for a parliamentary compromise (now a role for the Chief Whip's Office). Rosebery's government of 1894–95 could scarcely have lasted more than a few months without the mediating role between him and his Chancellor of the Exchequer undertaken by his principal private secretary. One reason the small office of Campbell-Bannerman (six people including the shorthand typist), worked so well in 1907 was that its principal private secretary had previously served in both the foreign service and party headquarters and could take the initiative on a wide range of both 'political' and 'official' tasks.

But the efficiency that could be obtained by using aides to save prime-ministerial time or to improve the quality of prime-ministerial business was, between the two world wars, often seen as threatening, overstepping constitutional and institutional boundaries. When the Lloyd George coalition collapsed in 1922, an election theme of his opponent, Bonar Law, was the abolition of Lloyd George's secretariat. Lloyd George's introduction into No. 10's garden of five policy advisers and eight clerks seems insignificant by the standards of 1999, but it made his Office nearly three times as large as that of his predecessor, Asquith. When combined with his use of the Committee of Imperial Defence secretariat (the new Cabinet secretariat) to record conclusions of War Cabinet deliberations and chase up their implementation by departments, it was easily portrayed as 'imperialism'. Some critics of the Cabinet secretariat mistakenly confused it with the 'Garden Suburb' policy secretariat, though the Treasury was not confused when it tried to absorb Cabinet secretariat staff. But their value to the prime minister was acknowledged when Bonar Law kept the Cabinet secretariat and the eight clerks. The creation of the Cabinet secretariat, now part of the Cabinet Office, as a separate entity from No. 10, is of major significance for today. It took on the recording and co-ordinating roles in the name of the Cabinet that before 1916 belonged to the prime minister and his aides. Its continued presence not only helped keep No. 10 compact, but gave sustenance to the constitutional convention of Cabinet government. In contrast 'the Lloyd George effect' made suspect the setting-up of any central policy secretariat, seen in the opprobrium with which Mrs Thatcher's policy unit was received more than 50 years later. The continuing effect of such suspicions, especially when the policy advice becomes too vocal, was confirmed in 1989 when the then Chancellor of the Exchequer, Nigel Lawson, resigned.

The continued presence of the clerks in Bonar Law's No. 10 was important too. During Lloyd George's premiership they had brought modern filing systems into No. 10, which were not comprehensively destroyed when Lloyd George left office, as had happened during previous changes of administration. Some clerks stayed for 40 years, constituting, along with their files, the institutional memory of No. 10's procedures and conventions. A comparison in numerical terms of the three or four officials closest to Gladstone, Campbell-Bannerman or Asquith with the dozen or so advisers performing similar roles in today's No. 10 might lead to a conclusion of 'not much change'. But that would underestimate the role of more junior staff, who make their impact by refining and concentrating the quality of the material fed to the core advisers. Above all, the number of appointees to No. 10, official or not, may not be the crucial measure. Interviewees who had worked for Lloyd George spoke of the hum and buzz of No. 10 as large numbers of people came and went, indicating a volume of activity that perhaps was a true reflection of its size and its impact on the political environment than the number of appointed staff.

Limits to growth

Setting to one side the problem of statistics, we found two reasons for the comparatively limited expansion of No. 10 until 1997, the first of which can be summarised as the devolution and transfer of prime-ministerial functions to other offices. Prime ministers over time devolve to others outside No. 10 tasks they no longer want or need to perform personally. Consequently, the aides in No. 10 no longer have the primary supporting role on these tasks, though they may still co-ordinate with those who have the responsibilities. Among this group of activities could be included the prime minister's role in leading the House of Commons, and in drafting legislation. Until well into the twentieth century, prime ministers introduced legislation in the House, and were often active in drafting the clauses of a bill. In 1868 one of Gladstone's earliest actions was to ask his newly-appointed secretary, West, to help draft a bill. West stood near Gladstone in parliament keeping the draft up-to-date as amendments were voted. In 1902–5, Balfour's private secretaries were active in support of his legislation, writing to potential supporters and rehearsing departmental officials in the arguments they might use. Campbell-Bannerman's private secretaries went as far as to draft a memorandum to parliament on the strong reform of the Lords they wanted. They pressed it successfully on the prime minister, having gained the support of the Speaker and many leading ministers. Though Lloyd George asked his policy advisers to draw up bills on foreign policy, after his departure prime ministers left legislation to other ministers, and consequently no longer required such comprehensive support from their aides.

The putting aside of some prime-ministerial activities may be part of a longer cycle in which No. 10 first establishes a co-ordinating role or function and then, as it becomes routine, transfers it to a more peripheral location. The planning of a 'Queen's Speech' programme of legislation, and obtaining Cabinet agreement, first became routine in Liberal governments under Gladstone. Before then, ministers used to introduce bills without informing their colleagues. Conservative governments were slower to adopt this co-ordinating procedure. But Salisbury's secretary McDonnell, in the late 1890s, used to remind Salisbury to urge his ministers at least to circulate bills to Cabinet. Campbell-Bannerman's pro-active aides helped him by collecting ideas from departments and writing the speeches on legislation that opened and closed each parliamentary session. In 1921, the young Cabinet Office started to involve itself in this role, though still working closely with No. 10. During the war years, Churchill delegated supervision of the legislative programme to a committee under a ministerial colleague. Attlee continued this arrangement after the war, confiding it to the Leader of the House, Herbert Morrison. Ministerial responsibility for drawing up and co-ordinating the legislative programme today belongs without question to one or other of the major sinecure ministers, usually working from the Privy Council Office and in close collaboration with the Chief Whip's Office. It is no longer a prime-ministerial role, and No. 10 aides do not need to be much involved.

In Victorian times, No. 10 private secretaries helped the prime minister organise Cabinet meetings and Cabinet committees, but that is now the job of the Cabinet Office. Gladstone would ask West to contact Lord Granville, the prime minister's closest colleague, requesting him to suggest a date. However, writing Cabinet minutes was never a task for No. 10 aides. This duty, from Disraeli to Asquith, was that of the Crown's chief servant, the prime minister, in the form of a letter to the monarch reporting discussions and decisions. On the rare occasions when the prime minister was incapacitated, a senior minister, such as the Leader of the Lords, would write the letter. It was a sign of unusual favour when Montagu Corry, Disraeli's secretary, was asked by Queen Victoria to report urgent Cabinet discussions on behalf of a sick Disraeli, and it was very much an exception to the rule. Lloyd George was scornful of these conventions and used the excuse of war to escape the traditions. The moment Lloyd George became prime minister the

War Cabinet secretary came into No. 10 immediately after Cabinet meetings to dictate notes from memory to his own secretary. The top copy went to the King, the others were circulated to ministers and the precedent for the circulation of printed 'conclusions' was set. Though this duty was not one transferred from No. 10 aides, it nevertheless forms one reason for the slow expansion of the Prime Minister's Office, since the growth of Cabinet business was supported by another element of the core institutions.

Other traditional responsibilities of the prime minister were devolved away from No. 10 by stages, first from the prime minister to the private secretaries, then elsewhere within Whitehall or Westminster. As well as the 'Cabinet letters' to the monarch, the prime minister was required to write him or her a letter reporting the day's events in the House of Commons. Since Gladstone and Balfour were in parliament every day as leaders of the Commons the work was tedious but practicable. Interviewees reported that Asquith preferred instead to go to the palace 'in his frock coat' and report in person. Lloyd George annoyed the palace by refusing to follow this procedure. Bonar Law in 1922–23 was the last prime minister to write the 'King's Letter' but until the death of George V in 1936, various members of No. 10, private or political secretaries, undertook what they regarded as a chore, writing a text culled from *The Times* or *Hansard* on a set of blank sheets already signed by the prime minister. At some stage the chore was successfully transferred to the Whip's Office and is now regularly reported in the press as being a traditional duty and honour of one of the senior whips. In contrast, some prime-ministerial prerogatives which derive from the Crown, such as the appointment of bishops, regius professors and the poet laureate, remain within No. 10. Though the day-to-day tasks of this role are handled by a specialised group of staff, and do not impinge much on the core advisers, it seems surprising that an overcrowded No. 10 still finds room for issues somewhat removed from government business.

Overall, there has been a decentralisation and transfer of tasks once undertaken in No. 10, which goes some way towards explaining why changes in the level of staffing, especially at senior level, have been limited. We must also take into account the high level of activity of Victorian prime ministers and aides in roles usually thought to have expanded in recent times. That is, the growth in No. 10 has been limited not only because some older tasks have ceased to be part of No. 10's work, but because some apparently newer tasks have in reality long been carried out there, though perhaps in a different form. Giving the prime minister substantial help on international affairs is often thought to be a relatively new task for No. 10 and an activity often criticised, as when Mrs Thatcher's No. 10 was deemed to be intervening in Foreign Office affairs. But Disraeli's private secretaries paid official visits to foreign ambassadors, helped him read and cipher foreign telegrams and accompanied him to overseas 'summits'. Gladstone tried to leave foreign affairs to the Foreign Secretary and believed that, constitutionally, he could not command the War Office. Yet parliament and public hold prime ministers responsible, and he was inevitably and reluctantly dragged into foreign affairs when mistakes were made and lives were lost. Diplomatic telegrams to the Foreign

Office were so routinely circulated to No. 10 that when it emerged that some 'had not crossed the street' from Rosebery in the Foreign Office to Gladstone in No. 10, it was regarded as a scandal. An examination of the work of the prime minister's aides from Disraeli onwards shows prime ministers ready to intervene in other departmental business where co-ordination of policies or the government's reputation are at stake. Prime ministers use their aides to conduct that business, some more overtly than others, and mostly successfully but at other times meeting rebuffs from offended ministers. In evaluating the changes that have taken place in No. 10 since 1868 we have to note both the work that has been delegated and shifted away, easing the load on the prime minister and his or her staff, but also the essential continuity of the prime-ministerial role.

Evolution and innovation

The description of changes we have given so far may make it appear that where change has occurred, it has been in the form of continuous evolution; that is, a task was performed until it was devolved or at least no longer formed a significant part of No. 10 work. But examination of the changes made over time for assistance with particular prime-ministerial roles shows that No. 10 did not develop in such a simple evolutionary way. Prime ministers would have reasons or find reasons not to undertake certain burdensome tasks, such as leading the House of Commons in its daily business, but then the burden would come back at a later date. Systems put in place during one premiership that were apparently effective could be dismantled under the next, because parliament required it, or because each prime minister's office was itself dismantled, or simply because 'the Book of Knowledge' that listed procedures about how to make appointments and conduct royal funerals had been taken away or not passed on. Gladstone constructed Cabinet agendas-cum-minutes that served as reminders of decisions taken and arguments made. Yet 40 years later his successors were still operating without records of what they had decided. Until Bonar Law decided to retain Lloyd George's filing clerks, all such systems were destroyed, perhaps not to be reinvented, when prime ministers left Downing Street. MacDonald's first Labour government in 1924 did not know how to co-ordinate parliamentary business (or even, at first, that it should): it was not until 1929 that one of his secretaries learned from a Cabinet Office official to contact departments.

Consolidation of experience and the development of institutional memory required that some senior staff remain in place when prime ministers changed and, in some spheres, the development of strong party organisations that outlasted leaders. It could take more than the term of one premiership for innovations to become part of the standing arrangements. Introductions had first to be resisted, then to become acceptable, and then to become the norm under all premiers. Wilson's personal and political secretary, Marcia Williams, said with bitterness and some justice that innovations which Wilson had to fight for (the right to a political secretary, or to policy advisers, the right to a room for political staff, her right to headed notepaper, or to glimpse the content of Cabinet papers), were conceded to succeeding Conservative prime ministers and their secretaries more willingly, and it then became easier for Labour prime ministers to be given those facilities. It is difficult to separate the events from the personalities (Heath's political secretary, Douglas Hurd, was more diplomatic, but he was also pushing at doors that Marcia Williams had already hammered down), but the interview evidence does seem to show a slight but consistent pattern, over the years, of Conservative prime ministers finding their wishes more easily accommodated than those desired by the more radical politicians, such as Lloyd George and Wilson. Some innovations, such as Lloyd George's policy secretariat, seem to have been effective in their own terms at the time, but were so associated in the collective political mind with the prime minister's other tactics that they became impossible to reintroduce, except cautiously and surreptitiously and in new guises.

Most of the efficient innovations we noted (Burnham and Jones 1999) were the result of conscious introductions by premiers, or by principal aides with the assent of the prime minister. In addition to Gladstone's Cabinet records and Lloyd George's willingness to let the 'secretary to the Cabinet' draw up Cabinet 'conclusions', examples are the regular preparation of answers to parliamentary questions by Nash for Campbell-Bannerman; the systematic filing by No. 10 clerks of parliamentary answers which J. C. C. Davidson's secretary, Miss Watson, prepared for Lloyd George and Bonar Law; or the common pool of material for the prime minister, first called the 'dip', invented by Churchill and Attlee's secretary, Rowan, which lets all the principal aides see and comment on the advice the prime minister receives. These efficient administrative innovations occur more frequently where long-serving aides, like Nash, Davidson, Watson and Rowan, have the chance to observe and to revise. The clearest example is the continuous improvement of the system for answering parliamentary questions by Miss Watson during her 30 years at No. 11 and No. 10. It was given further refinements, including those of a more political nature, by some of the 'high-flying' civil servants who succeeded her.

But other innovations, including some of the most effective and long-lasting, reveal surprising weaknesses at the heart of government, especially an inability to remove ineffective staff. Ronald Waterhouse, the first principal private secretary to remain to serve prime ministers from different parties, started the useful trend of 'permanent' principal private secretaries because it was impossible to dismiss him. He was clearly incompetent and idle, but he knew how Baldwin had become prime minister. During the Second World War, Anthony Bevir developed the useful specialised role of 'secretary for Crown appointments' because he could not cope with the pressures of a private secretary's work and the other staff found him this sideline. Wilson's appointment of two PPSs seemed at the time to be a reinvention of a successful innovation by Campbell-Bannerman and again by Baldwin. But, according to interviewees, his first PPS had made a serious error and was therefore 'doubled up'. At other times, two PPSs were appointed to cope with situations such as coalition or unreliable majorities in both houses (where there were two parties or two chambers to conciliate). In cases of this kind, an increase in the number of aides to the prime minister can indicate government weakness, not strength. The variety of the number, characters and roles of PPSs down the decades is less a matter of innovation than a difficulty in deciding who would be best-suited to the circumstances, either in persuading an MP to take on a particicular task, or indecision about what they should do. It appears to be the least systematically-organised of the No. 10 posts, perhaps because it must be adaptable in order to ensure liaison between an individual prime minister and an almost infinitely-variable chamber. It should be added that it is perhaps also the case that the significance of its role is under-estimated by many prime ministers and their chief civil service advisers.

Our conclusions from looking at the five apparently most innovative individuals between 1868 and 1997 – Gladstone, Lloyd George, Wilson, Waterhouse and Rowan – were that Waterhouse was innovative by default, and that Rowan, seen as the 'shining example' of principal private secretaries by many interviewees, introduced a large range of measures aimed at improving the administrative effectiveness of No. 10 but in uncontentious ways and with the approval of an administratively-effective prime minister, Attlee; Rowan could not have succeeded so well under Churchill. The three innovative prime ministers, all from the radical party groups of their times, introduced the most truly radical changes, but only Wilson had to confront an established and self-confident civil service. Individuals can innovate against the institutional conventions but it is not easily or frequently accomplished: one argument for not creating a more heavily-structured central department which will be harder for an incoming prime minister to modify.

Patterns of development or obsolescence?

These and the many other different patterns of changes we found can be summed up as fitting four broad patterns, and these are shown in Figure 10.1, above.

Pattern I refers to tasks undertaken by No. 10 aides on a continuous basis since the nineteenth century or earlier (preparation of answers to parliamentary questions, advice on Crown appointments). These categories of advice and assistance now seem 'institutionalised'; that is, their essential nature is assumed. They include 'constitutional' roles that would be difficult to devolve, but not all are politically salient in 2000. There is a danger governments fail to consider whether these activities could be diverted elsewhere; possible examples include Crown appointments of bishropics to the church and of regius professors to the universities or to the Privy Council Office.

Pattern II refers to tasks which the prime minister or his aides carried out in the nineteenth century (IIa) or adopted in the early twentieth century (IIb), but which have since been delegated to ministers or officials outside No. 10, perhaps only after a number of unsuccessful attempts to persuade other institutions to accept change (leadership of the House of Commons, Cabinet minutes, King's or Queen's Speech programme). Some of these changes were introduced easily, but the more significant 'constitutional' changes required tangible, legitimising reasons, such as war, illness or coalition, or even pretence that something had not occurred (MacDonald was still denying that an official took Cabinet minutes more than a decade after the practice began; and MacDonald and Churchill both appointed ministers who were *de facto* leaders of the Commons though this was not officially admitted). However, once change was accepted, the new arrangement so quickly became the new norm that the 'necessity' for the old arrangement was forgotten and return became unthinkable. Paradoxically, a premier's capacity to overcome the existing institutions is most easily demonstrated when the delegation is first resisted then eventually implemented (for example, delegating leadership of the Commons to another minister), whereas for some continuous activities in pattern (I), such as Crown appointments, it is not possible to be sure whether prime ministers have been unable to overcome resistance (by the Crown?), or whether no prime minister has considered the possibility of change.

Pattern III refers to 'new' forms of assistance, which were added in the twentieth century but now seem to have become insitutionalised. They were often introduced in an intermittent or low-key way, which soon became routine, perhaps after some debate about utility or propriety. The gradual infiltration of private secretaries into Cabinet, first sitting quietly behind a pillar, then taking notes, and later the attendance at Cabinet of the PPS to the prime minister, are examples of these developments, and followed the earlier introduction of the chief whip at a date in the 1940s or 1950s, which, significantly, is not accurately known. At first they are queried (by fellow ministers; by a new prime minister). Then they become so routine as to be unquestioned by prime ministers, even if the actors concerned are sceptical about their efficiency. For example, one of Mrs Thatcher's PPSs was doubtful about the value of his presence at Cabinet, but continued to go because it had been 'established', a confirmation of the pressure of convention.

The fourth pattern (IV), is one of no pattern, or of a wide range of possible forms of assistance with a particular task. One example is the role assigned to PPSs or even the number of PPSs that there should be. Do they work mainly in the Commons, or mainly at No. 10? Do they write prime-ministerial speeches, talk to MPs, attend backbench committees, or hold Commons tea-parties for the prime minister? Another example is the handling of letters to the prime ministers from MPs. Should all be answered by civil servants, or all by the political office, or only those from government MPs by the political office? This variability can support the hypothesis that premiers can choose their own provision, especially where they are seen to insist on a change from the previous premier's arrangement. But sometimes, as with the role of the PPS, 'no pattern' means no optimum structure has been found, perhaps because the task is strongly affected by fluctuating factors, such as interpersonal relationships, or the nature of the party system.

In summary, the many forms of assistance that have changed over time generally demonstrate that prime ministers can organise No. 10 to meet their own needs, though sometimes the changes indicate an inability to determine the optimum form of aid. Institutionalised routines generally indicate that a successful formula has been found, but they might also be unthinking continuations of old formulae. A flexible response, such as a willingness to rethink the role of a PPS, could be helpful in new circumstances, such as a reformed second chamber or coalition government.

Internal structure

The Prime Minister's Office has gradually split into specialised sections. Press, party and policy advisers were spun off in turn from the core private office. But these contemporary functions all had their parallel in the early multi-functional No. 10. It was easier for staff in the Victorian and Edwardian office to be multi-functional because it was accepted they could belong simultaneously to political and official worlds. They had family connections not only with the ministers they served but also with the leading members of the opposition. The three main players in Campbell-Bannerman's small but effective office had expertise in journalism, party organisation, the monarchy, the Foreign Office, the Treasury and parliament. Specialisation from Asquith's government onward, broken by the unusual period of Lloyd George (which perhaps acted as a confirmatory warning), was partly a response to the professionalisation of the civil service. Interviews showed No. 10 civil servants in the 1930s and beyond constructing conventions on what support they might properly give, and not give, a head of government who was also a political leader. There was always conflict for them in needing to appear non-political to remain in post and in the civil service under different prime ministers, and yet not wanting to allow political assistants to take over their roles. They instinctively and logically argued against Wilson's letters from MPs being answered by the political office because it reduced 'co-ordination' within the office and their control over events. But, almost by the same token, it was essential to the political office, if Wilson were to retain power, that MPs should be given a politically-aware response. Specialisation has disadvantages as well as advantages.

Roseveare, in his history of the Treasury, described the No. 10 private secretaries of Victorian times as 'high-class clerical valets, whose duties tended to render them unfit for return to the humdrum work of the divisions' (Roseveare 1969: 213). His interviews make clear that later high-flyers could not find in the Office a sufficient outlet for their policy-making skills. They worried they might lose the talents they required for more senior postings in departments and often seemed glad to escape No. 10. While the most senior staff do well in the service or, becoming too close to the premier, follow them out and into a City career, the junior private secretaries seem often to have had low-key endings to their professional lives.

The common characteristic of No. 10 aides was their devotion to serving the prime minister. However, nearly all prime ministers have, initially at least, mistrusted civil servants to some extent and have imported into No. 10 familiar supporters, who are among those sometimes accused of being 'powers behind the Prime Minister' (Petrie 1958). The claim comes nearest to being supported by the evidence in the cases of Balfour's Sandars and in Campbell-Bannerman's

Ponsonby and Nash. Yet although Sandars did a great deal for Balfour, he was carrying out Balfour's wishes with the full knowledge not only of Balfour himself but his leading party and Cabinet colleagues. They often resented it, but they knew about it and accepted it. Ponsonby and Nash went further, having their own independent views on Lords reform which they pressed on the premier, but only after gaining the support of the chief ministers and parliamentarians. In all other cases the research showed that the aides were 'shadows' of their 'chiefs'. If the prime ministers were interested and active in some role, then their advisers were active in their support.

No. 10: *primus inter pares*

When the Chief Whip's private secretary of the 1970s was described by a No. 10 secretary as 'an integral part of No. 10' it conveyed accurately the sense that no hard-and-fast boundary can be drawn around 'the Prime Minister's Office'. Though the focus of our research was 'No. 10', it is clear 'the Prime Minister's Office' has long been amorphous and permeable. Its shape and size vary, depending on time and activity. It can incorporate aides from a variety of Whitehall offices to work for the premier, or transfer to new or existing institutions roles at other times undertaken by No. 10. Its porous boundaries enable staff appointed to other ministers or offices to liaise so closely and so frequently with No. 10 that it becomes a technical point whether they work for the prime minister, or for the chief whip, the Cabinet or the Treasury. Creating a formal 'Prime Minister's Department', however, would tend to trap the current structural requirements – the posts that are currently linked closely to No. 10 – within institutional boundaries. As our research shows, persistence is needed to overcome existing institutional arrangements when a new prime minister, with different requirements, comes into office. Arrangements would become both less efficient and less versatile. Delineating a Prime Minister's Department would also expose to the light some relationships which remain ambiguous but which help efficient (not necessarily democratic) government, because it is not made too clear whether an official serves the prime minister or Cabinet, Parliament or the government.

The Prime Minister's Office has traditionally been seen as an entity which is internally as well as externally flexible. Staff from the different, specialised, sections of No. 10 share information to ensure the prime minister is briefed on all aspects of an issue, as symbolised by 'the dip'. There have been some notable 'teething difficulties' when incoming prime ministers clash with existing· conventions, a difficulty unlikely to be eased by any other structured arrangement which incorporates permanent staff. No. 10 seems to have found a workable compromise between the almost total loss of accumulated experience which accompanied changes of prime minister until 1922 and the inflexibility of a structure dominated by permanent officials. However, the professionalisation of the civil service, and the growth in numbers of staff and of activities at No. 10, all of which encourage specialisation, have harmed the capacity of an intimate group of No. 10 staff to provide within one shared office a wide variety of contacts, experiences and skills. By the Wilson premiership of the 1960s, separate sets of aides with legitimate but different priorities could be seen vying for the prime minister's time and attention. The increasing pressure for the prime minister to deal 'efficiently' with Parliament, to the neglect of relationships between government and backbenchers, illustrates this trend. The long-term impact of this trend is perhaps underestimated by the civil servants or former civil servants who dominate No. 10. There is a contrast to be made in other ways too between the large proportion of tasks which, after a century or more of trial and error, are performed ever more efficiently, and those for which no optimal procedures appear to have been found.

No. 10 has remained relatively compact for two principal reasons. First, tasks which were once performed by the prime minister or by the prime minister's aides, but which do not need the prime minister's continuous or close oversight, have been devolved or transferred to other ministers or other officials; a lesson for those who think improved co-ordination of every new issue needs a taskforce in or near No. 10. Second, there has been an ambiguous incorporation of many staff in other parts of Whitehall, who link the prime minister effectively to Cabinet, Parliament, party and the media. This strategy, if it can be called such (because it evolved and continues to evolve in an intermittent way), has provided the prime minister with the tools for efficient co-ordination of business, without threatening the political institutions of Cabinet and Parliament with the appearance of an over-mighty prime minister or government. The lesson for those who would re-fashion the core offices into a Prime Minister's Department is that a clear division of aides and tasks between prime-ministerial and not prime-ministerial would expose these ambiguities, break the links in the networks formed by mutual understandings and unwritten procedures, and put institutional obstacles in the way of evolution.

Part III
Agencies

11
Agencies and Accountability

Brian W. Hogwood, David Judge and Murray McVicar

Introduction

This chapter draws on research conducted for the project 'The Audit of Accountability: Agencies and their Multiple Constituencies'.* While we do explore the *concept* of accountability, our main concern was to explore what the accountability of agencies meant *in practice*. Our approach involved using observable indicators for all agencies, both quantitative indicators of parliamentary interest and documentary material. For a sample of 20 agencies, designed to cover a range of departments and a range of functions (regulatory, service-providing, funding), we conducted interviews in the agency and in the core departments to try to establish what accountability meant in practice for the participants and to pick up on accountability issues which are not otherwise observable. As the title of the project suggested, we were concerned not simply with formal accountability to ministers and Parliament, but with the full range of groups to which agencies felt they ought to give accounts of their activity. Because we wanted to avoid attributing any findings simply to agency status, we also explored a similarly sized sample of other bodies used by government for delivering policy, including non-ministerial departments, non-departmental bodies in the public sector, and bodies nominally not in the public sector but carrying out a policy delivery function.

In this chapter we start by providing some background information on the development of agencies, and place this in the context of the wider range of bodies through which departments deliver policies. We then explore the multilevel nature of the concept of accountability before setting out the formal basis of operation and accountability of agencies. We discuss what accountability to Parliament means in practice, whether through questions, letters from MPs, or select committee investigations. Given the crucial nature of the link with the minister in the accountability debate, we look at the wide variation in their involvement in practice. We then switch to the perspective from the agencies on the wide range of sources of demands for information and

* Funded by the ESRC as part of its Whitehall Programme (Award no.: L124251014).

scrutiny placed on them. MPs and core departments are only one of the constituencies to which agencies feel obliged to offer accounts of their activity, and we give illustrations of the range of such other constituencies. Throughout the chapter we draw on evidence both on Next Steps agencies and other bodies, but towards the end we identify some patterns of similarity and difference among the various categories.

Background: the development of agencies in context

This section sets out the development and characteristics of Next Steps agencies in British government. It sets this development in the context of other changes in public bureaucracy in Britain, since the implications of Next Steps agencies, including those for accountability, are often discussed in isolation from the implications of those other developments.

On 18 February 1988, Mrs Thatcher, the then British Prime Minister, announced her acceptance of a report produced by the efficiency unit within the Cabinet Office, *Improving Management in Government: the Next Steps* (The Ibbs Report 1988), which, she stated, 'recommended that to the greatest extent practicable the executive functions of government, as distinct from policy advice, should be carried out by units clearly designated within Departments, referred to as "agencies"' (HC Debates 18 February 1988, column 1149).

The data shown in Table 11.1 would appear to indicate that the agency initiative has been a resounding success, with 77 per cent of UK civil servants

Table 11.1   The development of Next Steps agencies

Year (April)	Number of UK agencies[a]	UK civil servants		
		In agencies	Including 'Next Steps' lines[b]	As % of all UK civil servants
1989	3	5 800	5 800	1
1990	26	60 800	60 800	11
1991	48	177 000	204 000	37
1992	66	197 000	287 000	51
1993	82	249 000	335 000	60
1994	91	252 000	334 000	63
1995	97	277 000	357 000	68
1996	102	275 000	350 000	71
1997	110	286 000	364 000	77
1998	112	277 000	356 000	77

Notes: a. Number of agencies excludes agencies of the Northern Ireland Civil Service (25 by September 1998) and the Forestry Commission (2).

b. The 'Next Steps lines' column adds staff of the 24 executive units of Customs and Excise (from 1991) and 24 executive offices of Inland Revenue (from 1992) and of the Crown Prosecution Service and the Serious Fraud Office (from 1997).

Sources: *Civil Service Statistics* (annual, Cabinet Office); *Next Steps Briefing* (occasional, Cabinet Office).

now in agencies or 'working on Next Steps lines'. It is worth noting that although the net number of agencies and their share of civil servants continued to grow after 1995, the number of staff in agencies did not rise overall, and actually fell between 1997 and 1998, reflecting not only civil service reductions overall, but also falls in many agencies, as well as the effects of privatising agencies. The process of establishing new agencies was still not complete at the end of 1998, despite being supposed to be complete by 1993. The candidates for newly established agencies are largely to be found in the Northern Ireland Civil Service and the Ministry of Defence, neither of which appear to have been the targets of the original initiative. Agencies have now been established sufficiently long that they are routinely subject to organisational succession in the form of privatisations, splittings and mergers; this makes the process of trying to track the process of agency formation by body count complex, since the totals may contain different sets of organisations.

Staff of agencies remain civil servants and also part of their department, except for those agencies which were already separate non-ministerial departments. A distinctively British feature is that the establishment of agencies, both in terms of the general principle and individual agencies, does not require any legislative action, even secondary legislation.

The implication of Mrs Thatcher's February 1988 statement appeared to be that the structure of government was to move from an old pattern of monolithic departments with no clear separation of policy and executive functions, in which ministers were responsible for all activities, however detailed, to a new standard pattern of small policy cores with nearly all executive activities carried out by agencies within departments, and with ministers not taking responsibility for day-to-day operational decisions. The acceptance of these before and after patterns is implicit in the early academic critiques voicing concern about the implications of the Next Steps initiative for ministerial responsibility for the actions of their departments (see, for example, Drewry 1990).

However, the view that the Next Steps initiative has entailed a move away from a previous standard monolithic pattern to a new simple core-agency pattern can be challenged. A monolithic pattern is a grossly inadequate characterisation of how the functions of central government were delivered prior to 1988, and the pattern which applies as the launch of new agencies nears completion has so many variations that a simple core-agency characterisation is insufficient. There are three main issues here (following Hogwood 1995):

1. The *pre-1988 picture* was not one of standard monolithic departments, which were the exception rather than the rule. One-quarter of the civil service were in non-ministerial departments (some of which are now also agencies), and many ministerial departments had distinct organisational units within them. A further quarter of the civil service was in the Ministry of Defence, with its distinctive intertwining of civil service and military staff at all levels.
2. The *process of organisational change* in British central government since 1988 cannot be adequately characterised as the identification of policy advice

cores with all executive functions then being assigned to agencies. The establishment of Next Steps agencies was only one of the many forms utilised by government in undertaking organisational change in the means of policy delivery. Others have included the use of statutory non-departmental public bodies, regulators of privatised industries with the status of non-ministerial departments, and the use made of nominally private or voluntary organisations for policy delivery.

3. The prospective *pattern on completion* of the Next Steps initiative is not one of policy advice cores with all central government executive actions being performed through Next Steps agencies. Rather, there are immense variations in the extent to which the residual department can be considered to be limited to a policy advice core as implied in Mrs Thatcher's statement, and in the extent to which separately identifiable units engaged in delivery take the form of Next Steps agencies. For example, the Department of Social Security has over 84 000 of its 87 000 staff in agencies (96.8 per cent) but sponsors only three non-departmental public bodies with a total staff of 100. By contrast, the Department of Culture, Media and Sport has only one agency, employing 231 out of its 612 staff, but sponsors 37 non-departmental public bodies, with a total staff of 12 400. The debate about accountability of agencies to ministers often focuses on the bilateral link between an agency and the minister, but clearly the relationship between agencies and ministers is bound to be different in a department with 44 agencies (Defence), compared to a department with one engaged in a core activity (the Employment Service in the Department for Education and Employment).

What is accountability?

The words 'accountability' and 'responsibility' are frequently used interchangeably, and where an attempt to differentiate them is made, the contrasted pair may be given the opposite meanings by different authors. Dictionary definitions often define one in terms of the other. *Chambers* gives one meaning of 'account' as: 'to answer as one responsible: to have the responsibility or credit'; 'responsible' has as one of its definitions: 'liable to be called to account as being in charge or control'. The distinction or lack of it is not simply a matter of semantics, since the issue of whether they can be differentiated lies at the heart of the debate in Britain about the relationship between ministers, civil servants and Parliament. This debate is not simply an academic one, but is hotly disputed in political argument. It is particularly relevant to Next Steps agencies as evidenced by the difference of view between the Treasury and Civil Service Committee (1994) and Sir Robin Butler on this issue and, more dramatically, the Learmont Report (1995) and the subsequent dismissal of the head of the Prison Service agency. However, as the Scott Report (1996) has shown, it has a broader application as well.

Accountability has normative implications. An examination of the derivation of the term accountability indicates that it does not necessarily carry connotations of democracy and participation – something, which some current uses of the word might imply. Historically, accountability might be to a king or tyrant, or even to God through the monarch. Accountability needs to be distinguished conceptually from democracy or participation, though particular manifestations of accountability may invoke or be invoked by such concepts. Interestingly, Day and Klein (1987) came to the conclusion that election was neither a necessary nor a sufficient condition for control or accountability:

> If members' perceptions of accountability are largely shaped by internalized feelings of a duty and an ability to explain and justify, as suggested by our evidence, election is not a necessary condition for bringing this about.

Further, on the issue of whether you can have too much of a good thing, too much calling to account may confuse the issue of who is responsible (see Hogwood, Judge and McVicar 1998). Calling to account may actively impede the ability of the management of an organisation to administer effectively the delivery of the services in relation to which they are to be called to account.

In this section we attempt to unpack the different meanings which can be embraced by the term accountability and its twin term responsibility. A range of these different meanings may apply to a particular individual or institution simultaneously, or they may be widely distributed among different postholders.

Accountability as the keeping and verification of a correct record

Here the concern is with veracity, fullness and timeliness of the keeping of records and summaries. Day and Klein (1987: 8) argue that 'the concept of accountability as verification is neither historically nor logically linked to ideas about political accountability seen as answerability to the people'. Day and Klein are concerned with the keeping of financial records, but the principle could be extended to keeping accurate records of other kinds relevant to the making and delivery of public policy. The role of Accounting Officer in the British Civil Service has this meaning as its starting, though not necessarily finishing, point. We might wish to make a further subdivision between the process of preparing accurate accounts and the verification of those accounts.

Accountability as the requirement (or obligation assumed) to provide information

In contrast to the keeping and verification of records, this meaning of accountability is concerned with providing information to a set of persons recognised or claiming to have a right to such information. This information might be provided either in a routinised form such as annual reports or annual accounts or specific instances where information is requested (such as a parliamentary question, Ombudsman investigation, or select committee investigation) or offered unprompted (such as a press release). In the widest sense, this involves rendering an account, but with a meaning much wider than numerical or financial reckoning or counting. This meaning involves answerability in the narrow sense of being expected to offer an answer. If it is to be differentiated from responsibility, then, as the Scott Report emphasised, the veracity, fullness (and also timeliness) of the provision of the information is crucial.

Redirecting responsibility

Dowding (1995: 155) uses the term *redirecting responsibility* to describe circumstances where a policy area or institution falls within the remit of a minister but the minister declines to provide the information and redirects the request. This could be either by referral by the minister or by the minister suggesting that the person requesting the information, even if a Member of Parliament, should direct the request to the chief executive of the body actually delivering the service, on the grounds that it is an 'operational' matter. Although Dowding does not discuss this point, there is a potential implication that, if the account given by the person to whom the enquirer is referred is unsatisfactory, there is a recourse to the minister (for whom read other appropriate person) with ultimate responsibility in this sense that the information be provided.

Responsibility as the formal recognition that the person or post is 'in charge or control'

This narrow, formal sense of responsibility does not directly imply blame-worthiness or praiseworthiness. The introduction of Next Steps agencies led to the public identification of chief executives as responsible for the operation of agencies within the framework document and annual plans for their agency. As we will see later, however, for some agencies the distinction between formal responsibility for policy matters (plus accountability in the narrow sense outlined above) of ministers and the operational responsibility of chief executives is difficult, perhaps meaningless to draw. In practice, people at different points of a chain of accountability and responsibility will have formal responsibility for different aspects of an organisation's work simultaneously. It may be particularly difficult to separate a minister's responsibility for policy, the framework documents and resource allocation from the operational responsibility of chief executives.

Although we can conceive of formal responsibility as a state in itself, it is in practice likely to be associated with at least one of the following three types: proclaiming, explaining or justifying; amendatory responsibility; and conferring or accepting praise or blame.

Proclaiming, explaining or justifying

Dowding (1995) refers to one sense of accountability as being 'explaining or justifying'; This latter implies going beyond a merely formal acceptance of responsibility to one which accepts a more substantive ownership of it, as would, for instance, proclaiming.

Amendatory responsibility

Dowding lists this type of responsibility and it perhaps can be caricatured as 'we're not to blame but accept that something needs to be done'. If this type of responsibility is regarded as distinct it implies a more than subtle distinction between formal *acceptance* of responsibility – perhaps for a *fait accompli* or response to uncontrollable and or one-off events – and responsibility which accepts that, while not blameworthy, *action* needs to be taken to cope in future with the same or similar circumstances or any other circumstances which might be covered by an investigation of the events under scrutiny. Dowding includes a range of responses including possibly symbolic investigation, through punishing individual civil servants, reorganisation and policy change.

Praiseworthy or blameworthy

Whether someone is identified as being formally in charge or control is different from whether that person will be praised if the organisation appears to be doing well, or blamed if it is doing badly. This distribution can arise in two, sometimes overlapping, ways:

1. it is accepted that there are factors beyond the control of the person in charge;
2. blame (or less likely, praise) is conferred on a person or persons identified as being more directly involved in the activity concerned.

Examples of (1) would be where an agency concerned with processing failed companies did not meet its targets as a result of a recession. Judgements of this kind are rarely likely to be clear-cut, however – even if an organisation is not in charge of events affecting its ability to deliver to target, how far should it anticipate such contingencies? The willingness of ministers to blame subordinates is seen by some commentators as undermining the essential nature of ministerial responsibility and the role of the civil service.

Reward or punishment

The conferment of praise or blame does not of itself produce a substantive reward or punishment, unless praise and blame are felt to be their own reward or punishment. Rewards may take the form of financial incentives, promotion and renewed contract. Punishments can take the form of loss of bonuses and forced resignation. Resignation or dismissal may be seen as the ultimate acceptance or imposition of substantive responsibility. Dowding refers to 'sacrificial or punitive responsibility'; the term sacrificial implies an undeserved punishment or at least one that should have been shared.

It may be worth separating out rewards or punishments while continuing to hold office from what Day and Klein (1987: 229) describe as 'accountability in the strict sense, that is the revocability of a mandate'.

The different meanings of accountability may be accepted by a post-holder or they may have that meaning imposed upon them: Derek Lewis did not accept that as chief executive of the Prison Service he was responsible in the sense of being blameworthy or punishable, and was sacked. The Home Secretary, while accepting that he was required to give an account and take amendatory action, did not accept blame or that he should resign, and was not sacked.

Accountability for what?

Accountability may not be seamless: the same person may have different types of accountability in relation to different aspects of an organisation's activity.

Day and Klein (1987: 24) suggest that responsibility *for* ensuring certain standards may override responsibility *to* particular persons or posts. In practice there may be a mixture. This mix is at heart of debate in Britain about whether civil servants can owe a responsibility to other than the government of the day.

Thus one can conceive in principle of:

- accountability for a particular aspect as an absolute value, leaving aside how this would be verified or enforced;
- accountability for different aspects to different actors.

Even a brief association with the history of accountability in practice indicates that accountability for different aspects may be owed either to different persons or through different routes to that person, even if one goes back, as Day and Klein do, to Athenian direct democracy.

The aspects of operations for which a person or organisation may be held accountable including the following:

- the formal legality of expenditure (both in terms of conformity to purpose and probity and avoidance of corruption);
- the accurate reporting of expenditure and other information, including issues of whether there has been a change in the basis on which it can be judged whether a policy is being properly conducted;
- efficiency in using resources;
- effectiveness at two levels;
  - effective implementation;
  - effectiveness of policy design in achieving outcomes;
- procedural correctness (avoidance of maladministration);
- correct determination of cases;
- customer care ('quality' of service rather than substantive treatment).

The timing of accountability requirements

A crucial issue in accountability as it relates to autonomy is the timing of accountability requirements in relation to the performance of tasks. Among the issues are the requirements or expectations of reporting prior to taking an action, and the formal or *de facto* ability of the person to whom a report is made to veto or impose an alternative to the proposed action. Examples would include pre-clearance of casework. We can distinguish between cases where an account is offered, but where the person to whom the account is given has no rights of veto of the action, and those where the person to whom the account of the proposed action is given has the right to determine the actual decision. Examples of the former would be the formal legal independence of the Charity Commission in deciding their actions in relation to a particular charity while informing the relevant Home Office Minister, and the right of the Highways Agency to proceed with the eviction of an elderly person in the path of an approved road while warning the minister concerned because of the possible political repercussions. Examples where pre-clearance is substantive include the role of the Home Secretary in the cases of individual prisoners, and of the Secretary of State for Industry in decisions about matters he or she has referred to the Competition Commission (formerly the Monopolies and Mergers Commission).

Another interesting issue relating to the timing of accountability is whether a department or minister sees the proposed answer which a chief executive of an agency or other body proposes to give to a Member of Parliament or other person, and whether the minister has the right or *de facto* ability to veto or rewrite the proposed answer. This issue is addressed empirically later in the chapter.

Accountability to whom?

Day and Klein (1987: 10–15) show that as modern welfare states developed, both the number of persons to whom an account has to be given and the complexity of the links grew. It is not simply a question of an organisation becoming more responsible to more than one other person or organisation, but that every actor is in some way accountable to one or more others, either directly or indirectly. Actors can be responsible by a number of different routes for different aspects of their work. The picture will look different depending on the particular con-stitutional arrangements and policy delivery structures in different countries, but in all developed countries we would expect a complex pattern. The significance of each type of link – to minister, to customer, to courts – will vary for different agencies.

The issue of accountability *through* whom is at least as important as the issue of accountability to whom. The traditional debate in Britain about ministerial responsibility is concerned in part with the accountability of civil servants through ministers to Parliament. For agencies the issue arises of the extent to which accountability links should be directed or mediated, for example, through agency boards, through civil servants (both agency official link and Permanent Secretaries), and through ministers, or indeed whether accountability in practice stops at the point of the intermediaries rather than the formal ultimate recipient of accounts of activity.

The 'standard' Next Steps model

Executive Agencies are based upon a nominal separation of policy and 'operational matters' within departments. The government accepted the Ibbs Report recommendation that 'agencies should be established to carry out the executive functions of government within a policy and resources framework set by a department' (Ibbs Report 1988: 9). The clear assumption was that:

> The main strategic control must lie with the Minister and Permanent Secretary. But once the policy objectives and budgets within the framework are set, the management of the agency should have as much independence as possible in deciding how these objectives are met ... the presumption must be that, provided management is operating within the strategic direction set by ministers, it must be left as free as possible to manage within that framework. (Ibbs Report 1988: 9)

The idea behind Next Steps is, thus, in Peter Kemp's words, 'essentially a most simple concept, in some ways almost naive' (HC 313-III 1996: 107). Or as Derek Lewis put it more graphically, the concept of agency status 'is not rocket science, it is very simple basic management principles' (HC 313-III 1996: 94, q. 606). Agencies are simply administrative arrangements within departments, the functions exercised by agencies are vested in the department and not in the agency itself, so that the division of responsibilities between agencies and departments is determined by the Framework Document and not by statute (see HC 313-II 1996: 35).

The staff of agencies are still civil servants, working under civil service terms and conditions, financed by public finances and accountable through ministers to Parliament (Kemp in HC 313-III 1996: 107) – with the non-trivial exceptions of military and other civil staff who also work in agencies, an element ignored in confining the agency debate to questions of ministerial–civil service relations. The delegation of tasks, and the extent of managerial devolution to the chief executive, is outlined in the Framework Document. The officially proclaimed expectation is that once authority has been delegated ministers effectively 'withdraw' from operational matters – the daily, routine matters that have no general policy implications (Brazier in HC 313-II, 1996: 11). In this sense there would be a 'depoliticisation' of operational matters, but the extent of depoliticisation is limited in practice by the overarching accountability of ministers to Parliament.

In addition to the initial Framework Document, agencies are subject to a five-year cycle of 'Prior Options' reviews, so called because they include consideration of whether the activity should continue at all, be privatised, or organised in a different way. If the decision is to continue the activity as an agency, a new Framework Document is prepared.

There are also annual corporate plans, some of which are kept confidential to the agency and its department for commercial reasons, and annual reports laid before Parliament. An important annual element is the setting of targets for performance indicators, with the results being published in the consolidated annual *Next Steps Review*.

So the officially proclaimed model is one of separation of policy and execution, operation within a Framework Document which specifies the roles of minister, main department and agency chief executive, and reporting on annual targets. Within that the chief executive is supposed to have operational autonomy, subject to the important *caveat* of continuing ministerial responsibility. The remainder of the chapter explores the extent to which this model applies in practice.

MPs and accountability

Parliamentary questions

Agencies attract the attention of MPs unequally. Our systematic analysis (using the POLIS database) of parliamentary coverage of agencies reveals that in quantitative terms written parliamentary questions (WPQs) are overwhelmingly the major recorded way in which MPs seek to call agencies to account through formal parliamentary mechanisms. Similarly, letters from MPs to ministers traditionally provide for a cost efficient and effective means of alerting ministers to backbench concerns. Taken together, parliamentary questions and letters from MPs provide, in quantitative terms alone, the most systematic formal indicator of MPs' collective interest in executive actions.

Agencies attract differing numbers of parliamentary questions (see Table 11.2) and letters from MPs (see Judge, Hogwood and McVicar 1997: Appendix 2). Since November 1992, letters sent by agency chief executives to MPs in response to parliamentary questions have been printed in the daily *Official Record*, beneath a standard statement by the minister with responsibility for the agency. As the then Leader of the House, Tony Newton, informed MPs: 'The arrangements apply to questions tabled on operational matters for which responsibility has been delegated by Ministers to agency chief executives' (*HC Debates*, 20 October 1992, vol. 212, cols 287–8w). A few agencies consistently attract more questions, and supply more answers directly from their chief executives than others. Half-a-dozen can be identified as the 'big fish' swimming in the waters closest to parliamentary view and interest; at an intermediate level there are a further half-dozen which are subject to lower levels of parliamentary questioning, and in the murkier depths are a host of agencies which attract few, or in some cases, no parliamentary questions in a three-month period.

This pattern is repeated if letters from MPs to ministers and chief executives are examined. Again the Employment Service, Prison Service, Benefits Agency and

Table 11.2   Agencies ranked by Written Parliamentary Questions (WPQs), 1995

Name of agency/Number of agencies in group	WPQs (N)
HM Prison Service	613
Child Support Agency	231
Benefits Agency	217
Employment Service	188
Highways Agency	187
Insolvency Service	109
Court Service	90
Defence Evaluation and Research Agency	87
Marine Safety Agency	84
Patent Office	69
Chemical and Biological Defence Establishment	59
Intervention Board	51
21 agencies	26–50
43 agencies	11–25
40 agencies	0–10

Note: Figures exclude HMSO and Central Statistical Office.
Source: Authors' database derived from Justis Parliament CD-ROM (POLIS).

Child Support Agency are at the forefront of MPs' (and their constituents') attention, while the War Pensions Agency also attracted over 1000 letters. A group of 8 agencies attracted intermediate levels of attention, between 101 and 1000 letters; 32 received between 11 and 100; followed by 38 agencies which received only between one and 10 letters in a year. 34 received no correspondence from MPs at all.

Our detailed content analysis of questions asked and answers provided in relation to selected agencies in sessions 1995–96 and 1996–97 enables us to identify just what MPs are concerned about when they ask questions (Hogwood and Judge 1998). Around a quarter of all answers to written parliamentary questions on agencies focus not on the work of any specific agency but on aspects of agencies or departments in general. For 9 out of 20 agencies in our sample, such WPQs accounted for 50 per cent or more of questions.

All WPQs are to an extent a manifestation of accountability, but only 6.5 per cent of questions required ministers or chief executives to respond directly to concerns about accountability, and for half the agencies the issue of accountability was not raised at all. Overall, just under 50 per cent of answers to MPs' queries related directly to substantive policies or decisions taken by the agency; apart from 'inspired' questions other questions related to issues of market testing or privatisation and to staffing and employment practices.

In terms of who asks the questions, the answer points overwhelmingly to an opposition-based form of accountability, rather than the nineteenth-century notion of the House acting as a corporate body collectively holding the executive to account for its actions. Questions from opposition frontbenchers (including Liberal Democrat spokespersons) accounted for 28 per cent of answers on agencies. Questions from backbenchers accounted for nearly two-thirds of answers, but 78 per cent of those were from opposition backbenchers.

The issue of who should answer questions was a very sensitive issue in the early stages of Next Steps. Replies from questions passed to chief executives for reply have been published in the Official Report since 1992. Nearly two-thirds (64 per cent) of answers in our sample were provided by chief executives. In early years there appeared to be inconsistency across departments in terms of whether similar questions were answered by ministers or chief executives. The findings from our sample is that the pattern seems to have settled down into a consistent one, which is not to say that the ambiguity of the distinction between policy and execution has been resolved in all matters relating to agencies.

Select committees

In their review of the achievements of select committees in scrutinising Next Steps agencies in the period 1988 to 1993, Natzler and Silk (1996: 73) concluded: 'The general perception is that they have done rather little. There has certainly been no systematic attempt either by select committees as a whole, or by individual select committees, to undertake a conscious programme of inquiries into agencies' (HC 323 1996–97: paragraph 29). In 1997, the Liaison Committee, in reviewing the activities of select committees in the 1992–97 Parliament, also concluded that 'to date Executive Agencies have not been sufficiently accountable' and that ways should be studied to improve the parliamentary scrutiny of agencies and other bodies. While recognising that some committees had far more agencies within their departmental remit, and that each committee had the right to determine its own work programme, nonetheless, the Liaison Committee believed that 'it would be appropriate, indeed essential, for the new committees to build into their forward programme examination of some if not all of the Agencies and other non-Departmental Bodies of whom they have an oversight' (HC 323 1996–97: paragraph 31).

Our general review of the activities of select committees in the sessions 1995–96 and 1996–97 confirms the unsystematic coverage afforded by departmental select committees to agencies, but also reveals that the investigations of committees brings them, of necessity, into contact with agency officials. Over the two sessions, representatives from a total of 12 executive agencies provided oral evidence before the departmental select committees. In 1995–96, five departmental committees heard evidence from 14 witnesses from these agencies, and in 1996–97 the corresponding figures were five committees and 16 witnesses. In the same sessions a number of committees received evidence from bodies which were later to become agencies. Thus, for example, the Northern Ireland Affairs Committee, in its investigation into the planning systems in Northern Ireland, questioned T. W. Stewart who, at the time, was the designate Chief Executive of the new Planning Agency (see HC 53 1995–96). Similarly, in 1996–97, Michael Finnigan, the then head of Statutory Services of ADAS and Chief Executive Designate of the Farming and Rural Conservation Agency, provided evidence to the Agriculture Committee during the course of its investigation into environmentally sensitive areas (see HC 45 1996–97).

In accordance with our wider findings about parliamentary questions, the high visibility agencies – the Child Support Agency, the Benefits Agency and the Prison Service – also attracted the attention of the relevant select committees. In the case of the Child Support Agency and Prison Service they were subject respectively to detailed examinations of their 'performance and operation' (Social Security Select Committee HC 50 1995–96) and 'management' (Home Affairs HC 57 1996–97).

As for the 20 selected agencies in our sample, only Lawrie Haynes, Chief Executive of the Highways Agency, and his colleague Peter Nutt, were called upon to provide oral evidence in the Transport Committee's inquiry into the road and bridge maintenance programme (HC 105 1996–97, see also below the Public Accounts Committee Report HC 83 1996–97). No other chief executives from the Next Steps agencies in the sample were called upon to provide oral evidence, nor submitted written memoranda to the departmental select committees. In contrast, executives from some of the other bodies in our sample appeared before select committees with some regularity. In 1996–97 alone, the Environment Agency provided evidence to the Agriculture Committee (HC 45 1996–97 – environmentally sensitive areas), the National Heritage Committee (HC 108 1996–97 – tourism) and twice to the Environment Committee (HC 22 1996–97 – contaminated land and HC 42 1996–97 – water conservation and supply). In the same session, the Chairman and Director General of the Health and Safety Executive appeared before the Environment Committee to provide evidence on the work of the Executive (HC 277 1996–97), and oral evidence was provided by representatives of the National Trust to both the Agriculture (HC 45 1996–97) and National Heritage Committees (HC 108 1996–97). Overall, some 82 other bodies provided oral evidence to departmental select committees during the course of the two sessions under study.

Despite little interest being shown in the activities of our sample of agencies, it is worth noting that in the first session of the 1997 Parliament the Select Committee on Defence undertook a detailed review of the Defence Evaluation and Research Agency (DERA). This review followed the Committee's earlier investigations into the Defence Medical Services (HC 142 1996–97). The Committee's inquiry was wide-ranging and covered DERA's performance, the issue of technology transfer, as well as the future status of DERA. The final report (HC 621 1997–98) followed upon the heels of a report from the National Audit Office (NAO) in December 1997 which focused upon the Agency's objective setting and use of performance indicators.

When the Defence Committee came to consider the future status of DERA, however, it encountered a problem that went directly to the heart of the issue of the accountability of agencies. When the committee requested a copy of DERA's 1998 Corporate Plan, which reviewed the options for the Agency's future status, ministers refused to provide a copy. The grounds for refusal were 'that the Plan fell under the classification of "advice to ministers" and should not, therefore, be disclosed to Parliament (HC 621 1997–98: paragraph 13). The report proceeded to note:

Access to such documents is essential if a select committee is to have a meaningful and well-informed scrutiny role. Restrictions on such access can only undermine departmental accountability to Parliament and should be used very sparingly. (HC 621 1997–98: paragraph 13)

Because the Committee was denied access to DERA's Corporate Plan it was unable to consider the respective merits and risks of all options being considered by ministers.

Public Accounts Committee and the National Audit Office

As Oliver and Drewry (1996: 84) note: 'Audit has always been a key parliamentary function'. Since 1861 the Public Accounts Committee, assisted since 1866 by the Comptroller and Auditor General (C&AG), has had the task of scrutinising the accounts of departments to ensure that money is spent legally and specifically for the purposes for which it was voted. Since 1983 and the National Audit Act, the Comptroller and Auditor General has been an officer of the House of Commons and the Head of the National Audit Office (NAO) and has been responsible for auditing the 'efficiency, effectiveness and economy' of public expenditure. In turn the C&AG and NAO report to the Public Accounts Committee of the House of Commons.

Alongside the traditional verification of financial legality and regularity, the NAO has in recent years placed particular emphasis upon undertaking value-for-money studies (see HC 323 1996–97: Appendix 19). From the inception of the Next Steps Programme the NAO has actively involved itself in advising on the form of agencies' accounts and in auditing those accounts (see Baines 1996: 99–102). By July 1993, the NAO had published eight value-for-money studies on the agencies. The first of these was largely a descriptive account of the work of the Next Steps Project Team and the efforts made by five departments to identify candidates for agency status and the arrangements made to establish these agencies. Thereafter, more detailed investigations were undertaken of the performance of specific agencies which occasionally resulted in combative and confrontational reports (see Baines 1996: 108–10).

Indeed, it has been argued that the 'use of the resources and powers of the National Audit Office formally to inquire into the reasonableness of the policy objectives of a Minister reduce the willingness of departments to engage in a constructive relationship with the C&AG' (HC 313 1995–96: paragraph 139). One good example of the often fraught relationship that has developed between the NAO and agencies is provided by the Child Support Agency. In 1995 the Public Accounts Committee (PAC) examined the creation and first two years of the operation of the CSA (HC 31 1995–96). The committee was gravely disturbed that at least 40 per cent of child maintenance assessments made in 1993–94 contained errors and severely criticised the Department and the Agency for allowing that state of affairs to arise. The PAC offered a number of recommendations aimed at improving the work of the Agency and its management of maintenance debt. On the basis of a further report by the C&AG in

1996–97 (HC 124 1997–98), the PAC returned to investigate the accuracy of assessments made by the Agency since 1995, the speed of processing work, and the management of outstanding debt (HC 313 1997–98). The committee also examined the challenges facing the Agency and its plans to improve the quality of service. Its conclusions were riddled with the words 'unacceptable' and 'appalled', phrases like 'continuing errors' 'cause hardship and distress to people at a difficult time of their lives'; and 'serious questions' were raised about whether the regulations under which the CSA operated could achieve fairness and equity in practice. The report went on to express its 'extreme disappointment' at the large numbers of outstanding reviews of assessments, and that it was 'disturbed' at the level of outstanding debt. Overall, the PAC questioned whether the Agency could deal with the immense task confronting it without 'radical action' in simplifying the very complex regulations and developing the need for greater sensitivity.

Of the 20 agencies in our sample only three had had aspects of their work investigated by the NAO by the end of the 1992–97 parliamentary session. In session 1994/95 the NAO conducted a value-for-money study of Historic Scotland's performance on protecting and presenting Scotland's heritage properties (HC 430 1994/95), and in the following session examined the extent and cost of sickness absence in HM Land Registry (HC 94 1995–96). The PAC followed the C&AG's Report with its own Report on this subject in which the Land Registry was criticised 'for allowing an increasingly serious problem [of sickness absence] to get away from them (HC 307 1995/96: paragraph 16).

The Bridge Programme of the Highways Agency was examined by the NAO in session 1995–96 (HC 282 1995–96). The Bridge Programme was inherited by the Agency from the Department of Transport and was halfway through its 15 year life. The NAO report considered the performance of the Agency in realising the programme's aims alongside a wider examination of the Agency's management of resources. On the basis of the C&AG's Report, the PAC undertook an investigation of the extent to which objectives of the Bridge Programme were being met and whether programme resources were being managed efficiently. In its characteristically strident style the PAC noted that it was 'disturbed' that the Agency was not keeping pace with the required maintenance programme, 'concerned' at the shortfall in the number of inspections carried out, and 'regretted' that an effective bridge management information system was not yet in place some eight years after the PAC had made such a recommendation to the Department of Transport (HC 83 1996–97).

When the Transport Select Committee came to investigate the road and bridge maintenance programme a few months later (HC 105 1996–97) no explicit reference to the NAO's report was made (other than in the written evidence of the Department of Transport itself HC 105 1996–97: 115). This was despite the Chairman of the Transport Committee having earlier identified 'merit in some more formal relationship between the NAO and departmental select committees. It would, for example be useful to be consulted formally by the NAO on its programme of work so that duplication of effort can be minimised' (HC 323-I

1996–97: Appendix 25). Undoubtedly, informal links between departmental committees and the NAO have been extended in recent years, and a clear case has been made for the further development of these links; nonetheless, there remains a reluctance within the House of Commons to formalise these relationships (see HC 323-I 1996/97: paragraph 26). How far this informal relationship would be transformed if select committees heeded the prompting of the Liaison Committee to 'build into their forward programme examination of some if not all of the Agencies and non-Departmental Bodies of whom they have an oversight' (HC 323-I 1996–97: paragraph 31) is open to conjecture. What is not open to speculation, however, is the widespread view in Westminster that in relation to select committees 'to date Executive Agencies have not been sufficiently accountable' (HC 323-I 1996–97: paragraph 29; see also HC 313 1995–96).

Ministers and accountability

One crucial link in the chain of accountability is that between the minister and the agency. One indicator of such involvement is frequency of meetings between Chief Executive and Secretary of State (see Hogwood, Judge and McVicar: Appendix 1, final column). The variations are extreme, with 43 meetings in the case of the Prison Service and no meetings in the case of many agencies. There are also variations in the extent to which agency chief executives may participate in weekly meetings of all senior civil servants in a department with ministers.

There are also structural differences in approach arising from the differing status of agencies. Some agencies, such as Companies House, do not formally report through civil servants in the minister's main department, but direct to the minister. This affords them the same status as other non-ministerial departments, such as the Charities Commission and the Office for Standards in Education. Other large agencies report through the Permanent Secretary, while smaller agencies may have as their primary contact either a lower rank civil servant or a departmental board. For the agencies associated with the Ministry of Defence there is a specified chain of command which often involves military officers, and through which agencies, large and small, report.

The handling of replies to parliamentary questions provides another indication of the variability in procedures affecting ministers and agencies (see list in HC 313-I 1996: xliii). Tony Wright's researches into whether ministers had amended replies from chief executives, revealed 'a sort of pick-and-mix system, some had, some had not, some had large figures, some had small figures' (HC 313-III 1996: 160, q 930). What he sought to discover, as 'a basic point about accountability', was 'who owns the answers?'. The response is that at one end of the spectrum there are those agencies where PQs are answered exclusively by the chief executive and which are unseen by ministers prior to finalisation (Northern Ireland); and, at the other end, there are those agencies in which ministers routinely 'approve' the replies of chief executives (Transport). However, the difference in formally-stated practice is among ministerial departments. For most, the standard practice is that the minister may see a copy of an answer but would not normally intervene (HC 313-I 1996: xliii). There is no evidence of different treatment in practice within a department according to agency characteristics or visibility. There is neither a standard constitutional practice about the role of ministers in relation to chief executives in accounting for operational matters, nor a systematic attempt to structure such relationships on the basis of special characteristics or sensitivities of individual agencies.

We noted earlier that the Prison Service scored highest on many indicators of parliamentary interest. It also provides an extreme and untypical example of involvement by the minister, with the two forms of interest being clearly related. The formally-stated position of the Prison Service is that it is structured so that the principal responsibility for prison *policy* rests with the Home Office. Prison *management* is the responsibility of the Director General, the Prisons Board and individual prison managers (Cooper 1995: 141). The concept of the division of labour is the inspiration behind the entire Next Steps initiative. However, the Home Office has traditionally been closely involved in Prison Service operational matters, contributing to a culture in which departmental interference has become the norm (Talbot 1995).

The absence of a Home Office corporate plan to set out strategy means that, in practice, the Director General has the role of attempting to specify prison policy, subject to various political and public pressures. The Director General is open to enquiries from Ministers, MPs and parliamentary questions. In Learmont's view, this takes up a 'detrimental' amount of time. Indeed, the amount of paperwork throughout the service is judged to have reached 'epidemic proportions' (Learmont 1995: 166). The Prison Services Framework Document specifies the role to be played by the Home Secretary:

> The Home Secretary is accountable to Parliament for the Prison Service. The Home Secretary allocates resources to the Prison service and approves its Corporate and Business Plans, including its key targets.

But the Framework Document is vague in the delineation of responsibility:

> The Home Secretary will not normally become involved in the day-to-day management of the Prison service but will expect to be consulted by the Director General on the handling of operational matters which could give rise to grave public or Parliamentary concern.

In Talbot's view, this allows the Home Secretary an important formal influence over operational matters as well as policy (1995: 17). For example, evidence submitted reveals that the Director General's answers to MPs' questions are cleared with ministers. Shortly after his dismissal (an example of 'sacrificial' responsibility), Derek Lewis complained in interview:

> Agency status was intended to bring greater operational autonomy to the prison service. This clearly has not happened. There are many observers

who now consider the Prison Service to have less autonomy than it did pre-Agency status. There has been very close Ministerial involvement in and scrutiny of operational decisions. (Newsnight, 16 October 1995, quoted in Talbot 1995: 17)

Of course, the Prison Service is politically salient – sensitive and central to the department. It is a core service, comprising nearly 80 per cent of Home Office staff. It is large in overall governmental terms, both in relation to staffing and finance. However, the evidence presented to the Learmont Inquiry indicate that the organisation suffered from pathological accountability – where management was forced to donate a disproportionate effort to meeting its responsibility to be 'accountable' (Learmont 1995). Learmont recorded over 1000 pieces of correspondence between the Prison Service and the Home Office during a four-month period, October 1994 to January 1995, 137 of which were 'substantive'. The inquiry concluded that upwards communication had become the 'raison d'être' of Prison Service headquarters and that a more balanced approach was needed. In particular, a balance needed to be struck between informing ministers and managing the Service (Recommendation 70).

Apart from the extreme case of the Prisons Service, there is substantial variation in patterns of ministerial involvement. We can distinguish in principle between underlying patterns and those associated with particular issues or events. A string of events and issues may lead to a longer term pattern of contact between agency executives and ministers. For example, the Meat Hygiene Service was different from most agencies in that it was not simply an existing civil service activity separated out into an agency. Problems with its establishment, and subsequently the BSE crisis, *e-coli* outbreaks in Scotland, and Labour's commitment to a Food Standards Agency, meant a high frequency of contact between the chief executive and ministers at all levels within the department. Other executives might be involved on relevant matters; for example, the finance director had several meetings within one month on issues concerning charging.

For other agencies, including many in the Ministry of Defence, there would be very little ministerial involvement, except when there was a high profile issue such as announcing a market test or a workshop closure, where the need to refer such matters to the minister's office could lead to delays.

The perspective from the agencies

Our research reveals a mixed picture in terms of whether the requirement to respond is seen by agencies or observers of them as positive or pathological (Hogwood, Judge and McVicar 1998). For most agencies and other bodies, parliamentary accountability is neither a real issue nor 'a problem'. It might even be regarded as a useful feedback mechanism. Lawrie Haynes, chief executive of the Highways Agency, who responded to the question, 'Do you think that answering questions from Members of Parliament ... takes up too much of your time':

> No I don't think so. I believe that there are some genuine questions which come in ... I find this very useful. It is actually quite a good mechanism for staff to be made aware that people are actually caring and looking at their actions. (HC 313-v 1996: 86)

Agencies generally deal diligently with answers to parliamentary questions. One interviewee drew attention to the importance of ensuring that answers were returned in good time, 'because there's nothing more embarrassing for a minister than having a member put down a reminder question about something that we as an agency have not got round to answering' (a Northern Ireland agency).

More generally, other commentators (see for example Norton, HC 313-II 1996: 74) have noted that agency responses to MPs' questions tend to be more extensive than those received directly from ministers; they also are more likely to express hopes that the answers have been helpful, and even in some instances actually to apologise for factual errors or inaccuracies – 'a response one would not associate with the normal run of departmental answers' (Norton in HC 313-II 1996: 74). Thus positive benefits appear to be derived by both agencies and parliament alike in the answering of parliamentary questions by chief executives.

However, for some agencies, there are considerable organisational disbenefits associated with MPs' written questions. Ironically, disbenefits were experienced and identified by some of the smallest and less visible agencies as well as by the most highly visible and larger agencies. Small agencies are particularly aggrieved by the phenomenon of 'trawling questions' where an MP with a general interest, in for example determining the educational background of public servants (see HC Debates 13 March 1998: vol. 307, cols. 383–9) or expenditure on market research by central government (see HC Debates 18 February 1998: vol. 305, cols. 849–51), asks the same question for all departments and agencies without being interested specifically in the work of any single department or agency. In these instances parliamentary responsibility was seen as a disbenefit of agency status.

Of more significance, however, is organisational displacement apparent within a few high profile agencies dealing with politically contentious or sensitive matters. Clearly, the need to respond to MPs' queries, and to be sensitive to a minister's accountability to Parliament, has had an organisational impact in these 'politically sensitive' agencies – to the extent of creating special Parliamentary Groups and Units in some. The sheer volume of MPs' queries and the relentlessness with which these are pursued can assume pathological proportions. Before examining this argument, however, it should be reiterated that for the overwhelming majority of agencies parliamentary scrutiny is not perceived to cause organisational problems. Typical of responses from mid-range agencies (in terms of volume of MPs' questions) was that of one NDPB director who noted: 'we have a couple of people who now deal with PQs on more or less a full-time basis. They are then cleared at the highest level within [the organisation]'.

For other agencies, most particularly the Prison Service, Child Support Agency, Benefits Agency and Employment Service, the persistent interest of MPs in their daily activities has had organisational consequences. Not all of these effects are pathological in themselves. Michael Bichard, ex-chief executive of the Benefits Agency, noted that by the time he left the agency he was signing 85 per cent of the replies to MPs' letters and that this procedure was positively beneficial as he obtained an overview of the agency by 'looking at the vast majority of the enquiries, complaints, suggestions we were getting from MPs' (HC 313-III 1996: 160). Armed with this information he felt that he was well placed both to review performance and also to 'raise any issues which were bubbling around in the organisation' at the monthly meeting between chief executive and minister.

The sheer volume of MPs' enquiries led to the creation of a Parliamentary Group at the centre of the Benefits Agency. Local managers reported to this Group and were expected to refer 'issues which were coming up more than once or were seriously contentious' (HC 313-III 1996: 160). The ex-chief executive of the agency pointed out that it was customary to send periodic guidance to MPs on how they might get the best responses to their queries by contacting local offices in the first instance, or, if it was a more wide-ranging operational matter, they were advised to contact the chief executive rather than the minister. This advice seems to have been heeded, because, by 1995, 65 to 70 per cent of MPs' letters were addressed directly to the chief executive rather than to the minister.

The impact of sustained questioning and interrogation by MPs upon an agency's organisational structure is also evident in the Child Support Agency. A special Task Force had to be created in 1993 in response to the exceptional volume of correspondence – some 5000 letters in one year – directed at Ros Hepplewhite (then Chief Executive). The 1993–94 Annual Report of the Agency noted the introduction of 'new systems to track and control the very high volumes of letters we are receiving from Members of Parliament' (Child Support Agency, 1994: 14). This resulted in the creation of a special Parliamentary Correspondence Unit (PCU) at the London headquarters to deal with letters from MPs. Within a year this unit was expanded and a new computer database developed to improve the quality and reply-time of replies to MPs. In 1994–95 it prepared replies to 12 374 letters from MPs, and CSA Centres (CSAC) around the country also answered around 100 letters a week from MPs (Child Support Agency, 1995: 12). In 1996–97 the PCU and CSAC managers prepared over 17 900 replies to letters from MPs. At the start of the year only

30 per cent of parliamentary correspondence was cleared within the departmentally stipulated 20-day deadline. Overall for 1996–97, the average clearance rate within 20 days improved to 78 per cent (Child Support Agency 1997: 16).

The organisational impact of the need to respond to MPs' queries and to be sensitive to a minister's accountability to Parliament can thus be seen in these 'politically sensitive' agencies. However, the pathological organisational effects – stemming from the tension between, on the one side, operational matters, efficiency and service delivery, and, on the other, policy matters, accountability and political sensitivity – are best illustrated in the case of the Prison Service under the Directorship of Derek Lewis. The former Director General, while finding it difficult to quantify the exact impact of responding directly to MPs' enquiries, was in no doubt that 'the level of detailed involvement and provision of information ... certainly was a distraction' (HC 313-v 1996: 99). The Learmont Report (1995) – a review of prison service security in the light of the escape from Parkhurst Prison on 3 January 1995 – also drew attention to the perceived tension between efficiency and accountability:

> The Director General is required to deal with a great number of ministerial queries, letters from MPs and parliamentary questions. These are now running at a total of 600 questions per year, many of which require discussion with Ministers to achieve a mutually acceptable answer, and 4000 MPs' letters. The Director General has not assumed this task voluntarily: it is assigned to him, as to Chief Executives of all Agencies. It occupies too much of his time, to the potential detriment of the efficient running of the Prison Service. (Learmont Report 1995: 93)

In the case of the Prison Service 'informatory accountability' was thus identified as a 'problem', and Learmont recommended that: 'The problem of the Director General's pre-occupation with Parliamentary matters must be overcome. He must redress the balance of keeping ministers informed and running the Service' (Cm 3020 1995: 110). For Derek Lewis, however, the 'problem' was never overcome, and he was left simply 'to groan every morning when confronted by the heap of letters' (Lewis 1997: 69).

Investigations by the National Audit Office, which reports directly to Parliament, have been a source of some friction, both as to the type of information requested and the resources which have had to be devoted to dealing with the investigation. Adverse publicity arising from reports by the Commons Committee of Public Accounts, such as those into the Child Support Agency, can hardly have been a welcome form of publicity at a time when the agency was already under great strain. For many other agencies, however, the results of wider investigations by departmental select committees are far less negative. Indeed, there is evidence that agencies are willing to use committee reports to sustain their claims to be meeting their stated objectives. Thus, for example, the 1996–97 Annual Report of the Prison Service (HC 274 1997) devoted a whole page to the report of the Home Affairs Committee on management in the prison service. The page was littered with references to the 'praise' from MPs, to 'commendable developments' within the Service, and to the 'congratulations' offered in the report for improvements in service delivery (HC 274 1997: 15). In his foreword to the Annual Report, Richard Tilt, Director General, recorded his 'delight' that 'an all-party group of MPs found so much to praise about the work of the Prison Service'. Certainly, in this instance at least, external accountability was not perceived to be all bad!

We saw above that some agencies attract more parliamentary, public and ministerial interest than others. This led us to ask at an early stage of research, when we had only examined available indicators of involvement by MPs and ministers, just what does accountability mean in practice when there is little or no ministerial or parliamentary interest over a period of a year, especially given the central role which accountability through ministers to Parliament is accorded in the British model? (Judge, Hogwood and McVicar: 1997). Our research, drawing on interviews with officials in agencies and other bodies, and in their core departments, has established that absence of ministerial and parliamentary interest does *not* imply absence of accountability. Even those least subject to MPs' questions or meetings with ministers are nevertheless subject to reporting and scrutiny, particularly by the core department, but also through system-wide reviews.

A number of officials commented to us in interviews that they had been disappointed with agency status and the lack of autonomy. *Repetition* of requests for information was a particular source of grievance, as were departmental-wide information-gathering exercises. One of the concerns from the agency perspective is that some accountability demands are made without reference to other possibly overlapping accountability requirements. For example, a research unit might be reviewed for research excellence under the academic Research Assessment Exercise, but despite achieving a good result may still be subjected to an internal governmental review of its viability as a research centre. Thus an agency may have to account in several different ways for the same aspects of its activities.

Closely related to this redundancy aspect is the perception that agencies are constantly having to show adequacy of procedures or substantive outcomes. Were such reviews confined to the annual target review and setting process and the five-yearly cycle of 'prior options' reviews there would be little complaint (though some executives consider that being accountable on pain of organisational death every five years is rather drastic). However, agencies are to varying degrees constantly being subjected to departmental reviews, system-wide reviews (sometimes as case studies), special reviews of particular functional categories of bodies such as research centres, market-testing, National Audit investigations, and so on.

The Prison Service is unique in the sheer scale of requests for giving an account (followed at some points by the Child Support Agency). However, these requests were largely concentrated on the related parliamentary and 'own' minister and departmental demands. For other organisations – with a range of request levels on the parliamentary side – it is the sheer *multiplicity of the sources of demands* which causes problems. Here the simple linear relationship implicit in the traditional model of ministerial accountability does not apply. The evidence from our interviews is that, while agencies may be happy to embrace many stakeholders in addition to their sponsoring department, such as some types of customers or scientific peers, they resent major demands for information which arrive either frequently or randomly from other sources.

Other constituencies

For all agencies, 'accountability' and the groups to whom they consider themselves to be accountable is wider than the technical definitions high-lighted in framework documents or financial memoranda. Organisations frequently cited constituencies of responsibility and accountability beyond the departmental.

Even the smallest, single function agencies had other constituencies. The Chief Executive and Head Teacher of the Queen Victoria School, Dunblane, considers himself accountable to the parents of the school's pupils and has been active in encouraging greater liaison between the school and parents. He also highlights his responsibility to the pupils in his care. In addition, the school is subject to scrutiny by HM Inspectors – accountable to an official source outwith the core department.

Some bodies may be subject to far greater scrutiny by those with a specialist interest than by Parliament. The Horse Race Levy Betting Board is scrutinised by a popular press whose field of expertise and reporting is specific to the Board's area of operation. So its activities and decisions are open to public assessment by experienced journalists writing for a highly-knowledgeable readership.

A number of the organisations we spoke to are subject to peer review. Cultural and heritage bodies operate in a highly inter-related environment, dealing with other government bodies and independent charities. Representation on each other's boards is a feature of this group. In the case of English Heritage and Historic Scotland, these government agencies also provide funding for charities such as the National Trust and the National Trust for Scotland. Many of the scientific bodies in our survey are also subject to scientific peer-review (often an obligation defined in their framework documents). This was true both of Next Steps agencies and non-departmental public bodies. Such reviews are not restricted to scientific bodies. For example, English Heritage has a range of peer assessment, such as scrutiny by members of professional bodies.

However, some organisations concerned with culture and heritage place an equal or greater emphasis on users. For example, the British Museum argued that responsibility to customers is more important than peer review:

> I don't think that there is any peer accountability ... I think there is responsibility to our customers in the sense that our Head of Public Services is

responsible for ensuring that the service is the kind of service the customer wants. (Interview)

Many agencies provide their services on a contractual basis. Many have 'customers' within both the core and other departments, and outwith government altogether. The customer, as the following quote makes clear, is in an important position:

> The customer truly has very powerful influence. ... I'm not accountable in the sense of a formal reporting system to the [Department], but if they spend some money with us, then I am accountable for ensuring that we deliver to them what is they have asked for and for the price they have asked for and when they've asked for it. (Interview)

Most agencies and NDPBs rejected the notion of the possibility of a conflict of interest between the 'customers' on the one hand and the constitutional responsibility to the department on the other, often because the customer belongs to the department. Many of the organisations we studied are themselves responsible for allocating grants and contracted works to other bodies (both within and outwith government). Therefore, they hold others to account as part of their own accountability. Most of those interviewed considered it essential to ensure that the work they contracted others to do was properly monitored and had systems in place to do so.

In short, all organisations have some form of accountability in addition to the departmental level. In some cases (especially for smaller bodies), they view this as more important than departmental accountability and resent the amount of time taken in dealing with routine requests for information from the core. For some, the accountability relationships are simple and restricted to just a few constituencies. For others, the network of accountability is both complex and diverse.

Comparison with other bodies

Do our findings about agencies also apply to other bodies which the government has established to deliver policy? This question covers both organisations established before the Next Steps initiative was launched and those established since, where the government has chosen not to use the Next Steps agency form. Our overall finding is that there is overlap on many aspects of accountability between the categories, and that variation within each category is more significant than differences between the two categories. We are not arguing that agencies and other bodies are the same, only that some are more similar to those in the other category than they are to those in the same category.

There are sources of convergence and continuing divergence between agencies and non-departmental public bodies. Perhaps the case for similarity was best made by one Chief Executive of a large organisation, who insisted in interview that his organisation was a Next Steps agency when it was in fact an executive NDPB. As with Next Steps agencies, executive NDPBs are subject to a quinquennial review, similar to Prior Options reviews for agencies, in which the continuing need for the activity is considered and whether the NDPB form is the most suited. The reviews look at past performance and problems, aims and objectives, management structures, financial systems, performance measures and targets and the content of the corporate plan (Office of Public Service, *Non-Departmental Public Bodies: a Guide for Departments*). All executive NDPBs are now required to publish annual reports. Summaries relating to the largest ones are, since 1998, published annually in an *Executive Non-Departmental Public Bodies Report*, similar in nature to the *Next Steps Annual Review*.

Many of the scrutiny requirements for agencies and NDPBs are similar, and both may be caught by system-wide reviews, such as that on public sector research establishments. Some reviews may be specific to NDPBs, but be similar in nature to reviews involving agencies. The evidence from our interviews and from questioning in select committee reports is that many concerns are similar. In illustrating the perspective from the agencies, we were often able to pair remarks from agencies with similar ones from NDPBs. Certainly, for some NDPBs, the idea that they are able to operate at arms length from government is not seen as conferring meaningful differences compared to agencies.

There are overlaps between the two types of body in the role of the chief executive as 'accounting officer' for the proper expenditure of money. It is chief executives of NDPBs, not the boards, who are responsible as individuals for finance, and this allocation can lead to a blurring between policy matters and the distribution of expenditure.

There are also sources of divergence, though many of them reflect different frequencies among the two categories rather than absolute differences. Some NDPBs are not directly audited by the National Audit Office, though the NAO has access to their accounts. Many NDPBs are paid through grant-in-aid, which makes it more difficult for a department to claw back money in a year to cope with general departmental funding problems. The publication of reports, though now standardised on annual reports, comes in a variety of forms – House of Commons Papers, Command Papers, published by the Stationery Office, or published by the body itself – whereas agency reports are now all House of Commons papers (although who reads them is another matter).

Boards of NDPBs are more likely to play a visible and significant role as an accountability route in their own right. For a few, though not most, NDPBs, the role of the chair of the board seems quasi-ministerial. The role of boards of Next Steps agency boards, while varying considerably, is more likely to be an avenue of control by departments, while involving less public visibility.

Some NDPBs (for example, Environment Agency, English Partnerships, English Heritage) seem to have particularly complex patterns of other constituencies to which they feel obliged to explain their activities, but this may in large part be related to function. For example, all research bodies, whether agencies or NDPBs, have complex patterns, as do all heritage bodies.

In our content analysis of MPs' questions we compared our selected agencies with a sample of other bodies, including non-departmental public bodies and non-ministerial departments which did not have agency status. We found that there was a substantial overlap between agencies and these other bodies in terms of levels of interest, with great variation within both categories. Non-agencies tended to have a thinner tail, with some bodies attracting no questions over a two-year period. The fact that replies from chief executives of non-agency bodies are not printed in the Official Report precludes a full comparison of content. Questions about accountability accounted for a higher proportion (13.1 per cent compared to 6.5 per cent) of questions than those directed at agencies, as did questions about substantive policy or decisions – at 61 per cent compared to 48 per cent. Questions for non-agency bodies were overwhelmingly answered directly by ministers, with only 7 per cent being answered with the statement that the chief executive would write, and those heavily concentrated in two bodies: the Office for Standards in Education (a non-ministerial department) and the Student Loans Company (originally treated as a private company, but now listed as a non-departmental public body.)

Status as an NDPB certainly does not provide protection from parliamentary scrutiny. We noted earlier in the chapter that 82 NDPBs gave evidence to departmental select committees in 1995–96 and 1996–97, compared to only 12 agencies. The evidence we have collected implies that non-departmental status for bodies with national (as opposed to regional or local) remits does not necessarily imply lack of accountability. For both NDPBs and agencies, a substantial part of any accountability gap is a failure systematically to call to account, rather than of bodies to offer an account when called on.

Conclusions

The debate about the accountability of Next Steps agencies has sometimes had an air of unreality about it. MPs and other commentators expressed concern that agencies would prove a barrier to their ability to call ministers to account. Yet most MPs are not interested in most agencies nearly all of the time. When they are interested they are rarely interested in accountability issues as such. From the evidence of their written Parliamentary Questions they focus on politically hot issues and constituency cases.

Parliamentary and ministerial interest varies from the persistently uninterested, through minor levels of the irritatingly irrelevant (as seen by the agency), through varying levels (sometimes seen as useful feedback), to very high levels in a small number of agencies. Very high levels of interest have the effect of diverting senior management attention and potentially blurring responsibility. In general, low levels of accounting to Parliament reflect low levels of calling to account. An important exception is the inability of Parliament to demand access to corporate plans deemed to be commercially confidential or to constitute advice to ministers.

Another element of unreality is the way in which the debate has often taken place without making it clear what aspects of accountability are being referred to. Making generalisations about the accountability of agencies and other bodies is difficult precisely because the most significant generalisation is that there is so much variety. Even for the simplest agency, a linear model of responsibility of the chief executive to Parliament through the minister can be misleading, both because of what it does stress and because of what it does not mention. For many agencies, direct contact with ministers or Parliament is minimal, but at the same time they will have intensive accountability links with other parts of government, and with constituencies outside government.

What can accountability mean when there is little formal calling to account by Parliament and ministers? In practice, all agencies face demands for information and scrutiny of agencies by host departments and other parts of government. The levels of these demands are only weakly related to levels of parliamentary and ministerial interest, and apply to bodies for which there is very limited parliamentary interest. Such demands range from regular requests to one-off scrutinies. They are not co-ordinated through the agency link in the department, resulting in resentment from agencies about the volume and repetition of demands.

Many discussions about accountability focus on a limited set of actors who have the right to call to account. Such discussions are often about matters of symbolic significance, possibly illustrated by a limited number of special cases. By looking at the full range of agencies, and by incorporating their perspective, we get a much fuller perspective on what accountability means in practice. Agencies themselves readily identify constituencies of responsibility and accountability beyond Parliament and beyond their parent departments.

The irony of our findings is that we have found both accountability gaps and accountability overload, often relating to the same agency. Agencies publish annual reports and other documents which are then ignored in Parliament. A newsletter to users or a scientific conference paper may achieve a wider readership than the formal documentation of accountability. At the same time as being ignored by politicians, agencies may feel swamped by requests for information they do not regard as central to their purpose.

The ultimate irony to emerge from our research is that no-one is accountable for the overall pattern of accountability.

12
Accountability and Control in Next Steps Agencies*

Neil C. M. Elder and Edward C. Page

Introduction

When the UK introduced 'Next Steps' agencies after 1988 there was speculation that what was being introduced owed some sort of debt to a Swedish model of organisation. One of the basic building blocks of the Swedish system of administration has been, since the seventeenth century, the agency. There is evidence that the Swedish experience played a part in the evolution of the Next Steps initiative in the United Kingdom, although it is important here not to overstate the importance of Scandinavian experience (McDonald 1992; cf. Zifcak 1994). In fact, the notion of an agency – an operational unit delivering national government services outside a ministry – is found in other European countries. Germany has had agency structures organisationally separate from ministries but with more or less direct ministerial supervision since at least the nineteenth century. While they were part of a 'new public management' thrust in Britain, institutions bearing at least a superficial resemblance to Next Steps agencies have been around for centuries.

Are there any characteristic patterns of behaviour associated with the existence of agency structures? In the early years of the development of Next Steps agencies many commentators, quite reasonably at the time, believed these constituted a fundamental restructuring of British government and administration. For example, Lewis (1989: 429) argued the reforms would 'transform the civil service as we know it ... there is no doubt that serious questions of accountability are posed'. O'Toole (1989: 41) commented on the 'well-grounded fears about the potential implications for the system of control and accountability in the central administrative machine'. The reality has proved less dramatic. Many of the suggestions about the constitutional significance of agencies have given way to a realisation that however significant the Next Steps changes have been, expectations of radical transformation have not been met.

---

* We would like to acknowledge the ESRC for funding our research (award number: L1242510008).

None of this is to suggest that agency structures do not have the potential radically to change the nature of British administration, but rather to acknowledge that the time scale of any such change is likely to be longer than originally envisaged. If one considers the mechanisms by which Next Steps agencies might have been expected to effect such a transformation in Britain, these are more likely to be long-term than short-term changes. The increased power of agencies that comes through their expertise in a particular area of public policy might take time to develop as the agency increases its reputation as a specialist in operational matters and grows in confidence as an organisation, and as the generation of ministerial officials that has memory of running the services now run by agencies is replaced by a new generation without any such memory. The notion that agencies are accountable for the affairs that they run and that the minister's responsibility is limited might similarly be expected to take generations to take effect in any radical way. Such perceptions among ministers, MPs, the press, groups and the public are likely to be altered by the decades of experience of ministerial responses to a variety of specific incidents and questions rather than by a one-off administrative change.

The purpose of this research was to look at the longer-term trends in the development of agency structures in two countries which have had them for much longer than Britain: Sweden and Germany. Sweden and Germany certainly represent very different political systems from that of the United Kingdom. Let us outline some of the more obvious differences. Sweden is generally classed as a 'social-democratic' welfare state with a tradition of corporatist institutions and is a unicameral parliamentary system with a strong tradition of tripartite corporatism and consensual decision-making different from the bicameral parliamentary system of Britain with a tradition of adversarial politics and an aversion to corporatism. Germany is a federal system governed by coalition governments, the United Kingdom is a unitary state governed by a single party.

However, while such differences must be borne in mind, they do not invalidate the exercise of examining Swedish and German experience for clues about the development of agency structures in Britain. The purpose of this study is to examine whether there is a distinctive pattern of relationship between political leadership and administrative institutions resulting from an agency structure. Since Germany and Sweden have had long experience of agency structures we might expect to be able to detect such effects in these countries above all. The design of our study was to examine in detail the operation of four German and four Swedish agencies.

The term 'agency' covers a wide variety of highly diverse organisations. If we were to look at the whole range of organisations that are included in the Swedish *Statskalender* as agencies, or which are included as German *Anstalten* or *Behörden* we would include, among other types of organisation, universities, cultural missions, libraries and judicial bodies. This study took a rather narrower definition of agency to examine those organisations that are responsible for nationwide service delivery and organisationally separate from national government ministries. We looked at The Swedish National Insurance Board

(*Riksförsäkringsverket* – RFV); The Swedish National Prison and Probation Administration (*Kriminalva[o]rdsstyrelsen* – KVS); The Swedish National Labour Market Administration (*Arbetsmarknadsverket* – AMV) and the Swedish Roads Agency (*Vägverket* – VV). In Germany we looked at the Federal Labour Institute (*Bundesanstalt für Arbeit* – BA); the Federal Meat Research Institute (*Bundesanstalt für Fleischforschung* – BfF); the Federal Office of Constitutional Protection (*Bundesamt für Verfassungsschutz* – BfV) and the Federal Office of Goods Transport (*Bundesamt für Güterverkehr* – BfG).

A further problem any such study must face is that within countries agencies are all different. In any one country agencies differ according to, for example, age, the nature of services the agency provides, the mode of service provision it employs, its internal constitution, its budget size, the level of unionisation and professionalisation of its staff, the political sensitivity of its tasks and so on. Within nation differences might also reflect cross-national similarities (see, for example, Hogwood 1994). For example, the range of activities involved in running a prison service differ from those involved in running a research laboratory. The functional similarities of the Labour Market Board in Sweden and the Federal Labour Institute in Germany might mean that they have, in many respects, stronger similarities to each other than they have with, say, the other agencies in their respective countries we have examined.

Agency structures and national administrative systems

Within nations, agencies are diverse institutions. There are also major cross-national differences notably between the general administrative–legal framework within which agencies operate. These frameworks generate substantial differences in their origins and in the character of the functions and powers delegated to them.

The origins of agency structures differ sharply. In Britain the origins of the Next Steps initiative is firmly rooted in the new public management movement of the 1980s. It would be a mistake to suggest that the objectives of the British reforms were ever entirely clear, but the arguments used by those who set up the agencies tended to include freeing the policy-making ministries from the burdens of detailed operational issues and improving operational delivery. Operational delivery was to be improved by giving greater autonomy to those running the agencies, and here it was envisaged that many chief executives would be recruited from the private sector, to organise and develop precisely how they would perform their tasks. Autonomy would be exercised within a framework of accountability dominated by annual reports evocative of the annual reports a listed company might place before its shareholders and by evaluation against performance targets set by the minister. In addition, the linkage of agency structures to a new public management approach was reinforced by the fact that 'prior options' reviews of agency activity were to be conducted in order to identify any possible areas of agency operation which could be contracted out or sold off to the private sector (for a discussion of the origins of Next Steps see

Greer 1994; Zifcak 1994). In Sweden, the agencies have certainly been the vehicles for new public management reforms of public services with, for example, the Prisons Agency being fundamentally restructured along with the institution of a system of internal leasing of agency property. However, the difference is that in Sweden such managerial innovations are developed within a long-established system of agencies which originated in vastly different circumstances to those of the British.

The modern origins of the British Next Steps agencies, then, differ radically from the origins of agency structures in Sweden and Germany. On much of the European Continent a ministry has historically been associated with a parliamentary tradition. The German administrative historian Otto Hintze points out: 'the stronger the [power of the monarch] ... the looser the structure of the ministries: the stronger the parliamentary control, the closer the integration of the ministry into a solidary unit. ... Parliamentary government needs a closed, unitary ministry as an organ of government' (Hintze 1962: 276). Indeed, the development of the agency structure in Sweden in the seventeenth century coincided with the growth of absolutist institutions. The first agencies were set up under the 1634 Constitution of *Gustavus Adolphus* (see Roberts 1973). The first ministries – seven in number – were brought into being two centuries later, in 1840. But these ministries were not given direct control over the administrative apparatus but were responsible for introducing business at the King's Council. With the growth of parliamentary democracy after the last quarter of the nineteenth century, ministries did not gain executive powers as parliament remained reluctant to agree to the ministries acquiring any individual concentrations of authority (Larsson 1988).

In Germany, the notion that ministries concentrate on broad policy advice leaving execution and delivery to agencies can be associated with a strong tradition in German legal thought, associated with the nineteenth-century theorist Otto von Gierke, who envisaged the state as a series of *Behörden*, authorities with clearly defined functions and with their relationship to other public bodies defined through law (Becker 1989: 224). In addition, Germany has always been a federal state – even under the *gleichgeschaltet* administration of the National Socialists, vestiges of the federal territorial deal struck by Bismarck to unite Germany could still be seen (Caplan 1988). This has meant that ministries in Germany have traditionally had a policy-making rather than policy-implementation function.

The general constitutional–legal status of agencies in Germany and Sweden is also very different from that of agencies in the UK. Agencies in the Swedish structure have a measure of constitutional protection. They feature in the constitution (Riks försäkringsverket, [RF]; see Chapter 11) alongside the law courts and they are insulated from all outside influences – governmental or parliamentary – when they exercise their often highly important quasi-judicial functions in deciding individual cases. At the same time they have been the main building block of Swedish administration, quite divorced from the ministerial model of administration in which ministers have direct responsibility for the execution of policy by a staff of civil servants working within a single organisation. In Sweden this model has been limited to the diplomatic service. Consequently, ministerial staffs, outside the Foreign Ministry, have remained small. Some ministries (including Culture, Transport and Communication, Agriculture and Public Administration) have staffs numbering below one hundred, including clerical staff. The Ministry of Foreign Affairs, with 2200 employees, and the Finance Ministry, with 324 employees, are the two largest ministries; the remainder have fewer than 200 employees. Swedish agencies, for their part, have a general duty of obedience to the government as a collectivity rather than any individual minister under the constitution (RF Chapter 11: paragraph 6) and can be abolished, amalgamated or otherwise re-shaped at the behest of the government. But as long as they exist, they exist at arm's length from government and they bear the formal responsibility for the decisions which they take.

In Germany, agencies are defined by a variety of provisions of constitutional and administrative law. The 1949 Constitution (article 87) gives the power to the federal government to 'set up independent (*selbständige*) federal authorities and new federal public law bodies and institutes in those areas where the federal government has legislative competence'. Each agency has its own constituting legislation; however, the constituting legislation generally defines the agency in terms of a wider variety of administrative law concepts. Perhaps the most important of these concepts for agencies is the distinction between the *rechtsfähig* and the *nicht rechtsfähig* organisation. Rechtsfähig means literally 'having legal capacity' and refers to the concept common in Roman Law countries of being able to act as a 'legal person'. The direct implications of acting as a legal personality in German law include rights to draw up a budget, to have a form of direct responsibility for the actions of its officials (known as *Dienstherr* status – literally 'service master') and the ability to be sued as a separate organisation. *Rechtsfähigkeit* distinguishes between two broad types of federal organisation. On the one hand there are the public-law corporations and institutes – *Körperschaften, Anstalten und Stiftungen* – which are fully or partially *rechtsfähig*. On the other there is a variety of authorities, institutes and bureaus – *Oberbehörde, Behörde, Anstalten* and *Zentralstellen*, which are not *rechtsfähig*. Within each of these two broad categories, there is a variety of different types of organisation. *Rechtsfähige Anstalten*, such as the most important *Bundesanstalt für Arbeit*, responsible for delivering a wide range of labour market services and social benefits, has a self-governing apparatus made up of representatives of labour, capital, the federal states and the federal government. The *Bundesbank* is a *rechtsfähige Anstalt* specifically mentioned in the constitution. Some of the *nicht rechtsfähige organisations* are called 'independent' – this term has relatively little real effect upon their status and powers.

In Germany and Sweden, as in Britain, the *form* of agency structure tends to reflect wider and basic features of the administrative system. Consistent with the characterisation of the German politico-administrative system as one which emphasises a legalistic rationalism, German agencies can only be understood in the context of the specific laws that led to the constitution of a particular agency, and by the status of that agency in relation to a variety of administrative law concepts. In Sweden, too, regulations establishing agencies likewise vest formal powers and obligations in them, but their position within the Swedish system can only be understood once one grasps the fact that the formal relationship between the agency and the political executive can only take place through the collective institution of the cabinet and not through direct contacts with ministers. For this reason, the issue of the informal contacts between an individual minister and an agency director has the status of a sensitive political issue. In Britain, agencies are in legal terms extensions of a longer-established principle of the delegation of authority. As Freedland (1996: 21) states, 'the setting up of these executive agencies has proceeded on the assumption that there has been no need to seek statutory authority to make their establishment lawful and valid'.

Since agency structures tend to reflect distinctive administrative traditions it would be mistaken to look at agencies as identical or even closely similar organisations in all three countries. They were set up at different times, by different means and for different purposes. This observation allows us to see Next Steps agencies in Britain as less of a radical break with the past than at first appears to be the case – their status is as typically British as those of our other two countries incorporate characteristic features of the politico-administrative system of Sweden and Germany respectively. Thus, claims that 'agencies' have the potential to restructure patterns of accountability and control have to be qualified since agency status is not an exogenous force for change, but at least in part a creation of prevailing patterns of accountability and control. Nevertheless, it remains possible to ask whether we can detect trends towards any increasing power of agencies and concomitant diminution of ministerial accountability and control in Germany and Sweden where operational service delivery has for centuries been vested in organisations separate from the ministerial bureaucracy.

Agency roles in policy making

Germany

Three of the four agencies we looked at in Germany were largely subordinate to their respective ministries. The *Bundesamt für Verfassungsschutz* (BfV) has the formal status of a *Zentralstelle* – a subordinate organisation within the Ministry of the Interior. In practice the BfV is to all intents and purposes a part of the Ministry of the Interior. The *Bundesamt für Güterverkehr* (Federal Office of Goods Transport) changed its status shortly before we examined it. Currently it is a *Bundesoberbehörde*, directly under the responsibility of the federal Ministry of Transport. It used to be, until 1993, the *Bundesanstalt für den Güterfernverkehr*, the Federal Institute for Long Distance Goods Transport, set up through the 1952 *Güterkraftverkehrsgesetz* (Goods Haulage Law). It used to be a 'legally independent', (but not rechtsfähig) organisation. The *Bundesanstalt für Fleischforschung* is a *nicht rechtsfähige* institute and is directly dependent upon the federal ministry. The first comment of its Director in interview was to explain that 'we are a subordinate service provider' (*nachgeordnete Dienststelle*).

In these three agencies the operational autonomy varied substantially, primarily because of the diverse nature of their tasks. The BfV had relatively little significant operational autonomy. Because its work (intelligence gathering on suspected subversives) is sensitive, there are a number of formal mechanisms designed to preserve citizens' liberties. Included among these are the political control by the Ministry of the Interior which has to clear all major operational decisions. Moreover, the minister can and does give direct instructions (Weisungen) to the President – these can be written but are usually oral; 'against these instructions there is no argument' one official explained, and these may be about 'all areas of activity and to any level of detail he wishes, whether this is about personnel, organisation or anything else'.

The Transport Ministry has similar direct powers over the *Bundesamt für Güterverkehr*, some that may be termed 'operational' matters of the *Bundesamt*. The nature of its work as an investigating authority – inspecting lorries to ensure conformity with safety and environmental regulations, usually through controls on motorways and other roads as well as monitoring and preparing statistics on goods transport, preparing statistics for the federal Ministry of Transport – generally means that the minister does not get involved in details of the logistics of such investigations. Officials within the BfG saw their role essentially as carrying out the level of roadside checks that are allowed for in the annual budget and according to the law which guides their activities (the *Güterkraftverkehrsgesetz*) without any direct interference from the ministry. 'Most of our work is carried out according to the law', a senior official added, 'and there is not much by way of detail the Minister can give'.

The *Bundesanstalt für Fleischforschung* (BfF), as a research institute, allows substantial scientific autonomy to researchers to determine research priorities. The sort of direct instruction that it might receive from the ministry is advice on a particular meat hygiene issue, usually associated with the European Union. As one respondent explained it 'Say the Danes have a new machine for classifying pigs, they ring us up and ask "is this sort of machine any use in Germany?" Mostly these come from the EU and only very rarely come from the Ministry's own initiative'. One respondent estimated that around one-tenth of BfF's resources were devoted to responding to such requests. Otherwise the research projects, developed within the stringent budgetary constraints set effectively by the ministry, are developed within planning and refereeing procedures over which the ministry has no direct control. The BfF advisory board is made up of representatives from universities, industry, food scientists, farmers and consumer groups with a ministry *auditeur* who is generally fairly junior, a *Referent* who, according to one respondent, '*never, ever* says anything'.

The *Bundesanstalt für Arbeit* differs from these three agencies not only because it is extremely large, employing 89 173 and spending DM99.45 billion marks in 1996, but also because it is a *rechtsfähig* agency with, at least on the face of it, greater decision-making autonomy. In practice this autonomy is highly limited because of the character of the agency activities and the stringency of the budget. The bulk of BA expenditure is paid out in social security transfers set at rates determined ultimately at ministerial level – one half of its expenditure is devoted to unemployment benefit. Transfer payments form a large part of its mandatory tasks. Its discretionary tasks cover mainly the active labour market policy parts of the budget and include job creation, training and retraining and associated employment subsidies. They account for a relatively small portion of BA expenditure, under a quarter, and have been consistently perceived by its officials as so squeezed that there is effectively little scope for developing policy in applying the non-mandatory portions.

In all four German agencies the budget for the agency is drawn up in-house and in collaboration with the ministry as the dominant partner. The BfF respondents felt the least involved in the budgetary process. One respondent commented that 'we don't have that much choice because we are told to keep the budget the same as last year'. While the Director and the senior finance official travel to Bonn to present their case for the budget they produce in-house, 'if Bonn says something we stand no chance of changing it'. The ministry also determines, with apparently little open consultation, the equipment grants which are given to the Institute – the bids of the BfF are in competition with bids from the other research institutes attached to the ministry. While as a security organisation the budget of the BfV is a sensitive issue (details are not published and only one summary line appears in the federal budget), a similar dominance of the ministry was noted. Only marginally greater influence on the budget was suggested by the BfG. Budget officials suggested a somewhat more active role for themselves – there is contact between the budget officials in the ministry and the *Bundesamt* 'to see if any proposal we want to put forward has any hope of getting through' and 'we usually get 10 per cent less than we ask for'. In the BA, the budget is drawn up in-house and is formally approved by the self-governing board (on which are represented employers, unions and state governments) which, in principle, can increase the budget. In 1995 it tried to do this by increasing the amount spent on non-mandatory activities. The ministry simply reinstated the lower budget.

In terms of their contribution to 'policy', the agencies in Germany are involved in offering policy advice. The impact of this advice seems to be highly variable. In the case of BfF the advice is technical and often in response to questions posed by the ministry. There was a general perception that the *Juristen* (lawyers) in Bonn had little understanding for the work of the natural scientists in Kulmbach, 200 miles away.

In some cases it is possible to interpret agency status as offering the director of the agency a particular standing – as a person to be consulted – that might not be offered to subordinate officials within a ministry. The President of the BfV attends the weekly meeting of the heads of all security services to discuss strategic security issues headed by a minister in the Federal Chancellor's Office.

Sweden

Swedish agencies enjoy a constitutional separation from the ministry but not from the government. All agencies are subject to the rules laid down in the General Instructions for Government Agencies (*Verksförordningen* 1995: 1322). These include provisions such as if an agency receives a critical report from the National Audit Bureau, then it must report to the government within a month on the action that it proposes to take (paragraph 15). Or again, the government must be kept fully briefed on European Union questions in which the agency is involved, and must supply staff to the government to deal with these questions (paragraph 16). Registers of unfinished items of business must be sent to the government's Chancellor of Justice on 1 March of each year (paragraph 30). Agency decisions involving the exercise of state authority in the legal sense must be fully documented and show who has decided the case, who has presented it for decision and who has been present at the hearing (paragraph 31).

On top of these, agencies have their own particular agency instructions which outline their specific tasks. For the Swedish National Insurance Board (*Riksförsäkringsverket* – RFV), a large agency, responsible for spending 17 per cent of GNP on a range of income maintenance programmes including old age pensions, sickness and child benefits. Its own Instruction requires it to lead and supervise the work of the social insurance offices (*försäkringskassorna*), to disseminate information and to provide training within the sector, to assess developments within the specialised branches in the field and to monitor the effectiveness of the measures taken. The Swedish National Labour Market Administration (*Arbetsmarknadsverket* – AMV) is charged with maximising employment, helping create an effective market for labour and protect the weaker groups in the labour market through job placements, counselling, occupational rehabilitation and active labour market measures.

In addition to these there are highly specific letters of regulation (*regleringsbrev*) which are issued when the estimates have been finalised by Parliament. These contain the agency's assignments for the year – a few general guidelines, broken down into quite detailed prescriptions, not unlike performance targets of British Next Steps agencies. The 1994/95 letters of regulation for the RFV included, for example, a request to show the effects of the rules system for housing allowances that was brought in at the start of 1994, to show the factors affecting costs in this area over the past five years, and to break down the expenditure involved between different types of household. Similarly, it had to provide an analysis of the effects of rule changes affecting levels of sickness benefit with particular reference to the introduction of a 'waiting day' before that benefit is payable. For the Swedish Roads Agency (VV) the 1997 letters of regulation targets included reducing the length of gravel roads by 110 kilometres, reducing the number of people living along the road network exposed to noise levels above 65db 'by at least 3000' and 'strengthening the competitiveness' of the road transport system (quantified as, for instance, an increase in the number of short distance journeys travelled by bus).

The letters of regulation are developed in a close dialogue between the agency's Director-General and senior staff on the one hand and the ministry on the other. Quite often the contents of the letters of regulation correspond to the agency's own proposals, but the crucial point about the letters of regulation is that while they are issued in the name of the government, they involve close collaboration between the ministry and the agencies. They are tied up with the budgetary process for agencies which form the focus for detailed discussions between agencies and ministries which continue throughout the year. For example, in the Swedish National Prison and Probation Administration (*Kriminalvårdsstyrelsen* – KVS), despite reforms in the mid 1990s of the budgetary process which sought to replace detailed regulation with broader 'goal steering', there developed increased co-operation between the Director General and the ministry and by the same token more frequent contacts between them. At the same time, trips by Stockholm-based staff to Norrköping for information briefings and for learning what is happening in the field are 'quite common'. Also, working groups within the ministry, with KVS participation, consider specific *ad hoc* questions such as electronic surveillance and treatment for drunken drivers. More generally, working groups similarly composed review the progress of experimental measures. The initiative on major reforms, one official explained to us, has come mainly from the ministry – though KVS has played a part in evolving programmes for prisoners, and also in shaping major reforms through its early involvement.

As in Germany, the operational autonomy of agencies depended substantially on the character of the agency's task. KVS has significant discretion in determining issues such as what kind of treatment offenders should receive, what programmes are best adapted to the needs of different types of offender, what type of training personnel in the system should receive, and so on. Its autonomy in this respect is strengthened by the consensus across political parties on a 'humane' rather than punitive prison policy whose emphasis should be on preparing offenders for life outside. AMV's work, by contrast, is highly politically charged and it has been under specific orders to pursue government priorities rather than its own. In its 1993/94 annual report, the agency took issue with the cuts that had been made in labour market training grants on the grounds that they had induced young unemployed people to seek cash assistance instead or to switch to work experience or YTS schemes – contrary to the agency's preferred policy. The VV's ability to plan and prioritise road schemes offers it substantial discretion, although this is limited by the increasingly stringent budgetary constraints on road-building. The RFV's room for manoeuvre is not only limited by the fact that the bulk of its expenditure goes on social benefits paid at rates determined by the government, but also by the fact that it presides over an administrative infrastructure of social insurance made up of regional insurance offices – formerly legally independent bodies on which local authorities, employers and trade unions are represented, but since the mid 1990s incorporated into RFV.

Have agencies served to involve 'operational' officials in policy making? In part this question depends on different definitions of what 'operational' means. As has already been suggested, because of a broad consensus in Swedish penal policy, the sorts of issue that would be regarded as sensitive policy questions in Britain are regarded as operational matters in Sweden. This was made clear by the Tidaholm prison riot in July 1994 which resulted in extensive fire damage to a major prison. Unlike a similar episode in Britain in which the Home Secretary sought direct involvement in detailed management of the riot, the Swedish Minister of Justice sought no such involvement. The riot was notified to the Minister of Justice on the Saturday morning after the outbreak, but otherwise was dealt with by KVS from start to finish. So it was KVS that handled the press conferences, analysed the causes (the immediate cause was a protest by the inmates against what they considered to be the unjust isolation of a prisoner), and devised and implemented the reforms that were judged necessary to prevent any recurrence. The Highways Agency, VV, has played a significant part in shaping policies. It was responsible, for example, for pro-posing that the wearing of seat-belts in cars should be made compulsory and that the training of drivers should start at sixteen. Sometimes it co-operates with interest groups – as with the organisation *Gröna bilister* (Green Motorists) in providing the car industry with arguments for producing and developing environmentally sound alternative technologies. A particularly influential pressure group within the sector is that of the Road Hauliers' Association – rather less so is the Swedish counterpart to the AA (*Motormännens riksförbund*). An agency initiative of a different kind had to be resorted to when there was a shortfall of money for building the E4 motorway from Hälsingborg to Sundsvall via Stockholm. So, VV experimented with a new type of road only half the width of earlier models using a pilot scheme to test cost, safety and environmental factors.

Despite the problems of defining the meaning of the term operational not only across different policy areas but also across nations, there is some evidence that agencies have in some circumstances enjoyed substantial involvement in policy making. The most striking example of this was the AMV in the postwar years. Created in 1948, AMV became the centrepiece of the celebrated 'Swedish Model' in which employment policy became a core strand in a more general economic policy. Under the influence of two economists from the research department of the Swedish Trade Union Confederation – Gösta Rehn and Rudolf Meidner – the pursuit of economic growth was reconciled with the maintenance of full employ-ment and a low rate of inflation by means of stringent fiscal policy and a highly active labour market policy.

In the contemporary fiscal climate, the initiative in labour market policy as well as social insurance (with the RFV) has shifted even more strongly towards the government and especially the Ministry of Finance. Most initiatives, as one would expect, originate with the government. Nevertheless, RFV can also point to some policy initiatives that originated within the agency. At the end of the 1980s, RFV drew the attention of the government to the fact that the administra-tive costs of the municipal housing allowance often exceeded the allowance paid – whereafter the government scrapped the allowance. Again, early in the 1990s, the agency alerted the government to the alarmingly steep rise in the cost of occupational injury insurance, with the result that the government cut back on the benefits payable.

The shape of accountability

Do agency structures pose problems for accountability? Are agencies and their heads likely to develop a degree of power of their own such that they become increasingly remote from institutions of political accountability? In Germany, the constitutional position of agencies in the democratic system is not substantially different to that of the United Kingdom where parliamentary control, including the powerful role of the Bundestag's Finance Committee, is exercised via the minister and not directly over the agency. The BfV (Office of Constitutional Protection) has its own distinctive arrangements for parliamentary scrutiny, by way of exception. Yet even here, as with most federal agencies, the close identity between the ministry and the agency as well as the strong possibilities for ministerial control and direction mean that agency status does not remove agencies from the sphere of ministerial accountability.

In the most autonomous of the German agencies we looked at, the Federal Labour Institute (BA), the President, although a household name who presides over the press release of unemployment figures each month, has tended not to become engaged in politically contentious issues. By tradition the appointment is that of a Christian Democrat. The Schmidt SPD-led government in the 1970s created a new post of Vice President, to be an SPD appointment, in order to balance the CDU President, but this was largely based not on the power of the President but on Schmidt's perception that the then President was making political capital for the CDU out of the rapidly rising level of unemployment. However, generally we found a reticence among senior agency officials to become involved in issues that involve political controversy (see Page and Elder 1999 for further discussion). The primacy of the ministry as a source of political decisions was illustrated graphically when the head of the BfF was being interviewed. There had been a television programme on BSE the night before which had mentioned BfF research – the Director was keen to say nothing but pointed the press to the ministry, explaining that normally they would talk to the press about the Institute's research, but not on anything remotely political. The accountability of agencies has not been a significant political issue in Germany in part because of the legal integration of agencies in the German ministerial structure as well as because the leaders of agencies tend not to challenge the political primacy of the ministry.

In Sweden, while agency influence in policy making varies according to the agency and the political circumstances, it is possible for agencies to have a somewhat broader role in making policy in Sweden than in Germany and Britain. One must be careful not to exaggerate this contrast since, as we have established, agencies are subject to influence from the government, and indirectly the Finance Ministry as well as the agency's cognate ministry, above all via the budgetary process and related letters of instruction. How is this possible without raising basic questions of accountability? Allowing for strong differences in parliamentary processes, the parliamentary forms of accountability in Sweden are no greater than in Germany or Britain.

Part of the answer lies, we believe, in the character of the policy-making system in Sweden. The notion that Sweden is a 'consensual democracy' has become an established part of our understanding of policy making in Sweden. Where there exists strong consensus over policy goals, decisions that may be perceived as policy issues in other countries are more likely to be understood as operational issues. At the heart of a definition of 'policy' is choice and conflict. Where choice and conflict is less marked as with, say, the importance of 'humane' penal policy or the postwar development of a social welfare state, we find that the role of the agency in structuring the nature of public services can be extensive. The role of agencies as part of a consensual policy-making structure is also reinforced by a number of structural features of the agencies. While the governing boards of agencies generally do not have a powerful role in developing agency strategies and decisions, nonetheless they do have a role, and along with the representative character of their boards, agencies can be seen as a symbol of the integration of interests into a broader consensual policy-making structure.

Related to the consensual system of policy making, and especially important when we come to consider the possibility for agency roles in the decision-making process, are the role of commissions in the formal institutions of policy initiation. Policy changes often start life in Commissions of Inquiry (*kommittéväsendet*), which further integrate agencies within domestic political structures. Their terms of reference and composition are in the hands of the government, and they produce between them an average of some 80–90 reports each year. They are composed mostly of civil servants – including representatives from the agencies – but they may also contain MPs and representatives of interest groups, although these last two have tended to dwindle in numbers in the past decade. Moreover, since Sweden joined the EU, many observers have noted a decline in the role of such commissions, as well as a shortening of the period which they have to consider any one particular issue, due to the pressures of an EU timetable. Nevertheless, they offer a rather visible means through which agency roles in the policy process can be observed, especially when seen in conjunction with the remiss procedure. This requires that the draft reports of commissions of inquiry and other proposals for reform are circulated to interested administrative agencies *inter alia* for their comments. These comments are public property under the general principle that a publicity rule should prevail in matters affecting the public interest. Also they are commonly included in an abridged form in the preamble to government bills which are submitted to the Riksdag. Thereby administrative agencies are enabled to publicise an independent stance should they feel it in their interest to do so. They have no constitutional duty to obey individual ministers and can act independently when they have not had a government directive on the matter in question.

Implications for the United Kingdom

Since we have established that the characteristics of agency structures in Sweden, Germany and the United Kingdom reflect the particular constitutional–legal conditions of each country, it is only with some caution that one can treat agency status as a variable which explains relationships between politicians, civil servants and the public. Even less is it possible to view agency status as an institutional innovation which has the power of transforming prevailing patterns of accountability and ministerial control in Britain towards a common Swedish or German 'model'. However, this does not prevent one from asking some rather more modest questions about the implications of German and Swedish agency practice for the United Kingdom.

On the question of the possible tendency for agencies to become the locus of expertise and thus gain a greater role in the policy process, we face the problem that operational officials, whether in agencies or ministries, have technical expertise in specific issues connected with service delivery that senior ministerial officials are not expected to possess in any of the three countries. Technical matters tend to involve specialised officials, and we believe this to be the case in British ministries prior to Next Steps and after Next Steps, as well as in parts of the administrative system not subject to Next Steps. German and Swedish experience suggests that the sort of transformation that can be expected is not in the form of a radical increase in the power of agencies and their directors or chief executives. The role of agencies in decision-making in Sweden derives from wider features of a consensual decision-making system rather than agency structures alone. Moreover, in both Germany and to a lesser extent Sweden, we detected a reticence by agency officials to challenge the political primacy of the government and the ministry. In this respect, the main difference that agency status is likely to imply for the United Kingdom is that it gives a clearer identity and status to those officials with the technical and administrative expertise in service delivery. As agencies with chief executives and their own structures, operational matters can be more easily represented at senior policy-making levels.

This is less a matter of agencies 'going it alone' on the basis of their expertise and more a matter of incorporating a recognised body of expertise into the decision-making process. Even in Sweden where, on the face of it, ministries have the least direct control over agencies, a variety of mechanisms, including budgetary power and the power to issue directions (albeit in the name of the government as a whole), bring ministerial officials into close contact with agency officials. In fact, the forms of ministerial (or, in the case of Sweden, government) influence over agency activities bear strong resemblance to each other – influence through the budgetary process and the ability to set targets and performance measures (although the constraints on a Swedish minister directly to give instructions to an agency is a major exception) – and bring the ministries into direct involvement in agency activity.

We can see no powerful implications of agency status on patterns of accountability in the UK from the Swedish and German cases (see also Elder and Page 1999). The involvement of agencies in the broader policy-making process in Sweden through the commissions of inquiry and *remiss* system offers, in fact, a glimpse of how UK agency status might be used to increase accountability through the agency's ability to participate in open and public policy debate.

If agency status in the UK develops to give agencies a standing which makes it easier for them to be incorporated in the policy process within Whitehall, it is possible to see the development of an agency role in wider processes of policy deliberation. At present the Next Steps initiative might be best characterised as an elaborate and effective programme of delegation within the existing constitutional framework. Nevertheless, procedures and devices which have enhanced accountability in Sweden might be adapted for United Kingdom circumstances and allow for greater public control and even permit more extensive delegation through providing the necessary democratic safeguards. Pre-legislative policy deliberations through the *remiss* procedure, could with some modifications offer useful extensions to democratic accountability in Britain. Above all, by making available to parliamentary scrutiny reports and other written documents that an agency produces in any pre-legislative discussion, the operational information on which changes in legislation are based might be identified and the important role of operational officials in policy formulation could be explicitly recognised.

There is no single 'agency model' of administration towards which the UK model appears to be progressing which involves fundamental shifts in patterns of accountability and control. The German and Swedish cases discussed above illustrate the range of features of administrative systems that limit the degree to which agencies are likely to become increasingly powerful in the policy-making system. Instead, the effects on the process of policy making in the UK are likely to be far more subtle and gradual – an increasing status as a source of expertise and technical knowledge. The Swedish example also offers glimpses of how Next Steps agencies may be developed, not only to enhance the quality of decision making in Whitehall but to bring greater openness and transparency in the wider public deliberation of policy.

13

The Politics of Managing the National Health Service[*]

Patricia Day and Rudolf Klein

Of all the ministries in Whitehall, none provides a better test case for exploring the impact of the new public management than the Department of Health. If we take the seven commandments of NPM (Hood 1991) as a check list, the department scores highly. It was one of the pioneers in developing performance measurements (Carter, Klein and Day 1992), moving from output to outcome indicators. It has sought to develop a hands-on professional management in the National Health Service, encouraging the adoption of private sector management styles. It has introduced the notion of market competition into the NHS, with the relationship between purchasers and providers based on contract not hierarchy. It anticipated the Next Steps initiative (Jenkins, Caines and Jackson 1988) by setting up an internal agency within the department in 1985. Further, it has been among the leaders in importing outsiders and now has more non-career civil servants at the top of the office than any other Whitehall department. And the common theme linking the various changes that have reshaped the department over the past decade, and the justification for them, is the need to promote greater efficiency in the use of resources.

All in all, there seems no better site for exploring the process by which Whitehall is reinventing itself and the extent to which restyling the machinery of government has led to a re-design of the engine of government: to look, as it were, below the streamlined bonnet. Specifically, this chapter address two questions. First, how realistic is the assumption shaping the Next Steps enterprise, and the creation of agencies, that management can be insulated from the policy process. Second, and related to this, what does the experience of the Department of Health teach us about the relationship between the policy makers at the centre and service delivers at the periphery – between steersmen and rowers?

To answer these questions, we analyse the changes that have taken place in the Department of Health since 1983 when the Griffiths Report (Griffiths 1983) inaugurated the period of managerialism. In all this, we concentrate exclusively

[*] We would like to acknowledge the ESRC for funding our research (award number: L1242511017).

on the Department of Health, although the Siamese twins of Health and Social Security were not parted until 1988. Again, within the Department of Health, we look primarily at its responsibilities for the NHS: thus we do not examine other aspects of its work, such as social services and public health. Finally, to complete our list of exclusions, our analysis is concerned only with England. The methodology used to generate our evidence, drawing on both published sources and interviews with 40 participants in the policy process, is set out in Day and Klein (1997). This chapter presents some of the findings reported in that study, although it is narrower in scope and more parsimonious in its presentation of evidence.

What's special about the Department of Health?

The Department of Health, with a budget in excess of £40 billion, is one of the biggest spenders in Whitehall. But its staff of about 4500 accounts for less than 1 per cent of the total for all departments. The reason for the large discrepancy between spending and the number of staff employed is as simple as its implications are profound. This is that the 760 000-strong staff (whole-time equivalents) of the NHS's hospital and community services are not employed by the department but by the health authorities or, overwhelmingly since the 1991 reforms, the provider trusts which they serve. Indeed some of those working in the NHS, notably general practitioners, are not even employed by health authorities but have always been free-standing contractors who hire their own staff.

So the Department of Health is emphatically a headquarters organisation and as such has a disproportionately large number of senior staff. It is also a department which ranks exceptionally high on the number of and status of the professional and occupational groups – doctors and nurses, catering specialists and building experts – represented among its staff (Hood and Dunsire 1981). It is therefore a paradigm example of Dunsire's 'Babel House' (Dunsire 1978) where 'a different tongue (concepts, vocabulary) is talked on each floor – amounting to a considerable linguistic disparity between top-floor speech and ground-floor speech – and different jargons and dialects are spoken on any floor'.

All this springs from the fact – crucial for any understanding of the institutional dilemmas and developments of the department – that the Secretary of State is accountable to Parliament for all spending in the NHS. He or she may not directly employ the staff of the NHS (although he or she is ultimately responsible for the nomination of the members of the authorities and trusts who do) but is answerable for their activities. As Aneurin Bevan put it: 'when a bedpan is dropped on a hospital floor, its noise should resound in the Palace of Westminster'. The Department of Health is thus unique in being accountable for the delivery of a service without exercising direct control over those who actually provide it. Moreover, it is a universal service with a high degree of visibility to the public at large, as well as great salience for those using it. In any year, there will be something like 300 million contacts – mainly with GPs – between consumers and the NHS. In short, the NHS is everyone's business. The Department of Health therefore operates in a peculiarly politically sensitive arena, where the noise of dropped bedpans is likely to reverberate not only through the corridors of Westminster but, perhaps more important these days, through the corridors of the television studios.

The search for new models

Long before the phrase became one of the fashionable mantras of the 1990s (Osborne and Gaebler 1992), the Department of Health had been in the business of steering but not rowing. The Department decided on the policies to be followed; the various NHS authorities implemented those policies. There was a clear distinction between setting the course and managing the system. Such, at least, was the theory. The practice, as we shall see, turned out to be rather more complicated. Indeed the story of the department's evolution – its successive attempts to reorganise itself internally as well as its relationship with the NHS – can be read as a cautionary tale about the problems involved in separating steering from rowing. For it is a story (to exaggerate only a little) of misunderstanding, suspicion and aggravation between steersmen and rowers.

The style of the Ministry of Health (the direct ancestor of the DoH) was set soon after it had given birth to the NHS. It was largely policy making through exhortation (Griffith 1966). Circulars poured out of the ministry, giving advice on policy as well as matters of detail – in particular, pay and conditions of work. But implementation was left to regional and local health authorities. The outcome was a sense of mutual frustration which was increasingly voiced from the 1960s onward as the centre switched from an essentially passive to a more active mode. Secretaries of State were left grumbling that their policies were being diluted or ignored by the periphery: the centre lacked power to make its policies stick (Crossman 1972). NHS managers at the periphery were left complaining that the centre was unrealistic in pouring out policy injunctions without regard to their financial implications and implementability, a problem further compounded by the department's complex internal structure and its failure to co-ordinate different policy streams (DHSS 1976).

The department itself was aware of some of the organisational weaknesses. For example, in the early 1970s, the department had reorganised its internal structure following a study carried out by the management consultants McKinseys in an attempt to achieve better co-ordination between policy making and implementation. But major organisational reform did not come until 1983, when the fuse of change was the Inquiry into the Management of the NHS (Griffiths 1983) led by Roy (later Sir Roy) Griffiths, managing director and deputy chairman of the Sainsbury group of stores. The main (revolutionary) aim of the report was to turn around the NHS by making it an output-rather than input-orientated service. Accordingly, it proposed a range of changes designed to make the NHS managerially more effective at all levels. Most important, for the purposes of our analysis, Griffiths put forward two proposals designed to transform the central direction of the NHS.

First, there was to be a Health Services Supervisory Board, chaired by the Secretary of State and including the Permanent Secretary, the Chief Medical Officer and 'two or three non-executive members with general management skills and experience'. The role of the Supervisory Board was to determine the objectives of the NHS, to take strategic decisions and to receive reports on performance. Second, and more crucial to the future organisation of the department as we shall see, there was to be a multi-professional NHS Management Board, accountable to the Supervisory Board, to take over 'all existing NHS management responsibilities' in the department. Its function would be 'to plan implementation of the policies approved by the Supervisory Board; to give leadership to the management of the NHS; to control performance; and to achieve consistency and drive over the long term'. The board's chairman, who would act as 'general manager, chief officer or director general' of the NHS, should have 'considerable experience and skill in effecting change in a large, service-orientated organisation'. The assumption was that the chairman and others would have to be recruited, at least initially, from outside the civil service and the NHS.

In all this, Griffiths aimed to emancipate the NHS 'from the present top-down approach to detailed management'. The NHS, the report argued in a phrase that was to capture the imagination, was 'swamped with directives without being given direction'. There should be less emphasis on requiring detailed information from health authorities and more stress on 'real output measurement, against clearly stated management objectives and budgets'.

The Griffiths model, in effect an agency within the department, represented a compromise. Griffiths himself would have preferred an independent commission or corporation: a model which, indeed, had been pushed by the Treasury as long ago as 1966 (Webster 1996). But he did not recommend the more radical option – and indeed explicitly rejected it in his report – because it would have required legislation and might have made the introduction of his package, in particular the various managerial reforms in the NHS, more difficult. But though the Griffiths model for the central direction of the NHS may have been a compromise, the implications of the report taken as a whole were radical – and in some respects threatening – for both the Department of Health and for the NHS. That its recommendations were accepted as soon as the report was published, and implemented with very little delay or change, can be put down to two sets of factors.

First, there were the factors endogenous to the NHS. The relationship between the policy makers at the centre and the managers at the periphery had long, as already noted, been troubled. The Griffiths report appeared, as the then Permanent Secretary – Sir Kenneth Stowe – remarked subsequently, to offer something to everyone (Stowe 1989). On the one hand, for NHS managers, the creation of the NHS Management Board seemed to mark 'the beginning of a long-awaited freedom from interference from Government'. On the other hand, there was 'the belief of Ministers and some officials that this was a body set up primarily to introduce into the management of the hospitals a competence, energy and discipline which had been manifestly lacking'. The possibility that these expectations might be contradictory – that it was a 'grand illusion', in Sir Kenneth's words, to expect that the Government would hand over billions of public money 'to be spent at the discretion of independent authorities with Ministers and their officials kept at arms length' – was only to emerge after the event.

Second, there were factors exogenous to the department and the NHS. By the time the Griffiths Report appeared, managerialism was already in the ascendancy in Whitehall (Gray and Jenkins 1991). Sir Derek (subsequently Lord) Rayner had been brought back to Whitehall as Margaret Thatcher's advisor on efficiency: Marks & Spencer, in other words, had already prepared the ground for Sainsbury's. The Financial Management Initiative had been launched a year before the publication of Griffiths. In short, the report – with its emphasis on managerial efficiency and effectiveness – spoke what was becoming the dominating language in Whitehall. Sir Roy himself – although dedicated to the notion of maintaining the NHS and far from being a New Right ideologue – became close to Margaret Thatcher. And, above all, the promise of achieving increased efficiency in the NHS by promoting managerial dynamism seemed to offer the government a way of resolving one of its central dilemmas: which was how to contain the growth of public spending, and if possible to cut it back, while yet meeting rising expectations and demands in services like the NHS.

Implementing the new model: stresses and strains

The new model of central governance that was officially launched in 1985 had a difficult birth and a troubled childhood. 'It was nearly a disaster', Sir Kenneth Stowe recorded. And over the following decade the model was to go through a number of different incarnations as successive attempts were made to resolve the tensions inherent in it. The attempt to separate policy making and implementation – to insulate, as it were, the management of the NHS from the day-to-day pressures of parliamentary accountability – proved to be beset with difficulties.

The first chairman of the new Management Board was Victor Paige, whose career had taken him from Boots to the National Freight Corporation, who was appointed with the rank of Second Permanent Secretary of the department. The rest of the board were a mix of civil servants, NHS managers and outsiders with specialist skills. The civil servants included Graham (later Sir Graham) Hart, a future Permanent Secretary, and Terri Banks, who in 1994 was to produce a report that reshaped the department (see below). The NHS managers included two regional administrators: Mike Fairey, who had been secretary of the working group that produced the 1976 chairmen's report, and Duncan (later Sir Duncan) Nichol, who was subsequently to become Chief Executive. The outsiders included Len (later Sir Len) Peach, IBM's Director of Personnel, Ian Mills, a senior partner in a management consultancy firm, and Idris Pearce, a senior partner in a firm of property advisers.

There was some cross-membership between the Management Board and the Supervisory Board, chaired by the Secretary of State. However, the latter also included other departmental ministers, the Permanent Secretary, and Roy

Griffiths. Its role, however, never became clearly defined: 'No one knew what to do with it, least of all the man running it' in the words of one civil servant closely involved in the work of the two boards. And it played no major role in the drama that soon followed the creation of the new system: the resignation of Victor Paige in June 1986.

In Paige's view, management was about taking decisions. But he discovered that, in practice, 'Ministers take all the important decisions, political, strategic and managerial. Because of that, the intention to devolve executive accountability and authority from the Secretary of State effectively did not happen' (Paige 1986). The consequence was that 'The Management Board and its Chairman did not "manage" in the way that would be understood in industry and commerce'. Its function, as Paige was reminded in a memorandum from the Permanent Secretary, was to advise, not to take decisions. Moreover, adding to Paige's frustration, the regional chairmen remained directly accountable to the Secretary of State, in effect bypassing the Management Board. They continued to act as the Secretary of State's 'kitchen cabinet', as one member of the board put it. The managerial hierarchy therefore remained, in effect, broken-backed. Finally, Norman Fowler as Secretary of State gave priority to avoiding political risks rather than to the Management Board's agenda and when controversial issues came up was inclined to compromise or retreat. In short, Paige discovered that managing the politicians had to come before managing the NHS. And it was his failure to achieve the former that precipitated his resignation.

Potentially, of course, the creation of the Management Board represented a threat to the department's civil servants – and perhaps most of all to the Permanent Secretary – since in effect it broke their monopoly of advice to ministers. But if the civil servants put the knife into Paige, it was done so skilfully that he did not notice it: he himself remained grateful for their support. Perhaps this lack of overt conflict was because he never achieved a sufficiently strong position with ministers to cause civil servants much anxiety. Perhaps, too, the strong representation of civil servants on the Management Board – the fact that the administrative structure of the department was not fundamentally changed by the infusion of a few newcomers at the top – helped to defuse any tension.

That was to change as the Management Board evolved into a body challenging the department's traditional role and structure more directly. But first there came an amicable period of co-existence under Paige's successor, Len Peach, who became Chief Executive in 1986 – a post he held until 1989. The Minister of Health, Tony Newton, took over the chairmanship of the board, with Griffiths as his deputy: thus 'fusing the political and managerial aspects of its work', as Griffiths put it (Griffiths 1987). And Peach's style did not challenge the civil servants. 'Len was not into ruffling feathers', as one of his colleagues put it. With his background in personnel rather than in line management, he saw himself as a persuader and a salesman of ideas, spreading the managerial message and converting those working in the NHS to the gospel of dynamic activism. Unlike Paige, he did not feel frustrated at not having direct management authority. The outside members of the board continued to be 'twinned' with civil service insiders. And, as one of the outsiders saw it, 'Ministers, when worried, would talk to civil servants'.

There was a certain irony in all these developments. The notion of a Management Board or 'General Staff' for the NHS had been urged in the 1970s (DHSS 1976) by health authorities in order to weaken the grip of the central department on the service. And the Griffiths Report, too, had stressed the need to move away from 'top-down' management. In the outcome, however, the introduction of the Management Board strengthened central control. For bringing about change meant greater intervention and activism by the centre, particularly in the implementation of the new managerial policies.

At the same time, however, there was a subtle shift in the nature of that control, with less emphasis on intervention in matters of detail and more stress on monitoring performance (Day and Klein 1985). The new era signalled also a policy of conscious birth-control over the propagation of advice, circulars and communications. The scale of this activity was documented by a departmental review that reported in 1985 (Fairey and Duffield 1985). This showed that the department (including the Management Board) issued some 500–600 circulars a year, on subjects ranging from the funding of the NHS to the supply and repair of European Hair wigs. The Personnel Division dealt with over 10 000 inquiries a year, mainly to do with the interpretation of Whitley agreements; the Regional Liaison Division annually dealt with some 19 000 inquiries from the field, making 15 000 telephone calls and sending out almost 5000 letters in turn. The review itself signalled an attempt to reduce the flow. However, the volume of communications continued to be an issue and remains one even today. Central paternalism remained a source of aggravation.

So, too, did the issue of co-ordination within the department. Specifically, there still was no effective mechanism for co-ordinating policy making and implementation, thereby generating a coherent set of priorities (Ham 1988). The departmental civil servants generating policy and the Management Board supervising implementation continued to work in separate compartments. The phenomenon of too many policies chasing too little money – a long-standing complaint among NHS managers – had survived the introduction of the new system of governance. The Supervisory Board – which might have been expected to play the role of strategic co-ordination – was little in evidence, meeting only very occasionally (Newton 1988).

Further evidence that all was not well, that a satisfactory co-ordination of policy work and management had yet to be achieved, was provided by an internal departmental review that reported in 1990 (Gwynn and Rook 1990). The Gwynn inquiry – which had involved interviews with senior officials – reported 'some perhaps understandable scepticism about the stability of the basic structure'. Boundaries were blurred; responsibilities were not always clear; there was too little consultation about the implications of policy work. The sceptics divided between those who thought that the longer term outcome would be that the NHS Management Executive (as the Board has been rechristened in 1989: see discussion below) would eventually be reabsorbed by the department and those who thought that it would be spun off as an independent body. Given that neither of these options reflected current ministerial policy, however, the report considered – only to reject – two less dramatic but still radical solutions: either allocating all health care responsibilities – policy as well as operational – to the Executive or making it clear that all health care policy issues were outside its remit.

The main reason for rejecting these radical options appears to have been the conviction that staff and line responsibilities – policy and management – were too intertwined to allow surgical separation: 'An issue may occur either in a management context, with the emphasis on finding day to day operational solutions, or as a more fundamental question requiring detailed analysis or review'. Similarly, there was a considerable degree of inter-dependence between health care and social care issues, with the Secretary of State being responsible for both while the Executive was responsible only for the former. And all activities were, in any case, carried out 'in support of an indivisible Secretary of State'. Accordingly, the report recommended re-drawing some boundaries, clarifying some responsibilities and more consultation. And it proposed that the Department's Management and Policy Group should be responsible for an annual review of all the Department's policy activities and relate these to the overall demands on the NHS's resources.

The Gwynn Report mirrored debate within the department. For it would be wrong to present the question of who should be responsible for policy as merely a turf war between civil servants and managers. Difficult organisational issues, as well as entrenched interests, were involved. Thus it was argued that handing over responsibility for service policy – hitherto organised around client groups – would strengthen provider interests. Similarly, there was the question of how best to handle issues cutting across NHS and local authority boundaries. Conversely, there was a recognition that the existing split of responsibilities between the department and the Management Board was inefficient, because it involved duplication, and ineffective, because the policy makers were not directly in touch with the field.

The Gwynn Report appeared in the aftermath of yet another reorganisation of the NHS and of the structure of central governance and was in part at least a response to a new situation. The fact that the review – and the debate in the department – did not lead to a resolution of the various tensions identified reflects the structural rigidities in the governance of health care that had characterised the system from 1948. This was only to happen as part of the more general shake-up of the health care system which followed in succeeding years and, as we shall see in the next section, brought on stage new and more powerful actors.

Management tanks on the Whitehall lawn

The publication of the 1989 White Paper, *Working for Patients* (Secretary of State for Health 1989), setting out the government's plans for introducing a mimic market system into the NHS, by separating the purchaser and provider roles, marked also the beginning of an era in which power shifted from the civil servants to the managers responsible for implementing the changes. There were two reasons for this. First, the new policy direction had been set not by the Department of Health but by a special review team of ministers and others handpicked by the prime minister (Day and Klein 1989). Departmental civil servants – although they contributed papers to the review and were to play a heroic part in fleshing out the somewhat skeletal proposals that emerged – were perceived, rightly or wrongly, to have played a somewhat negative role in the exercise. It was not to them, therefore, that Margaret Thatcher – whose attitude towards civil servants was at best ambivalent (Hennessy 1989) – looked for implementing her reforms.

Second, the proposals set out in the White Paper provoked a degree of opposition unprecedented in its intensity and virulence since the introduction of the NHS in 1948 (Klein 1995). The medical profession and the Labour Party mobilised to portray Mrs Thatcher and her Secretary of State, Kenneth Clarke, as intent on destroying the NHS. Given that the NHS commanded overwhelming public support, the government had much to lose if the reforms did not confound the prophecies of chaos and breakdown. Again, therefore, Mrs. Thatcher and her ministers looked to those with first-hand experience of management in the NHS to implement the new vision. Ministers were the steersmen: they simply wanted some enthusiastic rowers.

Ministerial attitudes are therefore more important in explaining the shifting balance of power in the 1990s than changes in the formal structure of governance: if anything the latter tended to follow the former. There were indeed changes in the structure. But it was the relationship between ministers and those responsible for executing policy which proved decisive. To exaggerate only a little, the crucial factor was that ministers looked more to managers, as the people who could speak with authority about what would or would not work in the NHS, than to civil servants. While in the 1980s it would have been unusual for Paige or Peach to see the Secretary of State unchaperoned by the Permanent Secretary, their successor established more direct and informal links, including chats over lunch at the House of Commons. Ministers and managers appeared to have a common stake in implementing and making a success of the changes that were brought into effect in 1991, since both were personally and publicly identified with the reforms in a way that civil servants were not.

The changes in governance announced by *Working for Patients* appeared, at first sight, largely to be an exercise in re-labelling. The Supervisory Board was reincarnated as the NHS Policy Board; the Management Board became the NHS Management Executive (ME). Once again, the radical option of spinning off the NHS as an independent authority or agency had, though considered and actively supported by John Major representing the Treasury, been rejected. The function of the Policy Board was to 'set objectives for the NHS Management Executive and monitor whether they are satisfactorily achieved'. The function of the Management Executive was to 'deal with all operational matters within the strategy and objectives set by the Policy Board'. In short, the distinction between steering and rowing was maintained. However, the position of the Management Executive was strengthened. Responsibility for family practitioner services was transferred to it. And the overall intention of the changes was 'to introduce *for the first time* (our emphasis) a clear and effective chain of management command running from the Districts through Regions to the Chief Executive and from there to the Secretary of State'.

Most immediately, it was the membership of the Policy Board which seemed to offer the most evidence of change. There was much continuity: ministers, the Permanent Secretary and the Chief Medical Officer remained as members, while Sir Roy Griffiths continued as deputy chairman to the Secretary of State. However, three industrialists – including the chairmen of the Rover Group of car companies and of British Steel – joined the Board as non-executive directors. Their role, as perceived by Griffiths who as the inventor of the two-tier system of governance remained its most enthusiastic advocate, was not only to bring in experience of running large organisations but also to restrain ministers from on-the-hoof policy making in response to headlines: to discipline the production of priorities by insisting on a strategic view.

In the outcome, the Policy Board appears to have played as unremarkable a role as the Supervisory Board which it replaced and disappears from our story at this point. Its membership changed over time but its lack of impact did not and debate about its proper role continued. 'I have written as many papers about the role of the Policy Board as you have had dinners', one senior civil servant remarked. Griffiths himself, until his death, tried to insist that it should carry out a monitoring role. But its actual role seems to have depended largely on the personality of the Secretary of State as chairman. Under Virginia Bottomley, Kenneth Clarke's successor, it engaged in 'breast beating sessions' about large issues; under her successor, Stephen Dorrell, it became rather more business-like with reports on progress. From the perspective of the NHS Management Executive, it represented a welcome buffer: its existence emphasised that the Executive's accountability to the Secretary of State was not mediated through the civil service but that the line ran through the Policy Board. The fact that this was a largely notional line made the arrangement all the more satisfactory.

The most important change in the membership of the NHS Management Executive was the arrival of Duncan Nichol as Chief Executive: the first health service manager to hold the post, so marking the beginning of a period which was to end with the domination of the Executive Board by former regional managers transmogrified into civil servants. However, for the time being, five out of the nine members remained career civil servants (including members of the department's medical and nursing hierarchy). Like his predecessors, Nichol was Accounting Officer for the NHS – answerable to the Public Accounts and other Committees of the House of Commons – with the rank of Permanent Secretary.

In his message introducing the new Executive to the NHS (NHS Management Executive, 1989), Nichol stressed that the changes were vital 'in establishing a clearer distinction between policy matters and operational issues'. Ministers and the Policy Board, he pointed out, rehearsing the well-known formula, would determine the policies and strategies while the Management Executive would be responsible for the implementation of policy within the overall framework set by the Policy Board. The distinction proved yet again impossible to sustain in practice and there is little evidence that Nichol thought that it was either feasible or desirable to maintain it. On the contrary, in the words of one insider, he 'drove his tanks on the Whitehall lawn'. The notion of 'operational policy' – that is, the acknowledged role of the Executive – proved elastic and capable of stretching ever more. And Nichol pushed it to breaking point. 'Operational policy' was increasingly interpreted to mean health service policy (i.e. everything to do with the NHS), leaving the department to deal with policy for health (i.e. the wider issues affecting the population's health).

The reason for this shift in the balance of influence, to reiterate the theme enunciated at the beginning of this section, had little to do with structure and everything to do with power. Nichol was in a position of power within the department because ministers looked to him and his executive to make a success of their NHS reforms: Margaret Thatcher had made it clear that she expected him to go out and sell the new NHS – to be a missionary for the government's policies. Given the controversy attending the reforms, this mission represented a much more formidable and risk-laden undertaking (and a much greater invest-ment of political capital by ministers and personal reputations by managers) than the original board's task to implement the Griffiths managerial reforms. It also represented a politically much more sensitive mission. Given Nichol's public commitment to making a success of the NHS reforms, it was widely assumed that he could not have survived in his post if Labour had won the 1992 General Election. But the converse, of course, was that ministers were dependent on him: hence, perhaps, his direct telephone line to them.

The 1990s therefore saw the NHS Management Executive developing its separate identity and its own style much more assertively than its predecessor had done. The sense of separateness was further strengthened when it was set in concrete and symbolised by geography: in 1992/93, the ME moved from Richmond House in London, the department's headquarters, to Quarry House in Leeds. Many officials preferred taking early retirement to moving, so giving the ME an opportunity to recruit people of their own choosing. The move prompted anxiety within the department about a 'two cultures' problem, even though by far the largest propor-tion of the ME's staff was still drawn from the civil service. One of the main beneficiaries of the move to Leeds was British Rail. Given that much of the ME's work revolved around the Secretary of State, commuting between London and Leeds became a way of life for some senior officials.

The next stage in the evolution of the ME came in 1993. Following yet another review – this time by a team chaired by Kate Jenkins, one of the authors of the Next Steps report, and later a member of the NHS Policy Board – a further round of change was announced (DoH 1993). The Functions and Manpower Review team had considered a variety of options, all familiar with long antecedents: the creation of an English National Health Authority (the independent corporation model), establishing the NHS Management Executive as an agency or retaining the ME within the Department 'but with greater clarity about roles and responsibility'. The first two options were rejected because the Secretary of State considered that they would be perceived to undermine the processes of parliamentary accountability. The task of achieving greater clarity was delegated to yet another review: see below.

Meanwhile, the immediate outcome was the abolition of the regional health authorities which, as many Secretaries of State had discovered (for example: Crossman 1972), had long been powerful actors in their own right, mediating and sometimes frustrating the policies of the centre. The 14 RHAs were to be replaced by eight regional offices of a 'streamlined' Executive whose role was seen to be increasingly 'strategic' rather than 'operational' as more responsibility was devolved to local managers. It was a decision that reflected increasing disillusion with the role of regions. Several had been embroiled in financial scandals of various kinds. And there was a widespread perception that regions were a cumbersome, over-staffed and ineffective mechanism for implementing central government policy. The regional managers were accordingly translated into the regional directors of the ME and, like their staff, were transmogrified into civil servants. They came in as Grade 2s (Deputy Secretary level) – a tribute, perhaps, to the heavy weight that was put on management experience in the emergent civil service – with the result that the Management Executive had far more officials at this level than the rest of the Department of Health.

The new machinery, although introduced in the name of devolving power, again strengthened the grip of the centre. Despite the emphasis, as mentioned above, on the Executive playing a 'strategic' rather than 'operational' role, in effect its grip on the NHS was strengthened. Implementing the 1991 reforms had meant an extremely interventionist style of action; so, too, did the government's drive to reduce waiting lists. Forcing people at the periphery to be free – that is, to take their own managerial decisions in the market place (the avowed philosophy of the reforms) – turned out, paradoxically, to involve central direction. Significantly, while control became tighter in many respects, it did change its character. There was less emphasis on detail and process. And there was more stress on the outcomes: the achievement of specific objectives (as in the case of waiting lists) or targets (as in meeting efficiency gains).

All this still left unresolved the central question which had provided the theme of so many reports and reviews: the relationship between the Siamese twins of policy-making and its managerial implementation. So we come to the 1994 Banks Report (Banks 1994). This was the report of a review team led by Terri Banks, a former civil servant in the Department of Health (and a contributor, almost 30 years earlier, to a submission to the Fulton Committee by a group of civil servants urging radical reform in the way government business was conducted: a further reminder that ideas may have a long gestation time). It accepted that ministers had decided that the top management of the NHS 'should remain within the central government framework as an integral part of the Department of Health, albeit a very special part with its own style and identity'.

But the central recommendation of the Banks review – accepted and implemented by the government – represented, in effect, an obituary of the notion that policy and management could be separated. It proposed that the NHS Executive (the word management had by now dropped out of its title) 'should take on responsibility at all stages for policies for services provided by the NHS, from policy development through implementation, monitoring and review'. The 'wider Department of Health' would, in turn, be structured round three business areas: a social care group, a public health group and a departmental resources and services group. Finally, the Departmental Management Board would play a more 'proactive' role than in the past in ensuring that issues cutting across organisational boundaries did not 'fall between the cracks' – assisted by a newly created Policy Management Unit responsible both for the co-ordination of different activities and for 'high-level scanning activity'.

The main recommendation flowed from the findings that previous reshuffles of responsibility had failed to deal with the problems they were meant to address and that indeed these might get worse as 'NHS Executive staff increasingly loosen their personal links with the wider Department of Health following the move to Leeds'. Responsibilities were still blurred. Many of the flaws identified in the Gwynn Report, Banks concluded, had still not been addressed. So, for example, 'Ministers have sometimes been concerned to find that different parts of the Department which should have been talking to each other about certain policy areas were not'. And, again, policy divisions in the wider Department of Health 'sometimes implement policies through their own service networks, while the NHS Executive sometimes takes the initiative in developing policy'. And, echoing earlier complaints, Banks commented: 'From the NHS Executive perspective, there is a perception of a worrying mismatch between policy aspirations and the capacity of the NHS'.

The post-Banks settlement suggests two conclusions. First, it appears – fairly unequivocally – to mark an acceptance that policy and management cannot be separated. But this, of course, raises a further and more general question: whether this conclusion undermines the whole Next Steps concept or only applies to the special circumstances of the NHS. Second, it appears to indicate a realignment of power, shifting the centre of NHS gravity from career civil servants to managers. Not only had the NHS Executive Board acquired responsibility for policy. But its composition had a strong managerial tone. By the time we leave the story, the NHS Executive Board was headed by Alan Langlands, a former regional manager who had been Duncan Nichol's deputy before succeeding him in 1994. In contrast, the scope of the Permanent Secretary's responsibilities had seemingly been reduced, although he or she remains responsible 'for advising the Secretary of State on the discharge of *all* (our emphasis) the duties' of the office (DoH 1995).

The managers who have moved into the Department of Health have helped to change, and in turn been changed by, the prevailing civil service culture (Day and Klein 1997). To survive effectively, they have had to adapt to prevailing norms, although the extent to which they have done so varies. The price that managers have had to pay for taking over responsibility for the NHS is that they have also had to take on the grinding task of dealing with parliamentary questions and helping ministers to survive politically. Conversely, civil service norms themselves have been changing: there has been a mass conversion, in form, if not always in spirit, to the philosophy of the new public management. Cultural cross-dressing has become the norm.

The emphasis on using resources effectively, on managing people as well as managing ministers, on driving through policy to the point of implementation, are in no way unique to the Department of Health. Rather, all these changes mirror the more general adoption of a managerial stance throughout Whitehall. If the Department of Health is in advance of the field in some respects, it may be because the need to incorporate the NHS Executive in its structure has forced the pace of change and because it is directly responsible for managing what is the most complex, comprehensive and politically sensitive service-delivery system in Whitehall: the NHS.

Implications and speculations

Two themes have shaped the analysis presented in this chapter. The first is that, in the case of the Department of Health, it has proved impossible to sustain the distinction between policy making and management required by the agency model. The second is that in the case of the NHS, the new public management approach has brought about greater centralisation. The second is perhaps more surprising and paradoxical than the first, given that NPM philosophy suggests that 'provided management is operating within the strategic direction set by ministers, it must be left as free as possible to manage within that framework', in the words of the Next Steps report. Griffiths's institutional device of a Policy Board – designed both to set the strategic framework and to act as buffer between politicians and managers – never achieved the status or the role which its inventor had hoped for.

The obvious explanation is 'the bedpan doctrine': that the requirements of parliamentary accountability for a highly visible service mean that ministers have to answer for everything that happens in the NHS, with the result that they inevitably become involved in managerial decision making at the periphery. But that is surely only a partial explanation. In the case of social security, for example, the agency model has been far more successful in introducing a buffer between political and managerial decisions. There appears to be no equivalent of the 'bedpan doctrine' in other centrally funded services and programmes.

So we are left searching for an additional explanation in the special characteristics of the NHS, distinguishing it from the normal run of agencies (Greer 1994). One of these, as noted in our introduction, is the political salience and sensitivity of the NHS: the one service perhaps which all citizens encounter with some regularity. Hospitals, unlike local benefits offices, can mobilise powerful constituencies when threatened with closure. But this effect is compounded by other factors. The services offered by the NHS are peculiarly heterogeneous and complex. They involve not the interpretation and use of national formulas by local officials – as in the case of social security – but individual judgements by autonomous professionals. The scope for discretion is much greater, as is uncertainty about what should be done in specific cases. The notion that accountability for the NHS might be translated into a technical exercise – read off, as it were, a series of dials – has therefore proved difficult to translate into practice. The search for a way of capturing the NHS's performance in a set of indicators has a long history (Carter, Klein and Day 1992) and still continues (NHS Executive 1998); similarly, there has been increasing emphasis on translating ministerial priorities into targets, waiting lists being the most notorious.

Nevertheless, managing the NHS remains essentially and stubbornly a political exercise insofar as it involves balancing competing priorities and conflicting claims at both the national and local levels within capped budgets. Successive Secretaries of State for Health have longingly mused – following retirement – about the possibility of transforming the NHS Executive into some kind of independent Commission (Fowler 1991). But the history of the NHS Executive itself suggests that this is to redescribe the problem without solving it. If the Executive has never succeeded in insulating management from politics – and indeed has increasingly become indistinguishable from the traditional civil service as the instrument of ministers – it is because it is far from self-evident that a preoccupation with technical efficiency should prevail over concern about public worries and local sensitivities.

So we come to what is perhaps the central problem in applying the new public management philosophy to a service like the NHS. The NPM philosophy requires the specification of clear goals and indicators which measure progress towards the achievement of those goals. If the currency of managerial accountability is clear (Day and Klein 1987), then it is possible to carve out a sphere of managerial autonomy. But these conditions do not apply, as we have sought to show, in the case of the NHS. The notion that the NHS's multiple, diverse and competing goals can be translated into a set of clearly defined, coherent and mutually consistent objectives, against which managerial performance can be measured, remains a mirage. And compounding the problem is the rhetorical insistence of successive governments that management should pursue national priorities while remaining responsive to local views: if management and the local community fail to agree, ministerial intervention is the result.

These tensions are evident in the policies of the Labour government's White Paper setting out its strategy for the NHS (Secretary of State for Health 1997). On the one hand, there is the rhetoric of localism and decentralisation: Primary Care Groups are supposed to be in 'the driving seat' of the NHS, interpreting the needs of their populations. On the other hand, the White Paper greatly strengthens the political grip of the centre on what happens at the periphery and represents (Klein 1998) a reversion to a command-and-control model. The emphasis is on developing national templates for services, all backed by the creation of a new central inspectorate designed to ensure the achievement of national standards. Just conceivably the development of such clear-cut benchmarks of performance could, in turn, encourage politicians to allow managers and professionals the kind of autonomy demanded by the NPM philosophy. But the odds seem stacked against such a development.

14
Conclusion: Interpreting British Government: the Governance Narrative

R. A. W. Rhodes

Introduction

The Whitehall Programme tells the distinctive story of *Governance*: of fragmentation, networks, unintended consequences and diplomacy. This story contrasts sharply with both the Westminster model and its story of a strong executive running a unitary state and new public management (NPM) with its story of the search for efficiency through markets and contracts (see Chapter 1). In other words, the Whitehall Programme provides a language for re-describing the world and, with the Local Governance Programme (Rhodes 1999b), played a part in challenging the dominant, managerial ideology of the 1980s. Both supported a view of the world in which networks rival markets and bureaucracy as the apt way of delivering services.

I build my story of change over the past two decades around nine aphorisms:

- from government to governance;
- more control over less;
- the hollowing-out of the state;
- the weakness of the core executive;
- the sour laws of unintended consequences;
- the loss of trust;
- it's the mix that matters;
- diplomacy and hands-off management;
- from deconcentration to devolution.

Each aphorism, is accompanied by a box which illustrates the point with either a vignette or relevant findings from projects on the Whitehall Programme. Finally, I paint a vainglorious picture of the Programme's achievement in challenging the language of NPM and putting governance on the agenda in the guise of 'joined-up government'. The aphorisms address the question, 'what happened'? I also address the question 'so what?' I try to draw lessons relevant to the continuing search to modernise government from my aphorisms. It should be obvious that, for a Programme with 23 projects, the findings point in many directions; this chapter is a personal interpretation.[1]

Governance

If the Westminster model and NPM are familiar stories about British government, governance is not. Defined here as 'steering networks' (see Rhodes 1997a: Chapter 3 and 1999c), it focuses on the shackles on leaders, undermining the 'leaders know best' strand of the British governmental tradition.

From government to governance

This aphorism summarises the shift from line bureaucracies to fragmented service delivery. After 1979, function-based policy networks based on central departments (or sections of them) changed in two ways. First, the membership of networks became broader, incorporating both the private and voluntary sectors. Second, the government swapped direct for indirect controls. British government privatised the utilities, swapping control through ownership for control by regulation. It contracted-out services to the private sector. It introduced quasi-markets through purchaser-provider splits when services could not be privatised. It bypassed local authorities for special-purpose bodies. It removed operational management from central departments and vested it in separate agencies (see Rhodes, 1997a: Chapters 5–7). Fragmentation not only created new networks but it also increased the membership of existing networks (see Box 14.1).

Box 14.1 Fragmentation

I live in Yorkshire in a quiet rural area with a few small towns. It is not the cosmopolitan capital of the western world. There is nightlife, but it shuts at 11 p.m. The government requires health and local authorities to provide for AIDS sufferers. To plan the service, 19 organisations come together to form the planning team. An unbelievable 39 organisations are involved in delivering the service. There is no hierarchy among the organisations. No one organisation can plan and command the others. And yet there are only 24 people who are HIV positive in the area. A tinge of black humour is unavoidable: there is only one clear policy choice – find a patient for each organisation (Rhodes 1997b).

Central departments are no longer either necessarily or invariably the fulcrum, or focal organisation, of a network. Power relations may remain unequal. The government can still set the boundaries to network actions. It funds the services. But it has also increased its dependence on multifarious networks. The policy of marketising public services speeded up differentiation and multiplied networks. Such trends make steering more difficult, so the mechanisms for integration multiply. Governance has become the defining narrative of British government at the start of the new century, challenging the commonplace notion of Britain as a unitary state with a strong executive.

More control over less

Government policy fragmented service delivery. It compensated for its loss of hands-on controls by reinforcing its control over resources. Decentralising service delivery was coupled with both centralised financial control and a massive extension of internal and external regulation. The government adopted a strategy of 'more control over less', with the 'freedom to manage' constrained by financial and regulatory controls (see Box 14.2).

Box 14.2   The growth of internal regulation

Christopher Hood and his colleagues (1998 and 1999) show that the loss of control, whether through privatisation or deconcentrating managerial authority, has fuelled regulatory growth.

Between 1976–95 the number of regulatory bodies increased by 22% from 110 to 134. Staffing increased by 60% to about 14,000. Spending increased by 106% to about £766 million, a figure doubled by including compliance costs.

They conclude government devotes as many resources to regulating itself as it does to private utilities; this regulation has become more formal, intensive, complex and specialised; like Topsy it just grew; and the regulators are unregulated.

The reasons for these changes have been often rehearsed. For example, Hood (1996: 273–82) focuses on 'English awfulness', right-wing party politics, poor economic performance, and scaling down big government (see also Wright 1994: 104–8). Rhodes (1999c) also points to the ways in which governmental traditions, or a set of beliefs about the institutions and history of government, resulted in different interpretations of public sector reform and its problems, leading to different aims, measures and outcomes.

So, the pace of change in Britain was greater than elsewhere in Western Europe because three characteristics of the British governmental tradition eased public sector reform.

First, a defining characteristic of the British governmental tradition is its strong executive. Margaret Thatcher exercised strong, directive, and, above all, persistent, executive leadership to push through reform of the civil service. Riddell (1997) argues that 'the Blair Presidency' continues the tradition.

Second, Britain has a written constitution but it does not entrench the rights of institutions or individuals. So, there are few constitutional constraints on executive leadership when the government has a majority in Parliament. Once the government decided on a change, it could force it through.

Finally, the Conservative government devised a clear set of political ideas to justify and 'sell' its various reform packages. It attacked big government and waste, used markets to create more individual choice and campaigned for the consumer.

One theme remains constant: containing public spending to provide more services for the same or less money. This imperative drove the search for management reform. Although a commonplace of the academic literature, it is worth stressing that administrative reform is always political. Since 1979, the reform of the civil service has been rooted in the political decision to cut government spending and to exert effective control over the administrative machine.

The hollowing out of the state

Governance is also the product of the hollowing-out of the state from above (for example, by international interdependencies), not just from below (by marketisation and networks), and sideways (by agencies) (Rhodes 1994: 138–9).

The European Union shows how transnational policy networks emerge when, for example, there is a high dependence in the policy sector; policy making is depoliticised and routinised; supra-national agencies are dependent on other agencies to deliver a service; and there is a need to aggregate interests. In the EU, multilevel governance links the Commission, national ministries and local and regional authorities. It is a specific example of the impact of international interdependencies on the state (see Box 14.3).

So, the hollowing-out thesis suggests that internal fragmentation and external dependence create many challenges to the capacity of core executives to steer. Day and Klein (1997), who argue the NHS Executive has hollowed out the Department of Health, and Norton (2000), who argues decentralising power to bodies outside government has further limited the capacity of ministers to have any independent impact on policy outcomes and is evidence of hollowing out, also support this conclusion.

The weakness of the core executive

The strong executive strand of the Westminster model overstated the power of the British centre which was always embedded in complex sets of dependencies (see Box 14.4).

NPM created a greater need for co-ordination while reducing governmental ability to co-ordinate. Concern for this decline in central capability was voiced by Sir Robin Butler (1993: 404), former Head of the Home Civil Service, when he wrote:

it is essential that it does not reach the point where individual Departments and their Agencies become simply different unconnected elements in the overall public sector, with ... *no real working mechanisms for policy co-ordination.* (emphasis added)

The Conservative government did not strengthen strategic capacity with the other changes. This search for co-ordination lies at the heart of New Labour's reforms. As Kavanagh and Seldon (2000) point out, we have seen prime ministerial centralisation in the guises of: institutional innovation and more resources for No. 10 and the Cabinet Office; and strong political and policy direction as No. 10

Box 14.3   **EU and hollowing-out**

Menon and Wright (1998) argue 'there is no doubt' the UK 'has 'forged an efficient policy making and co-ordinating machine' because the government speaks and acts with one voice. It has also been successful in its 'basic strategy of opening up and liberalising the EU's economy'. However, its 'unjustified reputation' for being at the margins of Europe is justified for EU constitution building and 'an effective and coherent policy making machine becomes ineffective when it is bypassed' for the history making decisions.

Bulmer and Burch (1998: 624) conclude:
'At the levels of policy and political management, the impact of EC-EU on the activities of the British government has been profound. Membership has brought new issues on to the agenda, given whole areas of policy a European dimension, required the development of new expertise on the part of officials and ministers, involved intensive and extensive negotiations with EU partners and raised significant problems about policy presentation and party management.'

Three epigrams from Richard Rose (2000) on the shrinking world of the British core executive
'All politics is international'
'There are two kinds of countries: those that are small and know it and those that are small and don't'.
'What goes on outside the world of Westminster is more important to the peace and prosperity of the British people than what is done by Her Majesty's Government, including its first minister.'

However, without denying the claim there has been some hollowing-out, Lowe and Rollings (2000) caution against the argument there was a unilinear increase in state intervention after 1900 and a hollowing-out after 1945. They record the rise and fall of governance this century: it was a core concept at the turn of the century, obsolete in the 1960s and reinvented in the 1980s.

---

seeks a strong grip on the government machine. The pendulum swings yet again as the centre promotes co-ordination and strategic oversight to combat Whitehall's departmentalism. Such 'power grabs' are 'a reaction to felt weakness, a frustration with the inability to pull effective levers'.

However, in spite of the strong pressures for more and pro-active co-ordination throughout Western Europe:

> the co-ordination activities of the core remain in practice modest in scope: most internal co-ordination takes place at lower levels of the state hierarchy; is rarely strategic or even directive, but selective, issue oriented and reactive; is negative in the sense that it is characterised by the toleration of heavily compartmentalised units pursuing mutual avoidance strategies to reduce tensions. ... All governments have resorted to a variety of measures to

reduce the burden of co-ordination, ... but with only limited success and ... many of the measures adopted have served only to complicate and even increase co-ordination requirements. (Hayward and Wright in Volume 2, Chapter 2)

Box 14.4   Power-dependence in the core executive

Martin Smith (1999: Ch. 2) usefully links the notion of the core executive to power-dependence (Rhodes 1999a) to show the constraints on leadership in British government (see Chapter 1 above).

Power-dependence means *all* actors within the core executive have resources and to achieve goals resources have to be exchanged. So, even actors with many resources, such as the prime minister, are dependent on other actors to achieve their goals. This distribution of resources, coupled with the strength of departments and their overlapping networks, mean the core executive is fragmented and central co-ordination is difficult.

Other projects discuss the weakness of the core executive rather than its dependency relationships

The core executive is 'elusive and fluid' and the notion needs to be 'widened' to include 'the strictly political dimension of policy making' and 'deepened' to cover 'the relatively low level at which ... key decisions are taken' (Lowe 1997).

Norton (2000) describes the core executive as baronial: 'Ministers are like medieval barons in that they preside over their own, sometimes vast, policy territory. Within that territory they are largely supreme. ... The ministers have their own policy space, their own castles – even some of the architecture of departments ... reinforces that perception – and their own courtiers. The ministers fight – or form alliances – with other barons in order to get what they want. They resent interference in their territory by other barons and will fight to defend it.'
In sum, power-dependence characterises the links between both barons and the barons and prime minister.

'It often feels like a very hostile world out there' said one former Prime Minister, 'and the fact was I could do very little about it' (quoted in Kavanagh and Seldon 1999)

Referring to the 1960s, Lowe and Rollings (2000) conclude: 'political and administrative fragmentation may have sapped the ability of the core executive to co-ordinate a strong central policy, but the fundamental impediment to modernisation remained the power of vested interests within the broader governance'.

Co-ordination is the philosopher's stone of modern government, ever sought, never found.

The sour laws of unintended consequences

Unintended consequences are not the result of Sod's law that 'if it can go wrong, it will go wrong'. They are not just the result of poor design or wayward implementation by other agencies. They are unavoidable because new knowledge does not increase control of the social world but alters that world and sets it off in new directions. Policies are theories about how to change the social world. Implementation provides findings of how that world is both changing and in so doing changing the policies. There is a juggernaut or heavy lorry quality to the impact of knowledge on political institutions.

Governance is no exception. Marketisation provides a vivid illustration of 'the sour laws of unintended consequences' (Hennessy 1992: 453). One clear, even dramatic, irony of marketisation was that it was undermined by networks while simultaneously undermining the effectiveness of the networks it increased.

The loss of trust

Networks are a distinctive way of co-ordinating and, therefore, a separate governing structure from markets and bureaucracies. Trust is their central co-ordinating mechanism in the same way that commands and price competition are the key mechanisms for bureaucracies and markets respectively.

The loss of trust is a general argument about marketisation and its effects. It is also a specific argument about eroding public service ethics. On trust, Newman *et al.* (1998: 105) conclude:

> Relational contracts involve a degree of trust between client and contractor. The client must be prepared to trust the contractor to behave within the spirit of the agreement on the assumption that the reputation and future business growth of the contractor depend on it. The contractor must be prepared to trust that the client understands the realities of the new situation, i.e. that the private sector needs to make a return on investment.

Managerialism, open competition, political impropriety and macho-ministers add up to a dilution of public service ethics. It is hard to provide incontestable evidence about marketisation and its effects but Box 14.5 provides a dramatic example (see also Committee of Public Accounts 1994).

It's the mix that matters

No governing structure works for all services in all conditions; one size does not fit all. The issue, therefore, is not the superiority of one governing structure over another but the conditions under which each works best.

The limits to markets and planning are well documented. The limits to governance as networks are less well known (see Box: 14.6). Also, network negotiation and co-ordination can be confounded by the political context in which they are embedded. Rapid rates of change, endemic social conflicts and short-term political, especially party political, interests can all undermine negotiations and the search for an agreed course of action. So, whatever the governing structure,

---

Box 14.5 **Marketisation and declining standards in public life**

Yorkshire RHA awarded a contract to Yorkshire Water for clinical waste incineration worth £7.2 million of capital and £2 million a year in revenue. It was not let competitively. It was for *fifteen* years. The Authority did not get NHS Executive approval. The Committee of Public Accounts (1997) was 'concerned' about a further eight instances of 'unacceptable' behaviour which they noted 'with surprise' and 'serious concern', including on one occasion, an 'appalled'.

The Regional General Manager defended his actions claiming he brought a more commercial attitude and a willingness to embrace risk to health services management. He embraced 'the rhetoric of the day (in summary the ministerial encouragement to break away from the bureaucratic stranglehold).' The point is of sufficient importance to warrant a lengthy quote from the former chief executive of Yorkshire RHA, Keith McLean.

'The culture of the day in the NHS should be recognised as a real factor. In the 1988–93 period, senior managers were encouraged *from the highest levels* to focus on the achievement of nationally desired results. The service was in the throes of radical structural change with the introduction of a market approach and, ..., it felt to me and perhaps others that the regulatory framework of the pre-reform era was relaxed to give local managers the space to achieve change quickly through the exercise of managerial discretion. The advent of the Chief Executive ... was a signal of the changing culture. Several of the regulations which are said to have been transgressed in Yorkshire have since been modified in the direction of greater flexibility ... and the coming changes were, inevitably, 'in the air' before they actually came about'. (Committee of Public Accounts 1997: 40 emphasis added)

Mr McLean accepted that he embraced 'the culture of the day too enthusiastically and uncritically in pursuit of successful outcomes' but insisted that his decisions must be placed in the broader context. His point about encouragement from the highest level is accurate. The impact of marketisation and the decline in standards could not be clearer.

---

there is a high probability that it will produce unintended consequences because of the political context, inappropriate conditions, and the unpredictable impact of social knowledge.

Finally, this concentration on the problems of networks should not lead to the conclusion that governance is an unworkable alternative. Networks also possess advantages. First, *all* governing structures fail. Networks work in conditions where other governing structures do not. The list of conditions in Box 14.6, below, are conditions under which markets fail; for example, where it is difficult to specify the price of a good or service. Second, networks bring together policy makers and the implementing agencies, and by so doing increase the available expertise and information. Third, networks bring together many actors to negotiate about a policy, increasing the acceptability of that policy and improving the likelihood of compliance. Fourth, networks increase the resources available for policy making by drawing together the public, private and voluntary sectors.

Diplomacy and hands-off management

I use 'diplomacy' to refer to management by negotiation. As Sir Douglas Wass said 'finesse and diplomacy are an essential ingredient in public service' (cited in Hennessy 1989: 150). Such skills lie at the heart of steering networks.

The idea is not new, although they can seem novel (see Box 14.7); they have just been temporarily misplaced. Nicholson (1950: 15) identifies seven diplomatic virtues: truthfulness; precision; calm; good temper; patience; modesty; and loyalty (to the government one serves). There is a charming quality to Nicholson's account. The budding diplomat is advised that: 'above everything, do not allow yourself to become excited about your work' (p. 116). He then adds:

Box 14.6   The limits to networks

Networks are effective when for example:
– actors need reliable, 'thicker' information;
– quality cannot be specified or is difficult to define and measure;
– commodities are difficult to price;
– professional discretion and expertise are core values;
– flexibility to meet localised, varied service demands is needed;
– cross-sector, multi-agency co-operation and production is needed;
– monitoring and evaluation incur high political and administrative costs; and
– implementation involves haggling.

The costs of networks include:
– closed to outsiders and unrepresentative;
– unaccountable for their actions;
– serve private interests, not the public interest (at both local and national levels of government);
– difficult to steer;
– inefficient because co-operation causes delay;
– immobilised by conflicts of interest; and
– difficult to combine with other governing structures (see Rhodes 1997a and 1997c).

'"But", the reader may object, "you have forgotten intelligence, knowledge, discernment, prudence, hospitality, charm, industry, courage and even tact". I have not forgotten them. I have taken them for granted.' (p. 126)

For all its slightly old-fashioned, even quaint, air, Nicholson signals an important shift in style to a language which stresses sitting where the other person sits and helping other people to realise their objectives.

Box 14.7 Diplomacy

Recently, I addressed the annual conference of the Queensland Division of the Institute of Public Administration Australia. I contrasted the style of the 'head kicker' – Australian for macho-manager – with that of the diplomat. As I mingled after the address, three female public servants working for the Queensland government approached me, congratulated me on my talk, 'but', they commented, 'they won't listen to you. That diplomacy is *"girlie talk"*.' My instant response was to laugh. On reflection, I realised that language about sitting where the other person sits and helping other people to realise their objectives was seen as 'soft'.

The new style of hands-off management involves setting the framework in which networks work but keeping an arm's length relationship. For example, a central department can: provide the policy framework and policy guidance; prod the network into action by systematic review and scrutiny of its work; use patronage to put 'one of its own' in key positions; mobilise resources and skills across sectors; regulate the network and its members; and provide advice and assistance (Cm 2811 1995; Rhodes 1997c and citations).

The new style also employs a colourful language. For example, civil servants in the Department of Health, confronted with the challenge of instilling financial discipline in doctors, liken their task to 'herding cats' and their management tools to 'rubber levers' which when pushed bend in the middle but effect little change on the ground.

From deconcentration to devolution

Decentralisation encompasses both deconcentration and devolution. Deconcentration refers to the redistribution of administrative responsibilities in central government. Devolution refers to the exercise of political authority by lay, elected, institutions within territorial areas. In the UK, most of the reforms of the 1980s and 1990s sought to deconcentrate managerial authority; for example, to agencies. Devolution was a feature of public sector reform elsewhere in Europe. With the advent of the Labour government, devolution became a political priority in Britain.

There was one important change relevant to devolution in the life of the Whitehall Programme: Government Offices for the Regions (GOs) (see Box 14.8)

Box 14.8 **Government Offices for the Regions**

The decision to set up GOs was 'a radical departure from the centralised and compartmentalised traditions of the civil service'. They have led to greater co-ordination in the regions. Although 'much remains to be done in developing the skills of civil servants in networking partnership development', none the less GOs are a key mechanism for developing holistic governance. Potentially, they are also 'the building blocks of a devolved democratically elected regional structure' (Mawson and Spencer 1997: 81–3).

The British unitary state was always a differentiated polity – a maze of divided functional authority. GOs were an embryo reform of that system. To a significant degree they will be supplanted by the Regional Development Agencies. It was their misfortune to be created by the Conservative government.

Devolution reinforces functional decentralisation with divided political authority. Under New Labour the extensive and entrenched functional representation of British government faces a challenge from territorial representation in the guise of both local and regional governments.

Conclusions

So what lessons can we draw from a view of the world in which networks rival markets and bureaucracy as a suitable means for delivering services? Too often academics seek to play the role of ersatz public servant. We try to provide data, even solutions, to present-day problems. But the social sciences offer only provisional knowledge. Prediction is an impossibility, only hindsight is a realistic goal. An awareness of our limits does not make the social sciences useless. If we cannot offer solutions, we can define and redefine problems in novel ways. We can tell the policy makers and administrators distinctive stories about their world and how it is governed. The new public management told a story of economy, efficiency and effectiveness which contrasted sharply with the story of the local government officer as professional with clients and the permanent secretary as policy adviser and fire-fighter for the minister.

The governance narrative stresses differentiation, networks, hollowing-out, trust and diplomacy. Its language contrasts sharply with that of managerialism, markets and contracts. The ESRC's 'Local Governance' and 'Whitehall' Programmes helped to change the language of the 1980s from managerialism to networks. If there is a simple lesson, it is that in the complex world of diplomacy in governance there are no simple solutions based on markets or bureaucracies or networks.

This lesson is broad. In fact, it is unpacked by each aphorism. The following lessons parallel the earlier sections of the chapter.

- fragmentation limits the centre's ability to command;
- regulation substitutes for control;
- external dependence further erodes the ability of the core executive to act;
- fragmentation confounds centralisation, undermining the ability of the core executive to co-ordinate;
- knowledge, or policy learning, has a juggernaut quality, changing problems as policies seek to solve them;
- marketisation corrodes trust, co-operation and shared professional values, undermining the networks it only partially replaces;
- all governing structures – markets, bureaucracies and networks – fail, so 'if it ain't broke don't fix it';
- steering networks needs diplomacy, so hands-off management is the only effective operating code.
- decentralisation is a key mechanism for developing holistic governance.

The maxim 'for every complex problem there is a simple solution and it is always wrong' may not be literally correct but it should instil a modicum of caution in the breast of the would-be reformer.

These lessons are directly relevant to many reforms under New Labour (see Box 14.9).

Box 14.9   White Paper on *Modernising Government* (Cm. 4130 1999)

This White Paper aspires to 'joined-up' or 'holistic' government (pp. 6, 7, 32 and 40). Both phrases are synonyms for steering networks.

The problem
'in general too little effort has gone into making sure that policies are devised and delivered in a consistent and effective way across institutional boundaries – for example between different Government departments and between central and local government'

The solution
'Our challenge, … , is to get different parts of government to work together' by, for example: 'designing policy around shared goals'; 'involving others in policy making'; 'integrating the European Union and international dimension in our policy making'; and regarding 'policy making as a continuous learning process'.

Specific proposals include: organising work around cross cutting issues; pooled budgets; cross-cutting performance measures; and appraisal systems which reward team working.

Their approach is instrumental and assumes the centre can devise and impose tools which will foster integration in and between networks to reach central government's objectives. To quote an official, departments must drop their 'arrogant and aloof stance' and accept that 'partnerships must be more equal' and involve more actors (personal correspondence). The problem of integration will be easily resolved. The reforms have a centralising thrust. They seek to co-ordinate departments and local authorities by imposing a new style of management on other agencies. So, they 'do not want to run local services from the centre' but 'The Government is not afraid to take action where standards slip'; an obvious instance of a command operating code.

A key mechanism of 'joined up government' is the action zone; that is, area-based initiatives in, for example, health and education which seek to co-ordinate service delivery between central and local government, the health service, the private sector and the voluntary sector. There are now 25 education action zones and 29 health action zones. These initiatives not only make the local service delivery map more complicated, especially for citizens, but raise the problem of who joins-up the zones? But the key problem is the costs of steering. The centre's command operating code, no matter how well disguised, runs the ever-present risk of recalcitrance from key actors and a loss of flexibility in dealing with localised problems. Control deficits are an ever-present unintended consequence of the top-down imposition of objectives. Network structures are characterised by a decentralised negotiating style which trades off control for agreement. Management by negotiation means agreeing with the objectives of others not just persuading them that you were right all along or resorting to sanctions when they disagree.

There is much to welcome in New Labour's modernising programme for central, local and devolved government. But the government lacks trust; it fears the independence it bestows. So, the White Paper on *Modernising Government* recognises the need to manage networks but fails to recognise the limits to central intervention as it tries to balance independence with central control.

My story stresses muddling through based on provisional knowledge and diverse, local policy responses to contested definitions of problems. There is no tool kit for the central steering of decentralised networks. 'Hands off' is the hardest lesson of all to learn.

Notes

1. The text covers mainly the publications of the Whitehall Programme. It is a personal 'best of', covering the items that support my argument. So, I apologise to those colleagues whose work is not given the prominence I am sure it will command elsewhere. To make some sense of 23 projects, such selectivity was unavoidable. I have also cited official publications and speeches and lectures by ministers and senior civil servants. I have not cited other relevant literature simply because I seek to show the distinctive contribution of the Whitehall Programme.

Bibliography

Ahmed and others v. The United Kingdom, European Court of Human Rights, 2 September 1998.

Alford, B. W. E., Lowe, R. and Rollings, N. (1992), *Economic Planning, 1943–1951*, London: HMSO.

Amery, L. (1938), 'A Weakness of Democracy', *The Times*, 10 April.

Ayres, I. and Braithwaite, J. (1992), *Responsive Regulation: Transcending the Deregulation Debate*, Oxford: Oxford University Press.

Baines, P. (1996), 'Financial Accountability: Agencies and Audit'. In P. Giddings (ed.), *Parliamentary Accountability: a Study of Parliament and Executive Agencies*, London: Macmillan.

Baker, D. and Seawright, D. (eds) (1998), *Britain For and Against Europe: British Politics and the Question of European Integration*, Oxford: Clarendon Press.

Baker, K. (1993), *The Turbulent Years: My Life in Politics*, London: Faber and Faber.

Balogh, T. (1959), 'The Apotheosis of the Dilettante'. In H. Thomas (ed.), *The Establishment*, London: Anthony Blond.

Baldwin, R. and McCrudden, C. (1987), *Regulation and Public Law*. London. Weidenfeld and Nicolson.

Bank of England, (1997a), 'Financial Regulation: Why, How and by Whom?', *Bank of England Quarterly Bulletin*, 37/1: 107–12.

Bank of England, (1997b), 'Reforms to the UK Monetary Policy Framework and Financial Services Regulation', *Bank of England Quarterly Bulletin*, 37.

Banks, T. (1994), *Review of the Wider Department of Health*, London: DoH.

Barker, A. (1982), *Quangos in Britain*, London: Macmillan.

Barker, A. (1998), 'Political Responsibility for UK Prison Security – Ministers Escape Again', *Public Administration*, 76: 1-23.

Barrow, L. and Bullock I. (1996), *Democratic Ideas and the British Labour Movement 1880–1914*, Cambridge: Cambridge University Press.

Battista, R. (1994), *Servicing the Stigma; the Implementation of AIDS Policy*, unpublished MA thesis, University of York.

Becker, B. (1989), *Öffentlicher Verwaltung, Lehrbuch für Wissenschaft und Praxis*, Percha: R. S. Schulz.

Beer, S. (1981), *Brain of the Firm*, Chichester: Wiley & Sons.

Beloff, M. (1960), Letter to the *Daily Telegraph*, 2 August.

Benson, J. K. (1982), 'A Framework for Policy Analysis'. In D. Rogers, D. Whitten and Associates, *Inter-organisation Co-ordination*, Ames Iowa-Iowa State University Press.

Bentham, J. (1983) [1830], *Constitutional Code*, Edited by F. Rosen and J. H. Burns, Oxford: Oxford University Press.

Beveridge, Sir W. (1942), Letter to *The Times*, 19 February.

Beveridge, W. H. (1953), *Power and Influence*, London: Hodder and Stoughton.

Bevir, M. and Rhodes, R. A. W. (1999), 'Narratives of British Government', *British Journal of Politics and International Relations* 1/2: 215–39.

Bichard, M. (1996), 'Shake-up Inspires New State of Mind', *People Management*, 8 February, 22-7.

Birch, A. H. (1964), *Representative and Responsible Government*, London: Allen & Unwin.

Black, D. (1976), *The Behaviour of Law*. New York: Academic Press.

Booth, A. (1983), 'The "Keynesian Revolution" in Economic Policy-Making', *Economic History Review*, 36: 103–23.

Booth, A. (1987), 'Britain in the 1930s: A Managed Economy?', *Economic History Review*, 40: 499–522.

Boothby, R. (1960), Letter to the *Daily Telegraph*, 4 August.

Brady, C. (1997), 'The Cabinet System and Management of the Suez Crisis', *Contemporary British History*, 11(2): 65–93.

Brady, C. and Catterall, P. (1997), 'Managing the Core Executive', *Public Administration*, 75: 509–29.

Braithwaite, C. (1938), *The Voluntary Citizen*, London: Methuen.

Brasnett, M. (1969), *Voluntary Social Action*, London: NCSS.

Brett, M. V. (ed.) (1934), *Journals and Letters of Reginald Viscount Esher: Vol II, 1903–1910*, London: Nicolson and Watson.

Bridgen, P. (Forthcoming), 'Making a Mess of Modernisation: the State, Redundancy Pay and Economic Policy-making in the Early 1960s', *Twentieth Century British History*, 10:

Bridgen, P. (forthcoming), 'The One Nation Idea and State Welfare: The Conservatives and Pensions', *Contemporary British History*, 14:

Bridgen, P. and Lowe, R. (1998), *Welfare Policy Under the Conservatives, 1951–1964*, London: PRO Publications.

Brittan, S. (1964), *The Treasury Under the Tories*, Harmondsworth: Pelican.

Brittan, S. (1969), *Steering the Economy*, London: Secker and Warburg.

Broadbent, Sir E. (1988), *The Military and Government: From Macmillan to Heseltine*, London: Macmillan.

Brook, N. (1961), *Cabinet Government*, London: Home Office Administration Series, no. 5.

Brooke, S. (1991), 'Problems of "Socialist Planning": Evan Durbin and the Labour Government of 1945', *Historical Journal*, 34: 687–702.

Bruce-Gardyne, J. and Lawson, N. (1976), *The Power Game*, London: Macmillan.

Bryson, J. M. and Crosby, B. C. (1992), *Leadership for the Common Good*. San Francisco: Jossey-Bass.

Buller, J. and Smith, M. J. (1997), 'Civil Service Attitudes to the European Union'. In D. Baker and D. Seawright (eds), *Britain For and Against Europe*, Oxford: Clarendon Press.

Bulmer, S. and Burch, M. (1998a), *The "Europeanisation" of Central Government: the UK and Germany in Historical Institutionalist Perspective*, Manchester Papers in Politics/EPRU Series no. 06/98.

Bulmer, S. and Burch, M. (1998b), 'Organising for Europe – Whitehall, the British State and the European Union', *Public Administration*, 76: 601–28.

Burch, M. (1988), 'British Cabinet: a Residual Executive', *Parliamentary Affairs*, 41: 34–47.

Burch, M. and Holliday, I. (1996), *The British Cabinet System*, London: Prentice-Hall.

Burk, K. (1982), 'The Treasury for Impotence to Power'. In K. Burk (ed.) *War and the State: the Transformation of British Government*, 1914–19, London: Allen & Unwin.

Burnham, J. and Jones, G. W. (1993), 'Advising Margaret Thatcher: the Prime Minister's Office and the Cabinet Office Compared', *Political Studies*, 41: 299–314.

Burnham, J. and Jones, G. W. (1999), 'Innovators at 10 Downing Street'. In K. Theakston (ed.), *Leadership in Whitehall*, Basingstoke: Macmillan.

Butler, D. and Butler, G. (1994), *British Political Facts 1900–1994*, London: Macmillan.

Butler, D. and Kavanagh, D. (1992), *The British General Election of 1992*, London: Macmillan.

Butler, Sir R. (1992), 'The New Public Management: the Contribution of Whitehall and Academia', *Public Policy and Administration*,7/3: 4–14.

Cabinet Office (1994), *Responsibilities for Recruitment to the Civil Service*, London: Cabinet Office.

Cabinet Office (1995a), *The Civil Service: Taking Forward Continuity and Change*, Cm. 2748, London: HMSO.

Cabinet Office (1995b), *The Ombudsman in Your Files*, London: HMSO.

Cabinet Office (1997), *Ministerial Code*, London: Cabinet Office.

Cabinet Office (1998), *Parliamentary Scrutiny of European Business*, Cm. 4095, London: Stationery Office.

Cabinet Office (Office of Public Service) (1996), *Next Steps Agencies in Government Review*, Cm. 3164, London: Stationery Office.

Cairncross, A. K. (1985), *Years of Recovery*, London: Methuen.

Cairncross, A. K. (1987), 'Prelude to Radcliffe', *Rivista di Storia Economica*, 2nd series 4, 189–211.

Cairncross, A. K. (1994), 'Economic Policy and Performance, 1945–64'. In R. Floud and D. McCloskey (eds), *The Economic History of Britain Since 1700, Vol 3*, Cambridge: Cambridge University Press.

Cairncross, A. K. (ed.) (1991), *The Robert Hall Diaries 1954–1961*, London: Unwin Hyman.

Cairncross, A. K. and Watts, N. (1989), *The Economic Section, 1939–1961*, London: Routledge.

Campbell, C. and Wilson, G. (1995), *The End of Whitehall: Death of a Paradigm*, Oxford: Blackwell.

Campbell, J. (1993), *Edward Heath: a Biography*, London: Jonathan Cape.

Capie, F. and Collins, M. (1992), *Have the Banks Failed British Industry?*, London: IEA.

Caplan, J. (1988), *Government Without Administration: State and Civil Service in Weimar and Nazi Germany*, Oxford: Clarendon Press.

Carper, W. B. and Stalker G. M. (1980), 'The Nature and Types of Organizational Taxonomies: an Overview', *Academy of Management Review*, 5: 65–75.

Carter, N., Klein, R. and Day, P. (1992), *How Organisations Measure Success*, London: Routledge.

Catterall, P. (1998), 'How Imperial was the Committee of Imperial Defence?', paper presented at 'The Dominion Concept' conference, University of Warwick.

Catterall, P. and Brady, C. (1998), 'Cabinet Committees in British Governance', *Public Policy and Administration*, 13(4): 67–84.

Catterall, P. and McDougall, S. (eds) (1996), *The Northern Ireland Question in British Politics*, Basingstoke: Macmillan.

Caulcott, T. H. and Mountfield, P. (1974), 'Decentralized Administration in Sweden', *Public Administration*, 52: 41–53.

Chester, D. and Willson, F. M. G. (1968) [1957] *The Organization/ British Central Government 1914-1964*. 2nd edition. London: Allen, Unwin.

Chester, D. N. (1950), 'Robert Morant and Michael Sadler', *Public Administration*, 28: 109–16.

Chester, D. N. (1979), 'Fringe Bodies, Quangos and All That', *Public Administration*, 57: 51–4.

Chester, D. N. (1953),'Public Corporations and the Classification of Administrative Bodies.' *Political Studies*, 1: 34–52.

Child Support Agency (1994), *Annual Report and Accounts 1993–94*, London: HMSO.

Child Support Agency (1995), *Annual Report and Accounts 1994–95*, London: HMSO.

Child Support Agency (1997), Annual Report and Accounts 1996–97, London: HMSO.

Churchill, W. S. (1948), *The Gathering Storm*, London: Cassell.

Clifford, C., McMillan, A. and McLean, I. (1997), *The Organisation of Central Government Departments: a History 1964–1992*, Oxford: Nuffield College, 3 vols in 5 parts.

Cm 2290 (1993), *Open Government*, London: HMSO.

Cm 2748 (1995), *The Civil Service. Taking Forward Continuity and Change*, London: HMSO.

Cm 2811 (1995), *Department of National Heritage Annual Report 1995*, London: HMSO.

Cm 3020 (1995), *Review of Prison Service Security in England and Wales and the Escape from Parkhurst Prison on Tuesday 3rd January 1995*, London: HMSO.

Cm 3579 (1996/7), *Next Steps Agencies in Government: Review 1996*, London: HMSO.

Cm 3557 (1997), *The Governance of Public Bodies: a Progress Report*, London: HMSO.

Cm 4310 (1999), *Modernising Government*, London: Stationery Office.

Collier, R. and Collier, D. (1991), *Shaping the Political Agenda: Critical Junctures, the Labor Movement, and Regime Dynamics in Latin America*, Princeton: Princeton University Press.

Committee of Public Accounts (1994), *The Proper Conduct of Public Business*, London: HMSO.

Committee of Public Accounts (1997), *The Former Yorkshire Regional Health Authority: the Inquiry Commissioned by the NHS Chief Executive*, HC 432 Session 1996–97, London: Stationery Office.

Cooper, Lord, of Culross (1957), *Selected Papers 1922–1954*, Edinburgh: Oliver and Boyd.

Cooper, P. (1995), 'Separating Policy From Operations in the Prison Service: a Case Study', *Public Policy and Administration*, 10 (4): 4–19.

Coopey, R., Fielding, S. and Tiratsoo, N. (1993), *The Wilson Governments 1964–1970*, London: Pinter.

Corbett, R. (1998), 'Governance and Institutions'. In *The European Union: Annual Review of Activities*, special issue of *Journal of Common Market Studies*, Oxford: Blackwell.

Council of Civil Service Unions v. Minister for the Civil Service [1985] Appeal Cases 374 (House of Lords).

Cronin, J. E. (1991), *The Politics of State Expansion*, London: Routledge.

Crooks, C. (1993), *100 Not Out: The Centenary of the Employment Department 1893–1993*, London: Employment Department Group.

Cross, J. A. (1970), 'The Regional Decentralization of British Government Departments', *Public Administration*, 48: 423–41.

Crossman, R. H. S. (1963), 'Introduction'. In Walter Bagehot, *The British Constitution*, Harmondsworth: Penguin.

Crossman, R. H. S. (1972), *A Politician's View of Health Service Planning*, Glasgow: University of Glasgow.

Daalder, H. (1963a), *Cabinet Reform in Britain 1914–63*, California: Stanford University Press.

Daalder, H. (1963b), 'The Haldane Committee and the Cabinet', *Public Administration*, 41: 117–35.

Daintith, T. and Page, A. (1999), *The Executive in the Constitution: Structure, Autonomy, Internal Control*, Oxford: Oxford University Press.

Daunton, M. (1996), 'Payment and Participation: Welfare and State Finance in Britain, 1900–1951', *Past and Present*, 150: 169–216.

Davies, P. L. and Rose, R. (1988), 'Are Programme Resources Related to Organizational Change?', *European Journal of Political Research*, 16: 73–98.

Dawkins, R. (1986), *The Blind Watchmaker*, Harlow: Longman.

Dawkins, R. (1995), *River Out of Eden: a Darwinian View of Life*, London: Weidenfeld & Nicolson.

Day, P. and Klein, R. (1985), 'Central Accountability and Local Decision Making: Towards a New NHS', *British Medical Journal*, 290: 1676–8.

Day, P. and Klein, R. (1987), *Accountabilities: Five Public Services*, London: Tavistock.

Day, P. and Klein, R. (1989), 'The Politics of Modernization: Britain's National Health Service in the 1980s', *The Millbank Quarterly*, 67(1): 1–34.

Day, P. and Klein, R. (1997), *Steering But Not Rowing? The Transformation of the Department of Health*, Bristol: The Policy Press.

De Callières, F. (1963) [1716], *On the Manner of Negotiating with Princes*, Washington: University of America Press.

Department of Health (1993), *Managing the New NHS*, London: DoH.

Department of Health (1995), *Statement of Responsibilities and Accountabilities*, London: DoH.

Department of Health and Social Security (1976), *Regional Chairmen's Enquiry Into the Working of the DHSS in Relation to Regional Health Authorities Report*, London: DHSS.

Dimsdale, N. H. (1991), 'British Monetary Policy Since 1945'. In N. F. R. Crafts and N. Woodward (eds), *The British Economy Since 1945*, Oxford: Oxford University Press.

Doty, D. H. and Glick, W. H. (1994), 'Typologies as a Unique Form of Theory Building: Toward Improved Understanding and Modelling', *Academy of Management Review*, 19 (2): 230–51.

Dow, J. C. R. (1965), *The Management of the British Economy 1945–1960*, Cambridge: Cambridge University Press.

Dowding, K. (1995), *The Civil Service*, London: Routledge.

Draper, D. (1997), *Blair's Hundred Days*, London: Faber.

Drewry, G. (1990), 'Next Steps: The Pace Falters', *Public Law*, Autumn: 322–9.

Dudley, G. (1994), 'The Next Steps Agencies, Political Salience and the Arm's-Length Principle: Barbara Castle at the Ministry of Transport 1965–68', *Public Administration*, 72: 219–40.

Dunleavy, P. (1985), 'Bureaucrats, Budgets and the Growth of the State: Reconstructing an Instrumental Model', *British Journal of Political Science*, 15: 299–328.

Dunleavy, P. (1989), 'The Architecture of the British Central State, Part I: Framework for Analysis', *Public Administration*, 67: 249–75.

Dunleavy, P. (1991), *Democracy, Bureaucracy and Public Choice*, Hemel Hempstead: Harvester Wheatsheaf.

Dunleavy, P. (1994), 'Estimating the Distribution of Influence in Cabinet Committees under Major'. In P. Dunleavy and J. Stanyer (eds), *Contemporary Political Studies 1994, I*, Belfast: Political Studies Association.

Dunleavy, P. and Rhodes, R. A. W. (1990), 'Core Executive Studies in Britain', *Public Administration*, 68: 3–28.

Dunsire, A. (1978), *Implementation in Bureaucracy Vol.1: the Execution Process*, London: Martin Robertson.

Dupree, M. (1987), *Lancashire and Whitehall: the Diary of Sir Raymond Streat*, Manchester: Manchester University Press.

Dynes, M. and Walker, D. (1995), *The New British State*, London: Times Books.

The Economist (1997), 'A Good Start', 10 May.

Efficiency Unit (1991), *Making the Most of Next Steps*, London: HMSO.

Efficiency Unit (1993), *Career Management and Succession Planning Study*, London: HMSO.

Ehrman, J. (1958), *Cabinet Government and War 1890–1940*, Cambridge: Cambridge University Press.

Elgie, R. and Thompson, H. (1998), *The Politics of Central Banks*, London: Routledge.

Elliott, L. and Thomas, R. (1995), 'Brown Targets Treasury', *The Guardian* 6 April.

Esher, Lord (1904), *Report of the War Office (Reconstitution) Committee*, Part I, Cd 1943, London: HMSO.

European Commission (1994), *Archives in the European Commission: Report of the Group of Experts on the Coordination of Archives*, Brussels: European Commission.

Fairey, M. J. and Duffield, L. J. (1985), *Review of Communications Between the DHSS and the NHS*, London: DHSS Mimeo.

Ferguson, R. B. (1988), 'The Legal Status of Non-Statutory Codes of Practice', *Journal of Business Law*: 12–19.

Fforde, J. (1992), *The Bank of England and Public Policy, 1941–1958*, Cambridge: Cambridge University Press.

Finer, S. E. (1970), *Comparative Government*, London: The Penguin Press.

Flynn, N. (1990), *Public Sector Management*. Brighton: Harvester Wheatsheaf.

Foreman, S. (1989), *Loaves and Fishes: an Illustrated History of the Ministry of Agriculture, Fisheries and Food 1889–1989*, London: HMSO.

Foster, C. D. and Plowden, F. J. (1996), *The State Under Stress*, Buckingham: Open University Press.

Fowler, h. W. (1965) [1926], *Modern English Usage*, Oxford: Oxford University Press.

Fowler, N. (1991), *Ministers Decide*, London: Chapman.

Freedland, M. (1996), 'The Rule Against Delegation and the Carltona Doctrine', *Public Law*, Spring: 19–30.

French, D. (1982), 'The Rise and Fall of Business as Usual'. In K. Burk (ed.) *War and the State: the Transformation of British Government, 1914–18*, Allen & Unwin.

Freund, E. (1932), *Legislative Regulation: A Study of the Ways and Means of Written Law*, New York: The Commonwealth Fund.

Friedmann, W. (1951), 'The Legal Status and Organization of the Public Corporation', *Law and Contemporary Problems*, 16, Autumn: 576–93.

Fry, G. K. (1993), *Reforming the Civil Service*, Edinburgh: Edinburgh University Press.

Fry, G. K. (1981), *The Administrative 'Revolution' in Whitehall*, London: Croom Helm.

Gains, F. (1998), *Relationships of Dependency Between Departments and Agencies*, unpublished PhD thesis, University of Sheffield.

Gamble, A. (1990), 'Theories of British Politics', *Political Studies*, 38: 404–20.

Garside, R. and Greaves, J. I. (1996), 'The Bank of England and Industrial Intervention in Interwar Britain', *Financial History Review*, 3: 69–86.

Geen, A. C. (1981), 'Educational Policy-making in Cardiff, 1944–70', *Public Administration*, 59: 85–104.

Goodin, R. E. (1996), 'Institutions and their Design', in R. Goodin (ed.), *The Theory of Institutional Design*. Cambridge: Cambridge University Press.

Grabosky, P. and Braithwaite, J. (1986), *Of Manners Gentle*, Melbourne: Oxford University Press.

Grant, C. (1998), *Can Britain Lead in Europe?*, London: Centre for European Reform.

Gray, A. and Jenkins, B., with Flynn, A. and Rutherford, B. (1991), 'The Management of Change in Whitehall: the Experience of the FMI', *Public Administration*, 69: 41–59.

Greaves, H. R. (1947), *Civil Service in the Changing State*, London: George G. Harrap.

Green, C., Tunstall, S. M. and Fordham, M. (1991), 'The Risks from Flooding: Which Risks and Whose Perception?' *Disaster* 15: 227–36.

Greenleaf, W. H. (1983), *The British Political Tradition: Volume 1. The Rise of Collectivism*, London: Methuen.

Greenleaf, W. H. (1987), *The British Political Tradition: Volume 3. A Much-Governed Nation, Part I*, London: Methuen.

Greer, P. (1994), *Transforming Central Government: the Next Steps Initiative*, Milton Keynes: Open University Press.

Greer, P. (1992), 'The Next Steps Initiative: an Examination of the Agency Framework Documents', *Public Administration*, 70 (1): 89–98.

Griffith, J. A. G. (1966), *Central Departments and Local Authorities*, London: Allen & Unwin.

Griffiths, R. (1983), *NHS Management Inquiry: Report*, London: DHSS. mimeo.

Griffiths, R. (1987), 'General Management Sharpens Decision-making in the NHS', *NHS Management Bulletin*, No. 3, January: 2–3.

Grunow, D. (1986), 'Internal Control in Public Administration'. In F.-X. Kaufmann, *Guidance, Control and Evaluation in the Public Sector*, Berlin and New York: W. de Gruyter.

Guardian, The (1998), 'Weathered Eddie is Ready For Almost Anything Now', 7 November.

Gulick, L. (1937), 'Notes on the Theory of Organization.' In L. Gulick and L. Urwick (eds), *Papers on the Science of Administration*, New York: Institute of Public Administration, Columbia University Press.

Gwynn, H. and Rook, R. (1990), *Functions and Structure of the Department of Health*, London: DoH.

Hague, D. C., Mackenzie, W. J. M. and Barker, A. (1975), *Public Policy and Private Interests*, London: Macmillan.

Haldane, Lord (1918), *Report of the Machinery of Government Committee* Cd 9230, London: HMSO.

Haldane, Viscount, of Cloan (1923), 'An Organised Civil Service', *Public Administration*, 6: 16.

Halevy, E. (1961), *The Rule of Democracy*, London: Benn.

Hall, P. (1986), *Governing the Economy*, Cambridge: Polity Press.

Ham, C. (1980), 'The NHS – Travelling Without Map or Compass', *The Health Service Journal*, 14 April: 412–13.

Hamilton, Sir H. P. (1951), 'Sir Warren Fisher and the Public Service', *Public Administration*, 29: 3–38.

Hammond, E. (1967), 'Dispersal of Government Offices: A Survey', *Urban Studies*, 4: 258–75.

Hammond, T. H. (1990), 'In Defence of Luther Gulick's "Notes on the Theory of Organization"', *Public Administration*, 68: 143–73.

Hanf, K. and Soetendorp, B. (eds) (1998), *Adapting to European Integration: Small States and the European Union*, Harlow: Addison Wesley, Longman Limited.

Hanson, A. H. (1956), 'The Labour Party and House of Commons Reform', *Parliamentary Affairs*, 10: 454–68.

Harris, J. (1990), 'State and Society in Twentieth-century Britain'. In F. M. L.Thompson, *The Cambridge Social History of Britain, Vol. 3*, Cambridge: Cambridge University Press.

Harris, J. (1992), 'Political Thought and the Welfare State, 1870–1940', *Past and Present*, 135: 116–41.

Harris, J. (1997), *William Beveridge*, Oxford: Oxford University Press.

Hart, J. (1972), 'The Genesis of the Northcote–Trevelyan Report'. In G. Sutherland (ed.), *Studies in the Growth of Government*, London: Routledge Kegan Paul.

Hawtrey, R. (1961), *The Pound at Home and Abroad*, London: Longman.

Hayes-Renshaw, F. and Wallace, H. (1997), *The Council of Ministers*, London: Macmillan.

HC 430 (1994–95), *Protecting and Presenting Scotland's Heritage Properties*, National Audit Office, London: HMSO.

HC 31 (1995–96), *First Report from the Public Accounts Committee, Session 1995–96*, London: HMSO.

HC 50 (1995–96), *Performance and Operation of the Child Support Agency, Second Report from the Select Committee on Social Security*, London: HMSO.

HC 51 (1995–96), *The Scrutiny of European Business', 27th Report of the Select Committee on European Legislation, Session 1995–96*, London: HMSO.

HC 53 (1995–96), *Planning Systems in Northern Ireland, First Report from the Northern Ireland Affairs Committee, Session 1995–96*, London: Stationery Office.

HC 94 (1995–96), *The Management of Sickness Absence in Her Majesty's Land Registry*, National Audit Office, London: HMSO.

HC 282 (1995–96), *Highways Agency: The Bridge Programme*, National Audit Office, London: HMSO.

HC 307 (1995–96), *Her Majesty's Land Registry: The Management of Sickness Absence, Thirty Fourth Report of the Committee of Public Accounts*, London: HMSO.

HC 313 (1995–96), *Ministerial Accountability and Responsibility, Second Report from the Public Service Committee, Session 1995–96*, London: HMSO.

HC 22 (1996–97), *Contaminated Land, Second Report from the Environment Committee, Session 1996–97*, London: Stationery Office.

HC 42 (1996–97), *Water Conservation and Supply, First Report from the Environment Committee*, London: Stationery Office.

HC 45 (1996–97), *Environmentally Sensitive Areas and Other Schemes under the Agri-environment Regulation, Second Report from the Select Committee on Agriculture*, London: Stationery Office.

HC 57 (1996–97), *Management of the Prison Service, Second Report from the Select Committee on Home Affairs, Session 1996–97*, London: Stationery Office.

HC 83 (1996–97), *Highways Agency: the Bridge Programme, Fifth Report from the Committee of Public Accounts, Session 1996–97*, London: Stationery Office.

HC 105 (1996–97), *The Road and Bridge Maintenance Programme, First Report from the Transport Committee, Session 1996–97*, London: Stationery Office.

HC 108 (1996–97), *Tourism, First Report from the National Heritage Committee*, London: Stationery Office.

HC 142 (1996–97), *Defence Medical Services, Third Report from the Defence Committee, Session 1996–97*, London: Stationery Office.

HC 277 (1996–97), *Work of the Health and Safety Executive, Fourth Report from the Environment Committee*, London: Stationery Office.

HC 323 (1996–97), *The Work of Select Committees, First Report from the Liaison Committee, Session 1996–97*, London: Stationery Office.

HC 274 (1997), *Prison Service: Annual Report and Accounts 1996–97*, London: Stationery Office.

HC 124 (1997–98), *Child Support Agency: Annual Report and Accounts 1996/97*, London: Stationery Office.

HC 313 (1995–96), *Ministerial Accountability and Responsibility*, Public Service Committee, Second Report, Session 1995–96. London: HMSO.

HC 313 (1997–98), *Child Support Agency: Client Funds Account, Twenty-first Report from the Select Committee on Public Accounts, Session 1997–98*, London: Stationery Office.

HC 621 (1997–98), *The Defence Evaluation and Research Agency, Sixth Report from the Defence Committee*, London: Stationery Office.

HC 791 (1997–98), *The Scrutiny of European Business, 7th Report of the Modernisation of the House of Commons Select Committee*, London: Stationery Office.

Heclo, H. and Wildavsky, A. (1974), *The Private Government of Public Money*, London: Macmillan.

Hennessy, P. (1985), 'The Quality of Cabinet Government in Britain', *Policy Studies*, 6(2): 15–45.

Hennessy, P. (1986), *Cabinet*, Oxford: Blackwell.

Hennessy, P. (1989), *Whitehall*, London: Fontana Press.

Hennessy, P. (1993), 'Access and Confidentiality'. In H. Forde and R. Seton (eds) *Archivists and Researchers: Mutual Perceptions and Requirements*, London: British Records Association/Society of Archivists.

Hennessy, P. (1994), 'Cabinet Government: a Commentary', *Contemporary Record*, 8: 484–94.

Hintze, O. (1962), 'Die Entstehung der Modernen Staatsministerien'. In O. Hintze, *Staat und Verfassung, (Gesammelte Abhandlungen zue allgemeinen Verfassungsgeschichte)*, Göttingen: Vandenhoeck und Ruprecht.

Hoggett, P. (1996), 'New Modes of Control in the Public Service', *Public Administration*, 74: 9–32.

Hogwood, B. W. (1994), 'A Reform Beyond Compare? The Next Steps Restructuring of British Central Government', *Journal of European Public Policy*, 2: 73–94.

Hogwood, B. W. (1995), 'Whitehall Families: Core Departments and Agency Forms in Britain', *International Review of Administrative Sciences*, 61: 511–30.

Hogwood, B. W. and Judge, D. (1998), 'Agencification and Ministerial Accountability in the UK, paper to 1998 British-German Workshop on Public Sector Modernisation in the United Kingdom and Germany, Berlin, 10–12 December 1998.

Hogwood, B. W. and Judge, D. and McVicar, M. (1998), 'Too Much of a Good Thing? The Pathology of Accountability', paper to the Political Studies Association Annual Conference, University of Keele, 7–9 April 1998.

Hogwood, B. W. (1988), 'The Rise and Fall and Rise of the Department of Trade and Industry'. In C. Campbell, and B. G. Peters, (eds), *Organising Governance, Governing Organisations*, Pittsburgh: University of Pittsburgh Press.

Hogwood, B. W. (1992), *Trends in British Public Policy*, Buckingham: Open University Press.

Hogwood, B. W. (1993), *The Uneven Staircase: Measuring up to Next Steps*, Glasgow: University of Strathclyde.

Hogwood, B. W. (1995a), 'The "Growth" of Quangos: Evidence and Explanations', *Parliamentary Affairs*, 48/2: 207–25.

Hogwood, B. W. (1995b), 'Whitehall Families: Core Departments and Agency Forms', *International Review of Administrative Sciences*, 61: 511–30.

Hood, C. (1991), 'A Public Management for All Seasons?', *Public Administration*, 69: 3–19.

Hood, C. (1995), 'Contemporary Public Management: A New Global Paradigm?', *Public Policy and Administration*, 10/2: 104–17.

Hood, C. (1996), 'Control Over Bureaucracy: Cultural Theory and Institutional Variety', *Journal of Public Policy*, 15: 207–30.

Hood, C. (1996), ' Exploring Variations in Public Management Reforms of the 1980s'. In H. A. G. M. Bekke, J. L. Perry and T. A. J. Toonen (eds), *Civil Service Systems in Comparative Perspective*, Bloomington: Indiana University Press.

Hood, C. (1998), *The Art of the State*, Oxford: Clarendon Press.

Hood, C., James, O., Jones, G. W., Scott, C. and Travers, T. (1998), 'Regulation Inside Government'. Where New Public Management Meets the Audit Explosion, *Public Money and Management*, 18(2): 61–8.

Hood, C., James, O., Jones, G. W., Scott, C. and Travers, T. (1999), *Regulation Inside Government: Waste-Watchers, Quality Police and Sleaze Busters*, Oxford: Oxford University Press.

Hood, C. and Dunsire, A. (1981), *Bureaumetrics*, Farnborough: Gower.

Hood, C., Dunsire, A. and Thompson, K. S. (1978), 'So You Think You Know What Government Departments Are...?', *Public Administration Bulletin*, 27, August: 20–32.

Hood, C., Huby, M. and Dunsire, A. (1985), 'Scale Economies and Iron Laws: Mergers and Demergers in Whitehall 1971–1984', *Public Administration*, 63: 61–78.

Howson, S. (1993), *British Monetary Policy 1945–51*, Oxford: Clarendon Press.

Howson, S. (1994), 'Money and Monetary Policy in Britain, 1945–1990'. In R. Floud and D. McCloskey (eds), *The Economic History of Britain Since 1700, Vol 3*, Cambridge: Cambridge University Press.

Howson, S. and Winch D. (1977), *The Economic Advisory Council 1930–1939: A Study in Economic Advice During Depression and Recovery*, Cambridge: Cambridge University Press.

Humphreys, J. (1996), *A Way Through the Woods: Negotiating in the European Union*, London: Department of the Environment.

Hunt, J. (1987), 'The United Kingdom'. In W. Plowden (ed.), *Advising the Rulers*, Oxford: Blackwell.

Hutter, B. M. (1997), *Compliance, Regulation and Environment*. Oxford: Clarendon Press.

Hutton, W. (1995), *The State We're In*, London: Jonathan Cape.

Ibbs Report (1988), *Improving Management in Government: The Next Steps: Report to the Prime Minister*, London: HMSO.

Ikenberry, J. (1988), *Reasons of State: Oil Politics and the Capacities of the American Government*, Ithaca: Cornell University Press.

Ingham, G. (1984), *Capitalism Divided: The City and Industry in British Social Development*, London: Macmillan.

Jacob, J. M. (1991), 'Lawyers Go To Hospital', *Public Law*, Summer: 255–81.

James, S. (1992), *British Cabinet Government*, London: Routledge.

Jefferson, C. W. and Trainor, M. (1996), 'Public Sector Relocation and Regional Development', *Urban Studies*, 33/1: 37–48.

Jenkins, K., Caines, K. and Jackson, A. (1988), *Improving Management in Government: the Next Steps*, London: HMSO.

Johnson, F. A. (1960), *Defence by Committee: The British Committee of Imperial Defence 1885–1959*, London: Oxford University Press.

Johnson, N. (1971), 'Editorial: The Reorganization of Central Government', *Public Administration*, 49: 1–12.

Jones, G. W. (1975), 'Development of the Cabinet'. In W. Thornhill (ed.), *The Modernisation of British Government*, London: Pitman.

Jones, G. W. (1998), 'Reforming No.10', *Talking Politics*, 11/1: 21–7.

Jones, G. W. (1976), 'The Prime Minister's Secretaries'. In J. A. G. Griffith (ed.), *From Policy to Administration*, London: George Allen & Unwin.

Jones, G. W. (1983), 'Prime Ministers' Departments Really Create Problems: a Rejoinder to Patrick Weller', *Public Administration*, 61: 79–84.

Jones, G. W. (1985), 'The Prime Minister's Aides'. In A. King (ed.), *The British Prime Minister*, London: Macmillan.

Jones, H. (1992), 'The Conservative Party and Social Policy, 1942–1955', unpublished PhD thesis, University of London.

Jordan, G. (1976), 'Hiving-off and Departmental Agencies', *Public Administration Bulletin*, 21, August: 37–51.

Jordan, G. (1992), *Next Steps Agencies: From Managing by Command to Managing by Contract?* Aberdeen Papers in Accountancy Finance and Management, Aberdeen: University of Aberdeen.

Jordan, G. (1994), *The British Administrative System: Principles Versus Practice*, London: Routledge.

Jubb, M. (1982), 'The Cabinet in the Reign of George I', *Bulletin of the Institute of Historical Research*, 55: 108–10.

Judge, D. (1993), *The Parliamentary State*, London: Sage.

Judge, D., Hogwood, B. W. and McVicar, M. (1997), 'The Pondlife of Executive Agencies: Parliament and Informatory Accountability', *Public Policy and Administration*, 12 (2): 95–115.

Kavanagh, D. and Seldon, A. (1999), *Advising No. 10*, London: HarperCollins.

Kellner, P and Crowther-Hunt, L. (1980), *The Civil Servants: An Enquiry into Britain's Ruling Class*, London: MacDonald.

Kemp, P. (1993), *Beyond Next Steps: A Civil Service for the 21st Century*, London: Social Market Foundation.

Kernaghan, K. (1993), 'Promoting Public Service Ethics: The Codification Option'. In R. Chapman (ed.), *Ethics in Public Service*, Edinburgh: Edinburgh University Press.

King, A. (1985), 'Margaret Thatcher: The Style of a Prime Minister'. In A. King (ed.), *The British Prime Minister*, Basingstoke: Macmillan.

Klein, R. (1995), *The New Politics of the NHS*, London: Longman.

Klein, R. (1998), 'Why Britain is Reorganizing its National Health Service – Yet Again', *Health Affairs*, 17(4): 111–25.

Krasner, S. (1988), 'Sovereignty: An Institutional Perspective', *Comparative Political Studies*: 21(1): 66–94.

Ladrech, R. (1994), 'Europeanization of Domestic Politics and Institutions: The Case of France', *Journal of Common Market Studies*, 32(1): 69–88.

Larsson, T. (1988), 'Förändringar i och problem med den svenska regerings och regeringskannliets organisation sedan 1840', *Nordisk Administrativt Tidskrift*, 2: 238–57.

Laughlin, R. and Broadbent, J. (1993), 'Accounting and Law: Partners in the Juridification of the Public Sector in the UK?', *Critical Perspectives in Accounting*, 4: 337–68.

Laughlin, R. and Broadbent, J. (1996), 'The New Public Management'. Reforms in Schools and GP Practices: a Comparative Study of Professional Resistance and the Role of Absorption and Absorbing Groups. *Working Paper*, University of Essex.

Laughlin, R. and Broadbent, J. (1997), 'Contracts and Competition? A Reflection on the Nature and Effects of Recent Legislation on Modes of Control in Schools'. *Cambridge Journal of Economics*, 21/2: 277–90.

Loughlin, M. and Scott, C. (1997), 'The Regulatory State', in P. Dunleavy, A. Gamble I. Holliday and G. Peele (eds), *Developments in British Politics 5*. London: Macmillan.

Lawson, N. (1992), *The View From No. 11*, London: Bantham Press.

Lawson, N. and Armstrong, R. (1994), 'Cabinet Government in the Thatcher Years', *Contemporary Record*, 8: 440–52.

Learmont Report (Sir John Learmont) (1995), *Review of Prison Service Security in England and Wales and the Escape from Parkhurst Prison on 3rd January 1995*, Cm 3020. London: HMSO.

Lee, J. M. (1977), *Reviewing the Machinery of Government 1942–1952*, London: Privately Printed.

Lee, J. M., Jones, G. W. and Burnham, J. (1998), *At the Centre of Whitehall*, Basingstoke: Macmillan.

Lewis, D. (1997), *Hidden Agendas: Politics, Law and Disorder*, London: Hamish Hamilton.

Lewis, N. (1989), 'The Case for a Standing Administrative Conference', *Political Quarterly*, 60: 421–32.

Lowe, R. (1986), *Adjusting to Democracy*, Oxford: Clarendon Press.

Lowe, R. (1989), 'Resignation at the Treasury: The Social Services Committee and the Failure to Reform the Welfare State, 1955–7', *Journal of Social Policy*, 18: 505–26.

Lowe, R. (1996), 'The Replanning of the British Welfare State, 1957–1964'. In M. Francis *et. al.*, (eds), *The Conservatives and British Society, 1880–1980*, Cardiff: University of Wales Press.

Lowe, R. (1997a), 'Plumbing New Depths? Contemporary Historians and the Public Record Office', *Twentieth Century British History*, 8: 239–65.

Lowe, R. (1997a), 'The Core Executive, Modernization and the Creation of PESC, 1960–64', *Public Administration*, 75: 602–15.

Lowe, R. (1997b), 'Milestone or Millstone? The 1959–61 Plowden Committee and its Impact on British Welfare Policy', *Historical Journal*, 40: 463–91.

Lowe, R. (1998), *The Welfare State in Britain since 1945*, Basingstoke: Macmillan.

Lowe, R. and Roberts, R. (1987), 'Sir Horace Wilson, 1900–1935: The Making of a Mandarin', *Historical Journal*, 30: 641–62.

Lowe, R. and Rollings, N. (2000), 'Modernising Britain, 1957–1964: A Classic Case of Centralisation and Fragmentation' in R. A. W. Rhodes (ed.), *Transforming British Government*. Vol. 1, Basingstoke: Macmillan.

Ludlow, N. P. (1997), *Dealing with Britain: The Six and the First UK Application to the EEC*, Cambridge: Cambridge University Press.

Mackintosh, J. P. (1962), *The Cabinet*, London: Stevens. 3rd edn, 1977.

Mackintosh, J. P. (1977), *The Politics and Government of Britain*, London: Hutchinson.

Mandelson, P. and Liddle, R. (1996), *The Blair Revolution: Can New Labour Deliver?* London: Faber & Faber.

Maor, M. and Stevens, H. (1997), 'Measuring the Impact of New Public Management and European Integration on Recruitment and Training in the UK Civil Service', *Public Administration*, 75: 531–51.

March, J. and Olsen, J. (1996), 'Institutional Perspectives on Political Institutions', *Governance*, 9: 247–64.

March, J. G. and Olsen, J. P. (1984), 'The New Institutionalism: Organizational Factors in Political Life', *American Political Science Review*, 78: 734–49.

Marquand, D. (1988), *The Unprincipled Society*, London: Fontana.

Marsh, D. and Rhodes, R. A. W. (1992) (eds), *Policy Networks in British Government*, Oxford: Clarendon Press.

Marsh, D. and Smith, M. J. (2000), 'Understanding Policy Networks: a Dialectical Approach', *Political Studies*, 48: 4–21.

Marshall, J. N. (1990), 'Reorganising the British Civil Service: How are the Regions Being Served?', *Area*, 22: 246–55.

Marshall, J. N. (1996), 'Civil Service Reorganization and Urban and Regional Development in Britain', *Service Industries Journal*, 16: 347–67.

Marshall, J. N. and Alderman, N. (1991), 'Rolling Back the Frontiers of the State: Civil Service Reorganization and Relocation in Britain', *Growth and Change*, Fall: 51–74.

Marshall, J. N., Alderman, N. and Thwaites, A. (1991), 'Civil Service Relocation and the English Regions', *Regional Studies*, 25: 499–510.

Mawson, J. and Spencer, K. (1997), 'The Government Offices for the English Regions: Towards Regional Governance?', *Policy and Politics*, 25: 71–84.

Mawson, J. and Spencer, K. (1997), 'The Origins and Operation of the Government Offices for the English Regions'. In J. Mawson and J. Bradbury (eds), *British Regionalism and Devolution: The Challenges of State Reform and European Integration*, London: Jessica Kingsley.

Mayne, J. (1990), 'Whitehall Watch', *The Independent*, October.

McDonald, O. (1992), *Swedish Models. The Swedish Model of Central Government*, London, Institute for Public Policy Research.

McKibbin, R. (1990), *The Ideologies of Class*, Oxford: Clarendon Press.

McLean, I. (1997), 'On Moles and the Habits of Birds: The Unpolitics of Aberfan', *Twentieth-century British History*, 8: 285–309.

Menon, A. and Wright, V. (1998), 'The Paradoxes of 'Failure': British EU Policy Making In Comparative Perspective', *Public Policy and Administration*, 13(4): 46–66.

Mercer, H. (1995), *Constructing a Competitive Order*, Cambridge: Cambridge University Press.

Mercer, H., Rollings, N. and Tomlinson, J. (1992), *Labour Governments and Private Industry: the Experience of 1945–51*, Edinburgh: Edinburgh University Press.

Michael, D. C. (1996), 'Co-operative Implementation of Federal Regulations', *Yale Journal on Regulation*, 13: 535–601.

Middlemas, K. (1986), *Power, Competition and the State: Volume 1, Britain in Search of Balance*, London: Macmillan.

Middleton, R. (1996), *Government versus the Market*, Cheltenham: Edward Elgar.

Moran, M. (1986), *The Politics of Banking*, London: Macmillan, 2nd edn.

Morgan, J. (1987), *Conflict and Order: The Police and Industrial Disputes in England and Wales, 1900–1939*, Oxford: Clarendon Press.

Nailor, P. (1991), *Learning from Precedent in Whitehall*, London: Institute of Contemporary British History/Royal Institute of Public Administration.

Natzler, D. and Silk, P. (1996), 'Departmental Select Committees and the Next Steps Programme'. In P. Giddings (ed.), *Parliamentary Accountability: A Study of Parliament and Executive Agencies*, London: Macmillan.

Newman, J., Richards, S., and Smith, P. (1998), 'Market Testing and Institutional Change in the UK Civil Service: Compliance, Non-compliance and Engagement', *Public Policy and Administration*, 13 (4): 96–110.

Newton, T. (1988), *Evidence of Minister of Health to the Social Services Committee. Resourcing the National Health Service. Minutes of Evidence*, 8 June, London: HMSO, H.C. 264-xll.

NHS Executive (1998), *The New NHS Modern and Dependable: a National Framework for Assessing Performance*, London: DoH.

NHS Management Executive (1989), *Message to NHS General Managers and FPC Administrators*, London: NHS Management Executive, EL (89) MB102.

Nicholson, H. (1950), *Diplomacy*, Oxford: Oxford University Press.

Niskanen, W. A. (1971), *Bureaucracy and Representative Government*, Chicago: Aldine.

Norton, P. (1997), 'Leaders or Led? Senior Ministers in British Government'. *Talking Politics*, 10 (2): 78–85.

Norton, P. (2000), 'Barons in a Shrinking Kingdom'. In R. A. W. Rhodes (ed.) (2000), *Transforming British Government*. 2 volumes. London: Macmillan.

Office of Public Service (1998), *Executive Non-Departmental Public Bodies 1997 Report*, London: Stationery Office.

Office of Public Service (occasional), *Non-Departmental Public Bodies: A Guide for Departments*, London: Cabinet Office.

Oliver, D. and Drewry, G. (1996), *Public Service Reforms: Issues of Accountability and Public Law*, London: Pinter.

Olsen, J. (1995), 'European Challenges to the Nation State', *Arena Working Paper*, 14/95, Oslo: University of Oslo.

Osborne, D. and Gaebler, T. (1992), *Reinventing Government*. Reading, Mass.: Addison-Wesley.

O'Toole, B. (1989), 'The 'Next Steps' and Control of the Civil Service: a Historical Perspective', *Public Policy and Administration*, 4(1): 41–52.

O'Toole, B. and Jordan, G. (1995), *Next Steps: Improving Management in Government*, Aldershot: Dartmouth.

Otte, T. (1996), 'A Question of Leadership: The Unionist Cabinet and Foreign Policy 1895–1900', unpublished seminar paper presented at the Institute of Historical Research, London, 20 March.

PRO (1917), LAB2/212/ML 1200/2, memorandum by Sir Thomas Phillips.

PRO (1930), CAB27/438/UP(30)15, minutes of a panel of ministers on unemployment, 25 October.

PRO (1961) CAB 129/105, C(61)94, Treasury, 'Economic Growth and National Efficiency: Report by Officials'.

PRO (1961) T291/14, CPE(SC1)10, memorandum of Committee I of the Plowden Committee, para.13.

PRO (1962) PREM 11/4520, note by Harold Macmillan for Cabinet, 25 October.

PRO (1964) PREM 11/4778, note by Sir Burke Trend, 21 January.

Padmore, Sir T. (1956), 'Civil Service Establishments and the Treasury'. In W. A. Robson (ed.), *The Civil Service in Britain and France*, London: The Hogarth Press.

Page, A. (1995), *Executive Self-Regulation in the United Kingdom*, London: Institute of Advanced Legal Studies.

Page, E. and Wouters, L. (1995), 'The Europeanization of National Bureaucracies?'. In J. Pierre (ed.), *Bureaucracy in the Modern State*, Aldershot: Edward Elgar.

Paige, V. (1986), 'The Development of General Management Within the NHS, With Particular Reference to the Role of the NHS Management Board', Memorandum to the *Social Services Committee of the House of Commons*, Mimeo.

Pardoe, C. H. B. and Williamson, I. F. (1979), 'The Road to Cardiff', *Management Services in Government*, 34(1): 27–37.

Parkinson, C. N. (1961), *Parkinson's Law*. Harmondsworth: Penguin Books.

Peden, G. C. (1983), 'Sir Richard Hopkins and the "Keynesian Revolution" in Employment Policy', *Economic History Review*, 36: 281–96.

Petrie, C. (1958), *The Powers Behind the Prime Ministers*, London: MacGibbon & Kee.

Pimlott, B. (1988), *Harold Wilson*, London: Harper Collins.

Pliatzky, L. (1989), *The Treasury Under Mrs Thatcher*, Oxford: Blackwell.

Pliatzky, Sir L. (1980), *Report on Non-Departmental Bodies*, London: HMSO.

Plumb, J. H. (1957), 'The Organisation of the Cabinet in the Reign of Queen Anne', *Transactions of the Royal Historical Society*, 5th series, 7: 137–57.

Pollard, S. (1982), *The Wasting of the Economy*, London: Croom Helm.

Pollitt, C. (1984), *Manipulating the Machine: Changing the Pattern of Ministerial Departments 1960–83*, London: George Allen & Unwin.

Pollitt, C. (1993), *Managerialism and the Public Services*. 2nd edition. Oxford: Blackwell.

Ponting, C. (1986), *Whitehall: Tragedy and Farce*, London: Hamish Hamilton.

Power, M. (1997), *The Audit Society*. Oxford: Oxford University Press.

Prime Minister/Minister for the Civil Service, (1970), *The Reorganisation of Central Government*, London: HMSO.

Pryce, S. (1997), *Presidentializing the Premiership*, London: Macmillan.

Public Records Office (1995), *Current Guide*, Kew: PRO.

Regina v. Lord Chancellor's Department, ex parte Nangle [1992] 1 *All England Law Reports* 897–909.

Radcliffe Committee (1959), *Report*, London: HMSO.

Radcliffe Committee (1960), *Minutes of Evidence*, London: HMSO.

Radcliffe, J. (1991), *The Reorganisation of British Central Government*, Aldershot: Dartmouth.

Rhodes, R. A. W. (1981), *Control and Power in Central–Local Government Relations*, Farnborough: Gower.

Rhodes, R. A. W. (1986), *The National World of Local Government*, London: Allen & Unwin.

Rhodes, R. A. W. (1988), *Beyond Westminster and Whitehall*, London: Unwin-Hyman. Reprinted Routledge, 1992.

Rhodes, R. A. W. (1994), 'The Hollowing Out of the State', *Political Quarterly*, 65: 138–51.

Rhodes, R. A. W. (1995), 'From Prime Ministerial Power to Core Executive'. In R. A. W. Rhodes and P. Dunleavy (eds), *Prime Minister, Cabinet and Core Executive*, London: Macmillan.

Rhodes, R. A. W. (1997a), *Understanding Governance*, Buckingham, Open University Press.

Rhodes, R. A. W. (1997b), 'Diplomacy in Governance', *Politics Today*, 7(3) 24–27.
Rhodes, R. A. W. (1997c), 'It's the Mix that Matters: From Marketisation to Diplomacy'. *Australian Journal of Public Administration*, 56: 40–53.
Rhodes, R. A. W. (1998a), 'The Changing Nature of Central Government in Britain: the ESRC's Whitehall Programme'. *Public Policy and Administration*, 13(4): 1–11.
Rhodes, R. A. W. (1998b), 'Different Roads To Unfamiliar Places: UK Experience in Comparative Perspective', *Australian Journal of Public Administration*, 57: 19–31.
Rhodes, R. A. W. (1999a) [1981], *Control and Power in Central-Local Government Relations*, Aldershot: Dartmouth. New edition.
Rhodes, R. A. W. (1999b), 'Foreword: Governance and Networks'. In G. Stoker (ed.), *The New Management of British Local Governance*, London: Macmillan.
Rhodes, R. A. W. (1999c), 'Traditions and Public Sector Reform', *Scandinavian Political Studies*, 22/4: 341–70.
Rhodes, R. A. W. and Dunleavy, P. (eds), (1995), *Prime Minister, Cabinet and Core Executive*, London: Macmillan.
Rhodes, R. A. W. (2000), 'Governance and Public Administration'. In J. Pierre (ed.), *Debating Governance*, Oxford: Oxford University Press.
Richards, D. (1997), *The Civil Service Under the Conservatives*, Sussex: Sussex Academic Press.
Richards, S., Smith, P., and Newman, J. (1996), 'Shaping and Reshaping Market Testing Policy', *Public Policy and Administration*, 1(2): 19–34.
Ridge v. Baldwin [1964] Appeal Cases 40 (House of Lords).
Riddell, P. (1997), 'Advising the Prime Minister', paper to the ESRC conference on 'Future Whitehall', Church House, London.
Ridley, N. (1973), *Industry and the Civil Service*, London: Aims of Industry, 11–12.
Ringe, A. (1998), 'Witness Seminar: The National Economic Development Council, 1962–67'. *Contemporary British History*, 12: 88–130.
Ringe, A. (forthcoming), '*Incomes Policy: A Case of Intransigence and Inconsequential Initiatives*'.
Ringe, A. and Rollings, N. (2000), 'Domesticating the 'Market Animal': The Treasury and the Bank of England, 1955–1960'. In R. A. W. Rhodes, (ed.) *Transforming British Government, Vol. 1 Changing Institutions*, London: Macmillan.
Ringe, A. and Rollings, N. (2000), 'Responding to Relative Decline: The Creation of the National Economic Development Council', *Economic History Review*, forthcoming.
Roberts, M. (1973), *Gustavus Adolphus and the Rise of Sweden*, London: English Universities Press.
Rollings, N. (1988), 'British Budgetary Policy, 1945–1954: A "Keynesian revolution"?', *Economic History Review*, 41: 283–98.
Rollings, N. (1992), 'The Reichstag Method of Governing? The Attlee Governments and Permanent Economic Controls'. In H. Mercer, N. Rollings and J. Tomlinson (eds), *Labour Governments and Private Industry: The Experience of 1945–51*, Edinburgh: Edinburgh University Press.
Rollings, N. (1994), 'Poor Mr. Butskell: A Short Life Wrecked by Schizophrenia'?, *Twentieth Century British History*, 5: 183–205.
Rollings, N. (1996), 'Butskellism, the Postwar Consensus and the Managed Economy'. In H. Jones and M. Kandiah (eds), *The Myth of Consensus*, Basingstoke: Macmillan.
Rometsch, D. and Wessels, W. (eds) (1996), *The European Union and Member States*, Manchester: Manchester University Press.
Rose, R. (2000), *The Paradox of Downing Street: The Prime Minister in a Shrinking World*, London: Macmillan.
Rosen, F. (1983), *Jeremy Bentham and Representative Democracy: a Study of the Constitutional Code*, Oxford: Clarendon Press.
Roseveare, S. (1997), 'Rethinking Regional Policy: the Board of Trade and the Tactics of Industrial Intervention, 1956–60', paper submitted to an ESRC conference on Whitehall in the 1950s and 1960s, London.

Roseveare, H. (1969), *The Treasury: The Evolution of a British Institution*, London: Allen Lane.

Salamon, L. M. (1981), 'The Goals of Reorganisation: A Framework for Analysis', *Administration and Society*, 12: 471–500.

Saward, M. (1997), 'In Search of the Hollow Crown'. In P. Weller, H. Bakvis, and R. A. W. Rhodes (eds), *The Hollow Crown: Countervailing Trends in Core Executives*, London: Macmillan.

Scott Report (Sir Richard Scott) (1996), *Report of the Inquiry into the Export of Defence Equipment and Dual-Use Goods to Iraq and Related Prosecutions*, Session 1995–96, HC 115. 5 vols. and index. London: HMSO.

Scottish Office (1991), '*The Scottish Office and the European Community – a Review: Summary of the Main Findings and Recommendations*', Edinburgh: Scottish Office Industry Department.

Scottish Office (1998), *Scotland's Parliament: Handling of European Business*, Edinburgh: Scottish Office Development Department.

Secretary of State for Health (1989), *Working for Patients*, Cm. 3807. London: HMSO, Cmnd.555.

Secretary of State for Health (1997), *The New NHS: Modern-Dependable*, London: HMSO, Cm 3807.

Sedgewick, R. R. (1919), 'The Inner Cabinet from 1739 to 1741', *English Historical Review*, 34: 270–302.

Seldon, A. (1995), 'The Ethos of the Cabinet Office: A Comment on the Testimony of Officials'. In R. A. W. Rhodes, and P. Dunleavy (eds), *Prime Minister, Cabinet and Core Executive*, London: Macmillan.

Seldon, A. (1997), *Major: A Political Life*, London: Weidenfeld and Nicolson.

Self, P. (1972), *Administrative Theories and Politics*, London: George Allen & Unwin.

Seymour-Ure, C. (1971), 'The "Disintegration" of the Cabinet and the Neglected Question of Cabinet Reform', *Parliamentary Affairs*, 24(3): 196–207.

Sharpe, L. J. (1977), 'Whitehall – Structures and People'. In D. Kavanagh and R. Rose (eds), *New Trends in British Political Science*, London: Sage.

Sieber, S. (1981), *Fatal Remedies: the Ironies of Social Intervention*. New York: Plenum.

Simms, M. M. (1974), *The Ministry of Technology 1964–70*, Manchester University, unpublished MSc Thesis.

Simon, B. (1991), *Education and the Social Order, 1940–1990*, London: Lawrence and Wishart.

Simon, H. A. (1947), *Administrative Behavior*, New York: The Free Press.

Sisson, C. H. (1966), *The Spirit of British Administration and Some European Comparisons*, 2nd edn., London: Faber & Faber.

Skowronek, S. (1982), *Building a New American State: the Expansion of National Administrative Capacities, 1877–1920*, New York: Cambridge University Press.

Smith, M. J. (1994), 'The Core Executive and the Resignation of Mrs Thatcher', *Public Administration*, 72: 341–63.

Smith, M. J. (1998), 'Theoretical and Empirical Challenges to British Central Government', *Public Administration*, 76: 45–72.

Smith, M. J. (1999), *The Core Executive in Britain*, London: Macmillan.

Smith, M. J., Marsh, D. and Richards, D. (1993), 'Central Government Departments and the Policy Process', *Public Administration*, 71: 567–94.

Stephen, Sir J. (1854), Letter in Papers Relating to the Re-organisation of the Civil Service, *Parliamentary Papers (1854–55)*, Vol. 20.

Stevens, R. (1993), *The Independence of the Judiciary: The View from the Lord Chancellor's Office*, Oxford: Clarendon Press.

Stowe, K. (1989), *On Caring for the National Health*, London: Nuffield Provincial Hospitals Trust.

Street, Sir A. and Griffith, J. A. G. (1952), *Principles of Administrative Law*, London: Pitman.

Talbot, C. (1995), 'The Prison Service: a Framework of Irresponsibility?' *Public Finance Foundation Review*, No. 8: 16–19.

Talbot, C. (1996), 'The Prison Service: a Framework of Irresponsibility?', *Public Money and Management*, January–March: 5–7.

Teague, P. (1996), 'The European Union and the Irish Peace Process', *Journal of Common Market Studies*, 34/4: 549–70.

Thain, C and Wright, M. (1995), *The Treasury and Whitehall*, Oxford: Clarendon Press.

Thain, C. (1984), 'The Treasury and Britain's Decline', *Political Studies*, 32: 581–95.

Thane, P. (1990), 'Government and Society in England and Wales, 1750–1914'. In F. M. L. Thompson (ed.), *The Cambridge Social History of Modern Britain, 1750–1950, Vol 3, Social Agencies and Institutions*, Cambridge: Cambridge University Press.

Theakston, K. (1995), *The Civil Service Since 1945*, Oxford: Blackwell.

Theakston, K. (1997), 'Comparative Biography and Leadership in Whitehall', *Public Administration*, 75: 651–67.

Theakston, K. (1997), 'New Labour, New Whitehall?', *Public Policy and Administration* 13(1): 13–34.

Theakston, K. (1999), *Leadership in Whitehall*, London: Macmillan.

Thelen, K. and Steinmo, S. (1992), 'Historical Institutionalism in Comparative Politics'. In K. Thelen, S. Steinmo and F. Longstreth (eds), *Structuring Politics: Historical Institutionalism in Comparative Analysis*, Cambridge: Cambridge University Press.

Thomas, R. (1978), *The British Philosophy of Administration*, London: Longman.

Thompson, M., Ellis, R. and Wildavsky, A. (1990), *Cultural Theory*, Boulder: Westview Press.

Thorneycroft, P. (1960), 'Policy in Practice'. In P. Thorneycroft *et al.*, *Not Unanimous*, London: IEA.

Tivey, L. (1988), *Interpretations of British Politics*. Brighton: Harvester-Wheatsheaf.

Tomlinson, J. (1997), *Democratic Socialism and Economic Policy: the Attlee Years 1945–1951*, Cambridge: Cambridge University Press.

Tomlinson, J. (1998), 'Why So Austere? The British Welfare State of the 1940s', *Journal of Social Policy*, 27, 63–77.

Tratt, J. (1966), *The Macmillan Government and Europe: a Study in the Process of Policy Development*, London: Macmillan.

HM Treasury (1989), *Government Accounting: a Guide on Accounting and Financial Procedures for the Use of Government Departments* (2 vols., loose-leaf), London: HMSO.

HM Treasury (1997), *Regularity and Propriety: a Handbook*, London: HM Treasury.

HM Treasury (1998a), *Stability and Investment in the Long Term: Economic and Fiscal Strategy Report 1998*, Cm. 3978. London: Stationery Office.

HM Treasury (1998b), *Public Services for the Future: Modernisation, Reform, Accountability. Comprehensive Spending Review: Public Service Agreements 1999–2002*, Cm. 4181. London: Stationery Office.

Treasury and Civil Service Committee (1994), *The Role of the Civil Service, Fifth Report, Session 1993–94*, HC 27 (3 vols.). London: HMSO.

Treasury Solicitor's Department (1987), *The Judge Over Your Shoulder: Judicial Review of Administrative Decisions*, London: Cabinet Office.

Treasury Solicitor's Department (1995), *Judge Over Your Shoulder. Judicial Review: Balancing the Scales*, London: Cabinet Office.

Trentmann, F. (1996), 'The Transformation of Fiscal Reform: Reciprocity, Modernization, and the Fiscal Debate Within the Business Community in the Early Twentieth Century', *Historical Journal*, 39: 1005–48.

Turner, E. R. (1930), *The Cabinet Council of England in the Seventeenth and Eighteenth Centuries 1622–1784, Vol II*, Baltimore: Johns Hopkins Press.

Turner, J. (1982), *British Politics and the Great War*, New Haven, Conn: Yale University Press.

Turner, J. (1994), *Macmillan*, Harlow: Longman.

Varcoe, I. M. (1972), *The Department of Scientific and Industrial Research: a Study in the Growth of Organised Science*, Oxford University DPhil Thesis.

Verney, D. (1991), 'Westminster Model'. In V. Bogdanor (ed.), *The Blackwell Encyclopaedia of Political Science*. Corrected paperback edition. Oxford: Blackwell.

Wallace, H. and Wallace, W. (1973), 'The Impact of Community Membership on the British Machinery of Government', *Journal of Common Market Studies*, 11/2: 243–62.

Watkins, A. (1991), *A Conservative Coup*, London: Duckworth.

Webster, C. (1996), *The Health Services Since The War, Vol.11: Government And Health Care: the British National Health Service*, London: HMSO.

Weller, P. (1983), 'Do Prime Ministers' Departments Really Create Problems?', *Public Administration*, 61: 59–78.

Wessels, W. (1997), 'An Ever Closer Fusion? A Dynamic Macropolitical View on Integration Processes', *Journal of Common Market Studies*, 35(2): 267–99.

Westlake, M. (1995), *The Council of the European Union*, Harlow: Cartermill Publishing.

Whitelaw, W. (1989), *The Whitelaw Memoirs*, London: Aurum.

Whiteside, N. (1983), 'Private Agencies for Public Purposes', *Journal of Social Policy*, 12: 165–94.

Whiteside, N. (1997), 'Regulating Markets: The Real Costs of Polycentric Administration Under the National Health Insurance Scheme, 1912–1946', *Public Administration*, 75: 467–85.

Wilding, R. (1982), 'A Triangular Affair: Quangos, Ministers, and MPs.' In A. Barker (ed.), *Quangos in Britain*, London: Macmillan.

Willetts, D. (1996), 'Public Service Reform' (speech delivered at Civil Service College 17 July).

Williams, P. M. (ed.) (1983), *The Diary of Hugh Gaitskell 1945–56*, London: Jonathan Cape.

Willson, F. M. G. (1955), 'Ministries and Boards: Some Aspects of Administrative Development since 1832', *Public Administration*, 33: 43–58.

Wilson, H. (1964), *Whitehall and Beyond*, London: BBC.

Wilson, J. Q. and Rachal, P. (1977), 'Can the Government Regulate Itself?', *The Public Interest* 46b (Winter): 3–14.

Winkler, V. (1990), 'Restructuring the Civil Service: Reorganization and Relocation 1962–1985', *International Journal of Urban and Regional Research*, 14(1): 135–57.

Wood, G. E., Mills, T. C. and Capie, F. (1993), *Central Bank Independence: What Is It and What Will It Do For Us?*, London: IEA.

Woods, Sir J. (1956), 'Treasury Control'. In W. A. Robson (ed.), *The Civil Service in Britain and France*, London: The Hogarth Press.

Wright, V. (1994), 'Reshaping the State: Implications For Public Administration', *West European Politics*, 17: 102–34.

Wright, V. (1996), 'The National Coordination of European Policy-making: Negotiating the Quagmire'. In J. Richardson (ed.), *European Union: Power and Policy-Making*, London: Routledge.

Wrong, D. (1988), *Power*, Oxford: Blackwell.

Young, H. (1998), *This Blessed Plot: Britain and Europe from Churchill to Blair*, London: Macmillan.

Zifcak, S. (1994), *New Managerialism. Administrative Reform in Whitehall and Canberra*, Milton Keynes: Open University Press.

Name Index

Subject Index